D. H. LAWRENCE

SELECTED LITERARY
CRITICISM

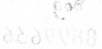

EDITED BY

ANTHONY BEAL

HEINEMANN

LONDON

Heinemann Educational Books Ltd
LONDON EDINBURGH MELBOURNE AUCKLAND TORONTO
HONG KONG SINGAPORE KUALA LUMPUR NEW DELHI
NAIROBI JOHANNESBURG LUSAKA IBADAN
KINGSTON

ISBN 0 435 18058 4

First published 1956
Reprinted 1960, 1964
First published in Mercury Books 1961
First published in HEB Paperbacks 1967
Reprinted 1969, 1973, 1978

Published by
Heinemann Educational Books Ltd
48 Charles Street, London W1X 8AH
Printed Offset Litho and bound in Great Britain by
Cox & Wyman Ltd, London, Fakenham and Reading

D. H. LAWRENCE

SELECTED LITERARY
CRITICISM

CONTENTS

*The Index (pp. 429–435) gives a complete list of topics,
authors and books*

INTRODUCTION   ix

I. AUTOBIOGRAPHICAL

1. AUTOBIOGRAPHICAL SKETCH   1
2. HYMNS IN A MAN'S LIFE   6
3–20. Extracts from Letters   11

II. PURITANISM AND THE ARTS

21–27. Extracts from Letters   23
28. Introduction to *Pansies*   26
29. Extract from Letter   30
30. PORNOGRAPHY AND OBSCENITY   32
31. Extract from Letter   52
32. From INTRODUCTION TO THESE PAINTINGS   52
33. From STUDY OF THOMAS HARDY   67

III. VERSE

34. Review of *Georgian Poetry: 1911–1912*   72
35–43. Extracts from Letters   76
44. Introduction to *New Poems*   84
45. From CHAOS IN POETRY   89
46. Review of *A Second Contemporary Verse Anthology*   92
47. From THE NIGHTINGALE   98

IV. CONTEMPORARIES AND THE IMPORTANCE OF THE NOVEL

48. WHY THE NOVEL MATTERS   102
49. MORALITY AND THE NOVEL   108
50. SURGERY FOR THE NOVEL—OR A BOMB   114
51. JOHN GALSWORTHY   118
52–56. Extracts from Letters   131
57. Review of *The World of William Clissold* (Wells)   133
58–64. Extracts from Letters   138
65. Review of Four Contemporary Books (by Robert
    Byron, Clough Williams-Ellis, Maurice Baring
    and W. Somerset Maugham)   140
66–73. Extracts from Letters   145
74. Review of *Hadrian the Seventh* (Corvo)   149
75. Introduction to *The Dragon of the Apocalypse*
    (Carter)   153
76. From STUDY OF THOMAS HARDY   166

V. CONTINENTALS

77–80. Extracts from Letters   229
81. Preface to *The Grand Inquisitor* (Dostoievsky)   233
82–83. Extracts from Letters   242
84. Preface to *All Things Are Possible* (Shestov)   242
85. Review of *Solitaria* (Rozanov)   245
86. Review of *Fallen Leaves* (Rozanov)   249
87. Extract from Letter   254
88. THE GOOD MAN   254
89. THOMAS MANN   260
90. Preface to *Max Havelaar* (E. D. Dekker)   266
91. On *Mastro-don Gesualdo* (Verga)   270
92. Introduction to *Cavalleria Rusticana* (Verga)   279
93. Preface to *The Mother* (Deledda)   291

VI. AMERICANS

94. THE SPIRIT OF PLACE   296
95. FENIMORE COOPER'S WHITE NOVELS   303
96. FENIMORE COOPER'S LEATHERSTOCKING NOVELS   314
97. EDGAR ALLAN POE   330
98. NATHANIEL HAWTHORNE AND 'THE SCARLET
    LETTER'   347
99. HERMAN MELVILLE'S 'TYPEE' AND 'OMOO'   363
100. HERMAN MELVILLE'S 'MOBY DICK'   376
101. WALT WHITMAN   392
102. Review of *Bottom Dogs* (Dahlberg)   407
103. Review of *Americans* (Sherman)   414
104. Review of Four American Novels (by Van
     Vechten, White, Dos Passos and Hemingway)   422

INDEX   429

Introduction

In his lifetime Lawrence published only one critical book, *Studies in Classic American Literature* (1924). Yet he was constantly engaged in literary criticism. He reviewed books; he contributed prefaces and introductions to works in which he was particularly interested; he wrote some of the most important essays that we have on the novel, its purpose and its relationship with morality and society, on pornography, obscenity, and the effect of Puritanism on the arts. He believed passionately that books should help us "to be alive, to be man alive, to be whole man alive", and in the light of this belief he surveyed a great deal of modern literature—English, American, European—and made his judgments and discriminations.

Much of this writing was done for ephemeral periodicals, while some of the best of it was not published at all in his lifetime. But six years after his death it was collected together in *Phoenix* (1936), with many other essays, sketches, articles and stories that had not appeared before in book form.

But this does not complete the range of Lawrence's criticism. His *Letters* (1932) are an invaluable source of literary opinions. There is hardly one without some comment on what he is writing or what he is reading at the time. We see him at work, struggling to bring his novels to completion and describing the effect that he hopes they will have. We hear his immediate reactions to the books he is reading and their authors; and some of Lawrence's most perceptive and illuminating remarks (together with some of his most devastating) are to be found here. This is Lawrence at his most impulsive, and it is possible that he might have had second thoughts about a few of his snap judgments before committing them to print. But they are as much a part of him as his more weighty and considered essays, and a selection of his literary criticism would be the poorer without them.

Since his death Lawrence's importance as a critic has been increasingly recognised. Many of his judgments and comments

have passed into critical parlance and any discussion of the
novel or the relation of literature to morality must heed his
views. But the reader looking for these opinions has had to
search through a number of books, looking for what he wants
amongst a great deal of extraneous material.

The object of this book then is to gather together in one
place for the first time all Lawrence's important writings on
literature. It does not contain everything he ever wrote concerning books or authors: a comprehensive book would have
become unwieldy, repetitive and scrappy. But it is hoped that
everything of real importance has been included here.

The selection contains over a hundred passages varying in
length from a single sentence to sixty pages, and in substance
from closely argued essays to spur-of-the-moment asides in
letters. How was such diverse material to be arranged in some
sort of order? It seemed to sort itself out finally into six main
groups, and the book has been divided accordingly.

I. AUTOBIOGRAPHICAL. The *Autobiographical Sketch* and
Hymns in a Man's Life give the background of Lawrence's childhood and early manhood and provide a key to many of his
beliefs, opinions and feelings. The rest of the section, drawn
from the letters, shows him mainly at the beginning of his
career, half-blindly, half-consciously evolving what he had to
say. From the first he believed that the main purpose of his
fiction was to explore the relationship between man and woman,
and this preoccupation leads to the subject of the next section.

II. PURITANISM AND THE ARTS. Lawrence wished to describe
sexual relationships fully, frankly and seriously, yet he started
writing in a society still ruled by Victorian conventions of what
could and what could not be said in print. A struggle was
inevitable. His fourth novel, *The Rainbow*, was seized by the
police, on grounds of obscenity, a few weeks after publication
in 1915; and the Bow Street magistrate ordered the seized
copies to be destroyed. For the rest of his life Lawrence was
harassed and persecuted by the official and unofficial guardians
of public morals—the censor-morons, as he called them, who
"hate the living and growing human consciousness". The
battle reached its height in the last two or three years of his
life, when *Lady Chatterley's Lover*, his "direct phallic book" was
suppressed in both Britain and America. Lawrence's case
against the censors, "the grey ones," profound in its psycho-

logical insight, brilliant in argument, and based on the history
of the last four hundred years, leaves nothing more to be said.
III. VERSE. Lawrence was a poet before he was a novelist,
and although for a time he was himself a "Georgian Poet", he
very soon put his finger on the weaknesses of the others in the
group. His verse criticism is not his greatest work, but at its
best it is very fine, with an originality, immediacy and freshness
that makes nearly all other modern writing about poetry
appear dry and pedantic.

IV. CONTEMPORARIES AND THE IMPORTANCE OF THE NOVEL.
Here at the heart of the book are the magnificent essays in
which Lawrence affirms his faith in the importance of the novel
not merely as "literature", but as a vital force in life. Here too
are his criticisms of the novelists who were his contemporaries—
criticisms which implicitly or explicitly help to define Lawrence's
own position amongst them.

V. CONTINENTALS. The beginning of the century saw the
first complete translations of the great Russian novelists into
English. To Lawrence, as to many others, this revelation of a
whole new literature "meant an enormous amount . . . I
thought them the greatest writers of all time". Later he became
convinced "how much finer and purer and more ultimate
our own stuff is", but his writing on the Russians and particularly on "the Russian spirit" are as relevant today as ever.
Lawrence lived for long periods on the Continent, and was
widely read in modern European literature. In discussing it
he sought always to penetrate to the local genius behind it—
French or Sicilian, German or Sardinian. Both as a critic and
a traveller he was intensely aware of the "spirit of place".

VI. AMERICANS. "The Spirit of Place" is the introductory
essay to *Studies in Classic American Literature*, and Lawrence's
ideas on the American character are never far below the
surface in these essays that represent his most sustained venture
into literary criticism. The whole book is reprinted here, with
the exception of four pieces that seemed of less literary interest
than the rest—those on Franklin, Crèvecœur, Dana and
Hawthorne's *Blithedale Romance*. After the *Studies* the section
concludes with Lawrence in his best reviewing style discussing
some American books of the 1920's—with a word of praise
for Mr. Ernest Hemingway.

These bald summaries are intended merely to indicate the plan of the book. Yet even the plan itself suggests some unique characteristics of Lawrence as a critic—the complete absence of the academic approach to literature, of the desire to fit literature into tidy categories; the way in which many of his important statements occur in reviews or essays on books now forgotten; the striking fact that he never sets out to write directly about any literature earlier than that of the century into which he was born (though European literature from Homer onwards was present in his mind to be drawn on where necessary to illustrate some point in contemporary work); and how in this respect, as in many others, he contrasts with that other dominating literary figure of his generation, T. S. Eliot.

But this Introduction is not a discussion of Lawrence's literary criticism. It is rather a direction sign pointing ahead to the wonderful vitality and variety of the work itself.

ANTHONY BEAL.

PART ONE

Autobiographical

[1]

AUTOBIOGRAPHICAL SKETCH

THEY ask me: "Did you find it very hard to get on and to become a success?" And I have to admit that if I can be said to have got on, and if I can be called a success, then I *did not* find it hard.

I never starved in a garret, nor waited in anguish for the post to bring me an answer from editor or publisher, nor did I struggle in sweat and blood to bring forth mighty works, nor did I ever wake up and find myself famous.

I was a poor boy. I *ought* to have wrestled in the fell clutch of circumstance, and undergone the bludgeonings of chance before I became a writer with a very modest income and a very questionable reputation. But I didn't. It all happened by itself and without any groans from me.

It seems a pity. Because I was undoubtedly a poor boy of the working classes, with no apparent future in front of me. But after all, what am I now?

I was born among the working classes and brought up among them. My father was a collier, and only a collier, nothing praiseworthy about him. He wasn't even respectable, in so far as he got drunk rather frequently, never went near a chapel, and was usually rather rude to his little immediate bosses at the pit.

He practically never had a good stall, all the time he was a butty, because he was always saying tiresome and foolish things about the men just above him in control at the mine. He offended them all, almost on purpose, so how could he expect them to favour him? Yet he grumbled when they didn't.

My mother was, I suppose, superior. She came from town,

and belonged really to the lower bourgeoisie. She spoke King's English, without an accent, and never in her life could even imitate a sentence of the dialect which my father spoke, and which we children spoke out of doors.

She wrote a fine Italian hand, and a clever and amusing letter when she felt like it. And as she grew older she read novels again, and got terribly impatient with *Diana of the Crossways* and terribly thrilled by *East Lynne*.

But she was a working man's wife, and nothing else, in her shabby little black bonnet and her shrewd, clear, "different" face. And she was very much respected, just as my father was not respected. Her nature was quick and sensitive, and perhaps really superior. But she was down, right down in the working class, among the mass of poorer colliers' wives.

I was a delicate pale brat with a snuffy nose, whom most people treated quite gently as just an ordinary delicate little lad. When I was twelve I got a county council scholarship, twelve pounds a year, and went to Nottingham High School.

After leaving school I was a clerk for three months, then had a very serious pneumonia illness, in my seventeenth year, that damaged my health for life.

A year later I became a school teacher, and after three years' savage teaching of collier lads I went to take the "normal" course in Nottingham University.

As I was glad to leave school, I was glad to leave college. It had meant mere disillusion, instead of the living contact of men. From college I went down to Croydon, near London, to teach in a new elementary school at a hundred pounds a year.

It was while I was at Croydon, when I was twenty-three, that the girl who had been the chief friend of my youth, and who was herself a school teacher in a mining village at home, copied out some of my poems, and without telling me, sent them to the *English Review*, which had just had a glorious rebirth under Ford Madox Hueffer.

Hueffer was most kind. He printed the poems, and asked me to come and see him. The girl had launched me, so easily, on my literary career, like a princess cutting a thread, launching a ship.

I had been tussling away for four years, getting out *The White Peacock* in inchoate bits, from the underground of my consciousness. I must have written most of it five or six times, but only in intervals, never as a task or a divine labour, or in the groans of parturition.

I would dash at it, do a bit, show it to the girl; she always admired it; then realise afterwards it wasn't what I wanted, and have another dash. But at Croydon I had worked at it fairly steadily, in the evenings after school.

Anyhow, it was done, after four or five years' spasmodic effort. Hueffer asked at once to see the manuscript. He read it immediately, with the greatest cheery sort of kindness and bluff. And in his queer voice, when we were in an omnibus in London, he shouted in my ear: "It's got every fault that the English novel can have."

Just then the English novel was supposed to have so many faults, in comparison with the French, that it was hardly allowed to exist at all. "But," shouted Hueffer in the bus, "you've got GENIUS."

This made me want to laugh, it sounded so comical. In the early days they were always telling me I had got genius, as if to console me for not having their own incomparable advantages.

But Hueffer didn't mean that. I always thought he had a bit of genius himself. Anyhow, he sent the MS. of *The White Peacock* to William Heinemann, who accepted it at once, and made me alter only four little lines whose omission would now make anybody smile. I was to have £50 when the book was published.

Meanwhile Hueffer printed more poems and some stories of mine in the *English Review*, and people read them and told me so, to my embarrassment and anger. I hated being an author, in people's eyes. Especially as I was a teacher.

When I was twenty-five my mother died, and two months later *The White Peacock* was published, but it meant nothing to me. I went on teaching for another year, and then again a bad pneumonia illness intervened. When I got better I did not go back to school. I lived henceforward on my scanty literary earnings.

It is seventeen years since I gave up teaching and started to live an independent life of the pen. I have never starved, and never even felt poor, though my income for the first ten years was no better, and often worse, than it would have been if I had remained an elementary school teacher.

But when one has been born poor a very little money can be enough. Now my father would think I am rich, if nobody else does. And my mother would think I have risen in the world, even if I don't think so.

But something is wrong, either with me or with the world, or with both of us. I have gone far and met many people, of all sorts and all conditions, and many whom I have genuinely liked and esteemed.

People, *personally*, have nearly always been friendly. Of critics we will not speak, they are different fauna from people. And I have *wanted* to feel truly friendly with some, at least, of my fellow-men.

Yet I have never quite succeeded. Whether I get on *in* the world is a question; but I certainly don't get on very well *with* the world. And whether I am a worldly success or not I really don't know. But I feel, somehow, not much of a human success.

By which I mean that I don't feel there is any very cordial or fundamental contact between me and society, or me and other people. There is a breach. And my contact is with something that is non-human, non-vocal.

I used to think it had something to do with the oldness and the worn-outness of Europe. Having tried other places, I know that is not so. Europe is, perhaps, the least worn-out of the continents, because it is the most lived in. A place that is lived in lives.

It is since coming back from America that I ask myself seriously: Why is there so little contact between myself and the people whom I know? Why has the contact no vital meaning?

And if I write the question down, and try to write the answer down, it is because I feel it is a question that troubles many men.

The answer, as far as I can see, has something to do with class. Class makes a gulf, across which all the best human flow is lost. It is not exactly the triumph of the middle classes that has made the deadness, but the triumph of the middle-class *thing*.

As a man from the working class, I feel that the middle class cut off some of my vital vibration when I am with them. I admit them charming and educated and good people often enough. *But they just stop some part of me from working.* Some part has to be left out.

Then why don't I live with my working people? Because their vibration is limited in another direction. They are narrow, but still fairly deep and passionate, whereas the middle class is broad and shallow and passionless. Quite passionless. At the best they substitute affection, which is the great middle-class positive emotion.

But the working class is narrow in outlook, in prejudice, and narrow in intelligence. This again makes a prison. One can belong absolutely to no class.

Yet I find, here in Italy, for example, that I live in a certain silent contact with the peasants who work the land of this villa. I am not intimate with them, hardly speak to them save to say good day. And they are not working for me; I am not their *padrone.*

Yet it is they, really, who form my *ambiente,* and it is from them that the human flow comes to me. I don't want to live with them in their cottages; that would be a sort of prison. But I want them to be there, about the place, their lives going on along with mine, and in relation to mine. I don't idealise them. Enough of that folly! It is worse than setting school-children to express themselves in self-conscious twaddle. I don't expect them to make any millennium here on earth, neither now nor in the future. But I want to live near them, because their life still flows.

And now I know, more or less, why I cannot follow in the footsteps even of Barrie or of Wells, who both came from the common people also and are both such a success. Now I know why I cannot rise in the world and become even a little popular and rich.

I cannot make the transfer from my own class into the middle class. I cannot, not for anything in the world, forfeit my passional consciousness and my old blood-affinity with my fellow-men and the animals and the land, for that other thin, spurious mental conceit which is all that is left of the mental consciousness once it has made itself exclusive.

[2]

HYMNS IN A MAN'S LIFE

NOTHING is more difficult than to determine what a child takes in, and does not take in, of its environment and its teaching. This fact is brought home to me by the hymns which I learned as a child, and never forgot. They mean to me almost more than the finest poetry, and they have for me a more permanent value, somehow or other.

It is almost shameful to confess that the poems which have meant most to me, like Wordsworth's *Ode to Immortality* and Keats's *Odes*, and pieces of *Macbeth* or *As You Like It* or *Midsummer Night's Dream*, and Goethe's lyrics, such as *Uber allen Gipfeln ist Ruh*, and Verlaine's *Ayant poussé la porte qui chancelle*— all these lovely poems which after all give the ultimate shape to one's life; all these lovely poems woven deep into a man's consciousness, are still not woven so deep in me as the rather banal Nonconformist hymns that penetrated through and through my childhood.

> Each gentle dove
> And sighing bough
> That makes the eve
> So fair to me
> Has something far
> Diviner now
> To draw me back
> To Galilee.
> O Galilee, sweet Galilee,
> Where Jesus loved so much to be,
> O Galilee, sweet Galilee,
> Come sing thy songs again to me!

To me the word Galilee has a wonderful sound. The Lake of Galilee! I don't want to know where it is. I never want to go to Palestine. Galilee is one of those lovely, glamorous worlds, not places, that exist in the golden haze of a child's half-formed imagination. And in my man's imagination it is just the same. It has been left untouched. With regard to the hymns which had such a profound influence on my childish consciousness, there has been no crystallising out, no dwindling into actuality, no hardening into the commonplace. They are the same to my man's experience as they were to me nearly forty years ago.

The moon, perhaps, has shrunken a little. One has been forced to learn about orbits, eclipses, relative distances, dead worlds, craters of the moon, and so on. The crescent at evening still startles the soul with its delicate flashing. But the mind works automatically and says: "Ah, she is in her first quarter. She is all there, in spite of the fact that we see only this slim blade. The earth's shadow is over her." And, willy-nilly, the intrusion of the mental processes dims the brilliance, the magic of the first apperception.

It is the same with all things. The sheer delight of a child's apperception is based on *wonder*; and deny it as we may, knowledge and wonder counteract one another. So that as knowledge increases wonder decreases. We say again: Familiarity breeds contempt. So that as we grow older, and become more familiar with phenomena, we become more contemptuous of them. But that is only partly true. It has taken some races of men thousands of years to become contemptuous of the moon, and to the Hindu the cow is still wondrous. It is not familiarity that breeds contempt: it is the assumption of knowledge. Anybody who looks at the moon and says, "I know all about that poor orb," is, of course, bored by the moon.

Now the great and fatal fruit of our civilisation, which is a civilisation based on knowledge, and hostile to experience, is boredom. All our wonderful education and learning is producing a grand sum-total of boredom. Modern people are inwardly thoroughly bored. Do as they may, they are bored.

They are bored because they experience nothing. And they experience nothing because the wonder has gone out of them. And when the wonder has gone out of a man he is dead. He is henceforth only an insect.

When all comes to all, the most precious element in life is wonder. Love is a great emotion, and power is power. But both love and power are based on wonder. Love without wonder is a sensational affair, and power without wonder is mere force and compulsion. The one universal element in consciousness which is fundamental to life is the element of wonder. You cannot help feeling it in a bean as it starts to grow and pulls itself out of its jacket. You cannot help feeling it in the glisten of the nucleus of the amœba. You recognise it, willy-nilly, in an ant busily tugging at a straw; in a rook, as it walks the frosty grass.

They all have their own obstinate will. But also they all live with a sense of wonder. Plant consciousness, insect consciousness, fish consciousness, animal consciousness, all are related by one permanent element, which we may call the religious element inherent in all life, even in a flea: the sense of wonder. That is our sixth sense. And it is the *natural* religious sense.

Somebody says that mystery is nothing, because mystery is something you don't know, and what you don't know is nothing to you. But there is more than one way of knowing.

Even the real scientist works in the sense of wonder. The pity is, when he comes out of his laboratory he puts aside his wonder along with his apparatus, and tries to make it all perfectly didactic. Science in its true condition of wonder is as religious as any religion. But didactic science is as dead and boring as dogmatic religion. Both are wonderless and productive of boredom, endless boredom.

Now we come back to the hymns. They live and glisten in the depths of the man's consciousness in undimmed wonder, because they have not been subjected to any criticism or analysis. By the time I was sixteen I had criticised and got over the Christian dogma.

It was quite easy for me; my immediate forebears had already done it for me. Salvation, heaven, Virgin birth, miracles, even the Christian dogmas of right and wrong— one soon got them adjusted. I never could really worry about them. Heaven is one of the instinctive dreams. Right and wrong is something you can't dogmatise about; it's not so easy. As for my soul, I simply don't and never did understand how I could "save" it. One can save one's pennies. But how can one save one's soul? One can only *live* one's soul. The business is to live, really alive. And this needs wonder.

So that the miracle of the loaves and fishes is just as good to

me now as when I was a child. I don't care whether it is
historically a fact or not. What does it matter? It is part of
the genuine wonder. The same with all the religious teaching
I had as a child, *apart* from the didacticism and sentimentalism.
I am eternally grateful for the wonder with which it filled my
childhood.

> Sun of my soul, thou Saviour dear,
> It is not night if Thou be near—

That was the last hymn at the board school. It did not mean
to me any Christian dogma or any salvation. Just the words,
"Sun of my soul, thou Saviour dear," penetrated me with
wonder and the mystery of twilight. At another time the last
hymn was:

> Fair waved the golden corn
> In Canaan's pleasant land—

And again I loved "Canaan's pleasant land". The wonder of
"Canaan", which could never be localised.

I think it was good to be brought up a Protestant: and among
Protestants, a Nonconformist, and among Nonconformists, a
Congregationalist. Which sounds pharisaic. But I should
have missed bitterly a direct knowledge of the Bible, and a
direct relation to Galilee and Canaan, Moab and Kedron,
those places that never existed on earth. And in the Church of
England one would hardly have escaped those snobbish
hierarchies of class, which spoil so much for a child. And the
Primitive Methodists, when I was a boy, were always having
"revivals" and being "saved", and I always had a horror of
being saved.

So, altogether, I am grateful to my "Congregational"
upbringing. The Congregationalists are the oldest Nonconformists, descendants of the Oliver Cromwell Independents.
They still had the Puritan traditional of no ritual. But they
avoided the personal emotionalism which one found among the
Methodists when I was a boy.

I liked our chapel, which was tall and full of light, and yet
still; and colour-washed pale green and blue, with a bit of

lotus pattern. And over the organ-loft, "O worship the Lord
in the beauty of holiness," in big letters.
    That was a favourite hymn, too:

> O worship the Lord, in the beauty of holiness,
> Bow down before Him, His glory proclaim;
> With gold of obedience and incense of lowliness
> Kneel and adore Him, the Lord is His name.

I don't know what the "beauty of holiness" is, exactly. It
easily becomes cant, or nonsense. But if you don't think about
it—and why should you?—it has a magic. The same with the
whole verse. It is rather bad, really, "gold of obedience" and
"incense of lowliness". But in me, to the music, it still produces
a sense of splendour.
    I am always glad we had the Bristol hymn-book, not Moody
and Sankey. And I am glad our Scotch minister on the whole
avoided sentimental messes such as *Lead, Kindly Light*, or even
Abide With Me. He had a healthy preference for healthy
hymns.

> At even, ere the sun was set,
>   The sick, O Lord, around Thee lay.
> Oh, in what divers pains they met!
> Oh, in what joy they went away!

And often we had "Fight the good fight with all thy might".
    In Sunday School I am eternally grateful to old Mr.
Remington, with his round white beard and his ferocity. He
made us sing! And he loved the martial hymns:

> Sound the battle-cry,
> See, the foe is nigh.
> Raise the standard high
> For the Lord.

The ghastly sentimentalism that came like a leprosy over
religion had not yet got hold of our colliery village. I remember
when I was in Class II in the Sunday School, when I was
about seven, a woman teacher trying to harrow us about the
Crucifixion. And she kept saying: "And aren't you sorry for
Jesus? Aren't you sorry?" And most of the children wept. I

believe I shed a crocodile tear or two, but very vivid is my
memory of saying to myself: "I don't *really* care a bit." And I
could never go back on it. I never *cared* about the Crucifixion,
one way or another. Yet the *wonder* of it penetrated very deep
in me.

Thirty-six years ago men, even Sunday School teachers, still
believed in the fight for life and the fun of it. "Hold the fort,
for I am coming." It was far, far from any militarism or gun-
fighting. But it was the battle-cry of a stout soul, and a fine
thing too.

> Stand up, stand up for Jesus,
> Ye soldiers of the Lord.

Here is the clue to the ordinary Englishman—in the Nonconformist hymns.

[First published in *The Evening News* (London), 13 October, 1928.]

[3]

Letter to H. C., 1909.

. . . I admit your accusation of impressionism and dog-
matism. Suddenly, in a world full of tones and tints and
shadows I see a colour and it vibrates on my retina. I dip a
brush in it and say, "See, *that's* the colour!" So it is, so it
isn't. . . .

[4]

Letter to SYDNEY S. PAWLING (of Heinemann's) 18 Oct., 1910

I am glad, and much relieved, to hear that you have the
MSS. of the *S. of S.** in your hands. (By the way, don't you
think the title idiotic? I am a failure there. How would *The
Livanters* do?) I shall wait with some curiosity to hear your
opinion of the work. It contains, I know, some rattling good
stuff. But if the whole is not to your taste, I shall not mind,
for I am not in the least anxious to publish that book. I am
content to let it lie for a few years. Of course, you have only

* *The Saga of Siegfried*, afterwards published as *The Trespasser*.

got the rapid work of three months. I should want, I do want, to overhaul the book considerably as soon as you care to return it to me. I am not anxious to publish it, and if you are of like mind, we can let the thing stay, and I will give you—with no intermediary this time—my third novel, *Paul Morel*,* which is plotted out very interestingly (to me), and about one-eighth of which is written. *Paul Morel* will be a novel—not a florid prose poem, or a decorated idyll running to seed in realism: but a restrained, somewhat impersonal novel. It interests me very much.

[5]

Letter to EDWARD GARNETT, 21 Jan., 1912

. . . I will send you herewith the 180 or 190 pages of the *Trespasser* which I have done. It won't take me much longer, will it? I hope the thing is knitted firm—I hate those pieces where the stitch is slack and loose. The *Stranger* piece is probably still too literary—I don't feel at all satisfied.

But this is a work one can't regard easily—I mean, at one's ease. It is so much oneself, one's naked self. I give myself away so much, and write what is my most palpitant, sensitive self, that I loathe the book, because it will betray me to a parcel of fools. Which is what any deeply personal or lyrical writer feels, I guess. I often think Stendhal must have writhed in torture every time he remembered *Le Rouge et le Noir* was public property: and Jefferies at *The Story of my Heart*. I don't like *The Story of my Heart*.

I wish the *Trespasser* were to be issued privately, to a few folk who had understanding. But I suppose by all the rules of life, it must take open chance, if it's good enough.

[6]

Letter to EDWARD GARNETT, 14 Nov., 1912

. . . I hasten to tell you I sent the MS. of the *Paul Morel* novel to Duckworth registered, yesterday. And I want to defend it, quick. I wrote it again, pruning it and shaping it

* Published as *Sons and Lovers*.

and filling it in. I tell you it has got form—*form*: haven't I
made it patiently, out of sweat as well as blood. It follows this
idea: a woman of character and refinement goes into the lower
class, and has no satisfaction in her own life. She has had a
passion for her husband, so the children are born of passion,
and have heaps of vitality. But as her sons grow up she selects
them as lovers—first the eldest, then the second. These sons
are *urged* into life by their reciprocal love of their mother—
urged on and on. But when they come to manhood, they can't
love, because their mother is the strongest power in their lives,
and holds them. It's rather like Goethe and his mother and
Frau von Stein and Christiana—As soon as the young men
come into contact with women, there's a split. William gives
his sex to a fribble, and his mother holds his soul. But the split
kills him, because he doesn't know where he is. The next
son gets a woman who fights for his soul—fights his mother.
The son loves the mother—all the sons hate and are jealous of
the father. The battle goes on between the mother and the
girl, with the son as object. The mother gradually proves
stronger, because of the tie of blood. The son decides to leave
his soul in his mother's hands, and, like his elder brother, go
for passion. He gets passion. Then the split begins to tell again.
But, almost unconsciously, the mother realises what is the
matter, and begins to die. The son casts off his mistress,
attends to his mother dying. He is left in the end naked of
everything, with the drift towards death.

It is a great tragedy, and I tell you I have written a great
book. It's the tragedy of thousands of young men in England—
it may even be Bunny's tragedy. I think it was Ruskin's, and
men like him.—Now tell me if I haven't worked out my theme,
like life, but always my theme. Read my novel. It's a great
novel. If *you* can't see the development—which is slow, like
growth—I can.

[7]

Letter to EDWARD GARNETT, 12 Jan., 1913

. . . I could do hack work, to a certain amount. But apply
my creative self where it doesn't want to be applied, makes me

feel I should burst or go cracked. I couldn't have done any more at that novel—at least for six months. I must go on producing, producing, and the stuff must come more and more to shape each year. But trim and garnish my stuff I cannot—it must go.

[8]

Letter to EDWARD GARNETT, 11 March, 1913
. . . I'm a damned curse unto myself. I've written rather more than half of a most fascinating (to me) novel. But nobody will ever dare to publish it. I feel I could knock my head against the wall. Yet I love and adore this new book. It's all crude as yet, like one of Tony's clumsy prehistorical beasts—most cumbersome and floundering—but I think it's great—so new, so really a stratum deeper than I think anybody has ever gone, in a novel. But there, you see, it's my latest. It is all analytical—quite unlike *Sons and Lovers*, not a bit visualised. But nobody will publish it. I wish I had never been born. But I'm going to stick at it, get it done, and then write another, shorter, absolutely impeccable—as far as morals go—novel. It is an oath I have vowed—if I have to grind my teeth to stumps, I'll do it—or else what am I going to live on, and keep Frieda on withal?

[9]

Letter to A. W. MCLEOD, 26 April, 1913
. . . Pray to your gods for me that *Sons and Lovers* shall succeed. People should begin to take me seriously now. And I do so break my heart over England when I read the *New Machiavelli*.* And I am so sure that only through a readjustment between men and women, and a making free and healthy of this sex, will she get out of her present atrophy. Oh, Lord, and if I don't "subdue my art to a metaphysic", as somebody very beautifully said of Hardy, I do write because I want folk—English folk—to alter, and have more sense.

* Lawrence's views on *New Machiavelli* and Wells are given on page 133.

[10]

Letter to Edward Garnett, 30 Dec., 1913

In a few days' time I shall send you the first half of *The Sisters**—which I should rather call *The Wedding Ring*—to Duckworth's. It is *very* different from *Sons and Lovers*: written in another language almost. I shall be sorry if you don't like it, but am prepared. I shan't write in the same manner as *Sons and Lovers* again, I think—in that hard, violent style full of sensation and presentation. You must see what you think of the new style.

[11]

Letter to Edward Garnett, 29 Jan., 1914

I am not very much surprised, nor even very much hurt by your letter—and I agree with you. I agree with you about the Templeman episode. In the scheme of the novel, however, I *must* have Ella get some experience before she meets her Mr. Birkin. I also felt that the character was inclined to fall into two halves—and gradations between them. It came of trying to graft on to the character of ———— the character, more or less, of ————. That I ought not to have done. To your two main criticisms, that the Templeman episode is wrong, and that the character of Ella is incoherent, I agree. Then about the artistic side being in the background. It is that which troubles me most. I have no longer the joy in creating vivid scenes, that I had in *Sons and Lovers*. I don't care much more about accumulating objects in the powerful light of emotion, and making a scene of them. I have to write differently. I am most anxious about your criticism of this, the second half of the novel, a hundred and fifty pages of which I send you to-morrow. Tell me *very* frankly what you think of it: and if it pleases you, tell me whether you think Ella would be possible, as she now stands, unless she had some experience of love and of men. I think, impossible. Then she must have a love episode, a significant one. But it must not be a Templeman episode.

* This was the first draft of the novel eventually published as *The Rainbow*.

I shall go on now to the end of the book. It will not take me long. Then I will go over it all again, and I shall be very glad to hear *all* you have to say. But if this, the second half, also disappoints you, I will, when I come to the end, leave this book altogether. Then I should propose to write a story with a plot, and to abandon the exhaustive method entirely— write pure object and story.

I am going through a transition stage myself. I am a slow writer, really—I only have great outbursts of work. So that I do not much mind if I put all this novel in the fire, because it is the vaguer result of transition. I write with everything vague—plenty of fire underneath, but, like bulbs in the ground, only shadowy flowers that must be beaten and sustained, for another spring. I feel that this second half of *The Sisters* is very beautiful, but it may not be sufficiently incorporated to please you. I do not try to incorporate it very much—I prefer the permeating beauty. It is my transition stage—but I must write to live, and it must produce its flowers, and if they be frail or shadowy, they will be all right if they are true to their hour. It is not so easy for one to be married. In marriage one must become something else. And I am changing, one way or the other. Thank you for the trouble you take for me. I shall be all the better in the end. Remember I am a slow producer, really.

[12]

Letter to EDWARD GARNETT, 22 April, 1914

... I am not after all a child working erratically. All the time, underneath, there is something deep evolving itself out in me. And it is *hard* to express a new thing, in sincerity. And you should understand, and help me to the new thing, not get angry and say it is *common*, and send me back to the tone of the old *Sisters*. In the *Sisters* was the germ of this novel: woman becoming individual, self-responsible, taking her own initiative. But the first *Sisters* was flippant and often vulgar and jeering. I had to get out of that attitude, and make my subject really worthy. You see—you tell me I am half a Frenchman and one-eighth a Cockney. But that isn't it. I have very often the vulgarity and disagreeableness of the common people, as you say Cockney, and I may be a Frenchman. But primarily I am a passionately religious man, and my novels must be written from the depth of my religious experience. That I must keep to, because I can only work like that. And my Cockneyism and commonness are only when the deep feeling doesn't find its way out, and a sort of jeer comes instead, and sentimentality, and purplism. But you should see the religious, earnest, suffering man in me first, and then the flippant or common things after. Mrs. Garnett says I have no true nobility—with all my cleverness and charm. But that is not true. It is there, in spite of all the littlenesses and commonnesses.

[13]

Letter to EDWARD GARNETT, 5 June, 1914

. . . I don't agree with you about the *Wedding Ring*. You will find that in a while you will like the book as a whole. I don't think the psychology is wrong: it is only that I have a different attitude to my characters, and that necessitates a different attitude in you, which you are not prepared to give. As for its being my *cleverness* which would pull the thing through—that sounds odd to me, for I don't think I am so very clever, in that way. I think the book is a bit futuristic—quite unconsciously so. But when I read Marinetti—"the profound intuitions of life added one to the other, word by word, according to their illogical conception, will give us the general lines of an intuitive physiology of matter"—I see something of what I am after. I translate him clumsily, and his Italian is obfuscated—and I don't care about physiology of matter—but somehow—that which is physic—non-human, in humanity, is more interesting to me than the old-fashioned human element—which causes one to conceive a character in a certain moral scheme and make him consistent. The certain moral scheme is what I object to. In Turgenev, and in Tolstoi, and in Dostoievsky, the moral scheme into which all the characters fit—and it is nearly the same scheme—is, whatever the extraordinariness of the characters themselves, dull, old, dead. When Marinetti writes: "It is the solidity of a blade of steel that is interesting by itself, that is, the incomprehending and inhuman alliance of its molecules in resistance to, let us say, a bullet. The heat of a piece of wood or iron is in fact more passionate, for us, than the laughter or tears of a woman"—then I know what he means. He is stupid, as an artist, for contrasting the heat of the iron and the laugh of the woman. Because what is interesting in the laugh of the woman is the same as the binding of the molecules of steel or their action in heat: it is the inhuman will, call it physiology, or like Marinetti—physiology of matter, that fascinates me. I don't so much care about what the woman *feels*—in the ordinary usage of the word. That presumes an *ego* to feel with. I only care about what the woman is—what she is —inhumanly, physiologically, materially—according to the use of the word: but for me, what she *is* as a phenomenon (or as representing some greater, inhuman will), instead of what she feels according to the human conception. That is where the futurists are stupid. Instead of looking for the new human phenomenon, they will only look for the phenomena of the science of physics to be found in human beings. They are crassly stupid. But if anyone would give them eyes, they would pull the right apples off the tree, for their stomachs are true in appetite. You mustn't look in my novel for the old stable *ego* of the character. There is another *ego*, according to whose action the individual is unrecognisable, and passes through, as it were, allotropic states which it needs a deeper sense than any we've been used to exercise, to discover are states of the same single radically unchanged element. (Like as diamond and coal are the same pure single element of carbon. The ordinary novel would trace the history of the diamond—but I say, "Diamond, what! This is carbon." And my diamond might be coal or soot, and my theme is carbon.) You must not say my novel is shaky—it is not perfect, because I am not expert in what I want to do. But it is the real thing, say what you like. And I shall get my reception, if not now, then before long. Again I say, don't look for the development of the novel to follow the lines of certain characters: the characters fall into the form of some other rhythmic form, as when one draws a fiddle-bow across a fine tray delicately sanded, the sand takes lines unknown.

[14]

Letter to A. W. McLeod, 2 June, 1914

. . . I have been interested in the futurists. I got a book of
their poetry—a very fat book too—and a book of pictures—and
I read Marinetti's and Paolo Buzzi's manifestations and essays
and Soffici's essays on cubism and futurism. It interests me
very much. I like it because it is the applying to emotions
of the purging of the old forms and sentimentalities. I like it
for its saying—enough of this sickly cant, let us be honest and
stick by what is in us. Only when folk say, "Let us be honest
and stick by what is in us"—they always mean, stick by those
things that have been thought horrid, and by those alone.
They want to deny every scrap of tradition and experience,
which is silly. They are very young, college-student and
medical-student at his most blatant. But I like them. Only I
don't believe in them. I agree with them about the weary
sickness of pedantry and tradition and inertness, but I don't
agree with them as to the cure and the escape. They will
progress down the purely male or intellectual or scientific line.
They will even use their intuition for intellectual and scientific
purpose. The one thing about their art is that it *isn't* art, but
ultra scientific attempts to make diagrams of certain physic or
mental states. It is ultra-ultra intellectual, going beyond
Maeterlinck and the Symbolistes, who are intellectual. There
isn't one trace of naïveté in the works—though there's plenty of
naïveté in the authors. It's the most self-conscious, intentional,
pseudo-scientific stuff on the face of the earth. Marinetti
begins: "Italy is like a great Dreadnought surrounded by her
torpedo boats." That is it exactly—a great mechanism. Italy
has got to go through the most mechanical and dead stage of
all—everything is appraised according to its mechanic value—
everything is subject to the laws of physics. This is the revolt
against beastly sentiment and slavish adherence to tradition
and the dead mind. For that I love it. I love them when they
say to the child, "All right, if you want to drag nests and torment
kittens, do it lustily." But I reserve the right to answer, "All
right, try it on. But if I catch you at it you get a hiding."

I think the only re-sourcing of art, revivifying it, is to make it more the joint work of man and woman. I think *the* one thing to do, is for men to have courage to draw nearer to women, expose themselves to them, and be altered by them: and for women to accept and admit men. That is the start—by bringing themselves together, men and women—revealing themselves each to the other, gaining great blind knowledge and suffering and joy, which it will take a big further lapse of civilisation to exploit and work out. Because the source of all life and knowledge is in man and woman, and the source of all living is in the interchange and the meeting and mingling of these two: man-life and woman-life, man-knowledge and woman-knowledge, man-being and woman-being.

[15]

Letter to J. B. PINKER, 16 Dec., 1915

. . . Tell Arnold Bennett that all rules of construction hold good only for novels which are copies of other novels. A book which is not a copy of other books has its own construction, and what he calls faults, he being an old imitator, I call characteristics. I shall repeat till I am grey—when they have as good a work to show, they may make their pronouncements *ex cathedra*. Till then, let them learn decent respect.

[16]

Letter to CURTIS BROWN, 23 June, 1925

. . . I think next week I'll send the MS. of *The Plumed Serpent* (*Quetzalcoatl*), my Mexican novel, to the New York office, asking them to make the corrections on the duplicate and forward a copy to you at once. I consider this my most important novel, so far.

[17]

Letter to ERNEST COLLINGS, 24 Dec., 1912

. . . I am a great admirer of my own stuff while it's new, but after a while I'm not so gone on it—like the true maternal instinct, that kicks off an offspring as soon as it can go on its own legs.

[18]

Letter to LADY OTTOLINE MORRELL, 5 Feb., 1929

. . . Don't you think it's nonsense when Murry says that my world is not the ordinary man's world and that I am a sort of animal with a sixth sense. Seems to me more likely he's a sort of animal with only four senses—the real sense of touch missing. They all seem determined to make a freak of me—to save their own short-failings, and make them "normal".

[19]

Letter to J. M. MURRY, 20 May, 1929

. . . You said in your review of my poems: "this is not life, life is not like that." And you have the same attitude to the real me. Life is not like that—*ergo*, there is no such animal. Hence my "don't care". I am tired of being told there is no such animal, by animals who are merely different. If I am a giraffe, and the ordinary Englishmen who write about me and say they know me are nice well-behaved dogs, there it is, the animals are different. And the me that you say you love is not me, but an idol of your own imagination. Believe me, you don't love me. The animal that I am you instinctively dislike—just as all the Lynds and Squires and Eliots and Goulds instinctively dislike it—and you all say there's no such animal, or if there is there ought not to be—so why not stick to your position?

[20]

Letter to ROLF GARDINER, 9 Aug., 1924

. . . Bah! If ever you edit another paper, take up a hatchet, not a dummy teat of commiseration. What we need is to smash a few big holes in European suburbanity, let in a little real fresh air. Oh, words are action good enough, if they're the right words. But all this blasted snivel of hopelessness and self-pity and "stars"—and "Wind among the trees" and "camp-fires"—and witanagemotery—It's courage we want, fresh air, and not suffused sentiments. Even the stars are stale, that way. If one is going to act, in words, one should go armed to the teeth, and fire carefully at the suburbanians—like Wells, White Fox, Barrie, Jack Squire—even Murry—all the lot. Piff! and down they go!

PART TWO

Puritanism and the Arts

[21]

Letter to Miss Pearn, 12 April, 1927
. . . I am in a quandary about my novel, *Lady Chatterley's Lover*. It's what the world would call very improper. But you know it's not really improper—I always labour at the same thing, to make the sex relation valid and precious, instead of shameful. And this novel is the furthest I've gone. To me it is beautiful and tender and frail as the naked self is, and I shrink very much even from having it typed. Probably the typist would want to interfere.

[22]

Letter to Martin Secker, 5 March, 1928
I posted off the MS. of the novel to Pollinger to-day—changed the title to: *John Thomas and Lady Jane*: which I hope you like, as it's much more suitable than the other. I don't at all know how much you'll react to the book, probably you'll hate it. Aldous Huxley and Maria liked it very much—so they said. —— went into a fearful rage over it—a moral rage. They're the only people who have read it so far.

Then the expurgations—I did a fair amount of blanking out and changing, then I sort of got colour-blind, and didn't know any more what was supposed to be proper and what not. So you must consider it. Don't all in a rush be scared and want to pull whole sections out. Just consider a bit patiently, in detail, what is *possible* and what isn't. I know it's not easy to judge. And then if there are little bits you can leave out without making obvious gaps, then I'm willing you should leave them out. But if you want any substantial alteration made, then consider the

23

thing carefully, in detail, and mark it carefully in blue pencil, and send me the pages you want changed, and I'll do my best. I think we ought to manage to make it feasible. . . .

Well, I hope you won't hate the novel—though you easily may. It's a bit of a revolution in itself—a bit of a bomb.

[23]

Letter to ROLF GARDINER, 17 March, 1928

. . . It is strictly a novel of the phallic consciousness as against the mental consciousness of to-day. For some things, you will probably dislike it: because you are still squeamish, and scared of the phallic reality. It is perfectly wholesome and normal, and man and a woman. But I protest against its being labelled "sex". Sex is a mental reaction nowadays, and a hopelessly cerebral affair: and what I believe in is the true phallic consciousness. But you'll see. So I shall send you a bunch of the little order-forms, and you must get me what orders you can, because the book must be read—it's a bomb, but to the living, a flood of urge—and I must sell it. And it's part of the crusade that we are both out for, and *una mano lava l'altra*—but I know you'll help me what you can. This is where I throw a straight bomb at the skull of idealistic Mammon. And of course it will in a way set me apart even more definitely than I am already set apart. It's destiny. *Tu stai con me, lo so.*

[24]

Letter to L. E. POLLINGER, 2 April, 1928

If you haven't sent over the MS. of *Lady C.* to Chatto's office, please don't send it. I don't want any more publishers trying to cover their nakedness with "large patches of sheer beauty" and sighing, "It's a great pity." It is!

[25]

Letter to HARRY CROSBY, Aug., 1928
 . . . Savage rumours that *Lady Chatterley* is to be suppressed in
London: and that it is stopped from entering America. *Lieber
Ding!* Better read it—it's a direct phallic book, i.e. the direct
nocturnal connection of a man with the sun—the path of the
dark sun.

[26]

Letter to D. V. LEDERHANDLER, 12 Sept., 1929
 . . . Yes, the paralysis of Sir Clifford is symbolic—all art is *au
fond* symbolic, conscious or unconscious. When I began
Lady C., of course I did not know what I was doing—I did
not deliberately work symbolically. But by the time the book
was finished I realised what the unconscious symbolism was.
And I wrote the book three times—I have three complete
MSS.—pretty different, yet the same. The wood is of course
unconscious symbolism—perhaps even the mines—even Mrs.
Bolton.

[27]

Letter to LADY OTTOLINE MORRELL, 28 Dec., 1928
 . . . About *Lady C.*—you mustn't think I advocate perpetual
sex. Far from it. Nothing nauseates me more than promiscuous
sex in and out of season. But I want, with *Lady C.*, to make an
adjustment in consciousness to the basic physical realities. I
realise that one of the reasons why the common people often
keep—or kept—the good *natural glow* of life, just warm life,
longer than educated people, was because it was still possible
for them to say ——!* or ——* without either a shudder or a

* The law being what it is, I have been compelled, reluctantly, to excise some
words.—(EDITOR'S NOTE to *The Letters of D. H. Lawrence*.)

sensation. If a man had been able to say to you when you were young and in love: an' if tha ——,* an' if tha ——,* I'm glad, I shouldna want a woman who couldna ——* nor ——* —surely it would have been a liberation to you, and it would have helped to keep your heart warm. Think of poor Swift's insane *But* of horror at the end of every verse of that poem to Celia. But Celia shits!—you see the very fact that it should horrify him, and simply devastate his consciousness, is all wrong, and a bitter shame to poor Celia. It's just the awful and truly unnecessary *recoil* from these things that I would like to break. It's a question of conscious acceptance and adjustment—only that. God forbid that I should be taken as urging loose sex activity. There is a brief time for sex, and a long time when sex is out of place. But when it is out of place as an activity there still should be the large and quiet space in the consciousness where it lives quiescent. Old people can have a lovely quiescent sort of sex, like apples, leaving the young quite free for *their* sort.

It's such a pity preachers have always dinned in: Go thou and do likewise! That's not the point. The point is: It is so, let it be so, with a generous heart.

[28]

INTRODUCTION TO *PANSIES*

THIS little bunch of fragments is offered as a bunch of *pensées*, *anglicé* pansies; a handful of thoughts. Or, if you will have the other derivation of pansy, from *panser*, to dress or soothe a wound, these are my tender administrations to the mental and emotional wounds we suffer from. Or you can have heartsease if you like, since the modern heart could certainly do with it.

Each little piece is a thought; not a bare idea or an opinion or a didactic statement, but a true thought, which comes as much from the heart and the genitals as from the head. A thought, with its own blood of emotion and instinct running in it like the

* The law being what it is, I have been compelled, reluctantly, to excise some words.—(EDITOR'S NOTE to *The Letters of D. H. Lawrence*.)

fire in a fire-opal, if I may be so bold. Perhaps if you hold up my pansies properly to the light, they may show a running vein of fire. At least, they do not pretend to be half-baked lyrics or melodies in American measure. They are thoughts which run through the modern mind and body, each having its own separate existence, yet each of them combining with all the others to make up a complete state of mind.

It suits the modern temper better to have its state of mind made up of apparently irrelevant thoughts that scurry in different directions, yet belong to the same nest; each thought trotting down the page like an independent creature, each with its own small head and tail, trotting its own little way, then curling up to sleep. We prefer it, at least the young seem to prefer it to those solid blocks of mental pabulum packed like bales in the pages of a proper heavy book. Even we prefer it to those slightly didactic opinions and slices of wisdom which are laid horizontally across the pages of Pascal's *Pensées* or La Bruyère's *Caractères*, separated only by *pattes de mouches*, like faint sprigs of parsley. Let every *pensée* trot on its own little paws, not be laid like a cutlet trimmed with a *patte de mouche*.

Live and let live, and each pansy will tip you its separate wink. The fairest thing in nature, a flower, still has its roots in earth and manure; and in the perfume there hovers still the faint strange scent of earth, the under-earth in all its heavy humidity and darkness. Certainly it is so in pansy-scent, and in violet-scent; mingled with the blue of the morning the black of the corrosive humus. Else the scent would be just sickly sweet.

So it is: we all have our roots in earth. And it is our roots that now need a little attention, need the hard soil eased away from them, and softened so that a little fresh air can come to them, and they can breathe. For by pretending to have no roots, we have trodden the earth so hard over them that they are starving and stifling below the soil. We have roots, and our roots are in the sensual, instinctive and intuitive body, and it is here we need fresh air of open consciousness.

I am abused most of all for using the so-called "obscene" words. Nobody quite knows what the word "obscene" itself means, or what it is intended to mean: but gradually all the *old* words that belong to the body below the navel, have come to be judged obscene. Obscene means to-day that the policeman thinks he has a right to arrest you, nothing else.

Myself, I am mystified at this horror over a mere word, a plain simple word that stands for a plain simple thing. "In the beginning was the Word, and the Word was God and the Word was with God." If that is true, then we are very far from the beginning. When did the Word "fall"? When did the Word become unclean "below the navel"? Because to-day, if you suggest that the word arse was in the beginning and was God and was with God, you will just be put in prison at once. Though a doctor might say the same of the word *ischial tuberosity*, and all the old ladies would piously murmur "Quite!" Now that sort of thing is idiotic and humiliating. Whoever the God was that made us, He made us complete. He didn't stop at the navel and leave the rest to the devil. It is too childish. And the same with the Word which is God. If the Word is God—which in the sense of the human it is—then you can't suddenly say that all the words which belong below the navel are obscene. The word arse is as much god as the word face. It must be so, otherwise you cut off your god at the waist.

What is obvious is that the words in these cases have been dirtied by the mind, by unclean mental associations. The words themselves are clean, so are the things to which they apply. But the mind drags in a filthy association, calls up some repulsive emotion. Well, then, cleanse the mind, that is the real job. It is the mind which is the Augean stables, not language. The word arse is clean enough. Even the part of the body it refers to is just as much me as my hand and my brain are me. It is not for *me* to quarrel with my own natural make-up. If I am, I am all that I am. But the impudent and dirty mind won't have it. It hates certain parts of the body, and makes the words representing these parts scapegoats. It pelts them out of the consciousness with filth, and there they hover, never dying, never dead, slipping into the consciousness again unawares, and pelted out again with filth, haunting the margins of the consciousness like jackals or hyenas. And they refer to parts of our own living bodies, and to our most essential acts. So that man turns himself into a thing of shame and horror. And his consciousness shudders with horrors that he has made for himself.

That sort of thing has got to stop. We can't have the consciousness haunted any longer by repulsive spectres which are no more than poor simple scapegoat words representing parts of man himself; words that the cowardly and unclean mind has driven out into the limbo of the unconscious, whence they return upon us looming and magnified out of all proportion, frightening us beyond all reasons. We must put an end to that. It is the self divided against itself most dangerously. The simple and natural "obscene" words must be cleaned up of all their depraved fear-associations, and readmitted into the consciousness to take their natural place. Now they are magnified out of all proportion, so is the mental fear they represent. We must accept the word arse as we accept the word face, since arses we have and always shall have. We can't start cutting off the buttocks of unfortunate mankind, like the ladies in the Voltaire story, just to fit the mental expulsion of the word.

This scapegoat business does the mind itself so much damage. There is a poem of Swift's which should make us pause. It is written to Celia, his Celia—and every verse ends with the mad, maddened refrain: "But—Celia, Celia, Celia shits!" Now that, stated baldly, is so ridiculous it is almost funny. But when one remembers the gnashing insanity to which the great mind of Swift was reduced by that and similar thoughts, the joke dies away. Such thoughts poisoned him, like some terrible constipation. They poisoned his mind. And why, in Heaven's name? The *fact* cannot have troubled him, since it applied to himself and to all of us. It was not the fact that Celia shits which so deranged him, it was the *thought*. His mind couldn't bear the thought. Great wit as he was, he could not see how ridiculous his revulsions were. His arrogant mind overbore him. He couldn't even see how much worse it would be if Celia didn't shit. His physical sympathies were too weak, his guts were too cold to sympathise with poor Celia in her natural functions. His insolent and sicklily squeamish mind just turned her into a thing of horror, because she was merely natural and went to the w.c. It is monstrous! One feels like going back across all the years to poor Celia, to say to her: It's all right, don't you take any notice of that mental lunatic.

And Swift's form of madness is very common to-day. Men with cold guts and over-squeamish minds are always thinking

those things and squirming. Wretched man is the victim of his
own little revulsions, which he magnifies into great horrors and
terrifying taboos. We are all savages, we all have taboos. The
Australian black may have the kangaroo for his taboo. And
then he will probably die of shock and terror if a kangaroo
happens to touch him. Which is what I would call a purely
unnecessary death. But modern men have even more dangerous
taboos. To us, certain words, certain ideas are taboo, and if
they come upon us and we can't drive them away, we die or
go mad with a degraded sort of terror. Which is what happened
to Swift. He was such a great wit. And the modern mind
altogether is falling into this form of degraded taboo-insanity.
I call it a waste of sane human consciousness. But it is very
dangerous, dangerous to the individual and utterly dangerous
to society as a whole. Nothing is so fearful in a mass-civilisation
like ours as a mass-insanity.

The remedy is, of course, the same in both cases: lift off the
taboo. The kangaroo is a harmless animal, the word shit is a
harmless word. Make either into a taboo, and it becomes more
dangerous. The result of taboo is insanity. And insanity,
especially mob-insanity, mass-insanity, is the fearful danger that
threatens our civilisation. There are certain persons with a
sort of rabies, who live only to infect the mass. If the young do
not watch out, they will find themselves, before so very many
years are past, engulfed in a howling manifestation of mob-
insanity, truly terrifying to think of. It will be better to be
dead than to live to see it. Sanity, wholeness, is everything. In
the name of piety and purity, what a mass of disgusting
insanity is spoken and written. We shall have to fight the mob,
in order to keep sane, and to keep society sane.

[From the edition of *Pansies* privately printed for subscribers by P. R.
Stephensen, London, 1929.]

[29]

Letter to MORRIS L. ERNST, 10 Nov., 1928
I have finished reading *To the Pure.* I find it a curious,
interesting, pertinent book, curiously moving. As the work of
lawyers rather than literary men, it conveys an impression that

no truly literary work would achieve. I look out with those unemotional lawyer's eyes, and have a queer experience. I am left feeling puzzled, uneasy and a little frightened, as if I had been watching a great unchained ape fumbling through his hairs for something—he doesn't quite know what—which he will squash if he gets it. I see that weird and horrible animal, Social Man, devoid of real individuality or personality, fumbling gropingly and menacingly for something he is afraid of, but he doesn't know what it is. It is a lawyer's vision, not an artist's—but it is the result of experience in dealing with the Social Man. The book, in its queer muddle—for legal precision is artistic muddle—creates the weird reactionary of the ageless censor-animal curiously and vividly. It leaves one feeling breathless, and makes one realise the necessity of keeping a chain on the beast. For censorship is one of the lower and debasing activities of social man—that is obvious.

Myself, I believe censorship helps nobody; and hurts many. But the book has brought it home to me much more grimly than before. Our civilisation cannot afford to let the censor-moron loose. The censor-moron does not really hate anything but the living and growing human consciousness. It is our developing and extending consciousness that he threatens—and our consciousness in its newest, most sensitive activity, its vital growth. To arrest or circumscribe the vital consciousness is to produce morons, and nothing but a moron would wish to do it.

No, the book is a good book—and the very effect of muddle which it has on me conveys most vividly the feeling of the groping atavistic working of the ageless censor, furtive, underhand, mean.

Print this letter if you like—or any bit of it. I believe in the living extending consciousness of man. I believe the consciousness of man has now to embrace the emotions and passions of sex, and the deep effects of human physical contact. This is the glimmering edge of our awareness and our field of understanding, in the endless business of knowing ourselves. And no censor must or shall or even can really interfere.

[30]

PORNOGRAPHY AND OBSCENITY

WHAT they are depends, as usual, entirely on the individual. What is pornography to one man is the laughter of genius to another.

The word itself, we are told, means "pertaining to harlots"— the graph of the harlot. But nowadays, what is a harlot? If she was a woman who took money from a man in return for going to bed with him—really, most wives sold themselves, in the past, and plenty of harlots gave themselves, when they felt like it, for nothing. If a woman hasn't got a tiny streak of a harlot in her, she's a dry stick as a rule. And probably most harlots had somewhere a streak of womanly generosity. Why be so cut and dried? The law is a dreary thing, and its judgments have nothing to do with life.

The same with the word *obscene*: nobody knows what it means. Suppose it were derived from *obscena*: that which might not be represented on the stage; how much further are you? None! What is obscene to Tom is not obscene to Lucy or Joe, and really, the meaning of a word has to wait for majorities to decide it. If a play shocks ten people in an audience, and doesn't shock the remaining five hundred, then it is obscene to ten and innocuous to five hundred; hence, the play is not obscene, by majority. But *Hamlet* shocked all the Cromwellian Puritans, and shocks nobody to-day, and some of Aristophanes shocks everybody to-day, and didn't galvanise the later Greeks at all, apparently. Man is a changeable beast, and words change their meanings with him, and things are not what they seemed, and what's what becomes what isn't, and if we think we know where we are it's only because we are so rapidly being translated to somewhere else. We have to leave everything to the majority, everything to the majority, everything to the mob, the mob, the mob. They know what is obscene and what isn't, they do. If the lower ten million doesn't know better than the upper ten men, then there's something wrong with mathematics. Take a vote on it! Show hands, and prove it by count! *Vox populi, vox Dei. Odi profanum vulgus! Profanum vulgus.*

So it comes down to this: if you are talking to the mob, the meaning of your words is the mob-meaning, decided by majority. As somebody wrote to me: the American law on obscenity is very plain, and America is going to enforce the law. Quite, my dear, quite, quite, quite! The mob knows all about obscenity. Mild little words that rhyme with spit or farce are the height of obscenity. Supposing a printer put "h" in the place of "p", by mistake, in that mere word spit? Then the great American public knows that this man has committed an obscenity, an indecency, that his act was lewd, and as a compositor he was pornographical. You can't tamper with the great public, British or American. *Vox populi, vox Dei,* don't you know. If you don't we'll let you know it. At the same time, this *vox Dei* shouts with praise over moving-pictures and books and newspaper accounts that seem, to a sinful nature like mine, completely disgusting and obscene. Like a real prude and Puritan, I have to look the other way. When obscenity becomes mawkish, which is its palatable form for the public, and when the *Vox populi, vox Dei* is hoarse with senti-mental indecency, then I have to steer away, like a Pharisee, afraid of being contaminated. There is a certain kind of sticky universal pitch that I refuse to touch.

So again, it comes down to this: you accept the majority, the mob, and its decisions, or you don't. You bow down before the *Vox populi, vox Dei,* or you plug your ears not to hear its obscene howl. You perform your antics to please the vast public, *Deus ex machina,* or you refuse to perform for the public at all, unless now and then to pull its elephantine and ignominious leg.

When it comes to the meaning of anything, even the simplest word, then you must pause. Because there are two great categories of meaning, for ever separate. There is mob-meaning, and there is individual meaning. Take even the word *bread.* The mob-meaning is merely: stuff made with white flour into loaves that you eat. But take the individual meaning of the word bread: the white, the brown, the corn-pone, the home-made, the smell of bread just out of the oven, the crust, the crumb, the unleavened bread, the shew-bread, the staff of life, sour-dough bread, cottage loaves, French bread, Viennese bread, black bread, a yesterday's loaf, rye, graham, barley, rolls, *Bretzeln*, *Kringeln*, scones, damper, matsen—there is no end to it all, and the word bread will take you to the ends of time and space, and far-off down avenues of memory. But this is individual. The word bread will take the individual off on his own journey, and its meaning will be his own meaning, based on his own genuine imagination reactions. And when a word comes to us in its individual character, and starts in us the individual responses, it is great pleasure to us. The American advertisers have discovered this, and some of the cunningest American literature is to be found in advertisements of soap-suds, for example. These advertisements are *almost* prose-poems. They give the word soap-suds a bubbly, shiny individual meaning, which is very skilfully poetic, would, perhaps, be quite poetic to the mind which could forget that the poetry was bait on a hook.

Business is discovering the individual, dynamic meaning of words, and poetry is losing it. Poetry more and more tends to far-fetch its word-meanings, and this results once again in mob-meanings, which arouse only a mob-reaction in the individual. For every man has a mob-self and an individual self, in varying proportions. Some men are almost all mob-self, incapable of imaginative individual responses. The worst specimens of mob-self are usually to be found in the professions, lawyers, professors, clergymen and so on. The business man, much maligned, has a tough outside mob-self, and a scared, floundering yet still alive individual self. The public, which is feeble-minded like an idiot, will never be able to preserve its individual reactions from the tricks of the exploiter. The public is always exploited and always will be exploited. The methods of exploitation merely vary. To-day the public is tickled into laying the golden egg. With imaginative words and individual meanings it is tricked into giving the great goose-cackle of mob-acquiescence. *Vox populi, vox Dei.* It has always been so, and will always be so. Why? Because the public has not enough wit to distinguish between mob-meanings and individual meanings. The mass is for ever vulgar, because it can't distinguish between its own original feelings and feelings which are diddled into existence by the exploiter. The public is always profane, because it is controlled from the outside, by the trickster, and never from the inside, by its own sincerity. The mob is always obscene, because it is always second-hand.

Which brings us back to our subject of pornography and obscenity. The reaction to any word may be, in any individual, either a mob-reaction or an individual reaction. It is up to the individual to ask himself: Is my reaction individual, or am I merely reacting from my mob-self?

When it comes to the so-called obscene words, I should say that hardly one person in a million escapes mob-reaction. The first reaction is almost sure to be mob-reaction, mob-indignation, mob-condemnation. And the mob gets no further. But the real individual has second thoughts and says: Am I really shocked? Do I *really* feel outraged and indignant? And the answer of any individual is bound to be: No, I am not shocked, not outraged, nor indignant. I know the word, and take it for what it is, and I am not going to be jockeyed into making a mountain out of a mole-hill, not for all the law in the world.

Now if the use of a few so-called obscene words will startle man or woman out of a mob-habit into an individual state, well and good. And word prudery is so universal a mob-habit that it is time we were startled out of it.

But still we have only tackled obscenity, and the problem of pornography goes even deeper. When a man is startled into his individual self, he still may not be able to know, inside himself, whether Rabelais is or is not pornographic: and over Aretino or even Boccaccio he may perhaps puzzle in vain, torn between different emotions.

One essay on pornography, I remember, comes to the conclusion that pornography in art is that which is calculated to arouse sexual desire, or sexual excitement. And stress is laid on the fact, whether the author or artist *intended* to arouse sexual feelings. It is the old vexed question of intention, become so dull to-day, when we know how strong and influential our unconscious intentions are. And why a man should be held guilty of his conscious intentions, and innocent of his unconscious intentions, I don't know, since every man is more made up of unconscious intentions than of conscious ones. I am what I am, not merely what I think I am.

However! We take it, I assume, that *pornography* is something base, something unpleasant. In short, we don't like it.

And why don't we like it? Because it arouses sexual feelings?
I think not. No matter how hard we may pretend otherwise,
most of us rather like a moderate rousing of our sex. It warms
us, stimulates us like sunshine on a grey day. After a century
or two of Puritanism, this is still true of most people. Only the
mob-habit of condemning any form of sex is too strong to let
us admit it naturally. And there are, of course, many people
who are genuinely repelled by the simplest and most natural
stirrings of sexual feeling. But these people are perverts who
have fallen into hatred of their fellow-men: thwarted, disappointed, unfulfilled people, of whom, alas, our civilisation
contains so many. And they nearly alway enjoy some
unsimple and unnatural form of sex excitement, secretly.

Even quite advanced art critics would try to make us believe
that any picture or book which had "sex appeal" was *ipso
facto* a bad book or picture. This is just canting hypocrisy.
Half the great poems, pictures, music, stories of the whole
world are great by virtue of the beauty of their sex appeal.
Titian or Renoir, the Song of Solomon or *Jane Eyre*, Mozart or
"Annie Laurie", the loveliness is all interwoven with sex
appeal, sex stimulus, call it what you will. Even Michelangelo,
who rather hated sex, can't help filling the Cornucopia with
phallic acorns. Sex is a very powerful, beneficial and necessary
stimulus in human life, and we are all grateful when we feel
its warm, natural flow through us, like a form of sunshine.

So we can dismiss the idea that sex appeal in art is pornography. It may be so to the grey Puritan, but the grey Puritan
is a sick man, soul and body sick, so why should we bother
about his hallucinations? Sex appeal, of course, varies enormously. There are endless different kinds, and endless degrees
of each kind. Perhaps it may be argued that a mild degree of
sex appeal is not pornographical, whereas a high degree is.
But this is a fallacy. Boccaccio at his hottest seems to me less
pornographical than *Pamela* or *Clarissa Harlowe* or even *Jane
Eyre*, or a host of modern books or films which pass uncensored.
At the same time Wagner's *Tristan and Isolde* seems to me very
near to pornography, and so, even, do some quite popular
Christian hymns.

What is it, then? It isn't a question of sex appeal, merely:
nor even a question of deliberate intention on the part of the

author or artist to arouse sexual excitement. Rabelais sometimes had a deliberate intention, so in a different way, did Boccaccio. And I'm sure poor Charlotte Brontë, or the authoress of *The Sheik*, did not have any deliberate intention to stimulate sex feelings in the reader. Yet I find *Jane Eyre* verging towards pornography and Boccaccio seems to me always fresh and wholesome.

The late British Home Secretary, who prides himself on being a very sincere Puritan, grey, grey in every fibre, said with indignant sorrow in one of his outbursts on improper books: "—and these two young people, who had been perfectly pure up till that time, after reading this book went and had sexual intercouse together! ! !" *One up to them!* is all we can answer. But the grey Guardian of British Morals seemed to think that if they had murdered one another, or worn each other to rags of nervous prostration, it would have been much better. The grey disease!

Then what is pornography, after all this? It isn't sex appeal or sex stimulus in art. It isn't even a deliberate intention on the part of the artist to arouse or excite sexual feelings. There's nothing wrong with sexual feelings in themselves, so long as they are straightforward and not sneaking or sly. The right sort of sex stimulus is invaluable to human daily life. Without it the world grows grey. I would give everybody the gay Renaissance stories to read, they would help to shake off a lot of grey self-importance, which is our modern civilised disease.

But even I would censor genuine pornography, rigorously. It would not be very difficult. In the first place, genuine pornography is almost always underworld, it doesn't come into the open. In the second, you can recognise it by the insult it offers, invariably, to sex, and to the human spirit.

Pornography is the attempt to insult sex, to do dirt on it. This is unpardonable. Take the very lowest instance, the picture postcard sold underhand, by the underworld, in most cities. What I have seen of them have been of an ugliness to make you cry. The insult to the human body, the insult to a vital human relationship! Ugly and cheap they make the human nudity, ugly and degraded they make the sexual act, trivial and cheap and nasty.

It is the same with the books they sell in the underworld.

They are either so ugly they make you ill, or so fatuous you can't imagine anybody but a cretin or a moron reading them, or writing them.

It is the same with the dirty limericks that people tell after dinner, or the dirty stories one hears commercial travellers telling each other in a smoke-room. Occasionally there is a really funny one, that redeems a great deal. But usually they are just ugly and repellent, and the so-called "humour" is just a trick of doing dirt on sex.

Now the human nudity of a great many modern people is just ugly and degraded, and the sexual act between modern people is just the same, merely ugly and degrading. But this is nothing to be proud of. It is the catastrophe of our civilisation. I am sure no other civilisation, not even the Roman, has showed such a vast proportion of ignominious and degraded nudity, and ugly, squalid dirty sex. Because no other civilisation has driven sex into the underworld, and nudity to the w.c.

The intelligent young, thank heaven, seem determined to alter in these two respects. They are rescuing their young nudity from the stuffy, pornographical hole-and-corner underworld of their elders, and they refuse to sneak about the sexual relation. This is a change the elderly grey ones of course deplore, but it is in fact a very great change for the better, and a real revolution.

But it is amazing how strong is the will in ordinary, vulgar people, to do dirt on sex. It was one of my fond illusions, when I was young, that the ordinary healthy-seeming sort of men in railway carriages, or the smoke-room of an hotel or a pullman, were healthy in their feelings and had a wholesome rough devil-may-care attitude towards sex. All wrong! All wrong! Experience teaches that common individuals of this sort have a disgusting attitude towards sex, a disgusting contempt of it, a disgusting desire to insult it. If such fellows have intercourse with a woman, they triumphantly feel that they have done her dirt, and now she is lower, cheaper, more contemptible than she was before.

It is individuals of this sort that tell dirty stories, carry indecent picture postcards, and know the indecent books. This is the great pornographical class—the really common men-in-the-street and women-in-the-street. They have as great a hate and contempt of sex as the greyest Puritan, and when an appeal is made to them, they are always on the side of the angels. They insist that a film-heroine shall be a neuter, a sexless thing of washed-out purity. They insist that real sex-feeling shall only be shown by the villain or villainess, low lust. They find a Titian or a Renoir really indecent, and they don't want their wives and daughters to see it.

Why? Because they have the grey disease of sex-hatred, coupled with the yellow disease of dirt-lust. The sex functions and the excrementory functions in the human body work so close together, yet they are, so to speak, utterly different in direction. Sex is a creative flow, the excrementory flow is towards dissolution, de-creation, if we may use such a word. In the really healthy human being the distinction between the two is instant, our profoundest instincts are perhaps our instincts of opposition between the two flows.

But in the degraded human being the deep instincts have gone dead, and then the two flows become identical. *This* is the secret of really vulgar and of pornographical people: the sex flow and the excrement flow is the same to them. It happens when the psyche deteriorates, and the profound controlling instincts collapse. Then sex is dirt and dirt is sex, and sexual excitement becomes a playing with dirt, and any sign of sex in a woman becomes a show of her dirt. This is the condition of the common, vulgar human being whose name is legion, and who lifts his voice and it is the *Vox populi, vox Dei*. And this is the source of all pornography.

And for this reason we must admit that *Jane Eyre* or Wagner's *Tristan* are much nearer to pornography than is Boccaccio. Wagner and Charlotte Brontë were both in the state where the strongest instincts have collapsed, and sex has become something slightly obscene, to be wallowed in, but despised. Mr. Rochester's sex passion is not "respectable" till Mr. Rochester is burned, blinded, disfigured, and reduced to helpless dependence. Then, thoroughly humbled and humiliated, it may be merely admitted. All the previous titillations are slightly indecent, as in *Pamela* or *The Mill on the Floss* or *Anna Karenina*. As soon as there is sex excitement with a desire to spite the sexual feelings, to humiliate it and degrade it, the element of pornography enters.

For this reason, there is an element of pornography in nearly all nineteenth-century literature and very many so-called pure people have a nasty pornographical side to them, and never was the pornographical appetite stronger than it is to-day. It is a sign of a diseased condition of the body politic. But the way to treat the disease is to come out into the open with sex and sex stimulus. The real pornographer truly dislikes Boccaccio, because the fresh healthy naturalness of the Italian story-teller makes the modern pornographical shrimp feel the dirty worm he is. To-day Boccaccio should be given to everybody, young or old, to read if they like. Only a natural fresh openness about sex will do any good, now we are being swamped by secret or semi-secret pornography. And perhaps the Renaissance story-tellers, Boccaccio, Lasca, and the rest, are the best antidote we can find now, just as more plasters of Puritanism are the most harmful remedy we can resort to.

The whole question of pornography seems to me a question of secrecy. Without secrecy there would be no pornography. But secrecy and modesty are two utterly different things. Secrecy has always an element of fear in it, amounting very often to hate. Modesty is gentle and reserved. To-day, modesty is thrown to the winds, even in the presence of the grey guardians. But secrecy is hugged, being a vice in itself. And the attitude of the grey ones is: Dear young ladies, you may abandon all modesty, so long as you hug your dirty little secret.

This "dirty little secret" has become infinitely precious to the mob of people to-day. It is a kind of hidden sore or inflammation which, when rubbed or scratched, gives off sharp thrills that seem delicious. So the dirty little secret is rubbed and scratched more and more, till it becomes more and more secretly inflamed, and the nervous and psychic health of the individual is more and more impaired. One might easily say that half the love novels and half the love films to-day depend entirely for their success on the secret rubbing of the dirty little secret. You can call this sex excitement if you like, but it is sex excitement of a secretive, furtive sort, quite special. The plain and simple excitement, quite open and wholesome, which you find in some Boccaccio stories is not for a minute to be confused with the furtive excitement aroused by rubbing the dirty little secret in all secrecy in modern best-sellers. This furtive, sneaking, cunning rubbing of an inflamed spot in the imagination is the very quick of modern pornography, and it is a beastly and very dangerous thing. You can't so easily expose it, because of its very furtiveness and its sneaking cunning. So the cheap and popular modern love novel and love film flourishes and is even praised by moral guardians, because you get the sneaking thrill fumbling under all the purity of dainty underclothes, without one single gross word to let you know what is happening.

Without secrecy there would be no pornography. But if pornography is the result of sneaking secrecy, what is the result of pornography? What is the effect on the individual?

The effect on the individual is manifold, and always pernicious. But one effect is perhaps inevitable. The pornography of to-day, whether it be the pornography of the rubber-goods shop or the pornography of the popular novel, film, and play, is an invariable stimulant to the vice of self-abuse, onanism, masturbation, call it what you will. In young or old, man or woman, boy or girl, modern pornography is a direct provocative of masturbation. It cannot be otherwise. When the grey ones wail that the young man and the young woman went and had sexual intercourse, they are bewailing the fact that the young man and the young woman didn't go separately and masturbate. Sex must go somewhere, especially in young people. So, in our glorious civilisation, it goes in masturbation. And the mass of our popular literature, the bulk of our popular amusements just exists to provoke masturbation. Masturbation is the one thoroughly secret act of the human being, more secret even than excrementation. It is the one functional result of sex-secrecy, and it is stimulated and provoked by our glorious popular literature of pretty pornography, which rubs on the dirty secret without letting you know what is happening.

Now I have heard men, teachers and clergymen, commend masturbation as the solution of an otherwise insoluble sex problem. This at least is honest. The sex problem is there, and you can't just will it away. There it is, and under the ban of secrecy and taboo in mother and father, teacher, friend, and foe, it has found its own solution, the solution of masturbation.

But what about the solution? Do we accept it? Do all the grey ones of this world accept it? If so, they must now accept it openly. We can none of us pretend any longer to be blind to the fact of masturbation, in young and old, man and woman. The moral guardians who are prepared to censor all open and plain portrayal of sex must now be made to give their only justification: We prefer that the people shall masturbate. If this preference is open and declared, then the existing forms of censorship are justified. If the moral guardians prefer that the people shall masturbate, then their present behaviour is correct, and popular amusements are as they should be. If sexual intercourse is deadly sin, and masturbation is comparatively pure and harmless, then all is well. Let things continue as they now are.

Is masturbation so harmless, though? Is it even comparatively pure and harmless? Not to my thinking. In the young, a certain amount of masturbation is inevitable, but not therefore natural. I think, there is no boy or girl who masturbates without feeling a sense of shame, anger, and futility. Following the excitement comes the shame, anger, humiliation, and the sense of futility. This sense of futility and humiliation deepens as the years go on, into a suppressed rage, because of the impossibility of escape. The one thing that it seems impossible to escape from, once the habit is formed, is masturbation. It goes on and on, on into old age, in spite of marriage or love affairs or anything else. And it always carries this secret feeling of futility and humiliation, futility and humiliation. And this is, perhaps, the deepest and most dangerous cancer of our civilisation. Instead of being a comparatively pure and harmless vice, masturbation is certainly the most dangerous sexual vice that a society can be afflicted with, in the long run. Comparatively pure it may be—purity being what it is. But harmless! ! !

The great danger of masturbation lies in its merely exhaustive nature. In sexual intercourse, there is a give and take. A new stimulus enters as the native stimulus departs. Something quite new is added as the old surcharge is removed. And this is so in all sexual intercourse where two creatures are concerned, even in the homosexual intercourse. But in masturbation there is nothing but loss. There is no reciprocity. There is merely the spending away of a certain force, and no return. The body remains, in a sense, a corpse, after the act of self-abuse. There is no change, only deadening. There is what we call dead loss. And this is not the case in any act of sexual intercourse between two people. Two people may destroy one another in sex. But they cannot just produce the null effect of masturbation.

The only positive effect of masturbation is that it seems to release a certain mental energy, in some people. But it is mental energy which manifests itself always in the same way, in a vicious circle of analysis and impotent criticism, or else a vicious circle of false and easy sympathy, sentimentalities. The sentimentalism and the niggling analysis, often self-analysis, of most of our modern literature, is a sign of self-abuse. It is the manifestation of masturbation, the sort of conscious activity stimulated by masturbation, whether male or female. The outstanding feature of such consciousness is that there is no real object, there is only subject. This is just the same whether it be a novel or a work of science. The author never escapes from himself, he pads along within the vicious circle of himself. There is hardly a writer living who gets out of the vicious circle of himself—or a painter either. Hence the lack of creation, and the stupendous amount of production. It is a masturbation result, within the vicious circle of the self. It is self-absorption made public.

And of course the process is exhaustive. The real masturbation of Englishmen began only in the nineteenth century. It has continued with an increasing emptying of the real vitality and the real *being* of men, till now people are little more than shells of people. Most of the responses are dead, most of the awareness is dead, nearly all the constructive activity is dead, and all that remains is a sort of shell, a half-empty creature fatally self-preoccupied and incapable of either giving or taking. Incapable either of giving or taking, in the vital self. And this is masturbation result. Enclosed within the vicious circle of the self, with no vital contacts outside, the self becomes emptier and emptier, till it is almost a nullus, a nothingness.

But null or nothing as it may be, it still hangs on the dirty little secret, which it must still secretly rub and inflame. For ever the vicious circle. And it has a weird, blind will of its own.

One of my most sympathetic critics wrote: "If Mr. Lawrence's attitude to sex were adopted, then two things would disappear, the love lyric and the smoking-room story." And this, I think, is true. But it depends on which love lyric he means. If it is the: *Who is Sylvia, what is she?*—then it may just as well disappear. All that pure and noble and heaven-blessed stuff is only the counterpart to the smoking-room story. *Du bist wie eine Blume!* Jawohl! One can see the elderly gentleman laying his hands on the head of the pure maiden and praying God to keep her for ever so pure, so clean and beautiful. Very nice for him! Just pornography! Tickling the dirty little secret and rolling his eyes to heaven! He knows perfectly well that if God keeps the maiden so clean and pure and beautiful—in his vulgar sense of clean and pure—for a few more years, then she'll be an unhappy old maid, and not pure nor beautiful at all, only stale and pathetic. Sentimentality is a sure sign of pornography. Why should "sadness strike through the heart" of the old gentleman, because the maid was pure and beautiful? Anybody but a masturbator would have been glad and would have thought: What a lovely bride for some lucky man!—But no, not the self-enclosed, pornographic masturbator. Sadness has to strike into his beastly heart!—Away with such love lyrics, we've had too much of their pornographic poison, tickling the dirty little secret and rolling the eyes to heaven.

But if it is a question of the sound love lyric, *My love is like a red, red rose——!* then we are on other ground. My love is like a red, red rose only when she's *not* like a pure, pure lily. And nowadays the pure, pure lilies are mostly festering, anyhow. Away with them and their lyrics. Away with the pure, pure lily lyric, along with the smoking-room story. They are counterparts, and the one is as pornographic as the other. *Du bist wie eine Blume* is really as pornographic as a dirty story: tickling the dirty little secret and rolling the eyes to heaven. But oh, if only Robert Burns had been accepted for what he is, then love might still have been like a red, red rose.

The vicious circle, the vicious circle! The vicious circle of masturbation! The vicious circle of self-consciousness that is never *fully* self-conscious, never fully and openly conscious, but always harping on the dirty little secret. The vicious circle of secrecy, in parents, teacher, friends—everybody. The specially vicious circle of family. The vast conspiracy of secrecy in the press, and at the same time, the endless tickling of the dirty little secret. The needless masturbation! and the endless purity! The vicious circle!

How to get out of it? There is only one way: Away with the secret! No more secrecy! The only way to stop the terrible mental itch about sex is to come out quite simply and naturally into the open with it. It is terribly difficult, for the secret is cunning as a crab. Yet the thing to do is to make a beginning. The man who said to his exasperating daughter: "My child, the only pleasure I ever had out of you was the pleasure I had in begetting you" has already done a great deal to release both himself and her from the dirty little secret.

How to get out of the dirty little secret! It is, as a matter of fact, extremely difficult for us secretive moderns. You can't do it by being wise and scientific about it, like Dr. Marie Stopes: though to be wise and scientific like Dr. Marie Stopes is better than to be utterly hypocritical, like the grey ones. But by being wise and scientific in the serious and earnest manner you only tend to disinfect the dirty little secret, and either kill sex altogether with too much seriousness and intellect, or else leave it a miserable disinfected secret. The unhappy "free and pure" love of so many people who have taken out the dirty little secret and thoroughly disinfected it with scientific words is apt to be more pathetic even than the common run of dirty-little-secret love. The danger is, that in killing the dirty little secret, you kill dynamic sex altogether, and leave only the scientific and deliberate mechanism.

This is what happens to many of those who become seriously "free" in their sex, free and pure. They have mentalised sex till it is nothing at all, nothing at all but a mental quantity. And the final result is disaster, every time.

The same is true, in an even greater proportion, of the emancipated Bohemians: and very many of the young are Bohemian to-day, whether they ever set foot in Bohemia or not. But the Bohemian is "sex free". The dirty little secret is no secret either to him or her. It is, indeed, a most blatantly open question. There is nothing they don't say: everything that can be revealed is revealed. And they do as they wish.

And then what? They have apparently killed the dirty little secret, but somehow, they have killed everything else too. Some of the dirt still sticks, perhaps; sex remains still dirty. But the

thrill of secrecy is gone. Hence the terrible dreariness and
depression of modern Bohemia, and the inward dreariness and
emptiness of so many young people of to-day. They have killed,
they imagine, the dirty little secret. The thrill of secrecy is
gone. Some of the dirt remains. And for the rest, depression,
inertia, lack of life. For sex is the fountain-head of our energetic
life, and now the fountain ceases to flow.

Why? For two reasons. The idealists along the Marie
Stopes line, and the young Bohemians of to-day have killed the
dirty little secret as far as their personal self goes. But they are
still under its dominion socially. In the social world, in the
press, in literature, film, theatre, wireless, everywhere purity
and the dirty little secret reign supreme. At home, at the dinner
table, it is just the same. It is the same wherever you go. The
young girl, and the young woman is by tacit assumption pure,
virgin, sexless. *Du bist wie eine Blume.* She, poor thing, knows
quite well that flowers, even lilies, have tippling yellow anthers
and a sticky stigma, sex, rolling sex. But to the popular mind
flowers are sexless things, and when a girl is told she is like a
flower, it means she is sexless and ought to be sexless. She
herself knows quite well she isn't sexless and she isn't merely like
a flower. But how bear up against the great social life forced
on her? She can't! She succumbs, and the dirty little secret
triumphs. She loses her interest in sex, as far as men are
concerned, but the vicious circle of masturbation and self-
consciousness encloses her even still faster.

This is one of the disasters of young life to-day. Personally,
and among themselves, a great many, perhaps a majority of
the young people of to-day have come out into the open with
sex and laid salt on the tail of the dirty little secret. And this
is a very good thing. But in public, in the social world, the
young are still entirely under the shadow of the grey elderly
ones. The grey elderly ones belong to the last century, the
eunuch century, the century of the mealy-mouthed lie, the
century that has tried to destroy humanity, the nineteenth
century. All our grey ones are left over from this century. And
they rule us. They rule us with the grey, mealy-mouthed,
canting lie of that great century of lies which, thank God, we
are drifting away from. But they rule us still with the lie, for
the lie, in the name of the lie. And they are too heavy and too

numerous, the grey ones. It doesn't matter what government it is. They are all grey ones, left over from the last century, the century of mealy-mouthed liars, the century of purity and the dirty little secret.

So there is one cause for the depression of the young: the public reign of the mealy-mouthed lie, purity and the dirty little secret, which they themselves have privately overthrown. Having killed a good deal of the lie in their own private lives, the young are still enclosed and imprisoned within the great public lie of the grey ones. Hence the excess, the extravagance, the hysteria, and then the weakness, the feebleness, the pathetic silliness of the modern youth. They are all in a sort of prison, the prison of a great lie and a society of elderly liars. And this is one of the reasons, perhaps the main reason, why the sex-flow is dying out of the young, the real energy is dying away. They are enclosed within a lie, and the sex won't flow. For the length of a complete lie is never more than three generations, and the young are the fourth generation of the nineteenth-century lie.

The second reason why the sex-flow is dying is, of course, that the young, in spite of their emancipation, are still enclosed within the vicious circle of self-conscious masturbation. They are thrown back into it, when they try to escape, by the enclosure of the vast public lie of purity and the dirty little secret. The most emancipated Bohemians, who swank most about sex, are still utterly self-conscious and enclosed within the narcissus-masturbation circle. They have perhaps less sex even than the grey ones. The whole thing has been driven up into their heads. There isn't even the lurking hole of a dirty little secret. Their sex is more mental than their arithmetic; and as vital physical creatures they are more non-existent than ghosts. The modern Bohemian is indeed a kind of ghost, not even narcissus, only the image of narcissus reflected on the face of the audience. The dirty little secret is most difficult to kill. You may put it to death publicly a thousand times, and still it reappears, like a crab, stealthily from under the submerged rocks of the personality. The French, who are supposed to be so open about sex, will perhaps be the last to kill the dirty little secret. Perhaps they don't want to. Anyhow, mere publicity won't do it.

You may parade sex abroad, but you will not kill the dirty

little secret. You may read all the novels of Marcel Proust, with everything there in all detail. Yet you will not kill the dirty little secret. You will perhaps only make it more cunning. You may even bring about a state of utter indifference and sex-inertia, still without killing the dirty little secret. Or you may be the most wispy and enamoured little Don Juan of modern days, and still the core of your spirit merely be the dirty little secret. That is to say, you will still be in the narcissus-masturbation circle, the vicious circle of self-enclosure. For whenever the dirty little secret exists, it exists as the centre of the vicious circle of masturbation self-enclosure. And whenever you have the vicious circle of masturbation self-enclosure, you have at the core the dirty little secret. And the most high-flown sex-emancipated young people to-day are perhaps the most fatally and nervously enclosed within the masturbation self-enclosure. Nor do they want to get out of it, for there would be nothing left to come out.

But some people surely do want to come out of the awful self-enclosure. To-day, practically everybody is self-conscious and imprisoned in self-consciousness. It is the joyful result of the dirty little secret. Vast numbers of people don't want to come out of the prison of their self-consciousness: they have so little left to come out with. But some people, surely, want to escape this doom of self-enclosure which is the doom of our civilisation. There is surely a proud minority that wants once and for all to be free of the dirty little secret.

And the way to do it is, first, to fight the sentimental lie of purity and the dirty little secret wherever you meet it, inside yourself or in the world outside. Fight the great lie of the nineteenth century, which has soaked through our sex and our bones. It means fighting with almost every breath, for the lie is ubiquitous.

Then secondly, in his adventure of self-consciousness a man must come to the limits of himself and become aware of something beyond him. A man must be self-conscious enough to know his own limits, and to be aware of that which surpasses him. What surpasses me is the very urge of life that is within me, and this life urges me to forget myself and to yield to the stirring half-born impulse to smash up the vast lie of the world, and make a new world. If my life is merely to go on in a vicious circle of self-enclosure, masturbating self-consciousness, it is worth nothing to me. If my individual life is to be enclosed within the huge corrupt lie of society to-day, purity and the dirty little secret, then it is worth not much to me. Freedom is a very great reality. But it means, above all things, freedom from lies. It is first, freedom from myself, from the lie of myself, from the lie of my all-importance, even to myself; it is freedom from the self-conscious masturbating thing I am, self-enclosed. And second, freedom from the vast lie of the social world, the lie of purity and the dirty little secret. All the other monstrous lies lurk under the cloak of this one primary lie. The monstrous lie of money lurks under the cloak of purity. Kill the purity-lie, and the money-lie will be defenceless.

We have to be sufficiently conscious, and self-conscious, to know our own limits and to be aware of the greater urge within us and beyond us. Then we cease to be primarily interested in ourselves. Then we learn to leave ourselves alone, in all the affective centres: not to force our feelings in any way, and never to force our sex. Then we make the great onslaught on to the outside lie, the inside lie being settled. And that is freedom and the fight for freedom.

The greatest of all lies in the modern world is the lie of purity and the dirty little secret. The grey ones left over from the nineteenth century are the embodiment of this lie. They dominate in society, in the press, in literature, everywhere. And, naturally, they lead the vast mob of the general public along with them.

Which means, of course, perpetual censorship of anything that would militate against the lie of purity and the dirty little secret, and perpetual encouragement of what may be called permissible pornography, pure, but tickling the dirty little secret under the delicate underclothing. The grey ones will pass and will commend floods of evasive pornography, and will suppress every outspoken word.

The law is a mere figment. In his article on the "Censorship of Books", in the *Nineteenth Century*, Viscount Brentford, the late Home Secretary, says: "Let it be remembered that the publishing of an obscene book, the issue of an obscene postcard or pornographic photograph—are all offences against the law of the land, and the Secretary of State who is the general authority for the maintenance of law and order most clearly and definitely cannot discriminate between one offence and another in discharge of his duty."

So he winds up, *ex cathedra* and infallible. But only ten lines above he has written: "I agree, that if the law were pushed to its logical conclusion, the printing and publication of such books as *The Decameron*, Benvenuto Cellini's *Life*, and Burton's *Arabian Nights* might form the subject of proceedings. But the ultimate sanction of all law is public opinion, and I do not believe for one moment that prosecution in respect of books that have been in circulation for many centuries would command public support."

Ooray then for public opinion! It only needs that a few more years shall roll. But now we see that the Secretary of State most clearly and definitely *does* discriminate between one offence and another in discharge of his duty. Simple and admitted discrimination on his part! Yet what is this public opinion? Just more lies on the part of the grey ones. They would suppress Benvenuto to-morrow, if they dared. But they would make laughing-stocks of themselves, because *tradition* backs up Benvenuto. It isn't public opinion at all. It is the grey ones afraid of making still bigger fools of themselves. But the case is simple. If the grey ones are going to be backed by a general public, then every new book that would smash the mealy-mouthed lie of the nineteenth century will be suppressed as it appears. Yet let the grey ones beware. The general public is nowadays a very unstable affair, and no longer loves its grey ones so dearly, with their old lie. And there is another public, the small public of the minority, which hates the lie and the grey ones that perpetuate the lie, and which has its own dynamic ideas about pornography and obscenity. You can't fool all the people all the time, even with purity and a dirty little secret.

And this minority public knows well that the books of many contemporary writers, both big and lesser fry, are far more pornographical than the liveliest story in *The Decameron*: because they tickle the dirty little secret and excite to private masturbation, which the wholesome Boccaccio never does. And the minority public knows full well that the most obscene painting on a Greek vase—*Thou still unravished bride of quietness*—

is not as pornographical as the close-up kisses on the film, which excite men and women to secret and separate masturbation.

And perhaps one day even the general public will desire to look the thing in the face, and see for itself the difference between the sneaking masturbation pornography of the press, the film, and present-day popular literature, and then the creative portrayals of the sexual impulse that we have in Boccaccio or the Greek vase-paintings or some Pompeian art, and which are necessary for the fulfilment of our consciousness.

As it is, the public mind is to-day bewildered on this point, bewildered almost to idiocy. When the police raided my picture show, they did not in the least know what to take. So they took every picture where the smallest bit of the sex organ of either man or woman showed. Quite regardless of subject or meaning or anything else: they would allow anything, these dainty policemen in a picture show, except the actual sight of a fragment of the human *pudenda*. This was the police test. The dabbing on of a postage stamp—especially a green one that could be called a leaf—would in most cases have been quite sufficient to satisfy this "public opinion".

It is, we can only repeat, a condition of idiocy. And if the purity-with-a-dirty-little-secret lie is kept up much longer, the mass of society will really be an idiot, and a dangerous idiot at that. For the public is made up of individuals. And each individual has sex, and is pivoted on sex. And if, with purity and dirty little secrets, you drive every individual into the masturbation self-enclosure, and keep him there, then you will produce a state of general idiocy. For the masturbation self-enclosure produces idiots. Perhaps if we are all idiots, we shan't know it. But God preserve us.

[First published in *This Quarter*, July–September 1929.]

[31]

Letter to DONALD CARSWELL, 5 Dec., 1927
    . . . Cath's idea of a Burns' book I like very much: I always
wanted to do one myself, but am not Scotchy enough. I read
just now Lockhart's bit of a life of Burns. Made me spit!
Those damned middle-class Lockharts grew lilies of the valley
up their ———, to hear them talk. If Cath is condescending to
Burns, I disown her. He was quite right, a man's a man for a'
that, and it's *not* a bad poem. He means what he says. My word,
you can't know Burns unless you can hate the Lockharts and
all the estimable bourgeois and upper classes as he really did—
the narrow-gutted pigeons. Don't, for God's sake, be mealy-
mouthed like them. *I'd* like to write a Burns life. Oh, why
doesn't Burns come to life again, and really salt them! I'm all
for Keir Hardie, my boy. Did you ever *know* Sir G. Trevelyan,
for example? Pfui! "I'm it, mealy-mouthed it!" No, my boy,
don't be on the side of the angels, it's too lowering.

[32]

From

INTRODUCTION TO THESE PAINTINGS
(Puritanism and the Arts)

THE reason the English produce so few painters is not that they
are, as a nation, devoid of a genuine feeling for visual art:
though to look at their productions, and to look at the mess
which has been made of actual English landscape, one might
really conclude that they were, and leave it at that. But it is
not the fault of the God that made them. They are made with
æsthetic sensibilities the same as anybody else. The fault lies
in the English attitude to life.
    The English, and the Americans following them, are paralysed
by fear. That is what thwarts and distorts the Anglo-Saxon

existence, this paralysis of fear. It thwarts life, it distorts vision, and it strangles impulse: this overmastering fear. And fear of what, in Heaven's name? What is the Anglo-Saxon stock to-day so petrified with fear about? We have to answer that before we can understand the English failure in the visual arts: for, on the whole, it is a failure.

It is an old fear, which seemed to dig in to the English soul at the time of the Renaissance. Nothing could be more lovely and fearless than Chaucer. But already Shakespeare is morbid with fear, fear of consequences. That is the strange phenomenon of the English Renaissance: this mystic terror of the consequences, the consequences of action. Italy, too, had her reaction, at the end of the sixteenth century, and showed a similar fear. But not so profound, so overmastering. Aretino was anything but timorous: he was bold as any Renaissance novelist, and went one better.

What appeared to take full grip on the northern consciousness at the end of the sixteenth century was a terror, almost a horror of sexual life. The Elizabethans, grand as we think them, started it. The real "mortal coil" in Hamlet is all sexual; the young man's horror of his mother's incest, sex carrying with it a wild and nameless terror which, it seems to me, it had never carried before. Œdipus and Hamlet are very different in this respect. In Œdipus there is no recoil in horror from sex itself: Greek drama never shows us that. The horror, when it is present in Greek tragedy, is against *destiny*, man caught in the toils of destiny. But with the Renaissance itself, particularly in England, the horror is sexual. Orestes is dogged by destiny and driven mad by the Eumenides. But Hamlet is overpowered by horrible revulsion from his physical connexion with his mother, which makes him recoil in similar revulsion from Ophelia, and almost from his father, even as a ghost. He is horrified at the merest suggestion of physical connexion, as if it were an unspeakable taint.

This, no doubt, is all in the course of the growth of the "spiritual-mental" consciousness, at the expense of the instinctive-intuitive consciousness. Man came to have his own body in horror, especially in its sexual implications: and so he began to suppress with all his might his instinctive-intuitive consciousness, which is so radical, so physical, so sexual.

Cavalier poetry, love poetry, is already devoid of body. Donne, after the exacerbated revulsion-attraction excitement of his earlier poetry, becomes a divine. "Drink to me only with thine eyes," sings the cavalier: an expression incredible in Chaucer's poetry. "I could not love thee, dear, so much, loved I not honour more," sings the Cavalier lover. In Chaucer the "dear" and the "honour" would have been more or less identical.

But with the Elizabethans the grand rupture had started in the human consciousness, the mental consciousness recoiling in violence away from the physical, instinctive-intuitive. To the Restoration dramatists sex is, on the whole, a dirty business, but they more or less glory in the dirt. Fielding tries in vain to defend the Old Adam. Richardson with his calico purity and his underclothing excitements sweeps all before him. Swift goes mad with sex and excrement revulsion. Sterne flings a bit of the same excrement humorously around. And physical consciousness gives a last song in Burns, then is dead. Wordsworth, Keats, Shelley, the Brontës, all are post-mortem poets. The essential instinctive-intuitive body is dead, and worshipped in death—all very unhealthy. Till Swinburne and Oscar Wilde try to start a revival from the mental field. Swinburne's "white thighs" are purely mental.

Now, in England—and following, in America—the physical self was not just fig-leafed over or suppressed in public, as was the case in Italy and on most of the Continent. In England it excited a strange horror and terror. And this extra morbidity came, I believe, from the great shock of syphilis and the realisation of the consequences of the disease. Wherever syphilis, or "pox", came from, it was fairly new in England at the end of the fifteenth century. But by the end of the sixteenth, its ravages were obvious, and the shock of them had just penetrated the thoughtful and the imaginative consciousness. The royal families of England and Scotland were syphilitic; Edward VI and Elizabeth born with the inherited consequences of the disease. Edward VI died of it, while still a boy. Mary died childless and in utter depression. Elizabeth had no eyebrows, her teeth went rotten; she must have felt herself, somewhere, utterly unfit for marriage, poor thing. That was the grisly horror that lay behind the glory of Queen Bess. And so the Tudors died out: and another syphilitic-born unfortunate came to the throne, in the person of James I. Mary Queen of Scots had no more luck than the Tudors, apparently. Apparently Darnley was reeking with the pox, though probably at first she did not know it. But when the Archbishop of St. Andrews was christening her baby James, afterwards James I of England, the old clergyman was so dripping with pox that she was terrified lest he should give it to the infant. And she need not have troubled, for the wretched infant had brought it into the world with him, from that fool Darnley. So James I of England slobbered and shambled, and was the wisest fool in Christendom, and the Stuarts likewise died out, the stock enfeebled by the disease.

With the royal families of England and Scotland in this condition, we can judge what the noble houses, the nobility of both nations, given to free living and promiscuous pleasure, must have been like. England traded with the East and with America; England, unknowing, had opened her doors to the disease. The English aristocracy travelled and had curious taste in loves. And pox entered the blood of the nation, particularly of the upper classes, who had more chance of infection. And after it had entered the blood, it entered the consciousness, and hit the vital imagination.

It is possible that the effects of syphilis and the conscious realisation of its consequences gave a great blow also to the Spanish psyche, precisely at this period. And it is possible that Italian society, which was on the whole so untravelled, had no connection with America, and was so privately self-contained, suffered less from the disease. Someone ought to make a thorough study of the effects of "pox" on the minds and the emotions and imaginations of the various nations of Europe, at about the time of our Elizabethans.

The apparent effect on the Elizabethans and the Restoration wits is curious. They appear to take the whole thing as a joke. The common oath, "Pox on you!" was almost funny. But how common the oath was! How the word "pox" was in every mind and in every mouth. It is one of the words that haunt Elizabethan speech. Taken very manly, with a great deal of Falstaffian bluff, treated as a huge joke! Pox! Why, he's got the pox! Ha-ha! What's he been after?

There is just the same attitude among the common run of
men to-day with regard to the minor sexual diseases. Syphilis
is no longer regarded as a joke, according to my experience.
The very word itself frightens men. You could joke with the
word "pox". You can't joke with the word "syphilis". The
change of word has killed the joke. But men still joke about
clap! which is a minor sexual disease. They pretend to think it
manly, even, to have the disease, or to have had it. "What!
never had a shot of clap!" cries one gentleman to another.
"Why, where have you been all your life?" If we change the
word and insisted on "gonorrhœa", or whatever it is, in place
of "clap", the joke would die. And anyhow I have had young
men come to me green and quaking, afraid they've caught a
"shot of clap".

Now, in spite of all the Elizabethan jokes about pox, pox was
no joke to them. A joke may be a very brave way of meeting a
calamity, or it may be a very cowardly way. Myself, I consider
the Elizabethan pox joke a purely cowardly attitude. They
didn't think it funny, for by God it *wasn't* funny. Even poor
Elizabeth's lack of eyebrows and her rotten teeth were not
funny. And they all knew it. They may not have known it was
the direct result of pox: though probably they did. This fact
remains, that no man can contract syphilis, or any deadly
sexual disease, without feeling the most shattering and profound
terror go through him, through the very roots of his being.
And no man can look without a sort of horror on the effects of a
sexual disease in another person. We are so constituted that we
are all at once horrified and terrified. The fear and dread has
been so great that the pox joke was invented as an evasion, and
following that, the great hush! hush! was imposed. Man was
too frightened: that's the top and bottom of it.

But now, with remedies discovered, we need no longer be
too frightened. We can begin, after all these years, to face the
matter. After the most fearful damage has been done.

For an overmastering fear is poison to the human psyche.
And this overmastering fear, like some horrible secret tumour,
has been poisoning our consciousness ever since the Elizabethans, who first woke up with dread to the entry of the
original syphilitic poison into the blood.

I know nothing about medicine and very little about diseases, and my facts are such as I have picked up in casual reading. Nevertheless I am convinced that the secret awareness of syphilis, and the utter secret terror and horror of it, has had an enormous and incalculable effect on the English consciousness and on the American. Even when the fear has never been formulated, there it has lain, potent and overmastering. I am convinced that *some* of Shakespeare's horror and despair, in his tragedies, arose from the shock of his consciousness of syphilis. I don't suggest for one moment Shakespeare ever contracted syphilis. I have never had syphilis myself. Yet I know and confess how profound is my fear of the disease, and more than fear, my horror. In fact, I don't think I am so very much afraid of it. I am more horrified, inwardly and deeply, at the idea of its existence.

All this sounds very far from the art of painting. But it is not so far as it sounds. The appearance of syphilis in our midst gave a fearful blow to our sexual life. The real natural innocence of Chaucer was impossible after that. The very sexual act of procreation might bring as one of its consequences a foul disease, and the unborn might be tainted from the moment of conception. Fearful thought! It is truly a fearful thought, and all the centuries of getting used to it won't help us. It remains a fearful thought, and to free ourselves from this fearful dread we should use all our wits and all our efforts, not stick our heads in the sand of some idiotic joke, or still more idiotic don't-mention-it. The fearful thought of the consequences of syphilis, or of any sexual disease, upon the unborn gives a shock to the impetus of fatherhood in any man, even the cleanest. Our consciousness is a strange thing, and the knowledge of a certain fact may wound it mortally, even if the fact does not touch us directly. And so I am certain that *some* of Shakespeare's father-murder complex, *some* of Hamlet's horror of his mother, of his uncle, of all old men came from the feeling that fathers may transmit syphilis, or syphilis-consequences, to children. I don't know even whether Shakespeare was actually aware of the consequences to a child born of a syphilitic father or mother. He may not have been, though most probably he was. But he certainly was aware of the effects of syphilis itself, especially on men. And this awareness struck at his deep sex imagination, at his instinct for fatherhood, and brought in an element of terror and abhorrence there where men should feel anything but terror and abhorrence, into the pro-creative act.

The terror-horror element which had entered the imagina-tion with regard to the sexual and procreative act was at least partly responsible for the rise of Puritanism, the beheading of the king-father Charles, and the establishment of the New England colonies. If America really sent us syphilis, she got back the full recoil of the horror of it, in her puritanism.

But deeper even than this, the terror-horror element led to the crippling of the consciousness of man. Very elementary in man is his sexual and procreative being, and on his sexual and procreative being depend many of his deepest instincts and the flow of his intuition. A deep instinct of kinship joins men together, and the kinship of flesh-and-blood keeps the warm flow of intuitional awareness streaming between human beings. Our true awareness of one another is intuitional, not mental. Attraction between people is really instinctive and intuitional, not an affair of judgment. And in mutual attraction lies perhaps the deepest pleasure in life, mutual attraction which may make us "like" our travelling companion for the two or three hours we are together, then no more; or mutual attraction that may deepen to powerful love, and last a lifetime.

The terror-horror element struck a blow at our feeling of physical communion. In fact, it almost killed it. We have become ideal beings, creatures that exist in idea, to one another, rather than flesh-and-blood kin. And with the collapse of the feeling of physical, flesh-and-blood kinship, and the substitution of our ideal, social or political oneness, came the failing of our intuitive awareness, and the great unease, the *nervousness* of mankind. We are *afraid* of the instincts. We are *afraid* of the intuition within us. We suppress the instincts, and we cut off our intuitional awareness from one another and from the world. The reason being some great shock to the procreative self. Now we know one another only as ideal or social or political entities, fleshless, bloodless, and cold, like Bernard Shaw's creatures. Intuitively we are dead to one another, we have all gone cold.

But by intuition alone can man *really* be aware of man, or of the living, substantial world. By intuition alone can man live

and know either woman or world, and by intuition alone can
he bring forth again images of magic awareness which we call
art. In the past men brought forth images of magic awareness,
and now it is the convention to admire these images. The
convention says, for example, we must admire Botticelli or
Giorgione, so Baedeker stars the pictures, and we admire them.
But it is all a fake. Even those that get a thrill, even when they
call it ecstasy, from these old pictures are only undergoing
cerebral excitation. Their deeper responses, down in the
intuitive and instinctive body, are not touched. They cannot
be, because they are dead. A dead intuitive body stands there
and gazes at the corpse of beauty: and usually it is completely
and honestly bored. Sometimes it feels a mental coruscation
which it calls an ecstasy or an æsthetic response.

Modern people, but particularly English and Americans,
cannot feel anything with the whole imagination. They can see
the living body of imagery as little as a blind man can see
colour. The imaginative vision, which includes physical,
intuitional perception, they *have not got*. Poor things, it is dead
in them. And they stand in front of a Botticelli Venus, which
they know as conventionally "beautiful", much as a blind man
might stand in front of a bunch of roses and pinks and monkey-
musk, saying: "Oh, do tell me which is red; let me feel red!
Now let me feel white! Oh, let me feel it! What is this I am
feeling? Monkey-musk? Is it white? Oh, do you say it is
yellow blotched with orange-brown? Oh, but I can't feel it!
What *can* it be? Is white velvety, or just silky?"

So the poor blind man! Yet he may have an acute perception
of alive beauty. Merely by touch and scent, his intuitions being
alive, the blind man may have a genuine and soul-satisfying
experience of imagery. But not pictorial images. These are
for ever beyond him.

So those poor English and Americans in front of the Botticelli
Venus. They stare so hard; they do so *want* to see. And their
eyesight is perfect. But all they can see is a sort of nude woman
on a sort of shell on a sort of pretty greenish water. As a rule
they rather dislike the "unnaturalness" or "affectation" of it.
If they are high-brows they may get a little self-conscious thrill
of æsthetic excitement. But real imaginative awareness, which
is so largely physical, is denied them. *Ils n'ont pas de quoi*, as the

Frenchman said of the angels, when asked if they made love in Heaven.

Ah, the dear high-brows who gaze in a sort of ecstasy and get a correct mental thrill! Their poor high-brow bodies stand there as dead as dust-bins, and can no more feel the sway of complete imagery upon them than they can feel any other real sway. *Ils n'ont pas de quoi.* The instincts and the intuitions are so nearly dead in them, and they fear even the feeble remains. Their fear of the instincts and intuitions is even greater than that of the English Tommy who calls: "Eh, Jack! Come an' look at this girl standin' wi' no clothes on, an' two blokes spittin' at 'er." That is his vision of Botticelli's Venus. It is, for him, complete, for he is void of the image-seeing imagination. But at least he doesn't have to work up a cerebral excitation, as the highbrow does, who is really just as void.

All alike, cultured and uncultured, they are still dominated by that unnamed, yet overmastering dread and hate of the instincts deep in the body, dread of the strange intuitional awareness of the body, dread of anything but ideas, which *can't* contain bacteria. And the dread all works back to a dread of the procreative body, and is partly traceable to the shock of the awareness of syphilis.

The dread of the instincts included the dread of intuitional awareness. "Beauty is a snare"—"Beauty is but skin-deep" —"Handsome is as handsome does"—"Looks don't count"— "Don't judge by appearances"—if we only realised it, there are thousands of these vile proverbs which have been dinned into us for over two hundred years. They are all of them false. Beauty is not a snare, nor is it skin-deep, since it always involves a certain loveliness of modelling, and handsome doers are often ugly and objectionable people, and if you ignore the look of the thing you plaster England with slums and produce at last a state of spiritual depression that is suicidal, and if you don't judge by appearances, that is, if you can't trust the impression which things make on you, you are a fool. But all these base-born proverbs, born in the cash-box, hit direct against the intuitional consciousness. Naturally, man gets a great deal of his life's satisfaction from beauty, from a certain sensuous pleasure in the look of the thing. The old Englishman built his hut of a cottage with a childish joy in its appearance, purely intuitional and direct. The modern Englishman has a few borrowed ideas, simply doesn't know *what* to feel, and makes a silly mess of it: though perhaps he is improving, hopefully, in this field of architecture and house-building. The intuitional faculty, which alone relates us in direct awareness to physical things and substantial presences, is atrophied and dead, and we don't know *what* to feel. We know we ought to feel something, but what?—Oh, tell us what! And this is true of all nations, the French and Italians as much as the English. Look at new French suburbs! Go through the crockery and furniture departments in the *Dames de France* or any big shop. The blood in the body stands still, before such *crétin* ugliness. One has to decide that the modern bourgeois is a *crétin*.

This movement against the instincts and the intuition took on a moral tone in all countries. It started in hatred. Let us never forget that modern morality has its roots in hatred, a deep, evil hate of the instinctive, intuitional, procreative body. This hatred is made more virulent by fear, and an extra poison is added to the fear by unconscious horror of syphilis. And so we come to modern bourgeois consciousness, which turns upon the secret poles of fear and hate. That is the real pivot of all bourgeois consciousness in all countries: fear and hate of the instinctive, intuitional, procreative body in man or woman. But of course this fear and hate had to take on a righteous appearance, so it became moral, said that the instincts, intuitions and all the activities of the procreative body were evil, and promised a *reward* for their suppression. That is the great clue to bourgeois psychology: the reward business. It is screamingly obvious in Maria Edgeworth's tales, which must have done unspeakable damage to ordinary people. Be good, and you'll have money. Be wicked, and you'll be utterly penniless at last, and the good ones will have to offer you a little charity. This is sound working morality in the world. And it makes one realise that, even to Milton, the true hero of *Paradise Lost* must be Satan. But by this baited morality the masses were caught and enslaved to industrialism before ever they knew it; the good got hold of the goods, and our modern "civilisation" of money, machines, and wage-slaves was inaugurated. The very pivot of it, let us never forget, being fear and hate, the most intimate fear and hate, fear and hate of one's own instinctive, intuitive body, and fear and hate of every other man's and every other woman's warm, procreative body and imagination.

Now it is obvious what result this will have on the plastic arts, which depend entirely on the representation of substantial bodies, and on the intuitional perception of the *reality* of substantial bodies. The reality of substantial bodies can only be perceived by the imagination, and the imagination is a kindled state of consciousness in which intuitive awareness predominates. The plastic arts are all imagery, and imagery is the body of our imaginative life, and our imaginative life is a great joy and fulfilment to us, for the imagination is a more powerful and more comprehensive flow of consciousness than our ordinary flow. In the flow of true imagination we know in full, mentally and physically at once, in a greater, enkindled awareness. At the maximum of our imagination we are religious. And if we deny our imagination, and have no imaginative life, we are poor worms who have never lived.

In the seventeenth and eighteenth centuries we have the deliberate denial of intuitive awareness, and we see the results on the arts. Vision became more optical, less intuitive and painting began to flourish. But what painting! Watteau, Ingres, Poussin, Chardin have some real imaginative glow still. They are still somewhat free. The puritan and the intellectual has not yet struck them down with his fear and hate obsession. But look at England! Hogarth, Reynolds, Gainsborough, they all are already bourgeois. The coat is really more important than the man. It is amazing how important clothes suddenly become, how they *cover* the subject. An old Reynolds colonel in a red uniform is much more a uniform than an individual, and as for Gainsborough, all one can say is: What a lovely dress and hat! What really expensive Italian silk! This painting of garments continued in vogue, till pictures like Sargent's seem to be nothing but yards and yards of satin from the most expensive shops, having some pretty head popped on the top. The imagination is quite dead. The optical vision, a sort of flashy coloured photography of the eye, is rampant.

In Titian, in Velasquez, in Rembrandt, the people are there inside their clothes all right, and the clothes are imbued with the life of the individual, the gleam of the warm procreative body comes through all the time, even if it be an old, half-blind woman or a weird, ironic little Spanish princess. But modern people are nothing inside their garments, and a head sticks out at the top and hands stick out of the sleeves, and it is a bore. Or, as in Lawrence or Raeburn, you have something very pretty but almost a mere cliché, with very little instinctive or intuitional perception to it.

After this, and apart from landscape and water-colour, there is strictly no English painting that exists. As far as I am concerned, the pre-Raphaelites don't exist; Watts doesn't, Sargent doesn't, and none of the moderns.

There is the exception of Blake. Blake is the only painter of imaginative pictures, apart from landscape, that England has produced. And unfortunately there is so little Blake, and even in that little the symbolism is often artificially imposed. Nevertheless, Blake paints with real intuitional awareness and solid instinctive feeling. He dares handle the human body, even if he sometimes make it a mere ideograph. And no other Englishman has even dared handle it with alive imagination. Painters of composition-pictures in England, of whom perhaps the best is Watts, never quite get beyond the level of cliché, sentimentalism, and *funk*. Even Watts is a failure, though he made some sort of try: even Etty's nudes in York fail imaginatively, though they have some feeling for flesh. And the rest, the Leightons, even the moderns don't really do anything. They never get beyond studio models and clichés of the nude. The image never gets across to us, to seize us intuitively. It remains merely optical.

Landscape, however, is different. Here the English exist and hold their own. But, for me, personally, landscape is always waiting for something to occupy it. Landscape seems to be *meant* as a background to an intenser vision of life, so to my feeling painted landscape is background with the real subject left out.

Nevertheless, it can be very lovely, especially in water-colour, which is a more bodiless medium, and doesn't aspire to very substantial existence, and is so small that it doesn't try to make a very deep seizure on the consciousness. Water-colour will always be more of a statement than an experience.

And landscape, on the whole, is the same. It doesn't call up the more powerful responses of the human imagination, the sensual, passional responses. Hence it is the favourite modern form of expression in painting. There is no deep conflict. The instinctive and intuitional consciousness is called into play, but lightly, superficially. It is not confronted with any living, procreative body.

Hence the English have delighted in landscape, and have succeeded in it well. It is a form of escape for them, from the actual human body they so hate and fear, and it is an outlet for their perishing æsthetic desires. For more than a century we have produced delicious water-colours, and Wilson, Crome, Constable, Turner are all great landscape-painters. Some of Turner's landscape compositions are, to my feelings, among the finest that exist. They still satisfy me more even than van Gogh's or Cézanne's landscapes, which make a more violent assault on the emotions, and repel a little for that reason. Somehow I don't want landscape to make a violent assault on my feelings. Landscape is background with the figures left out or reduced to minimum, so let it stay back. Van Gogh's surging earth and Cézanne's explosive or rattling planes worry me. Not being profoundly interested in landscape, I prefer it to be rather quiet and unexplosive.

But, of course, the English delight in landscape is a delight in escape. It is always the same. The northern races are so innerly afraid of their own bodily existence, which they believe fantastically to be an evil thing—you could never find them feel anything but uneasy shame, or an equally shameful gloating, over the fact that a man was having intercourse with his wife, in his house next door—that all they cry for is an escape. And, especially, art must provide that escape.

It is easy in literature. Shelley is pure escape: the body is sublimated into sublime gas. Keats is more difficult—the body can still be *felt* dissolving in waves of successive death—but the death-business is very satisfactory. The novelists have even a better time. You can get some of the lasciviousness of Hetty Sorrell's "sin", and you can enjoy condemning her to penal servitude for life. You can thrill to Mr. Rochester's *passion*, and you can enjoy having his eyes burnt out. So it is, all the way: the novel of "passion"!

But in paint it is more difficult. You cannot paint Hetty

Sorrell's sin or Mr. Rochester's passion without being really shocking. And you *daren't* be shocking. It was this fact that unsaddled Watts and Millais. Both might have been painters if they hadn't been Victorians. As it is, each of them is a wash-out.

Which is the poor, feeble history of art in England, since we can lay no claim to the great Holbein. And art on the Continent, in the last century? It is more interesting, and has a fuller story. An artist *can* only create what he really religiously *feels* is truth, religious truth really *felt*, in the blood and the bones. The English could never think anything connected with the body *religious*—unless it were the eyes. So they painted the social appearance of human beings, and hoped to give them wonderful eyes. But they *could* think landscape religious, since it had no sensual reality. So they felt religious about it and painted it as well as it could be painted, maybe, from their point of view.

And in France? In France it was more or less the same, but with a difference. The French, being more rational, decided that the body had its place, but that it should be rationalised. The Frenchman of to-day has the most reasonable and rationalised body possible. His conception of sex is basically hygienic. A certain amount of copulation is good for you. *Ça fait du bien au corps!* sums up the physical side of a Frenchman's idea of love, marriage, food, sport, and all the rest. Well, it is more sane, anyhow, than the Anglo-Saxon terrors. The Frenchman is afraid of syphilis and afraid of the procreative body, but not quite so deeply. He has known for a long time that you can take precautions. And he is not profoundly imaginative.

Therefore he has been able to paint. But his tendency, just like that of all the modern world, has been to get away from the body, while still paying attention to its hygiene, and still not violently quarrelling with it. Puvis de Chavannes is really as sloppy as all the other spiritual sentimentalisers. Renoir is jolly: *ça fait du bien au corps!* is his attitude to the flesh. If a woman didn't have buttocks and breasts, she wouldn't be paintable, he said, and he was right. *Ça fait du bien au corps!* What do you paint with, Maître?—With my penis, and be damned! Renoir didn't try to get away from the body. But he had to dodge it in some of its aspects, rob it of its natural terrors, its natural demonishness. He is delightful, but a trifle banal. *Ça fait du bien au corps!* Yet how infinitely much better he is than any English equivalent.

Courbet, Daumier, Degas, they all painted the human body. But Daumier satirised it, Courbet saw it as a toiling thing, Degas saw it as a wonderful instrument. They all of them deny it its finest qualities, its deepest instincts, its purest intuitions. They prefer, as it were, to industrialise it. They deny it the best imaginative existence.

And the real grand glamour of modern French art, the real outburst of delight came when the body was at last dissolved of its substance, and made part and parcel of the sunlight-and-shadow scheme. Let us say what we will, but the real grand thrill of modern French art was the discovery of light, the discovery of light, and all the subsequent discoveries of the impressionists, and of the post-impressionists, even Cézanne. No matter how Cézanne may have reacted from the impressionists, it was they, with their deliriously joyful discovery of light and "free" colour, who really opened his eyes. Probably the most joyous moment in the whole history of painting was the moment when the incipient impressionists discovered light, and with it, colour. Ah, then they made the grand, grand escape into freedom, into infinity, into light and delight. They escaped from the tyranny of solidity and the menace of mass-form. They escaped, they escaped from the dark procreative body which so haunts a man, they escaped into the open air, *plein air* and *plein soleil:* light and almost ecstasy.

Like every other human escape, it meant being hauled back later with the tail between the legs. Back comes the truant, back to the old doom of matter, of corporate existence, of the body sullen and stubborn and obstinately refusing to be transmuted into pure light, pure colour, or pure anything. It is not concerned with purity. Life isn't. Chemistry and mathematics and ideal religion are, but these are only small bits of life, which is itself bodily, and hence neither pure nor impure.

After the grand escape into impressionism and pure light, pure colour, pure bodilessness—for what is the body but a shimmer of lights and colours!—poor art came home truant and sulky, with its tail between its legs. And it is this return which now interests us. We know the escape was illusion, illusion, illusion. The cat had to come back. So now we despise the "light" blighters too much. We haven't a good word for them. Which is nonsense, for they too are wonderful, even if their escape was into *le grand néant*, the great nowhere.

But the cat came back. And it is the home-coming tom that now has our sympathy: Renoir, to a certain extent, but mostly Cézanne, the sublime little grimalkin, who is followed by Matisse and Gauguin and Derain and Vlaminck and Braque and all the host of other defiant and howling cats that have come back, perforce, to form and substance and *thereness*, instead of delicious nowhereness. . . .

(*The remainder of the essay deals specifically with French painting.*)

[First published in *The Paintings of D. H. Lawrence*, London, 1929; reprinted *complete* in *Phoenix* and in *Sex, Literature and Censorship*.]

[33]

From

STUDY OF THOMAS HARDY*

(Maleness and Femaleness in Art)

. . . Thus Correggio leads on to the whole of modern art, where the male still wrestles with the female, in unconscious struggle, but where he gains ever gradually over her, reducing her to nothing. Ever there is more and more vibration, movement, and less and less stability, centralisation. Ever man is more and more occupied with his own experience, with his own overpowering of resistance, ever less and less aware of any resistance in the object, less and less aware of any stability, less and less aware of anything unknown, more and more preoccupied with that which he knows, till his knowledge tends to become an abstraction, because it is limited by no unknown.

* This is a part of the essay on Hardy that is (as Lawrence himself said) "about everything but Hardy". The material that does refer to Hardy will be found on pp. 166–228.

It is the contradiction of Dürer, as the Parthenon Frieze was the contradication of Babylon and Egypt. To Dürer woman did not exist; even as to a child at the breast, woman does not exist separately. She is the overwhelming condition of life. She was to Dürer that which possessed him, and not that which he possessed. Her being overpowered him, he could only see in her terms, in terms of stability and of stable, incontrovertible being. He is overpowered by the vast assurance at whose breast he is suckled, and, as if astounded, he grasps at the unknown. He knows that he rests within some great stability, and, marvelling at his own power for movement, touches the objects of this stability, becomes familiar with them. It is a question of the starting-point. Dürer starts with a sense of that which he does not know and would discover; Correggio with the sense of that which he has known, and would re-create.

And in the Renaissance, after Botticelli, the motion begins to divide in these two directions. The hands no longer clasp in perfect union, but one clasp overbears the other. Botticelli develops to Correggio and to Andrea del Sarto, develops forward to Rembrandt, and Rembrandt to the Impressionists, to the male extreme of motion. But Botticelli, on the other hand, becomes Raphael, Raphael and Michelangelo.

In Raphael we see the stable, architectural developing out further, and becoming the geometric: the denial or refusal of all movement. In the *Madonna degli Ansidei* the child is drooping, the mother stereotyped, the picture geometric, static, abstract. When there is any union of male and female, there is no goal of abstraction: the abstract is used in place, as a means of a real union. The goal of the male impulse is the announcement of motion, endless motion, endless diversity, endless change. The goal of the female impulse is the announcement of infinite oneness, of infinite stability. When the two are working in combination, as they must in life, there is, as it were, a dual motion, centrifugal for the male, fleeing abroad, away from the centre, outward to infinite vibration, and centripetal for the female, fleeing in to the eternal centre of rest. A combination of the two movements produces a sum of motion and stability at once, satisfying. But in life there tends always to be more of one than the other. The Cathedrals, Fra Angelico, frighten us or [bore] us with their final annunciation of centrality and stability. We want to escape. The influence is too female for us. In Botticelli, the architecture remains, but there is the wonderful movement outwards, the joyous, if still clumsy, escape from the centre. His religious pictures tend to be stereotyped, resigned. The Primavera herself is static, melancholy, a stability become almost a negation. It is as if the female, instead of being the great, unknown Positive, towards which all must flow, became the great Negative, the centre which denied all motion. And the Aphrodite stands there not as a force, to draw all things unto her, but as the naked, almost unwilling pivot, as the keystone which endured all thrust and remained static. But still there is the joy, the great motion around her, sky and sea, all the elements and living, joyful forces.

Raphael, however, seeks and finds nothing there. He goes to the centre to ask: "What is this mystery we are all pivoted upon?" To Fra Angelico it was the unknown Omnipotent. It was a goal, to which man travelled inevitably. It was the desired, the end of the long horizontal journey. But to Raphael it was the negation. Still he is a seeker, an aspirant, still his art is religious art. But the Virgin, the essential female, was to him a negation, a neutrality. Such must have been his vivid experience. But still he seeks her. Still he desires the stability, the positive keystone which grasps the arch together, not the negative keystone neutralising the thrust, itself a neutrality. And reacting upon his own desire, the male reacting upon itself, he creates the Abstraction, the geometric conception of life. The fundament of all is the geometry of all. Which is the Plato conception. And the desire is to formulate the complete geometry.

So Raphael, knowing that his desire reaches out beyond the range of possible experience, sensible that he will not find satisfaction in any one woman, sensible that the female impulse does not, or cannot unite in him with the male impulse sufficiently to create a stability, an eternal moment of truth for him, or realisation, closes his eyes and his mind upon experience, and abstracting himself, reacting upon himself, produces the geometric conception of the fundamental truth, departs from religion, from any God idea, and becomes philosophic.

Raphael is the real end of Renaissance in Italy; almost he is the real end of Italy, as Plato was the real end of Greece. When the God-idea passes into the philosophic or geometric idea, then there is a sign that the male impulse has thrown the female impulse, and has recoiled upon itself, has become abstract, asexual.

Michelangelo, however, too physically passionate, containing too much of the female in his body ever to reach the geometric abstraction, unable to abstract himself, and at the same time, like Raphael, unable to find any woman who in her being should resist him and reserve still some unknown from him, strives to obtain his own physical satisfaction in his art. He is obsessed by the desire of the body. And he must react upon himself to produce his own bodily satisfaction, aware that he can never obtain it through woman. He must seek the moment, the consummation, the keystone, the pivot, in his own flesh. For his own body is both male and female.

Raphael and Michelangelo are men of different nature placed in the same position and resolving the same question in their several ways. Socrates and Plato are a parallel pair, and, in another degree, Tolstoi and Turgenev, and, perhaps, St. Paul and St. John the Evangelist, and, perhaps, Shakespeare and Shelley.

The body it is which attaches us directly to the female. Sex, as we call it, is only the point where the dual stream begins to divide, where it is nearly together, almost one. An infant is of no very determinate sex: that is, it is of both. Only at adolescence is there a real differentiation, the one is singled out to predominate. In what we call happy natures, in the lazy, contented people, there is a fairly equable balance of sex. There is sufficient of the female in the body of such a man as to leave him fairly free. He does not suffer the torture of desire of a more male being. It is obvious even from the physique of such a man that in him there is a proper proportion between male and female, so that he can be easy, balanced, and without excess. The Greek sculptors of the "best" period, Phidias and then Sophocles, Alcibiades, then Horace, must have been fairly well-balanced men, not passionate to any excess, tending to voluptuousness rather than to passion. So also Victor Hugo and Schiller and Tennyson. The real voluptuary is a man who is female as well as male, and who lives according to the female side of his nature, like Lord Byron.

The pure male is himself almost an abstraction, almost bodiless, like Shelley or Edmund Spenser. But, as we know humanity, this condition comes of an omission of some vital part. In the ordinary sense, Shelley never lived. He transcended life. But we do not want to transcend life, since we are of life.

Why should Shelley say of the skylark:

"Hail to thee, blithe Spirit!—bird thou never wert!—"? Why should he insist on the bodilessness of beauty, when we cannot know of any save embodied beauty? Who would wish that the skylark were not a bird, but a spirit? If the whistling skylark were a spirit, then we should all wish to be spirits. Which were impious and flippant.

I can think of no being in the world so transcendently male as Shelley. He is phenomenal. The rest of us have bodies which contain the male and the female. If we were so singled out as Shelley, we should not belong to life, as he did not belong to life. But it were impious to wish to be like the angels. So long as mankind exists it must exist in the body, and so long must each body pertain both to the male and the female.

In the degree of pure maleness below Shelley are Plato and Raphael and Wordsworth, then Goethe and Milton and Dante, then Michelangelo, then Shakespeare, then Tolstoi, then St. Paul.

A man who is well balanced between male and female, in his own nature, is, as a rule, happy, easy to mate, easy to satisfy, and content to exist. It is only a disproportion, or a dissatisfaction, which makes the man struggle into articulation. And the articulation is of two sorts, the cry of desire or the cry of realisation, the cry of satisfaction, the effort to prolong the sense of satisfaction, to prolong the moment of consummation.

[The *Study of Thomas Hardy* was first published posthumously in *Phœnix*.]

PART THREE

Verse

[34]

GEORGIAN POETRY: 1911–1912

Georgian Poetry is an anthology of verse which has been published during the reign of our present king, George V. It contains one poem of my own, but this fact will not, I hope, preclude my reviewing the book.

This collection is like a big breath taken when we are waking up after a night of oppressive dreams. The nihilists, the intellectual, hopeless people—Ibsen, Flaubert, Thomas Hardy —represent the dream we are waking from. It was a dream of demolition. Nothing was, but was nothing. Everything was taken from us. And now our lungs are full of new air, and our eyes see it is morning, but we have not forgotten the terror of the night. We dreamed we were falling through space into nothingness, and the anguish of it leaves us rather eager.

But we are awake again, our lungs are full of new air, our eyes of morning. The first song is nearly a cry, fear and the pain of remembrance sharpening away the pure music. And that is this book.

The last years have been years of demolition. Because faith and belief were getting pot-bound, and the Temple was made a place to barter sacrifices, therefore faith and belief and the Temple must be broken. This time art fought the battle, rather than science or any new religious faction. And art has been demolishing for us: Nietzsche, the Christian religion as it stood; Hardy, our faith in our own endeavour; Flaubert, our belief in love. Now, for us, it is all smashed, we can see the whole again. We were in prison, peeping at the sky through loop-holes. The great prisoners smashed at the loop-holes, for lying to us. And behold, out of the ruins leaps the whole sky.

It is we who see it and breathe in it for joy. God is there, faith, belief, love, everything. We are drunk with the joy of it, having got away from the fear. In almost every poem in the book comes this note of exultation after fear, the exultation in the vast freedom, the illimitable wealth that we have suddenly got.

> But send desire often forth to scan
> The immense night that is thy greater soul,

says Mr. Abercrombie. His deadly sin is Prudence, that will not risk to avail itself of the new freedom. Mr. Bottomley exults to find men for ever building religions which yet can never compass all.

> Yet the yielding sky
> Invincible vacancy was there discovered.

Mr. Rupert Brooke sees

> every glint
> Posture and jest and thought and tint
> Freed from the mask of transiency
> Triumphant in eternity,
> Immote, immortal

and this at Afternoon Tea. Mr. John Drinkwater sings:

> We cherish every hour that strays
> Adown the cataract of days:
> We see the clear, untroubled skies,
> We see the glory of the rose——

Mr. Wilfrid Wilson Gibson hears the "terror turned to tenderness," then

> I watched the mother sing to rest
> The baby snuggling on her breast.

And to Mr. Masefield:

> When men count
> Those hours of life that were a bursting fount
> Sparkling the dusty heart with living springs,
> There seems a world, beyond our earthly things,
> Gated by golden moments.

It is all the same—hope, and religious joy. Nothing is really wrong. Every new religion is a waste-product from the last, and every religion stands for us for ever. We love Christianity for what it has brought us, now that we are no longer upon the cross.

The great liberation gives us an overwhelming sense of joy, *joie d'être, joie de vivre*. This sense of exceeding keen relish and appreciation of life makes romance. I think I could say every poem in the book is romantic, tinged with a love of the marvellous, a joy of natural things, as if the poet were a child for the first time on the seashore, finding treasures. "Best trust the happy moments," says Mr. Masefield, who seems nearest to the black dream behind us. There is Mr. W. H. Davies's lovely joy, Mr. De La Mare's perfect appreciation of life at still moments, Mr. Rupert Brooke's brightness, when he "lived from laugh to laugh", Mr. Edmund Beale Sargant's pure, excited happiness in the woodland—it is all the same, keen zest in life found wonderful. In Mr. Gordon Bottomley it is the zest of activity, of hurrying, labouring men, or the zest of the utter stillness of long snows. It is a bookful of Romance that has not quite got clear of the terror of realism.

There is no *carpe diem* touch. The joy is sure and fast. It is not the falling rose, but the rose for ever rising to bud and falling to fruit that gives us joy. We have faith in the vastness of life's wealth. We are always rich: rich in buds and in shed blossoms. There is no winter that we fear. Life is like an orange tree, always in leaf and bud, in blossom and fruit.

And we ourselves, in each of us, have everything. Somebody said: "The Georgian poets are not love poets. The influence of Swinburne has gone." But I should say the Georgian poets are just ripening to be love poets. Swinburne was no love poet. What are the Georgian poets, nearly all, but just bursting into a thick blaze of being? They are not poets of passion, perhaps, but they are essentially passionate poets. The time to be impersonal has gone. We start from the joy we have in being ourselves, and everything must take colour from that joy. It is the return of the blood, that has been held back, as when the heart's action is arrested by fear. Now the warmth of blood is in everything, quick, healthy, passionate blood. I look at my hands as I write and know they are mine, with red blood running its way, sleuthing out Truth and pursuing it to eternity, and I am full of awe for this flesh and blood that holds this pen. Everything that ever was thought and ever will be thought, lies in this body of mine. This flesh and blood sitting here writing, the great impersonal flesh and blood, greater than me, which I am proud to belong to, contains all the future. What is it but the quick of all growth, the seed of all harvest, this body of mine? And grapes and corn and birds and rocks and visions, all are in my fingers. I am so full of wonder at my own miracle of flesh and blood that I could not contain myself, if I did not remember we are all alive, have all of us living bodies. And that is a joy greater than any dream of immortality in the spirit, to me. It reminds me of Rupert Brooke's moment triumphant in its eternality; and of Michelangelo, who is also the moment triumphant in its eternality; just the opposite from Corot, who is the eternal triumphing over the moment, at the moment, at the very point of sweeping it into the flow.

Of all love poets, we are the love poets. For our religion is loving. To love passionately, but completely, is our one desire.

What is "The Hare" but a complete love poem, with none of the hackneyed "But a bitter blossom was born" about it, nor yet the Yeats, "Never give all the heart." Love is the greatest of all things, no "bitter blossom" nor suchlike. It is sex-passion, so separated, in which we do not believe. The *Carmen* and *Tosca* sort of passion is not interesting any longer, because it can't progress. Its goal and aim is possession, whereas possession in love is only a means to love. And because passion cannot go beyond possession, the passionate heroes and heroines—Tristans and what-not—must die. We believe in the love that is happy ever after, progressive as life itself.

I worship Christ, I worship Jehovah, I worship Pan, I worship Aphrodite. But I do not worship hands nailed and running with blood upon a cross, nor licentiousness, nor lust. I want them all, all the gods. They are all God. But I must serve in real love. If I take my whole, passionate, spiritual and physical love to the woman who in return loves me, that is how I serve God. And my hymn and my game of joy is my work. All of which I read in the anthology of *Georgian Poetry*.

[Review in *Rhythm*, March 1913.]

[35]

Letter to EDWARD GARNETT, 3 March, 1913

. . . I should think Masefield's masterpieces will do for a sort of heavy *hors d'œuvres*—pickled herring, though not so good —to introduce my elegant dishes. He's a horrible sentimentalist —the cheap Byron of the day—his stuff is Lara 1913.

[36]

Letter to ERNEST COLLINGS, 14 Nov., 1912

. . . I can see all the poetry at the *back* of your verse—but there isn't much inside the lines. It's the rhythm and the sound that don't penetrate the blood—only now and then. I don't like the crackly little lines, nor the "thou wouldest" style, nor "mighty hills" and garlands and voices of birds and caskets—none of that. I can remember a few things, that nearly made poems in themselves.

> We met again, and for a short laughing
> Did play with words; till suddenly
> I knew—didst thou?

And then all the rest is inconsequent to me.

> The coverings of the doorway
> Are flung open:
> Superb thou standest, wild-eyed, eager girl,
> Letting fall thy gown to feel the little
> Winds of the morning soothe thy breasts and
>   shoulders.

Then you go on "Walk the earth in gladness"—but that girl isn't going to *walk the earth.*
   The first stanza of "Adventure" is so nice, and I love

> Now—go thy way.
> Ah, through the open door
> Is there an almond tree
> Aflame with blossom!

A little longer stay—
Why do tears blind me?
Nay, but go thy way.

That's a little poem, sufficient in itself. Then you go off to the
"Love did turn to hate" business. And fancy anybody saying
"Boy, whither away?" Then I like

I think you must have died last night,
For in my dreams you came to me——

then the rest isn't good. Do them in better form—put them in
blank verse or something. Your rhythms aren't a bit good.

Forgive me if I'm nasty. That's what I say to myself, what
I say to you.

[37]

Letter to EDWARD MARSH, 18 Aug., 1913

. . . I think you will find my verse smoother—not because I
consciously attend to rhythms, but because I am no longer so
criss-crossy in myself. I think, don't you know, that my
rhythms fit my mood pretty well, in the verse. And if the mood
is out of joint, the rhythm often is. I have always tried to get an
emotion out in its own course, without altering it. It needs the
finest instinct imaginable, much finer than the skill of the
craftsmen. That Japanese Yone Noguchi tried it. He doesn't
quite bring it off. Often I don't—sometimes I do. Sometimes
Whitman is perfect. Remember skilled verse is dead in fifty
years—I am thinking of your admiration of Flecker.

[38]

Letter to EDWARD MARSH, 28 Oct., 1913

. . . Poor Davies*—he makes me so furious, and so sorry.
He's really like a linnet that's got just a wee little sweet song,
but it only sings when it's wild. And he's made himself a

* W. H. Davies.

tame bird—poor little devil. He makes me furious. "I shall be all right now the winter is coming," he writes, "now I can sit by the fire and work." As if he could sing when he's been straining his heart to make a sound of music, for months. It isn't as if he were a passionate writer, writing his "agon". Oh, my God, he's like teaching a bull-finch to talk. I think one ought to be downright cruel to him, and drive him back: say to him, Davies, your work is getting like Birmingham tin-ware; Davies, you drop your h's, and everybody is tempering the wind to you, because you are a shorn lamb; Davies, your accent is intolerable in a carpeted room; Davies, you hang on like the mud on a lady's silk petticoat. Then he might leave his Sevenoaks room, where he is rigged up as a rural poet, proud of the gilt mirror and his romantic past: and he might grow his wings again, and chirrup a little sadder song.

And now I've got to quarrel with you about the Ralph Hodgson poem: because I think it is banal in utterance. The feeling is there, right enough—but not in itself, only represented. It's like "I asked for bread, and he gave me a penny." Only here and there is the least touch of personality in the poem: it is the currency of poetry, not poetry itself. Every single line of it is poetic currency—and a good deal of emotion handling it about. But it isn't really poetry. I hope to God you won't hate me and think me carping, for this. But look:

> the ruby's and the rainbow's song
> the nightingale's—all three

There's the emotion in the rhythm, but it's loose emotion, inarticulate, common—the words are mere currency. It is exactly like a man who feels very strongly for a beggar, and gives him a sovereign. The feeling is at either end, for the moment, but the sovereign is a dead bit of metal. And this poem is the sovereign. "Oh, I do want to give you this emotion," cries Hodgson, "I do." And so he takes out his poetic purse, and gives you a handful of cash, and feels very strongly, even a bit sentimentally over it.

> ——the sky was lit
> The sky was stars all over it,
> I stood, I knew not why

No one should say, "I knew not why" any more. It is as
meaningless as "yours truly" at the end of a letter.

[39]

Letter to EDWARD MARSH, 19 Nov., 1913
    You *are* wrong. It makes me open my eyes. I think I read
my poetry more by length than by stress—as a matter of
movements in space than footsteps hitting the earth.

Just a few of the roses we gathered by the Isar
Are fallen, and their blood-red petals on the cloth,
Float like boats on a river, waiting
For a fairy wind to wake them from their sloth.

I think more of a bird with broad wings flying and lapsing
through the air, than anything, when I think of metre.—So I
read

I wonder if that is quite intelligible. I am sure I am right.
There is a double method of scanning verse—if you'll notice it.

I have | forgot much|, Cynara! | gone with the | wind
Flung roses|, roses | riotously | with the | throng,|
Dancing | to put | thy pale|, lost lil|ies out |of mind;
But I | was des|olate|, and sick | of an old | passion,|
        Yea, all the time because the dance was long:
    I have been faithful to thee Cynara, in my fashion.

Would you scan like that? I hate an on-foot method of reading.
I should go:

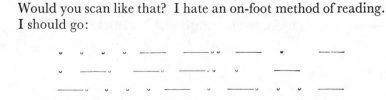

It all depends on the *pause*—the natural pause, the natural
lingering of the voice according to the feeling—it is the hidden
emotional pattern that makes poetry, not the obvious form.

Ĭ have forgŏt much, Cynara, gone with the wind.

It is the lapse of the feeling, something as indefinite as expression
in the voice carrying emotion. It doesn't depend on the ear,
particularly, but on the sensitive soul. And the ear gets a habit,
and becomes master, when the ebbing and lifting emotion
should be master, and the ear the transmitter. If your ear
has got stiff and a bit mechanical, *don't* blame my poetry.
That's why you like *Golden Journey to Samarkand*—it fits your
habituated ear, and your feeling crouches subservient and a bit
pathetic. "It satisfies my ear," you say. Well, I don't write for
your ear. This is the constant war, I reckon, between new
expression and the habituated, mechanical transmitters and
receivers of the human constitution.

I can't tell you what *pattern* I see in any poetry, save one
complete thing. But surely you don't class poetry among the
decorative or conventional arts. I always wonder if the Greeks
and Romans really did scan, or if scansion wasn't a thing
invented afterwards by the schoolmaster. Yet I seem to find
about the same number of long lingering notes in each line. I
know nothing about it. I only know you aren't right.

You are wrong, I think, about the two rhymes—why need
you notice they are rhymes? You are a bit of a policeman in
poetry. I *never* put them in because they are rhymes.

"Drearisome," I am guilty of—peccavi.

"Sloth," I feel a *bit* guilty about—not quite so guilty as you
would have me. I'm not sure about "Purity"—I always felt
suspicious of it, and yet I am inclined to think it is good.

"The land of her glad surmise" is a penny, not a sovereign. I always knew it was shocking bad. I must think about that ballad.

I rather suspect you of being a young Philistine with the poetry of youth on you, and the——

But I *am* being a David that throws stones.

Don't mind me. I find it frightfully easy to theorise and say all the things I don't mean, and frightfully difficult to find out, even for myself, what I do mean.

I only *know* that the verse you quote against me is right, and you are wrong. And I am a poor, maligned, misunderstood, patronised and misread poet, and soon I shall burst into tears.

But thanks be to God above, my poetry doesn't stick to me. My wife has a beastly habit of comparing poetry—all literature in fact—to the droppings of the goats among the rocks—mere excreta that fertilises the ground it falls on.

I think I came a *real* cropper in my belief in metre, over Shelley. I tried all roads to scan him, but could never *read* him as he could be scanned. And I thought what bit of Latin scansion I did was a *horrible* fake: I never believed for an instant in the Sapphic form—and Horace is already a bit of a mellow varsity man who never quite forgot Oxford.

[40]

Letter to EDWARD MARSH, 17 Dec., 1913

. . . About metres, I shall have to pray for grace from God. But (scissors!) I think Shelley a million thousand times more beautiful than Milton.

[41]

Letter to EDWARD MARSH, 24 May, 1914

. . . The other day I got the second *New Numbers*. I was rather disappointed, because I expected Abercrombie's long poem to be great indeed. I can't write to Wilfrid* because I think I have never seen him to worse advantage than in this quarter.

* W. W. Gibson

And it is no good your telling me Lascelles' *End of the World* is great, because it isn't. There are some fine bits of rhetoric, as there always are in Abercrombie. But oh, the spirit of the thing altogether seems mean and rather vulgar. When I remember even H. G. Wells' *Country of the Blind*, with which this poem of Abercrombie's had got associated beforehand in my mind, then I see how beautiful is Wells' conception, and how paltry this other. Why, why, in God's name, is Abercrombie messing about with Yokels and Cider and runaway wives? No, but it is *bitterly* disappointing. He who loves *Paradise Lost* must don the red nose and rough-spun cloak of Masefield and Wilfrid. And you encourage it—it is too bad. Abercrombie, if he does anything, surely ought to work upon rather noble and rather chill subjects. I hate and detest his ridiculous imitation yokels and all the silly hash of his bucolics; I loathe his rather nasty efforts at cruelty, like the wrapping frogs in paper and putting them for cartwheels to crush; I detest this irony with its clap-trap solution of everything being that which it seemeth not; and I hate that way of making what Meredith called Cockney metaphors:—moons like a white cat and meteors like a pike fish. And nearly all of this seems to me an Abercrombie turning cheap and wicked. What is the matter with the man? There's something wrong with his soul. *Mary and the Bramble* and *Sale of St. Thomas* weren't like this. They had a certain beauty of soul, a certain highness which I loved:—though I didn't like the Indian horrors in the *St. Thomas*. But here everything is mean and rather sordid, and full of rancid hate. He talked of *Sons and Lovers* being all *odi et amo*. Well, I wish I could find the "amo" in this poem of his. It is sheer "odi", and rather mean hatred at that. The best feeling in the thing is a certain bitter gloating over the coming destruction. What has happened to him? Something seems to be going bad in his soul. Even in the poem before this, the one of the *Shrivelled Zeus*, there was a gloating over nasty perishing which was objectionable. But what is the matter with him? The feelings in these late things are corrupt and dirty. What has happened to the man? I wish to heaven he were writing the best poems that were ever written, and then he turns out this.

[42]

Letter to HARRIET MONROE, 17 NOV., 1914

. . . To-day came the War Number of *Poetry*, for which also I thank you. It put me into such a rage—how dare Amy talk about bohemian glass and stalks of flame?—that in a real fury I had to write my war poem, because it breaks my heart, this war.

I hate, and hate, and hate the glib irreverence of some of your contributors—Aldington with his "Do you know what it's all about, brother Jonathan? We don't." It is obvious he doesn't. And your nasty, obscene, vulgar in the last degree—"Hero" ———— may God tread him out—why did you put him in? You shouldn't.

At least I like the woman who wrote *Metal Checks*—her idea, her attitude—but her poetry is pretty bad. I rather like the suggestion of Marian Ramie's *Face I shall never see—man I shall never see.* And *Unser Gott* isn't bad—but unbeautifully ugly. Your people have such little pressure: their safety valve goes off at the high scream when the pressure is still so low. Have you no people with any force in them? Aldington almost shows most—if he weren't so lamentably imitating Hueffer.

I don't care what you do with my war poem. I don't particularly care if I don't hear of it any more. The war is dreadful. It is the business of the artist to follow it home to the heart of the individual fighters—not to talk in armies and nations and numbers—but to track it home—home—their war—and it's at the bottom of almost every Englishman's heart—the war— the desire of war—the *will* to war—and at the bottom of every German's.

Don't put common things in like the *Campfollower*—why do you? They are only ugly, ugly—"putrid lips"—it is something for the nasty people of this world to batten on.

[43]

Letter to CATHERINE CARSWELL, 11 Jan., 1916

. . . The essence of poetry with us in this age of stark and unlovely actualities is a stark directness, without a shadow of a lie, or a shadow of deflection anywhere. Everything can go, but this stark, bare, rocky directness of statement, this alone makes poetry, to-day. That poem is *very good*, the best yet. My scribblings on it are only impertinent suggestions.

But you know it isn't rhythmed at all, metrically. So why rhyme if you don't rhythm. I mean that for your other poems. This has got its own form as it stands. But in general, why use rhyme when you don't use metrical rhythm?—which you don't—you'd lose all reality if you did. Use rhyme *accidentally*, not as a sort of draper's rule for measuring lines off.

The second poem is not good. It is again not created. Do it in free verse accidentally rhymed, and let us see.

I send you the *Spoon River Anthology*. It is good, but too static, always stated, not really art. Yet that is the line poetry will take, a free, essential verse, that cuts to the centre of things, without any flourish.

[44]

INTRODUCTION TO *NEW POEMS*

IT seems when we hear a skylark singing as if sound were running into the future, running so fast and utterly without consideration, straight on into futurity. And when we hear a nightingale, we hear the pause and the rich, piercing rhythm of recollection, the perfected past. The lark may sound sad, but with the lovely lapsing sadness that is almost a swoon of hope. The nightingale's triumph is a pæan, but a death-pæan.

So it is with poetry. Poetry is, as a rule, either the voice of the far future, exquisite and ethereal, or it is the voice of the past, rich, magnificent. When the Greeks heard the *Iliad* and the *Odyssey*, they heard their own past calling in their hearts, as men far inland sometimes hear the sea and fall weak with powerful, wonderful regret, nostalgia; or else their own future rippled its time-beats through their blood, as they followed the painful, glamorous progress of the Ithacan. This was Homer to the Greeks: their Past, splendid with battles won and death achieved, and their Future, the magic wandering of Ulysses through the unknown.

With us it is the same. Our birds sing on the horizons. They sing out of the blue, beyond us, or out of the quenched night. They sing at dawn and sunset. Only the poor, shrill, tame canaries whistle while we talk. The wild birds begin before we are awake, or as we drop into dimness, out of waking. Our poets sit by the gateways, some by the east, some by the west. As we arrive and as we go out our hearts surge with response. But whilst we are in the midst of life, we do not hear them.

The poetry of the beginning and the poetry of the end must have that exquisite finality, perfection which belongs to all that is far off. It is in the realm of all that is perfect. It is of the nature of all that is complete and consummate. This completeness, this consummateness, the finality and the perfection are conveyed in exquisite form: the perfect symmetry, the rhythm which returns upon itself like a dance where the hands link and loosen and link for the supreme moment of the end. Perfected bygone moments, perfected moments in the glimmering futurity, these are the treasured gem-like lyrics of Shelley and Keats.

But there is another kind of poetry: the poetry of that which is at hand: the immediate present. In the immediate present there is no perfection, no consummation, nothing finished. The strands are all flying, quivering, intermingling into the web, the waters are shaking the moon. There is no round, consummate moon on the face of running water, nor on the face of the unfinished tide. There are no gems of the living plasm. The living plasm vibrates unspeakably, it inhales the future, it exhales the past, it is the quick of both, and yet it is neither. There is no plasmic finality, nothing crystal, permanent. If we try to fix the living tissue, as the biologists fix it with formation, we have only a hardened bit of the past, the bygone life under our observation.

Life, the ever-present, knows no finality, no finished crystallisation. The perfect rose is only a running flame, emerging and flowing off, and never in any sense at rest, static, finished. Herein lies its transcendent loveliness. The whole tide of all life and all time suddenly heaves, and appears before us as an apparition, a revelation. We look at the very white quick of nascent creation. A water-lily heaves herself from the flood, looks around, gleams, and is gone. We have seen the incarnation, the quick of the ever-swirling flood. We have seen the invisible. We have seen, we have touched, we have partaken of the very substance of creative change, creative mutation. If you tell me about the lotus, tell me of nothing changeless or eternal. Tell me of the mystery of the inexhaustible, forever-unfolding creative spark. Tell me of the incarnate disclosure of the flux, mutation in blossom, laughter and decay perfectly open in their transit, nude in their movement before us.

Let me feel the mud and the heavens in my lotus. Let me feel the heavy, silting, sucking mud, the spinning of sky winds. Let me feel them both in purest contact, the nakedness of sucking weight, nakedly passing radiance. Give me nothing fixed, set, static. Don't give me the infinite or the eternal: nothing of infinity, nothing of eternity. Give me the still, white seething, the incandescence and the coldness of the incarnate moment: the moment, the quick of all change and haste and opposition: the moment, the immediate present, the Now. The immediate moment is not a drop of water running downstream. It is the source and issue, the bubbling up of the stream. Here, in this very instant moment, up bubbles the stream of time, out of the wells of futurity, flowing on to the oceans of the past. The source, the issue, the creative quick.

There is poetry of this immediate present, instant poetry, as well as poetry of the infinite past and the infinite future. The seething poetry of the incarnate Now is supreme, beyond even the everlasting gems of the before and after. In its quivering momentaneity it surpasses the crystalline, pearl-hard jewels, the poems of the eternities. Do not ask for the qualities of the un-fading timeless gems. Ask for the whiteness which is the seethe of mud, ask for that incipient putrescence which is the skies falling, ask for the never-pausing, never-ceasing life itself. There must be mutation, swifter than iridescence, haste, not rest, come-and-go, not fixity, inconclusiveness, immediacy, the quality of life itself, without denouement or close. There must be the rapid momentaneous association of things which meet and pass on the for ever incalculable journey of creation: everything left in its own rapid, fluid relationship with the rest of things.

This is the unrestful, ungraspable poetry of the sheer present, poetry whose very permanency lies in its wind-like transit.

Whitman's is the best poetry of this kind. Without beginning and without end, without any base and pediment, it sweeps past for ever, like a wind that is for ever in passage, and unchainable. Whitman truly looked before and after. But he did not sigh for what is not. The clue to all his utterance lies in the sheer appreciation of the instant moment, life surging itself into utterance at its very well-head. Eternity is only an abstraction from the actual present. Infinity is only a great reservoir of recollection, or a reservoir of aspiration: man-made. The quivering nimble hour of the present, this is the quick of Time. This is the immanence. The quick of the universe is the *pulsating, carnal self,* mysterious and palpable. So it is always.

Because Whitman put this into his poetry, we fear him and respect him so profoundly. We should not fear him if he sang only of the "old unhappy far-off things", or of the "wings of the morning". It is because his heart beats with the urgent, insurgent Now, which is even upon us all, that we dread him. He is so near the quick.

From the foregoing it is obvious that the poetry of the instant present cannot have the same body or the same motion as the poetry of the before and after. It can never submit to the same conditions. It is never finished. There is no rhythm which returns upon itself, no serpent of eternity with its tail in its own mouth. There is no static perfection, none of that finality which we find so satisfying because we are so frightened.

Much has been written about free verse. But all that can be said, first and last, is that free verse is, or should be, direct utterance from the instant, whole man. It is the soul and the mind and body surging at once, nothing left out. They speak all together. There is some confusion, some discord. But the confusion and the discord only belong to the reality, as noise belongs to the plunge of water. It is no use inventing fancy laws for free verse, no use drawing a melodic line which all the feet must toe. Free verse toes no melodic line, no matter what drill-sergeant. Whitman pruned away his clichés—perhaps his clichés of rhythm as well as of phrase. And this is about all we can do, deliberately, with free verse. We can get rid of the stereotyped movements and the old hackneyed associations of sound or sense. We can break down those artificial conduits and canals through which we do so love to force our utterance.

We can break the stiff neck of habit. We can be in ourselves spontaneous and flexible as flame, we can see that utterance rushes out without artificial form or artificial smoothness. But we cannot positively prescribe any motion, any rhythm. All the laws we invent or discover—it amounts to pretty much the same—will fail to apply to free verse. They will only apply to some form of restricted, limited unfree verse.

All we can say is that free verse does *not* have the same nature as restricted verse. It is not of the nature of reminiscence. It is not the past which we treasure in its perfection between our hands. Neither is it the crystal of the perfect future, into which we gaze. Its tide is neither the full, yearning flow of aspiration, nor the sweet, poignant ebb of remembrance and regret. The past and the future are the two great bournes of human emotion, the two great homes of the human days, the two eternities. They are both conclusive, final. Their beauty is the beauty of the goal, finished, perfected. Finished beauty and measured symmetry belong to the stable, unchanging eternities.

But in free verse we look for the insurgent naked throb of the instant moment. To break the lovely form of metrical verse, and to dish up the fragments as a new substance, called *vers libre*, this is what most of the free-versifiers accomplish. They do not know that free verse has its own *nature*, that it is neither star nor pearl, but instantaneous like plasm. It has no goal in either eternity. It has no finish. It has no satisfying stability, satisfying to those who like the immutable. None of this. It is the instant; the quick; the very jetting source of all will-be and has-been. The utterance is like a spasm, naked contact with all influences at once. It does not want to get anywhere. It just takes place.

For such utterance any externally applied law would be mere shackles and death. The law must come new each time from within. The bird is on the wing in the winds, flexible to every breath, a living spark in the storm, its very flickering depending upon its supreme mutability and power of change. Whence such a bird came: whither it goes: from what solid earth it rose up, and upon what solid earth it will close its wings and settle, this is not the question. This is a question of before and after. Now, *now*, the bird is on the wing in the winds.

Such is the rare new poetry. One realm we have never con-quered: the pure present. One great mystery of time is *terra incognita* to us: the instant. The most superb mystery we have hardly recognised: the immediate, instant self. The quick of all time is the instant. The quick of all the universe, of all creation, is the incarnate, carnal self. Poetry gave us the clue: free verse: Whitman. Now we know.

The ideal—what is the ideal? A figment. An abstraction. A static abstraction, abstracted from life. It is a fragment of the before or the after. It is a crystallised aspiration, or a crystal-lised remembrance: crystallised, set, finished. It is a thing set apart, in the great storehouse of eternity, the storehouse of finished things.

We do not speak of things crystallised and set apart. We speak of the instant, the immediate self, the very plasm of the self. We speak also of free verse.

All this should have come as a preface to *Look! We Have Come Through!* But is it not better to publish a preface long after the book it belongs to has appeared? For then the reader will have had his fair chance with the book, alone.

[From *New Poems* by D. H. Lawrence, New York, 1920.]

[45]

From

CHAOS IN POETRY

POETRY, they say, is a matter of words. And this is just as much true as that pictures are a matter of paint, and frescoes a matter of water and colour-wash. It is such a long way from being the whole truth that it is slightly silly if uttered sen-tentiously.

Poetry is a matter of words. Poetry is a stringing together of words into a ripple and jingle and a run of colours. Poetry is an interplay of images. Poetry is the iridescent suggestion of an idea. Poetry is all these things, and still it is something else. Given all these ingredients, you have something very like poetry, something for which we might borrow the old romantic name of poesy. And poesy, like bric-à-brac, will for ever be in fashion. But poetry is still another thing.

The essential quality of poetry is that it makes a new effort of attention, and "discovers" a new world within the known world. Man, and the animals, and the flowers, all live within a strange and for ever surging chaos. The chaos which we have got used to we call a cosmos. The unspeakable inner chaos of which we are composed we call consciousness, and mind, and even civilisation. But it is, ultimately, chaos, lit up by visions, or not lit up by visions. Just as the rainbow may or may not light up the storm. And, like the rainbow, the vision perisheth.

But man cannot live in chaos. The animals can. To the animal all is chaos, only there are a few recurring motions and aspects within the surge. And the animal is content. But man is not. Man must wrap himself in a vision, make a house of apparent form and stability, fixity. In his terror of chaos he begins by putting up an umbrella between himself and the everlasting whirl. Then he paints the underside of his umbrella like a firmament. Then he parades around, lives and dies under his umbrella. Bequeathed to his descendants, the umbrella becomes a dome, a vault, and men at last begin to feel that something is wrong.

Man fixes some wonderful erection of his own between himself and the wild chaos, and gradually goes bleached and stifled under his parasol. Then comes a poet, enemy of convention, and makes a slit in the umbrella; and lo! the glimpse of chaos is a vision, a window to the sun. But after a while, getting used to the vision, and not liking the genuine draught from chaos, commonplace man daubs a simulacrum of the window that opens on to chaos, and patches the umbrella with the painted patch of the simulacrum. That is, he has got used to the vision; it is part of his house-decoration. So that the umbrella at last looks like a glowing open firmament, of many aspects. But alas! it is all simulacrum, in innumerable patches. Homer and Keats, annotated and with glossary.

This is the history of poetry in our era. Someone sees Titans in the wild air of chaos, and the Titan becomes a wall between succeeding generations and the chaos they should have inherited. The wild sky moved and sang. Even that became a great umbrella between mankind and the sky of fresh air;

then it became a painted vault, a fresco on a vaulted roof, under which men bleach and go dissatisfied. Till another poet makes a slit on to the open and windy chaos.

But at last our roof deceives us no more. It is painted plaster, and all the skill of all the human ages won't take us in. Dante or Leonardo, Beethoven or Whitman: lo! it is painted on the plaster of our vault. Like St. Francis preaching to the birds in Assisi. Wonderfully like air and birdy space and chaos of many things—partly because the fresco is faded. But even so, we are glad to get out of that church, and into the natural chaos.

This is the momentous crisis for mankind, when we have to get back to chaos. So long as the umbrella serves, and poets make slits in it, and the mass of people can be gradually educated up to the vision in the slit: which means they patch it over with a patch that looks just like the vision in the slit: so long as this process can continue, and mankind can be educated up, and thus built in, so long will a civilisation continue more or less happily, completing its own painted prison. It is called completing the consciousness.

The joy men had when Wordsworth, for example, made a slit and saw a primrose! Till then, men had only seen a primrose dimly, in the shadow of the umbrella. They saw it through Wordsworth in the full gleam of chaos. Since then, gradually, we have come to see primavera nothing but primrose. Which means, we have patched over the slit.

And the greater joy when Shakespeare made a big rent and saw emotional, wistful man outside in the chaos, beyond the conventional idea and painted umbrella of moral images and iron-bound paladins, which had been put up in the Middle Ages. But now, alas, the roof of our vault is simply painted dense with Hamlets and Macbeths, the side walls too, and the order is fixed and complete. Man can't be any different from his image. Chaos is all shut out.

The umbrella has got so big, the patches and plaster are so tight and hard, it can be slit no more. If it were slit, the rent would no more be a vision, it would only be an outrage. We should dab it over at once, to match the rest.

So the umbrella is absolute. And so the yearning for chaos becomes a nostalgia. And this will go on till some terrific wind blows the umbrella to ribbons, and much of mankind to oblivion. The rest will shiver in the midst of chaos. For chaos is always there, and always will be, no matter how we put up umbrellas of visions.

What about the poets, then, at this juncture? They reveal the inward desire of mankind. What do they reveal? They show the desire for chaos, and the fear of chaos. The desire for chaos is the breath of their poetry. The fear of chaos is in their parade of forms and technique. Poetry is made of words, they say. So they blow bubbles of sound and image, which soon burst with the breath of longing for chaos, which fills them. But the poetasters can make pretty shiny bubbles for the Christmas-tree, which never burst, because there is no breath of poetry in them, but they remain till we drop them.

[Written in 1928 as part of Preface to *Chariot of the Sun* by Harry Crosby (Paris, 1931), but first published as "Chaos in Poetry" in *Exchanges*, December 1929.]

[46]

A SECOND CONTEMPORARY VERSE ANTHOLOGY

"It is not merely an assembly of verse, but the spiritual record of an entire people."—This from the wrapper of *A Second Contemporary Verse Anthology*. The spiritual record of an entire people sounds rather impressive. The book as a matter of fact is a collection of pleasant verse, neat and nice and easy as eating candy.

Naturally, any collection of contemporary verse in any country at any time is bound to be more or less a box of candy. Days of Horace, days of Milton, days of Whitman, it would be pretty much the same, more or less a box of candy. Would it be at the same time the spiritual record of an entire people? Why not? If we had a good representative anthology of the poetry of Whitman's day, and if it contained two poems by Whitman, then it would be a fairly true spiritual record of the American people of that day. As if the whole nation had whispered or chanted its inner experience into the horn of a gramophone.

And the bulk of the whisperings and murmurings would be

candy: sweet nothings, tender trifles and amusing things. For of such is the bulk of the spiritual experience of any entire people.

The Americans have always been good at "occasional" verse. Sixty years ago they were very good indeed: making their little joke against themselves and their century. To-day there are fewer jokes. There are also fewer footprints on the sands of time. Life is still earnest, but a little less real. And the soul has left off asserting that dust it isn't nor to dust returneth. The spirit of verse prefers now a "composition salad" of fruits of sensation, in a cooked mayonnaise of sympathy. Odds and ends of feelings smoothed into unison by some prevailing sentiment:

> My face is wet with the rain
> But my heart is warm to the core. . . .

Or you can call it a box of chocolate candies. Let me offer you a sweet! Candy! Isn't everything candy?

> There be none of Beauty's daughters
>   With a magic like thee—
> And like music on the waters
>   Is thy sweet voice to me.

Is that candy? Then what about this?

> But you are a girl and run
>   Fresh bathed and warm and sweet,
> After the flying ball
>   On little, sandalled feet.

One of those two fragments is a classic. And one is a scrap from the contemporary spiritual record.

> The river boat had loitered down its way,
> The ropes were coiled, and business for the day
> Was done——

> Now fades the glimmering landscape on the sight,
> And all the air a solemn stillness holds;
> Save where——

Two more bits. Do you see any intrinsic difference between them? After all, the one *means* as much as the other. And what is there in the mere stringing together of words?

For some mysterious reason, there is everything.

When lilacs last in the dooryard bloomed——

It is a string of words, but it makes me prick my innermost ear. So do I prick my ear to: "Fly low, vermilion dragon." But the next line: "With the moon horns," makes me lower that same inward ear once more, in indifference.

There is an element of danger in all new utterance. We prick our ears like an animal in a wood at a strange sound.

Alas! though there is a modicum of "strange sound" in this contemporary spiritual record, we are not the animal to prick our ears at it. Sounds sweetly familiar, linked in a new crochet pattern. "Christ, what are patterns for?" But why invoke Deity? Ask the *Ladies' Home Journal*. You may know a new utterance by the element of danger in it. "My heart aches," says Keats, and you bet it's no joke.

Why do I think of stairways
With a rush of hurt surprise?

Heaven knows, my dear, unless you once fell down.

The element of danger. Man is always, all the time and for ever on the brink of the unknown. The minute you realise this, you prick your ears in alarm. And the minute any man steps alone, with his whole naked self, emotional and mental, into the everlasting hinterland of consciousness, you hate him and you wonder over him. Why can't he stay cozily playing word-games around the camp fire?

Now it is time to invoke the Deity, who made man an adventurer into the everlasting unknown of consciousness.

The spiritual record of any people is 99 per cent a record of games around a camp fire: word-games and picture-games. But the one per cent is a step into the grisly dark, which is for ever dangerous and wonderful. Nothing is wonderful unless it is dangerous. Dangerous to the *status quo* of the soul. And therefore to some degree detestable.

When the contemporary spiritual record warbles away about the wonder of the blue sky and the changing seas, etc., etc., etc., it is all candy. The sky is a blue hand-mirror to the modern poet and he goes on smirking before it. The blue sky of our particular heavens is painfully well known to us all. In fact, it is like the glass bowl to the goldfish, a *ne plus ultra* in which he sees himself as he goes round and round.

The actual heavens can suddenly roll up like the heavens of Ezekiel. That's what happened at the Renaissance. The old heavens shrivelled and men found a new empyrean above them. But they didn't get at it by playing word-games around the camp fire. Somebody has to jump like a desperate clown through the vast blue hoop of the upper air. Or hack a slow way through the dome of crystal.

Play! Play! Play! All the little playboys and playgirls of the western world, playing at goodness, playing at badness, playing at sadness, and playing deafeningly at gladness. Playboys and playgirls of the western world, harmlessly fulfilling their higher destinies and registering the spiritual record of an entire people. Even playing at death, and playing with death. Oh, poetry, you child in a bathing-dress, playing at ball!

You say nature is always nature, the sky is always the sky. But sit still and consider for one moment what sort of nature it was the Romans saw on the face of the earth, and what sort of heavens the medievals knew above them, and your sky will begin to crack like glass. The world is what it is, and the chimerical universe of the ancients was always child's play. The camera cannot lie. And the eye of man is nothing but a camera photographing the outer world in colour-process.

This sounds very well. But the eye of man photographs the chimera of nature, as well as the so-called scientific vision. The eye of man photographs gorgons and chimeras, as the eye of the spider photographs images unrecognisable to us and the eye of the horse photographs flat ghosts and looming motions. We are at the phase of scientific vision. This phase will pass and this vision will seem as chimerical to our descendants as the medieval vision seems to us.

The upshot of it all is that we are pot-bound in our consciousness. We are like a fish in a glass bowl, swimming round and round and gaping at our own image reflected on the walls

of the infinite: the infinite being the glass bowl of our conception of life and the universe. We are prisoners inside our
own conception of life and being. We have exhausted the
possibilities of the universe, as we know it. All that remains is
to telephone to Mars for a new word of advice.

Our consciousness is pot-bound. Our ideas, our emotions, our
experiences are all pot-bound. For us there is nothing new
under the sun. What there is to know, we know it already, and
experience adds little. The girl who is going to fall in love
knows all about it beforehand from books and the movies. She
knows what she wants and she wants what she knows. Like
candy. It is still nice to eat candy, though one has eaten it
every day for years. It is still nice to eat candy. But the spiritual
record of eating candy is a rather thin noise.

There is nothing new under the sun, once the consciousness
becomes pot-bound. And this is what ails all art to-day. But
particularly American art. The American consciousness is
peculiarly pot-bound. It doesn't even have that little hole in
the bottom of the pot through which desperate roots straggle.
No, the American consciousness is not only potted in a solid
and everlasting pot, it is placed moreover in an immovable
ornamental vase. A double hide to bind it and a double bond
to hide it.

European consciousness still has cracks in its vessel and a
hole in the bottom of its absoluteness. It still has strange roots
of memory groping down to the heart of the world.

But American consciousness is absolutely free of such
danglers. It is free from all loop-holes and crevices of escape.
It is absolutely safe inside a solid and ornamental concept of
life. There it is Free! Life is good, and all men are meant to
have a good time. Life is good! that is the flower-pot. The
ornamental vase: Having a good time.

So they proceed to have it, even with their woes. The young
maiden knows exactly when she falls in love: she knows exactly
how she feels when her lover or husband betrays her or when
she betrays him: she knows precisely what it is to be a forsaken
wife, an adoring mother, an erratic grandmother. All at the
age of eighteen.

Vive la vie!

There is nothing new under the sun, but you can have a jolly good old time all the same with the old things. A nut sundae or a new beau, a baby or an automobile, a divorce or a troublesome appendix: my dear, that's Life! You've got to get a good time out of it, anyhow, so here goes!

In which attitude there is a certain piquant stoicism. The stoicism of having a good time. The heroism of enjoying yourself. But, as I say, it makes rather thin hearing in a spiritual record. *Rechauffés* of *rechauffés*. Old soup of old bones of life, heated up again for a new consommé. Nearly always called *printanière*.

> I know a forest, stilly-deep . . .

Mark the poetic novelty of stilly-deep, and then say there is nothing new under the sun.

> My soul-harp never thrills to peaceful tunes;

I should say so.

> For after all, the thing to do
> Is just to put your heart in song——

Or in pickle.

> I sometimes wish that God were back
> In this dark world and wide;
> For though some virtues he might lack,
> He had his pleasant side.

"Getting on the pleasant side of God, and how to stay there."—Hints by a Student of Life.

> Oh, ho! Now I am masterful!
> Now I am filled with power.
> Now I am brutally myself again
> And my own man.

> For I have been among my hills today,
> On the scarred dumb rocks standing;

And it made a man of him . . .
Open confession is good for the soul.
The spiritual record of an entire . . . what?

[Review in New York *Evening Post Literary Review*, 29 September, 1923.]

[47]

From

THE NIGHTINGALE

. . . The nightingale, let us repeat, is the most unsad thing in the world; even more unsad than the peacock full of gleam. He has nothing to be sad about. He feels perfect with life. It isn't conceit. He just feels life-perfect, and he trills it out—shouts, jugs, gurgles, trills, gives long, mock-plaintiff calls, makes declarations, assertions, and triumphs; but he never reflects. It is pure music, in so far as you could never put words to it. But there are words for the feelings aroused in us by the song. No, even that is not true. There are no words to tell what one really feels, hearing the nightingale. It is something so much purer than words, which are all tainted. Yet we can say, it is some sort of feeling of triumph in one's own life-perfection.

> 'Tis not through envy of thy happy lot,
>   But being too happy in thy happiness,—
>   That thou, light-wingèd Dryad of the trees,
>   In some melodious plot
> Of beechen green, and shadows numberless,
>   Singest of summer in full-throated ease.

Poor Keats, he has to be "too happy" in the nightingale's happiness, not being very happy in himself at all. So he wants to drink the blushful Hippocrene, and fade away with the nightingale into the forest dim.

> Fade far away, dissolve, and quite forget
>   What thou among the leaves hast never known,
> The weariness, the fever, and the fret. . . .

It is such sad, beautiful poetry of the human male. Yet the next line strikes me as a bit ridiculous.

> Here, where men sit and hear each other groan;
> Where palsy shakes a few, sad, last gray hairs. . . .

This is Keats, not at all the nightingale. But the sad human male still tries to break away, and get over into the nightingale world. Wine will not take him across. Yet he will go.

> Away! away! for I will fly to thee,
>   Not charioted by Bacchus and his pards,
>   But on the viewless wings of Poesy. . . .

He doesn't succeed, however. The viewless wings of Poesy carry him only into the bushes, not into the nightingale world. He is still outside.

> Darkling I listen; and for many a time
>   I have been half in love with easeful Death. . . .

The nightingale never made any man in love with easeful death, except by contrast. The contrast between the bright flame of positive pure self-aliveness, in the bird, and the uneasy flickering of yearning selflessness, for ever yearning for something outside himself, which is Keats:

> To cease upon the midnight with no pain,
>   While thou art pouring forth thy soul abroad
>   In such an ecstasy!
> Still wouldst thou sing, and I have ears in vain,—
>   To thy high requiem become a sod.

How astonished the nightingale would be if he could be made to realise what sort of answer the poet was answering to his song. He would fall off the bough with amazement.

Because a nightingale, when you answer him back, only shouts and sings louder. Suppose a few other nightingales pipe up in neighbouring bushes—as they always do. Then the blue-white sparks of sound go dazzling up to heaven. And suppose you, mere mortal, happen to be sitting on the shady bank having an altercation with the mistress of your heart, hammer and tongs, then the chief nightingale swells and goes at it like Caruso in the Third Act—simply a brilliant, bursting frenzy of music, singing you down, till you simply can't hear yourself speak to quarrel.

There was, in fact, something very like a nightingale in

Caruso—that bird-like, bursting, miraculous energy of song, and fullness of himself, and self-luxuriance.

> Thou wast not born for death, immortal Bird!
> No hungry generations tread thee down.

Not yet in Tuscany, anyhow. They are twenty to the dozen. Whereas the cuckoo seems remote and low-voiced, calling his low, half secretive call as he flies past. Perhaps it really is different in England.

> The voice I hear this passing night was heard
> In ancient days by emperor and clown:
> Perhaps the self-same song that found a path
> Through the sad heart of Ruth, when, sick for home,
> She stood in tears amid the alien corn.

And why in tears? Always tears. Did Diocletian, I wonder, among the emperors, burst into tears when he heard the nightingale, and Æsop among the clowns? And Ruth, really? Myself, I strongly suspect that young lady of setting the nightingale singing, like the nice damsel in Boccaccio's story, who went to sleep with the lively bird in her hand, "*—tua figliuola è stata sì vaga dell'usignuolo, ch'ella l'ha preso e tienlosi in mano!*"

And what does the hen nightingale think of it all, as she mildly sits upon the eggs and hears milord giving himself forth? Probably she likes it, for she goes on breeding him as jaunty as ever. Probably she prefers his high cockalorum to the poet's humble moan:

> Now more than ever seems it rich to die,
> To cease upon the midnight with no pain. . . .

That wouldn't be much use to the hen nightingale. And one sympathises with Keats's Fanny, and understands why she wasn't having any. Much good such a midnight would have been to *her!*

Perhaps, when all's said and done, the female of the species gets more out of life when the male isn't wanting to cease upon the midnight, with or without pain. There are better uses for midnights. And a bird that sings because he's full of his own bright life, and leaves her to keep the eggs cosy, is perhaps preferable to one who moans, even with love of her.

Of course, the nightingale is utterly unconscious of the little dim hen, while he sings. And he never mentions her name. But she knows well enough that the song is half her: just as she knows the eggs are half him. And just as she doesn't want him coming in and putting a heavy foot down on her little bunch of eggs, he doesn't want her poking into his song, and fussing over it, and mussing it up. Every man to his trade, and every woman to hers:

Adieu! adieu! thy plaintive anthem fades. . . .

It never was a plaintive anthem—it was Caruso at his jauntiest. But don't try to argue with a poet.

[*The Nightingale*, in *Forum*, September 1927, and *Spectator*, 10 September, 1927.]

PART FOUR

Contemporaries and the Importance of the Novel

[48]

WHY THE NOVEL MATTERS

We have curious ideas of ourselves. We think of ourselves as a body with a spirit in it, or a body with a soul in it, or a body with a mind in it. *Mens sana in corpore sano.* The years drink up the wine, and at last throw the bottle away, the body, of course, being the bottle.

It is a funny sort of superstition. Why should I look at my hand, as it so cleverly writes these words, and decide that it is a mere nothing compared to the mind that directs it? Is there really any huge difference between my hand and my brain? Or my mind? My hand is alive, it flickers with a life of its own. It meets all the strange universe in touch, and learns a vast number of things, and knows a vast number of things. My hand, as it writes these words, slips gaily along, jumps like a grasshopper to dot an *i*, feels the table rather cold, gets a little bored if I write too long, has its own rudiments of thought, and is just as much *me* as is my brain, my mind, or my soul. Why should I imagine that there is a *me* which is more *me* than my hand is? Since my hand is absolutely alive, me alive.

Whereas, of course, as far as I am concerned, my pen isn't alive at all. My pen *isn't me* alive. Me alive ends at my finger-tips.

Whatever is me alive is me. Every tiny bit of my hands is alive, every little freckle and hair and fold of skin. And whatever is me alive is me. Only my finger-nails, those ten little weapons between me and an inanimate universe, they cross the mysterious Rubicon between me alive and things like my pen, which are not alive, in my own sense.

So, seeing my hand is all alive, and me alive, wherein is it just a bottle, or a jug, or a tin can, or a vessel of clay, or any of the rest of that nonsense? True, if I cut it it will bleed, like a can of cherries. But then the skin that is cut, and the veins that bleed, and the bones that should never be seen, they are all just as alive as the blood that flows. So the tin can business, or vessel of clay, is just bunk.

And that's what you learn, when you're a novelist. And that's what you are very liable *not* to know, if you're a parson, or a philosopher, or a scientist, or a stupid person. If you're a parson, you talk about souls in heaven. If you're a novelist, you know that paradise is in the palm of your hand, and on the end of your nose, because both are alive; and alive, and man alive, which is more than you can say, for certain, of paradise. Paradise is after life, and I for one am not keen on anything that is *after* life. If you are a philosopher, you talk about infinity, and the pure spirit which knows all things. But if you pick up a novel, you realise immediately that infinity is just a handle to this self-same jug of a body of mine; while as for knowing, if I find my finger in the fire, I know that fire burns, with a knowledge so emphatic and vital, it leaves Nirvana merely a conjecture. Oh, yes, my body, me alive, *knows*, and knows intensely. And as for the sum of all knowledge, it can't be anything more than an accumulation of all the things I know in the body, and you, dear reader, know in the body.

These damned philosophers, they talk as if they suddenly went off in steam, and were then much more important than they are when they're in their shirts. It is nonsense. Every man, philosopher included, ends in his own finger-tips. That's the end of his man alive. As for the words and thoughts and sighs and aspirations that fly from him, they are so many tremulations in the ether, and not alive at all. But if the tremulations reach another man alive, he may receive them into his life, and his life may take on a new colour, like a chameleon creeping from a brown rock on to a green leaf. All very well and good. It still doesn't alter the fact that the so-called spirit, the message or teaching of the philosopher or the saint, isn't alive at all, but just a tremulation upon the ether, like a radio message. All this spirit stuff is just tremulations upon the ether. If you, as man alive, quiver from the tremulation of the ether into new life, that is because you are man alive, and you take sustenance and stimulation into your alive man in a myriad ways. But to say that the message, or the spirit which is communicated to you, is more important than your living body, is nonsense. You might as well say that the potato at dinner was more important.

Nothing is important but life. And for myself, I can absolutely see life nowhere but in the living. Life with a capital L is only man alive. Even a cabbage in the rain is cabbage alive. All things that are alive are amazing. And all things that are dead are subsidiary to the living. Better a live dog than a dead lion. But better a live lion than a live dog. *C'est la vie!*

It seems impossible to get a saint, or a philosopher, or a scientist, to stick to this simple truth. They are all, in a sense, renegades. The saint wishes to offer himself up as spiritual food for the multitude. Even Francis of Assisi turns himself into a sort of angel-cake, of which anyone may take a slice. But an angel-cake is rather less than man alive. And poor St. Francis might well apologise to his body, when he is dying: "Oh, pardon me, my body, the wrong I did you through the years!" It was no wafer, for others to eat.

The philosopher, on the other hand, because he can think, decides that nothing but thoughts matter. It is as if a rabbit, because he can make little pills, should decide that nothing but little pills matter. As for the scientist, he has absolutely no use for me so long as I am man alive. To the scientist, I am dead. He puts under the microscope a bit of dead me, and calls it me. He takes me to pieces, and says first one piece, and then another piece, is me. My heart, my liver, my stomach have all been scientifically me, according to the scientist; and nowadays I am either a brain, or nerves, or glands, or something more up-to-date in the tissue line.

Now I absolutely flatly deny that I am a soul, or a body, or a mind, or an intelligence, or a brain, or a nervous system, or a bunch of glands, or any of the rest of these bits of me. The whole is greater than the part. And therefore, I, who am man alive, am greater than my soul, or spirit, or body, or mind, or consciousness, or anything else that is merely a part of me. I am a man, and alive. I am man alive, and as long as I can, I intend to go on being man alive.

For this reason I am a novelist. And being a novelist, I consider myself superior to the saint, the scientist, the philosopher, and the poet, who are all great masters of different bits of man alive, but never get the whole hog.

The novel is the one bright book of life. Books are not life. They are only tremulations on the ether. But the novel as a tremulation can make the whole man alive tremble. Which is more than poetry, philosophy, science, or any other book-tremulation can do.

The novel is the book of life. In this sense, the Bible is a great confused novel. You may say, it is about God. But it is really about man alive. Adam, Eve, Sarai, Abraham, Isaac, Jacob, Samuel, David, Bath-Sheba, Ruth, Esther, Solomon, Job, Isaiah, Jesus, Mark, Judas, Paul, Peter: what is it but man alive, from start to finish? Man alive, not mere bits. Even the Lord is another man alive, in a burning bush, throwing the tablets of stone at Moses's head.

I do hope you begin to get my idea, why the novel is supremely important, as a tremulation on the ether. Plato makes the perfect ideal being tremble in me. But that's only a bit of me. Perfection is only a bit, in the strange make-up of man alive. The Sermon on the Mount makes the selfless spirit of me quiver. But that, too, is only a bit of me. The Ten Commandments set the old Adam shivering in me, warning me that I am a thief and a murderer, unless I watch it. But even the old Adam is only a bit of me.

I very much like all these bits of me to be set trembling with life and the wisdom of life. But I do ask that the whole of me shall tremble in its wholeness, some time or other.

And this, of course, must happen in me, living.

But as far as it can happen from a communication, it can only happen when a whole novel communicates itself to me. The Bible—but *all* the Bible—and Homer, and Shakespeare: these are the supreme old novels. These are all things to all men. Which means that in their wholeness they affect the whole man alive, which is the man himself, beyond any part of him. They set the whole tree trembling with a new access of life, they do not just stimulate growth in one direction.

I don't want to grow in any one direction any more. And, if I can help it, I don't want to stimulate anybody else into some

particular direction. A particular direction ends in a *cul-de-sac*.
We're in a *cul-de-sac* at present.

I don't believe in any dazzling revelation, or in any supreme
Word. "The grass withereth, the flower fadeth, but the Word
of the Lord shall stand for ever." That's the kind of stuff we've
drugged ourselves with. As a matter of fact, the grass withereth,
but comes up all the greener for that reason, after the rains.
The flower fadeth, and therefore the bud opens. But the Word
of the Lord, being man-uttered and a mere vibration on the
ether, becomes staler and staler, more and more boring, till at
last we turn a deaf ear and it ceases to exist, far more finally
than any withered grass. It is grass that renews its youth like
the eagle, not any Word.

We should ask for no absolutes, or absolute. Once and for all
and for ever, let us have done with the ugly imperialism of any
absolute. There is no absolute good, there is nothing absolutely
right. All things flow and change, and even change is not
absolute. The whole is a strange assembly of apparently
incongruous parts, slipping past one another.

Me, man alive, I am a very curious assembly of incongruous
parts. My yea! of to-day is oddly different from my yea! of
yesterday. My tears of to-morrow will have nothing to do with
my tears of a year ago. If the one I love remains unchanged
and unchanging, I shall cease to love her. It is only because she
changes and startles me into change and defies my inertia, and
is herself staggered in her inertia by my changing, that I can
continue to love her. If she stayed put, I might as well love the
pepper-pot.

In all this change, I maintain a certain integrity. But woe
betide me if I try to put my finger on it. If I say of myself, I
am this, I am that!—then, if I stick to it, I turn into a stupid
fixed thing like a lamp-post. I shall never know wherein lies
my integrity, my individuality, my me. I *can* never know it. It
is useless to talk about my ego. That only means that I have
made up an *idea* of myself, and that I am trying to cut myself
out to pattern. Which is no good. You can cut your cloth to fit
your coat, but you can't clip bits off your living body, to trim
it down to your idea. True, you can put yourself into ideal
corsets. But even in ideal corsets, fashions change.

Let us learn from the novel. In the novel, the characters can do nothing but *live*. If they keep on being good, according to pattern, or bad, according to pattern, or even volatile, according to pattern, they cease to live, and the novel falls dead. A character in a novel has got to live, or it is nothing.

We, likewise, in life have got to live, or we are nothing.

What we mean by living is, of course, just as indescribable as what we mean by *being*. Men get ideas into their heads, of what they mean by Life, and they proceed to cut life out to pattern. Sometimes they go into the desert to seek God, sometimes they go into the desert to seek cash, sometimes it is wine, woman, and song, and again it is water, political reform, and votes. You never know what it will be next: from killing your neighbour with hideous bombs and gas that tears the lungs, to supporting a Foundlings' Home and preaching infinite Love, and being co-respondent in a divorce.

In all this wild welter, we need some sort of guide. It's no good inventing Thou Shalt Nots!

What then? Turn truly, honourably to the novel, and see wherein you are man alive, and wherein you are dead man in life. You may love a woman as man alive, and you may be making love to a woman as sheer dead man in life. You may eat your dinner as man alive, or as a mere masticating corpse. As man alive you may have a shot at your enemy. But as a ghastly simulacrum of life you may be firing bombs into men who are neither your enemies nor your friends, but just things you are dead to. Which is criminal, when the things happen to be alive.

To be alive, to be man alive, to be whole man alive: that is the point. And at its best, the novel, and the novel supremely, can help you. It can help you not to be dead man in life. So much of a man walks about dead and a carcass in the street and house, to-day: so much of women is merely dead. Like a pianoforte with half the notes mute.

But in the novel you can see, plainly, when the man goes dead, the woman goes inert. You can develop an instinct for life, if you will, instead of a theory of right and wrong, good and bad.

In life, there is right and wrong, good and bad, all the time. But what is right in one case is wrong in another. And in the novel you see one man becoming a corpse, because of his so-called goodness, another going dead because of his so-called wickedness. Right and wrong is an instinct: but an instinct of the whole consciousness in a man, bodily, mental, spiritual at once. And only in the novel are *all* things given full play, or at least, they may be given full play, when we realise that life itself, and not inert safety, is the reason for living. For out of the full play of all things emerges the only thing that is anything, the wholeness of a man, the wholeness of a woman, man alive, and live woman.

[First published posthumously in *Phoenix*.]

[49]

MORALITY AND THE NOVEL

THE business of art is to reveal the relation between man and his circumambient universe, at the living moment. As mankind is always struggling in the toils of old relationships, art is always ahead of the "times", which themselves are always far in the rear of the living moment.

When van Gogh paints sunflowers, he reveals, or achieves, the vivid relation between himself, as man, and the sunflower, as sunflower, at that quick moment of time. His painting does not represent the sunflower itself. We shall never know what the sunflower itself is. And the camera will *visualise* the sunflower far more perfectly than van Gogh can.

The vision on the canvas is a third thing, utterly intangible and inexplicable, the offspring of the sunflower itself and van Gogh himself. The vision on the canvas is for ever incommensurable with the canvas, or the paint, or van Gogh as a human organism, or the sunflower as a botanical organism. You cannot weigh nor measure nor even describe the vision on the canvas. It exists, to tell the truth, only in the much-debated fourth dimension. In dimensional space it has no existence.

It is a revelation of the perfected relation, at a certain moment, between a man and a sunflower. It is neither man-in-the-mirror nor flower-in-the-mirror, neither is it above or below or across anything. It is between everything, in the fourth dimension.

And this perfected relation between man and his circumambient universe is life itself, for mankind. It has the fourth-dimensional quality of eternity and perfection. Yet it is momentaneous.

Man and the sunflower both pass away from the moment, in the process of forming a new relationship. The relation between all things changes from day to day, in a subtle stealth of change. Hence art, which reveals or attains to another perfect relationship, will be for ever new.

At the same time, that which exists in the non-dimensional space of pure relationship is deathless, lifeless, and eternal. That is, it gives us the *feeling* of being beyond life or death. We say an Assyrian lion or an Egyptian hawk's head "lives". What we really mean is that it is beyond life, and therefore beyond death. It gives us that feeling. And there is something inside us which must also be beyond life and beyond death, since that "feeling" which we get from an Assyrian lion or an Egyptian hawk's head is so infinitely precious to us. As the evening star, that spark of pure relation between night and day, has been precious to man since time began.

If we think about it, we find that our life *consists in* this achieving of a pure relationship between ourselves and the living universe about us. This is how I "save my soul" by accomplishing a pure relationship between me and another person, me and other people, me and a nation, me and a race of men, me and the animals, me and the trees or flowers, me and the earth, me and the skies and sun and stars, me and the moon: an infinity of pure relations, big and little, like the stars of the sky: that makes our eternity, for each one of us, me and the timber I am sawing, the lines of force I follow; me and the dough I knead for bread, me and the very motion with which I write, me and the bit of gold I have got. This, if we knew it, is our life and our eternity: the subtle, perfected relation between me and my whole circumambient universe.

And morality is that delicate, for ever trembling and changing *balance* between me and my circumambient universe, which precedes and accompanies a true relatedness.

Now here we see the beauty and the great value of the novel.

Philosophy, religion, science, they are all of them busy nailing things down, to get a stable equilibrium. Religion, with its nailed-down One God, who says *Thou shalt, Thou shan't*, and hammers home every time; philosophy, with its fixed ideas; science with its "laws": they, all of them, all the time, want to nail us on to some tree or other.

But the novel, no. The novel is the highest example of subtle inter-relatedness that man has discovered. Everything is true in its own time, place, circumstance, and untrue outside of its own place, time, circumstance. If you try to nail anything down, in the novel, either it kills the novel, or the novel gets up and walks away with the nail.

Morality in the novel is the trembling instability of the balance. When the novelist puts his thumb in the scale, to pull down the balance to his own predilection, that is immorality.

The modern novel tends to become more and more immoral, as the novelist tends to press his thumb heavier and heavier in the pan: either on the side of love, pure love: or on the side of licentious "freedom".

The novel is not, as a rule, immoral because the novelist has any dominant *idea*, or *purpose*. The immorality lies in the novelist's helpless, unconscious predilection. Love is a great emotion. But if you set out to write a novel, and you yourself are in the throes of the great predilection for love, love as the supreme, the only emotion worth living for, then you will write an immoral novel.

Because *no* emotion is supreme, or exclusively worth living for. *All* emotions go to the achieving of a living relationship between a human being and the other human being or creature or thing he becomes purely related to. All emotions, including love and hate, and rage and tenderness, go to the adjusting of the oscillating, unestablished balance between two people who amount to anything. If the novelist puts his thumb in the pan, for love, tenderness, sweetness, peace, then he commits an immoral act: he *prevents* the possibility of a pure relationship, a pure relatedness, the only thing that matters: and he makes inevitable the horrible reaction, when he lets his thumb go, towards hate and brutality, cruelty and destruction.

Life is so made that opposites sway about a trembling centre of balance. The sins of the fathers are visited on the children.

If the fathers drag down the balance on the side of love, peace, and production, then in the third or fourth generation the balance will swing back violently to hate, rage, and destruction. We must balance as we go.

And of all the art forms, the novel most of all demands the trembling and oscillating of the balance. The "sweet" novel is more falsified, and therefore more immoral, than the blood-and-thunder novel.

The same with the smart and smudgily cynical novel, which says it doesn't matter what you do, because one thing is as good as another, anyhow, and prostitution is just as much "life" as anything else.

This misses the point entirely. A thing isn't life just because somebody does it. This the artist ought to know perfectly well. The ordinary bank clerk buying himself a new straw hat isn't "life" at all: it is just existence, quite all right, like everyday dinners: but not "life".

By life, we mean something that gleams, that has the fourth-dimensional quality. If the bank clerk feels really piquant about his hat, if he establishes a lively relation with it, and goes out of the shop with the new straw on his head, a changed man, be-aureoled, then that is life.

The same with the prostitute. If a man establishes a living relation to her, if only for one moment, then it is life. But if it *doesn't:* if it is just money and function, then it is not life, but sordidness, and a betrayal of living.

If a novel reveals true and vivid relationships, it is a moral work, no matter what the relationships may consist in. If the novelist *honours* the relationship in itself, it will be a great novel.

But there are so many relationships which are not real. When the man in *Crime and Punishment* murders the old woman for sixpence, although it is *actual* enough, it is never quite real. The balance between the murderer and the old woman is gone entirely; it is only a mess. It is actuality, but it is not "life", in the living sense.

The popular novel, on the other hand, dishes up a *réchauffé* of old relationships: *If Winter Comes.* And old relationships dished up are likewise immoral. Even a magnificent painter like Raphael does nothing more than dress up in gorgeous new dresses relationships which have already been experienced.

And this gives a gluttonous kind of pleasure of the mass: a voluptuousness, a wallowing. For centuries, men say of their voluptuously ideal woman: "She is a Raphael Madonna." And women are only just learning to take it as an insult.

A new relation, a new relatedness hurts somewhat in the attaining; and will always hurt. So life will always hurt. Because real voluptuousness lies in re-acting old relationships, and at the best, getting an alcoholic sort of pleasure out of it, slightly depraving.

Each time we strive to a new relation, with anyone or anything, it is bound to hurt somewhat. Because it means the struggle with and the displacing of old connexions, and this is never pleasant. And moreover, between living things at least, an adjustment means also a fight, for each party, inevitably, must "seek its own" in the other, and be denied. When, in the parties, each of them seeks his own, her own, absolutely, then it is a fight to the death. And this is true of the thing called "passion". On the other hand, when, of the two parties, one yields utterly to the other, this is called sacrifice, and it also means death. So the Constant Nymph died of her eighteen months of constancy.

It isn't the nature of nymphs to be constant. She should have been constant in her nymph-hood. And it is unmanly to accept sacrifices. He should have abided by his own manhood.

There is, however, the third thing, which is neither sacrifice nor fight to the death: when each seeks only the true relatedness to the other. Each must be true to himself, herself, his own manhood, her own womanhood, and let the relationship work out of itself. This means courage above all things: and then discipline. Courage to accept the life-thrust from within oneself, and from the other person. Discipline, not to exceed oneself any more than one can help. Courage, when one has exceeded oneself, to accept the fact and not whine about it.

Obviously, to read a really new novel will *always* hurt, to some extent. There will always be resistance. The same with new pictures, new music. You may judge of their reality by the fact that they do arouse a certain resistance, and compel, at length, a certain acquiescence.

The great relationship, for humanity, will always be the relation between man and woman. The relation between man and man, woman and woman, parent and child, will always be subsidiary.

And the relation between man and woman will change for ever, and will for ever be the new central clue to human life. It is the *relation itself* which is the quick and the central clue to life, not the man, nor the woman, nor the children that result from the relationship, as a contingency.

It is no use thinking you can put a stamp on the relation between man and woman, to keep it in the *status quo*. You can't. You might as well try to put a stamp on the rainbow or the rain.

As for the bond of love, better put it off when it galls. It is an absurdity, to say that men and women *must love*. Men and women will be for ever subtly and changingly related to one another; no need to yoke them with any "bond" at all. The only morality is to have man true to his manhood, woman to her womanhood, and let the relationship form of itself, in all honour. For it is, to each, *life itself*.

If we are going to be moral, let us refrain from driving pegs through anything, either through each other or through the third thing, the relationship, which is for ever the ghost of both of us. Every sacrificial crucifixion needs five pegs, four short ones and a long one, each one an abomination. But when you try to nail down the relationship itself, and write over it *Love* instead of *This is the King of the Jews*, then you can go on putting in nails for ever. Even Jesus called it the Holy Ghost, to show you that you can't lay salt on its tail.

The novel is a perfect medium for revealing to us the changing rainbow of our living relationships. The novel can help us to live, as nothing else can: no didactic Scripture, anyhow. If the novelist keeps his thumb out of the pan.

But when the novelist *has* his thumb in the pan, the novel becomes an unparalleled perverter of men and women. To be compared only, perhaps, to that great mischief of sentimental hymns, like "Lead, Kindly Light," which have helped to rot the marrow in the bones of the present generation.

[First published in *Calendar of Modern Letters,* December 1925.]

[50]

SURGERY FOR THE NOVEL—OR A BOMB

You talk about the future of the baby, little cherub, when he's in the cradle cooing; and it's a romantic, glamorous subject. You also talk, with the parson, about the future of the wicked old grandfather who is at last lying on his death-bed. And there again you have a subject for much vague emotion, chiefly of fear this time.

How do we feel about the novel? Do we bounce with joy thinking of the wonderful novelistic days ahead? Or do we grimly shake our heads and hope the wicked creature will be spared a little longer? Is the novel on his death-bed, old sinner? Or is he just toddling round his cradle, sweet little thing? Let us have another look at him before we decide this rather serious case.

There he is, the monster with many faces, many branches to him, like a tree: the modern novel. And he is almost dual, like Siamese twins. On the one hand, the pale-faced, high-browed, earnest novel, which you have to take seriously; on the other, that smirking, rather plausible hussy, the popular novel.

Let us just for the moment feel the pulses of *Ulysses* and of Miss Dorothy Richardson and M. Marcel Proust, on the earnest side of Briareus; on the other, the throb of *The Sheik* and Mr. Zane Grey, and, if you will, Mr. Robert Chambers and the rest. Is *Ulysses* in his cradle? Oh, dear! What a grey face! And *Pointed Roofs*, are they a gay little toy for nice little girls? And M. Proust? Alas! You can hear the death-rattle in their throats. They can hear it themselves. They are listening to it with acute interest, trying to discover whether the intervals are minor thirds or major fourths. Which is rather infantile, really.

So there you have the "serious" novel, dying in a very long-drawn-out fourteen-volume death-agony, and absorbedly, childishly interested in the phenomenon. "Did I feel a twinge in my little toe, or didn't I?" asks every character of Mr. Joyce or of Miss Richardson or M. Proust. Is my aura a blend of frankincense and orange pekoe and boot-blacking, or is it myrrh and bacon-fat and Shetland tweed? The audience round the death-bed gapes for the answer. And when, in a sepulchral tone, the answer comes at length, after hundreds of pages: "It is none of these, it is abysmal chloro-coryambasis," the audience quivers all over, and murmurs: "That's just how I feel myself."

Which is the dismal, long-drawn-out comedy of the death-bed of the serious novel. It is self-consciousness picked into such fine bits that the bits are most of them invisible, and you have to go by smell. Through thousands and thousands of pages Mr. Joyce and Miss Richardson tear themselves to pieces, strip their smallest emotions to the finest threads, till you feel you are sewed inside a wool mattress that is being slowly shaken up, and you are turning to wool along with the rest of the woolliness.

It's awful. And it's childish. It really is childish, after a certain age, to be absorbedly self-conscious. One has to be self-conscious at seventeen: still a little self-conscious at twenty-seven; but if we are going it strong at thirty-seven, then it is a sign of arrested development, nothing else. And if it is still continuing at forty-seven, it is obvious senile precocity.

And there's the serious novel: senile-precocious. Absorbedly, childishly concerned with *what I am*. "I am this, I am that, I am the other. My reactions are such, and such, and such. And, oh, Lord, if I liked to watch myself closely enough, if I liked to analyse my feelings minutely, as I unbutton my gloves, instead of saying crudely I unbuttoned them, then I could go on to a million pages instead of a thousand. In fact, the more I come to think of it, it is gross, it is uncivilised bluntly to say: I unbuttoned my gloves. After all, the absorbing adventure of it! Which button did I begin with?" etc.

The people in the serious novels are so absorbedly concerned with themselves and what they feel and don't feel, and how they react to every mortal button; and their audience as frenziedly absorbed in the application of the author's discoveries to their own reactions: "That's me! That's exactly it! I'm just finding myself in this book!" Why, this is more than death-bed, it is almost post-mortem behaviour.

Some convulsion or cataclysm will have to get this serious novel out of its self-consciousness. The last great war made it worse. What's to be done? Because, poor thing, it's really young yet. The novel has never become fully adult. It has never quite grown to years of discretion. It has always youthfully hoped for the best, and felt rather sorry for itself on the last page. Which is just childish. The childishness has become very long-drawn-out. So very many adolescents who drag their adolescence on into their forties and their fifties and their sixties! There needs some sort of surgical operation, somewhere.

Then the popular novels—the *Sheiks* and *Babbitts* and Zane Grey novels. They are just as self-conscious, only they do have more illusions about themselves. The heroines do think they are lovelier, and more fascinating, and purer. The heroes do see themselves more heroic, braver, more chivalrous, more fetching. The mass of the populace "find themselves" in the popular novels. But nowadays it's a funny sort of self they find. A sheik with a whip up his sleeve, and a heroine with weals on her back, but adored in the end, adored, the whip out of sight, but the weals still faintly visible.

It's a funny sort of self they discover in the popular novels. And the essential moral of *If Winter Comes*, for example, is so shaky. "The gooder you are, the worse it is for you, poor you, oh, poor you. Don't you be so blimey good, it's not good enough." Or *Babbitt*: "Go on, you make your pile, and then pretend you're too good for it. Put it over the rest of the grabbers that way. They're only pleased with themselves when they've made their pile. You go one better."

Always the same sort of baking-powder gas to make you rise: the soda counteracting the cream of tartar, and the tartar counteracted by the soda. Sheik heroines, duly whipped, wildly adored. Babbitts with solid fortunes, weeping from self-pity. Winter-Comes heroes as good as pie, hauled off to jail. *Moral:* Don't be too good, because you'll go to jail for it. *Moral:* Don't feel sorry for yourself till you've made your pile and don't need to feel sorry for yourself. *Moral:* Don't let him adore you till he's whipped you into it. Then you'll be partners in mild crime as well as in holy matrimony.

Which again is childish. Adolescence which *can't* grow up. Got into the self-conscious rut and going crazy, quite crazy in it. Carrying on their adolescence into middle age and old age, like the looney Cleopatra in *Dombey and Son*, murmuring "Rose-coloured curtains" with her dying breath.

The future of the novel? Poor old novel, it's in a rather dirty, messy tight corner. And it's either got to get over the wall or knock a hole through it. In other words, it's got to grow up. Put away childish things like: "Do I love the girl, or don't I?"— "Am I pure and sweet, or am I not?"—"Do I unbutton my right glove first, or my left?"—"Did my mother ruin my life by refusing to drink the cocoa which my bride had boiled for her?" These questions and their answers don't really interest me any more, though the world still goes sawing them over. I simply don't care for any of these things now, though I used to. The purely emotional and self-analytical stunts are played out in me. I'm finished. I'm deaf to the whole band. But I'm neither *blasé* nor cynical, for all that. I'm just interested in something else.

Supposing a bomb were put under the whole scheme of things, what would we be after? What feelings do we want to carry through into the next epoch? What feelings will carry us through? What is the underlying impulse in us that will provide the motive power for a new state of things, when this democratic-industrial-lovey-dovey-darling-take-me-to-mamma state of things is bust?

What next? That's what interests me. "What now?" is no fun any more.

If you wish to look into the past for what-next books, you can go back to the Greek philosophers. Plato's Dialogues are queer little novels. It seems to me it was the greatest pity in the world, when philosophy and fiction got split. They used to be one, right from the days of myth. Then they went and parted, like a nagging married couple, with Aristotle and Thomas Aquinas and that beastly Kant. So the novel went sloppy, and philosophy went abstract-dry. The two should come together again—in the novel.

You've got to find a new impulse for new things in mankind, and it's really fatal to find it through abstraction. No, no; philosophy and religion, they've both gone too far on the algebraical tack: Let X stand for sheep and Y for goats: then X minus Y equals Heaven, and X plus Y equals Earth, and Y minus X equals Hell. Thank you! But what coloured shirt does X have on?

The novel has a future. It's got to have the courage to tackle new propositions without using abstractions; it's got to present us with new, really new feelings, a whole line of new emotion, which will get us out of the emotional rut. Instead of snivelling about what is and has been, or inventing new sensations in the old line, it's got to break a way through, like a hole in the wall. And the public will scream and say it is sacrilege: because, of course, when you've been jammed for a long time in a tight corner, and you get really used to its stuffiness and its tightness, till you find it suffocatingly cosy; then, of course, you're horrified when you see a new glaring hole in what was your cosy wall. You're horrified. You back away from the cold stream of fresh air as if it were killing you. But gradually, first one and then another of the sheep filters through the gap and finds a new world outside.

[From *International Book Review*, April 1923.]

[51]

JOHN GALSWORTHY

LITERARY criticism can be no more than a reasoned account of the feeling produced upon the critic by the book he is criticising. Criticism can never be a science: it is, in the first place, much too personal, and in the second, it is concerned with values that science ignores. The touchstone is emotion, not reason. We judge a work of art by its effect on our sincere and vital emotion, and nothing else. All the critical twiddle-twaddle about style and form, all this pseudo-scientific classifying and analysing of books in an imitation-botanical fashion, is mere impertinence and mostly dull jargon.

A critic must be able to *feel* the impact of a work of art in all its complexity and its force. To do so, he must be a man of force and complexity himself, which few critics are. A man with a paltry, impudent nature will never write anything but paltry, impudent criticism. And a man who is *emotionally* educated is rare as a phœnix. The more scholastically educated a man is generally, the more he is an emotional boor.

More than this, even an artistically and emotionally educated man must be a man of good faith. He must have the courage to admit what he feels, as well as the flexibility to *know* what he feels. So Sainte-Beuve remains, to me, a great critic. And a man like Macaulay, brilliant as he is, is unsatisfactory, because he is not honest. He is emotionally very alive, but he juggles his feelings. He prefers a fine effect to the sincere statement of the æsthetic and emotional reaction. He is quite intellectually capable of giving us a true account of what he feels. But not morally. A critic must be emotionally alive in every fibre, intellectually capable and skilful in essential logic, and then morally very honest.

Then it seems to me a good critic should give his reader a few standards to go by. He can change the standards for every new critical attempt, so long as he keeps good faith. But it is just as well to say: This and this is the standard we judge by.

Sainte-Beuve, on the whole, set up the standard of the "good man". He sincerely believed that the great man was essentially the good man in the widest range of human sympathy. This remained his universal standard. Pater's standard was the lonely philosopher of pure thought and pure æsthetic truth. Macaulay's standard was tainted by a political or democratic bias, he must be on the side of the weak. Gibbon tried a purely moral standard, individual morality.

Reading Galsworthy again—or most of him, for all is too much—one feels oneself in need of a standard, some conception of a real man and a real woman, by which to judge all these Forsytes and their contemporaries. One cannot judge them by the standard of the good man, nor of the man of pure thought, nor of the treasured humble nor the moral individual. One would like to judge them by the standard of the human being, but what, after all, is that? This is the trouble with the Forsytes. They are human enough, since anything in humanity is human, just as anything in nature is natural. Yet not one of them seems to be a really vivid human being. They are social beings. And what do we mean by that?

It remains to define, just for the purpose of this criticism, what we mean by a social being as distinct from a human being. The necessity arises from the sense of dissatisfaction which these Forsytes give us. Why can't we admit them as human beings? Why can't we have them in the same category as

Sairey Gamp for example, who is satirically conceived, or of Jane Austen's people, who are social enough? We can accept Mrs. Gamp or Jane Austen's characters or even George Meredith's Egoist as human beings in the same category as ourselves. Whence arises this repulsion from the Forsytes, this refusal, this emotional refusal, to have them identified with our common humanity? Why do we feel so instinctively that they are inferiors?

It is because they seem to us to have lost caste as human beings, and to have sunk to the level of the social being, that peculiar creature that takes the place in our civilisation of the slave in the old civilisations. The human individual is a queer animal, always changing. But the fatal change to-day is the collapse from the psychology of the free human individual into the psychology of the social being, just as the fatal change in the past was a collapse from the freeman's psyche to the psyche of the slave. The free moral and the slave moral, the human moral and the social moral: these are the abiding antitheses.

While a man remains a man, a true human individual, there is at the core of him a certain innocence or naïveté which defies all analysis, and which you cannot bargain with, you can only deal with it in good faith from your own corresponding innocence or naïveté. This does not mean that the human being is nothing but naïve or innocent. He is Mr. Worldly Wiseman also to his own degree. But in his essential core he.is naïve, and money does not touch him. Money, of course, with every man living goes a long way. With the alive human being it may go as far as his penultimate feeling. But in the last naked him it does not enter.

With the social being it goes right through the centre and is the controlling principle no matter how much he may pretend, nor how much bluff he may put up. He may give away all he has to the poor and still reveal himself as a social being swayed finally and helplessly by the money-sway, and by the social moral, which is inhuman.

It seems to me that when the human being becomes too much divided between his subjective and objective conscious-ness, at last something splits in him and he becomes a social being. When he becomes too much aware of objective reality, and of his own isolation in the face of a universe of objective reality, the core of his identity splits, his nucleus collapses, his innocence or his naïveté perishes, and he becomes only a subjective-objective reality, a divided thing hinged together but not strictly individual.

While a man remains a man, before he falls and becomes a social individual, he innocently feels himself altogether within the great continuum of the universe. He is not divided nor cut off. Men may be against him, the tide of affairs may be rising to sweep him away. But he is one with the living continuum of the universe. From this he cannot be swept away. Hamlet and Lear feel it, as does Œdipus or Phædra. It is the last and deepest feeling that is in a man while he remains a man. It is there the same in a deist like Voltaire or a scientist like Darwin: it is there, imperishable, in every great man: in Napoleon the same, till material things piled too much on him and he lost it and was doomed. It is the essential innocence and naïveté of the human being, the sense of being at one with the great universe-continuum of space-time-life, which is vivid in a great man, and a pure nuclear spark in every man who is still free.

But if man loses his mysterious naïve assurance, which is his innocence; if he gives *too* much importance to the external objective reality and so collapses in his natural innocent pride, then he becomes obsessed with the idea of objectives or material assurance; he wants to *insure* himself, and perhaps everybody else: universal insurance. The impulse rests on fear. Once the individual loses his naïve at-oneness with the living universe he falls into a state of fear and tries to insure himself with wealth. If he is an altruist he wants to insure everybody, and feels it is the tragedy of tragedies if this can't be done. But the whole necessity for thus materially insuring oneself with wealth, money, arises from the state of fear into which a man falls who has lost his at-oneness with the living universe, lost his peculiar nuclear innocence and fallen into fragmentariness. Money, material salvation is the only salvation. What is salvation is God. Hence money is God. The social being may rebel even against this god, as do many of Galsworthy's characters. But that does not give them back their innocence. They are only anti-materialists instead of positive materialists. And the anti-materialist is a social being just the same as the materialist,

neither more nor less. He is castrated just the same, made a
neuter by having lost his innocence, the bright little individual
spark of his at-oneness.

When one reads Mr. Galsworthy's books it seems as if there
were not on earth one single human individual. They are all
these social beings, positive and negative. There is not a free
soul among them, not even Pendyce, or June Forsyte. If money
does not actively determine their being, it does negatively.
Money, or property, which is the same thing. Mrs. Pendyce,
lovable as she is, is utterly circumscribed by property. Ultimately, she is not lovable at all, she is part of the fraud, she is
prostituted to property. And there is nobody else. Old Jolyon
is merely a sentimental materialist. Only for one moment do
we see a man, and that is the road-sweeper in *Fraternity* after
he comes out of prison and covers his face. But even *his* manhood has to be explained away by a wound in the head: an
abnormality.

Now it looks as if Mr. Galsworthy set out to make that very
point: to show that the Forsytes were not full human individuals,
but social beings fallen to a lower level of life. They have lost
that bit of free manhood and free womanhood which makes
men and women. *The Man of Property* has the elements of a
very great novel, a very great satire. It sets out to reveal the
social being in all his strength and inferiority. But the author
has not the courage to carry it through. The greatness of the
book rests in its new and sincere and amazingly profound
satire. It is the ultimate satire on modern humanity, and done
from the inside, with really consummate skill and sincere
creative passion, something quite new. It seems to be a real
effort to show up the social being in all his weirdness. And
then it fizzles out.

Then, in the love affair of Irene and Bosinney, and in the
sentimentalising of old Jolyon Forsyte, the thing is fatally
blemished. Galsworthy had not quite enough of the superb
courage of his satire. He faltered, and gave in to the Forsytes.
It is a thousand pities. He might have been the surgeon the
modern soul needs so badly, to cut away the proud flesh of our
Forsytes from the living body of men who are fully alive.
Instead, he put down the knife and laid on a soft, sentimental
poultice, and helped to make the corruption worse.

Satire exists for the very purpose of killing the social being, showing him what an inferior he is and, with all his parade of social honesty, how subtly and corruptly debased. Dishonest to life, dishonest to the living universe on which he is parasitic as a louse. By ridiculing the social being, the satirist helps the true individual, the real human being, to rise to his feet again and go on with the battle. For it is always a battle, and always will be.

Not that the majority are necessarily social beings. But the majority is only *conscious* socially: humanly, mankind is helpless and unconscious, unaware even of the thing most precious to any human being, that core of manhood or womanhood, naïve, innocent at-oneness with the living universe-continuum, which alone makes a man individual and, as an individual, *essentially* happy, even if he be driven mad like Lear. Lear was essentially happy, even in his greatest misery. A happiness from which Goneril and Regan were excluded as lice and bugs are excluded from happiness, being social beings, and, as such, parasites, fallen from true freedom and independence.

But the tragedy to-day is that men are only materially and socially conscious. They are unconscious of their own manhood, and so they let it be destroyed. Out of free men we produce social beings by the thousand every week.

The Forsytes are all parasites, and Mr. Galsworthy set out, in a really magnificent attempt, to let us see it. They are parasites upon the thought, the feelings, the whole body of life of really living individuals who have gone before them and who exist alongside with them. All they can do, having no individual life of their own, is out of fear to rake together property, and to feed upon the life that has been given by living men to mankind. They have no life, and so they live for ever, in perpetual fear of death, accumulating property to ward off death. They can keep up convention, but they cannot carry on a tradition. There is a tremendous difference between the two things. To carry on a tradition you must add something to the tradition. But to keep up a convention needs only the monotonous persistency of a parasite, the endless endurance of the craven, those who fear life because they are not alive, and who cannot die because they cannot live—the social beings.

As far as I can see, there is nothing but Forsyte in Galsworthy's

books: Forsyte positive or Forsyte negative, Forsyte successful or
Forsyte *manqué*. That is, every single character is determined by
money: either the getting it, or the having it, or the wanting it,
or the utter lacking it. Getting it are the Forsytes as such;
having it are the Pendyces and patricians and Hilarys and
Biancas and all that lot; wanting it are the Irenes and Bosinneys
and young Jolyons; and utterly lacking it are all the char-
women and squalid poor who form the background—the
shadows of the "having" ones, as old Mr. Stone says. This is
the whole Galsworthy gamut, all absolutely determined by
money, and not an individual soul among them. They are all
fallen, all social beings, a castrated lot.

Perhaps the overwhelming numerousness of the Forsytes
frightened Mr. Galsworthy from utterly damning them. Or
perhaps it was something else, something more serious in him.
Perhaps it was his utter failure to see what you were when you
weren't a Forsyte. What was there *besides* Forsytes in all the wide
human world? Mr. Galsworthy looked, and found nothing.
Strictly and truly, after his frightened search, he had found
nothing. But he came back with Irene and Bosinney, and
offered us that. Here! he seems to say. Here is the anti-
Forsyte! Here! Here you have it! Love! Pa-assion!
PASSION.

We look at this love, this PASSION, and we see nothing but a
doggish amorousness and a sort of anti-Forsytism. They are
the *anti* half of the show. Runaway dogs of these Forsytes,
running in the back garden and furtively and ignominiously
copulating—this is the effect, on me, of Mr. Galsworthy's
grand love affairs, Dark Flowers or Bosinneys, or Apple Trees
or George Pendyce—whatever they be. About every one of
them something ignominious and doggish, like dogs copulating
in the street, and looking round to see if the Forsytes are
watching.

Alas! this is the Forsyte trying to be freely sensual. He can't
do it; he's lost it. He can only be doggishly messy. Bosinney is
not only a Forsyte, but an anti-Forsyte, with a vast grudge
against property. And the thing a man has a vast grudge
against is the man's determinant. Bosinney is a property
hound, but he has run away from the kennels, or been born
outside the kennels, so he is a rebel. So he goes sniffing round

the property bitches, to get even with the successful property hounds that way. One cannot help preferring Soames Forsyte, in a choice of evils.

Just as one prefers June or any of the old aunts to Irene. Irene seems to me a sneaking, creeping, spiteful sort of bitch, an anti-Forsyte, absolutely living off the Forsytes—yes, to the very end; absolutely living off their money and trying to do them dirt. She is like Bosinney, a property mongrel doing dirt in the property kennels. But she is a real property prostitute, like the little model in *Fraternity*. Only she is *anti*! It is a type recurring again and again in Galsworthy: the parasite upon the parasites, "Big fleas have little fleas, etc." And Bosinney and Irene, as well as the vagabond in *The Island Pharisees*, are among the little fleas. And as a tramp loves his own vermin, so the Forsytes and the Hilarys love these, their own particular body parasites, their *antis*.

It is when he comes to sex that Mr. Galsworthy collapses finally. He becomes nastily sentimental. He wants to make sex important, and he only makes it repulsive. Sentimentalism is the working off on yourself of feelings you haven't really got. We all *want* to have certain feelings: feelings of love, of passionate sex, of kindliness, and so forth. Very few people really feel love, or sex passion, or kindliness, or anything else that goes at all deep. So the mass just fake these feelings inside themselves. Faked feelings! The world is all gummy with them. They are better than real feelings, because you can spit them out when you brush your teeth; and then to-morrow you can fake them afresh.

Shelton, in *The Island Pharisees*, is the first of Mr. Galsworthy's lovers, and he might as well be the last. He is almost comical. All we know of his passion for Antonia is that he feels at the beginning a "hunger" for her, as if she were a beefsteak. And towards the end he once kisses her, and expects her, no doubt, to fall instantly at his feet overwhelmed. He never for a second feels a moment of gentle sympathy with her. She is class-bound, but she doesn't seem to have been inhuman. The inhuman one was the lover. He can gloat over her in the distance, as if she were a dish of pig's trotters, *pieds truffés*: she can be an angelic *vision* to him a little way off, but when the poor thing has to be just a rather ordinary middle-class girl to

him, quite near, he hates her with a comical, rancorous hate.
It is most queer. He is helplessly *anti*. He hates her for even
existing as a woman of her own class, for even having her own
existence. Apparently she should just be a floating female sex-
organ, hovering round to satisfy his little "hungers", and then
basta. Anything of the real meaning of sex, which involves the
whole of a human being, never occurs to him. It is a function,
and the female is a sort of sexual appliance, no more.

And so we have it again and again, on this low and bastard
level, all the human correspondence lacking. The sexual level
is extraordinarily low, like dogs. The Galsworthy heroes are
all weirdly in love with themselves, when we know them better,
afflicted with chronic narcissism. They know just three types of
women: the Pendyce mother, prostitute to property: the Irene,
the essential *anti* prostitute, the floating, flaunting female organ;
and the social woman, the mere lady. All three are loved and
hated in turn by the recurrent heroes. But it is all on the
debased level of property, positive or *anti*. It is all a doggy
form of prostitution. Be quick and have done.

One of the funniest stories is *The Apple Tree*. The young man
finds, at a lonely Devon farm, a little Welsh farm-girl who,
being a Celt and not a Saxon, at once falls for the Galsworthian
hero. This young gentleman, in the throes of narcissistic love
for his marvellous self, falls for the maid because she has fallen
so utterly and abjectly for him. She doesn't call him "My
King", not being Wellsian; she only says: "I can't live away
from you. Do what you like with me. Only let me come with
you!" The proper prostitutional announcement!

For this, of course, a narcissistic young gentleman just down
from Oxford falls at once. Ensues a grand pa-assion. He goes
to buy her a proper frock to be carried away in, meets a college
friend with a young lady sister, has jam for tea and stays the
night, and the grand pa-assion has died a natural death by the
time he spreads the marmalade on his bread. He has returned
to his own class, and nothing else exists. He marries the young
lady, true to his class. But to fill the cup of his vanity, the maid
drowns herself. It is funny that maids only seem to do it for
these narcissistic young gentlemen who, looking in the pool for
their own image, desire the added satisfaction of seeing the
face of drowned Ophelia there as well; saving them the

necessity of taking the narcissus plunge in person. We have gone one better than the myth. Narcissus, in Mr. Galsworthy, doesn't drown himself. He asks Ophelia, or Megan, kindly to drown herself instead. And in this fiction she actually does. And he feels so *wonderful* about it!

Mr. Galsworthy's treatment of passion is really rather shameful. The whole thing is doggy to a degree. The man has a temporary "hunger"; he is "on the heat" as they say of dogs. The heat passes. It's done. Trot away, if you're not tangled. Trot off, looking shamefacedly over your shoulder. People have been watching! Damn them! But never mind, it'll blow over. Thank God, the bitch is trotting in the other direction. She'll soon have another trail of dogs after her. That'll wipe out my traces. Good for that! Next time I'll get properly married and do my doggishness in my own house.

With the fall of the individual, sex falls into a dog's heat. Oh, if only Mr. Galsworthy had had the strength to satirise this too, instead of pouring a sauce of sentimental savouriness over it. Of course, if he had done so he would never have been a popular writer, but he would have been a great one.

However, he chose to sentimentalise and glorify the most doggy sort of sex. Setting out to satirise the Forsytes, he glorifies the *anti*, who is one worse. While the individual remains real and unfallen, sex remains a vital and supremely important thing. But once you have the fall into social beings, sex becomes disgusting, like dogs on the heat. Dogs are social beings, with no true canine individuality. Wolves and foxes don't copulate on the pavement. Their sex is wild and in act utterly private. Howls you may hear, but you will never see anything. But the dog is tame—and he makes excrement and copulates on the pavement, as if to spite you. He is the Forsyte *anti*.

The same with human beings. Once they become tame they become, in a measure, exhibitionists, as if to spite everything. They have no real feelings of their own. Unless somebody "catches them at it" they don't really feel they've felt anything at all. And this is how the mob is to-day. It is Forsyte *anti*. It is the social being spiting society.

Oh, if only Mr. Galsworthy had satirised *this* side of Forsytism, the anti-Forsyte posturing of the "rebel", the narcissus and the exhibitionist, the dogs copulating on the pavement! Instead of that, he glorified it, to the eternal shame of English literature.

The satire, which in *The Man of Property* really had a certain noble touch, soon fizzles out, and we get that series of Galsworthian "rebels" who are, like all the rest of the modern middle-class rebels, not in rebellion at all. They are merely social beings behaving in an anti-social manner. They worship their own class, but they pretend to go one better and sneer at it. They are Forsyte *antis*, feeling snobbish about snobbery. Nevertheless, they want to attract attention and make money. That's why they are *anti*. It is the vicious circle of Forsytism. Money means more to them than it does to a Soames Forsyte, so they pretend to go one better, and despise it, but they will do anything to have it—things which Soames Forsyte would not have done.

If there is one thing more repulsive than the social being positive, it is the social being negative, the mere *anti*. In the great debacle of decency this gentleman is the most indecent. In a subtle way Bosinney and Irene are more dishonest and more indecent than Soames and Winifred, but they are *anti*, so they are glorified. It is pretty sickening.

The introduction to *The Island Pharisees* explains the whole show: "Each man born into the world is born to go a journey, and for the most part he is born on the high road. . . . As soon as he can toddle, he moves, by the queer instinct we call the love of life, along this road: . . . his fathers went this way before him, they made this road for him to tread, and, when they bred him, passed into his fibre the love of doing things as they themselves had done them. So he walks on and on. . . . Suddenly, one day, without intending to, he notices a path or opening in the hedge, leading to right or left, and he stands looking at the undiscovered. After that he stops at all the openings in the hedge; one day, with a beating heart, he tries one. And this is where the fun begins."—Nine out of ten get back to the broad road again, and sidetrack no more. They snuggle down comfortably in the next inn, and think where they might have been. "But the poor silly tenth is faring on. Nine times out of ten he goes down in a bog; the undiscovered has engulfed him." But the tenth time he gets across, and a new road is opened to mankind.

It is a class-bound consciousness, or at least a hopeless social consciousness which sees life as a high road between two hedges. And the only way out is gaps in the hedge and excursions into naughtiness! These little *anti* excursions, from which the wayfarer slinks back to solid comfort nine times out of ten; an odd one goes down in a bog; and a very rare one finds a way across and opens out a new road.

In Mr. Galsworthy's novels we see the nine, the ninety-nine, the nine hundred and ninety-nine slinking back to solid comfort; we see an odd Bosinney go under a bus, because he hadn't guts enough to do something else, the poor *anti?* but that rare figure sidetracking into the unknown we do *not* see. Because, as a matter of fact, the whole figure is faulty at that point. If life is a great highway, then it must forge on ahead into the unknown. Sidetracking gets nowhere. That is mere *anti*. The tip of the road is always unfinished, in the wilderness. If it comes to a precipice and a cañon—well, then, there is need for some exploring. But we see Mr. Galsworthy, after *The Country House*, very safe on the old highway, very secure in comfort, wealth, and renown. He at least has gone down in no bog, nor lost himself striking new paths. The hedges nowadays are ragged with gaps, anybody who likes strays out on the little trips of "unconventions". But the Forsyte road has not moved on at all. It has only become dishevelled and sordid with excursionists doing the *anti* tricks and being "unconventional", and leaving tin cans behind.

In the three early novels, *The Island Pharisees*, *The Man of Property*, *Fraternity*, it looked as if Mr. Galsworthy might break through the blind end of the highway with the dynamite of satire, and help us out on to a new lap. But the sex ingredient of his dynamite was damp and muzzy, the explosion gradually fizzled off in sentimentality, and we are left in a worse state than before.

The later novels are purely commercial, and, if it had not been for the early novels, of no importance. They are popular, they sell well, and there's the end of them. They contain the explosive powder of the first books in minute quantities, fizzling as silly squibs. When you arrive at *To Let*, and the end, at least the *promised* end, of the Forsytes, what have you? Just money! Money, money, money and a certain snobbish silliness, and

many more *anti* tricks and poses. Nothing else. The story is
feeble, the characters have no blood and bones, the emotions
are faked, faked, faked. It is one great fake. Not necessarily of
Mr. Galsworthy. The characters fake their own emotions. But
that doesn't help us. And if you look closely at the characters,
the meanness and low-level vulgarity are very distasteful. You
have all the Forsyte meanness, with none of the energy. Jolyon
and Irene are meaner and more treacherous to their son than
the older Forsytes were to theirs. The young ones are of a
limited, mechanical, vulgar egoism far surpassing that of
Swithin or James, their ancestors. There is in it all a vulgar
sense of being rich, and therefore we do as we like: an utter
incapacity for anything like *true* feeling, especially in the women,
Fleur, Irene, Annette, June: a glib crassness, a youthful
spontaneity which is just impertinence and lack of feeling; and
all the time, a creeping, "having" sort of vulgarity of money
and self-will, money and self-will, so that we wonder sometimes if
Mr. Galsworthy is not treating his public in real bad faith, and
being cynical and rancorous under his rainbow sentimentalism.

Fleur he destroys in one word: she is "having". It is perfectly
true. We don't blame the young Jon for clearing out. Irene he
destroys in a phrase out of Fleur's mouth to June: "Didn't she
spoil your life too?"—and it is precisely what she did. Sneaking
and mean, Irene prevented June from getting her lover.
Sneaking and mean, she prevents Fleur. She is the bitch in the
manger. She is the sneaking *anti*. Irene, the most beautiful
woman on earth! And Mr. Galsworthy, with the cynicism of a
successful old sentimentalist, turns it off by making June say:
"Nobody can spoil a life, my dear. That's nonsense. Things
happen, but we bob up."

This is the final philosophy of it all. "Things happen, but we
bob up." Very well, then, write the book in that key, the
keynote of a frank old cynic. There's no point in sentimentalising it and being a sneaking old cynic. Why pour out masses
of feelings that pretend to be genuine and then turn it all off
with: "Things happen, but we bob up"?

It is quite true, things happen, and we bob up. If we are
vulgar sentimentalists, we bob up just the same, so nothing has
happened and nothing can happen. All is vulgarity. But it
pays. There is money in it.

Vulgarity pays, and cheap cynicism smothered in sentimentalism pays better than anything else. Because nothing
can happen to the degraded social being. So let's pretend it
does, and then bob up!

It is time somebody began to spit out the jam of sentimentalism, at least, which smothers the "bobbing-up" philosophy. It is time we turned a straight light on this horde of
rats, these younger Forsyte sentimentalists whose name is
legion. It is sentimentalism which is stifling us. Let the social
beings keep on bobbing up while ever they can. But it is time
an effort was made to turn a hosepipe on the sentimentalism
they ooze over everything. The world is one sticky mess, in
which the little Forsytes indeed may keep on bobbing still, but
in which an honest feeling can't breathe.

But if the sticky mess gets much deeper, even the little
Forsytes won't be able to bob up any more. They'll be
smothered in their own slime along with everything else.
Which is a comfort.

[From *Scrutinies* by various writers, London, 1928.]

[52]

Letter to A. W. McLeod, 6 Oct., 1912

... I have read *Anna of the Five Towns* to-day, because it is
stormy weather. For five months I have scarcely seen a word
of English print, and to read it makes me feel fearfully queer.
I don't know where I am. I am so used to the people going by
outside, talking or singing some foreign language, always
Italian now: but to-day, to be in Hanley, and to read almost
my own dialect, makes me feel quite ill. I hate England and its
hopelessness. I hate Bennett's resignation. Tragedy ought
really to be a great kick at misery. But *Anna of the Five Towns*
seems like an acceptance—so does all the modern stuff since
Flaubert. I hate it. I want to wash again quickly, wash off
England, the oldness and grubbiness and despair.

[53]

Letter to EDWARD GARNETT, 30 Oct., 1912
Thanks so much for the books. I hate Strindberg—he seems
unnatural, forced, a bit indecent—a bit wooden, like Ibsen,
a bit skin-erupty. The Conrad, after months of Europe, makes
me furious—and the stories are *so* good. But why this giving
in before you start, that pervades all Conrad and such folks—
the Writers among the Ruins. I can't forgive Conrad for being
so sad and for giving in.

[54]

Letter to EDWARD GARNETT, 1 Feb., 1913
. . . I believe that, just as an audience was found in Russia
for *Tchekhov*, so an audience might be found in England for
some of my stuff, if there were a man to whip 'em in. It's the
producer that is lacking, not the audience. I am sure we are
sick of the rather bony, bloodless drama we get nowadays—it is
time for a reaction against Shaw and Galsworthy and Barker
and Irishy (except Synge) people—the rule and measure
mathematical folk. But you are of them and your sympathies
are with your own generation, not with mine. I think it is
inevitable. You are about the only man who is willing to let a
new generation come in. It will seem a bit rough to me, when I
am 45, and must see myself and my tradition supplanted. I
shall bear it badly. Damn my impudence, but don't dislike
me. But I don't want to write like Galsworthy nor Ibsen, nor
Strindberg, nor any of them, not even if I could. We have to
hate our immediate predecessors, to get free from their authority.
But Lord, I can't be sententious and keep my dignity.

[55]

Letter to MARTIN SECKER, 24 July, 1928
Many thanks for the books. I have great fun reading
Hardy's stories again. What a commonplace genius he has; or a

genius for the commonplace, I don't know which. He doesn't
rank so terribly high, really. But better than Bernard Shaw,
even then. I'm afraid *The Intelligent Woman's Guide* I shall
have to leave to the intelligent woman: it is too boring for the
intelligent man, if I'm any sample. Too much gas-bag.

[56]

Letter to A. W. McLeod, 26 April, 1913
. . . I am wading through *New Machiavelli*. It depresses me.
I sometimes find it too long. But it is awfully interesting. I
like Wells, he is so warm, such a passionate declaimer or
reasoner or whatever you like. But, ugh!—he hurts me. He
always seems to be looking at life as a cold and hungry little
boy in the street stares at a shop where there is hot pork. I do
like him and esteem him, and wish I knew half as much about
things.

[57]

THE WORLD OF WILLIAM CLISSOLD

By H. G. Wells

The World of William Clissold is, we are told, a novel. We are
assured it is a novel, and nothing but a novel. We are not
allowed to think of it even as a "mental autobiography" of
Mr. Wells. It is a novel.

Let us hope so. For, having finished this first volume, nothing
but hope of finding something in the two volumes yet to appear
will restrain us from asserting, roundly and flatly, that this is
simply not good enough to be called a novel. If *Tono-Bungay*
is a novel, then this is not one.

We have with us the first volume of *The World of William
Clissold*. The second volume will appear on October 1st, the
third on November 1st. We may still hope, then, if we wish to.

This first volume consists of "A Note before the Title-Page,"
in which we are forbidden to look on this book as anything but

a novel, and especially forbidden to look on it as a *roman à clef:* which means we mustn't identify the characters with any living people such as, for instance, Mr. Winston Churchill or the Countess of Oxford and Asquith; which negative command is very easy to obey, since, in this first volume, at least, there are no created characters at all: it is all words, words, words, about Socialism and Karl Marx, bankers and cave-men, money and the superman. One would welcome any old scarecrow of a character on this dreary, flinty hillside of abstract words.

The next thing is the title-page: "The World of William Clissold: A Novel from a New Angle"—whatever that pseudo-scientific phrase may mean.

Then comes Book I: "The Frame of the Picture." All right, we think! If we must get the frame first, and the picture later, let's make the best of the frame.

The frame consist of William Clissold informing us that he is an elderly gentleman of fifty-nine, and that he is going to tell us all about himself. He is quite well off, having made good in business, so that now he has retired and has bought a house near Cannes, and is going to tell us everything, absolutely everything about himself: insisting rather strongly that he is and always has been a somewhat scientific gentleman with an active mind, and that his mental activities have been more important than any other activity in his life. In short, he is not a "mere animal", he is an animal with a ferocious appetite for "ideas", and enormous thinking powers.

Again, like a submissive reader, we say: "Very well! Proceed!" and we sit down in front of this mental gentleman. William Clissold immediately begins to tell us what he believes, what he always has believed, and what he hasn't always believed, and what he won't believe, and we feel how superior he is to other people who believe other mere things. He talks about God, is very uneasy because of Roman Catholics—like an Early Victorian—and is naughtily funny about Mr. G.— which can mean either Mr. Gladstone or Mr. God.

But we bear up. After all, God, or Mr. G., is only the frame for William Clissold. We must put up with a frame of some sort. And God turns out to be Humanity in its nobler or disin-terestedly scientific aspect: or the Mind of Men collectively: in short, William Clissold himself, in a home-made halo. Still, after all, it is only a frame. Let us get on to the picture. Mr. Clissold, being somewhat of an amateur at making a self-portrait and framing it, has got bits of the picture stuck on to the frame, and great angular sections of the frame occupying the space where the picture should be. But patience! It is a sort of futuristic interpenetration, perhaps.

The first bit of the story is a little boy at a country house, sitting in a boat and observing the scientific phenomena of refraction and reflection. He also observes some forget-me-nots on the bank, and rather likes the look of them. So, scrambling carefully down through mud and sedges, he clutches a handful of the blue flowers, only to find his legs scratched and showing blood, from the sedges. " 'Oh! Oh!' I cried in profound dismay. . . . Still do I remember most vividly my astonishment at the treachery of that golden, flushed, and sapphire-eyed day.—That it should turn on me!"

This "section" is called "The Treacherous Forget-me-nots." But since, after all, the forget-me-nots had never asked the boy to gather them, wherein lay the treachery?

But they represent poetry. And perhaps William Clissold means to convey that, scrambling after poetry, he scratched his legs, and fell to howling, and called the poetry treacherous.

As for a child thinking that the sapphire-eyed day had turned on him—what a dreary old-boy of a child, if he did! But it is elderly-gentleman psychology, not childish.

The story doesn't get on very fast, and is extremely sketchy. The elderly Mr. Clissold is obviously bored by it himself. Two little boys, their mother and father, move from Bexhill to a grand country house called Mowbray. In the preface we are assured that Mowbray does not exist on earth, and we can well believe it. After a few years, the father of the two boys, a mushroom city magnate, fails, is arrested as a swindler, convicted, and swallows potassium cyanide. We have no vital glimpse of him. He never says anything, except "Hello, Sonny!" And he does ask the police to have some *déjeuner* with him, when he is arrested. The boys are trailed round Belgium by a weeping mother, who also is not created, and with whom they are only bored. The mother marries again: the boys go to the London University: and the story is lost again in a vast grey drizzle of words.

William Clissold, having in "The Frame" written a feeble résumé of Mr. Wells's *God the Invisible King*, proceeds in The Story, Book II, to write a much duller résumé of Mr. Wells's *Outline of History*. Cave-men, nomads, patriarchs, tribal Old Men, out they all come again, in the long march of human progress. Mr. Clissold, who holds forth against "systems", cannot help systematising us all into a gradual and systematic uplift from the ape. There is also a complete *exposé* of Socialism and Karl Marxism and finance, and a denunciation of Communism. There is a little feeble praise of the pure scientist who does physical research in a laboratory, and a great contempt of professors and dons who lurk in holes and study history. Last, and not least, there is a contemptuous sweeping of the temple, of all financiers, bankers, and money-men: they are all unscientific, untrained semi-idiots monkeying about with things they know nothing of.

And so, rather abruptly, end of Vol. I.

Except, of course, William Clissold has been continually taking a front seat in the picture, aged fifty-nine, in the villa back of Cannes. There is a slim slip of a red-haired Clem, who ruffles the old gentleman's hair.

" 'It's no good!' she said. 'I can't keep away from you to-day.' And she hasn't! She has ruffled my hair, she has also ruffled my mind"—much more important, of course, to William C.

This is the young Clementina: "She has a mind like one of those water-insects that never get below the surface of anything. . . . She professes an affection for me that is altogether monstrous"—I should say so—"and she knows no more about my substantial self than the water-insect knows of the deeps of the pond. . . . She knows as little about the world."

Poor Clementina, that lean, red-haired slip of a young thing. She is no more to him than an adoring sort of mosquito. But oh! wouldn't we like to hear all she *does* know about him, this sexagenarian bore, who says of her: "the same lean, red-haired Clem, so absurdly insistent that she idolises me, and will have no other man but me, invading me whenever she dares, and protecting me," etc.

Clementina, really, sounds rather nice. What a pity *she* didn't herself write *The World of William Clissold:* it would have been a novel, then. But she wouldn't even look at the frame-work of that world, says Clissold. And we don't blame her.

What is the elderly gentleman doing with her at all? Is it his "racial urge", as he calls it, still going on, rather late in life? We imagine the dear little bounder saying to her: "You are the mere object of my racial urge." To which, no doubt, she murmurs in the approved Clissold style: "My King!"

But it is altogether a poor book: the effusion of a peeved elderly gentleman who has nothing to grumble at, but who peeves at everything, from Clem to the High Finance, and from God, or Mr. G., to Russian Communism. His effective self is disgruntled, his ailment is a peevish, ashy indifference to *everything*, except himself, himself as centre of the universe. There is not one gleam of sympathy with anything in all the book, and not one breath of passionate rebellion. Mr. Clissold is too successful and wealthy to rebel and too hopelessly peeved to sympathise.

What has got him into such a state of peevishness is a problem: unless it is his insistence on the Universal Mind, which he, of course, exemplifies. The emotions are to him irritating aberrations. Yet even he admits that even thought must be preceded by some obscure physical happenings, some kind of confused sensation or emotion which is the necessary coarse body of thought and from which thought, living thought, arises or sublimates.

This being so, we wonder that he so insists on the Universal or racial *mind* of man, as the only hope or salvation. If the mind is fed from the obscure sensations, emotions, physical happenings inside us, if the mind is really no more than an exhalation of these, is it not obvious that without a full and subtle emotional life the mind itself must wither: or that it must turn itself into an automatic sort of grind-mill, grinding upon itself?

And in that case the superficial Clementina no doubt knows far more about the "deeps of the pond" of Mr. Clissold than that tiresome gentleman knows himself. He grinds on and on at the stale bones of sociology, while his actual living goes to pieces, falls into a state of irritable peevishness which makes his "mental autobiography" tiresome. His scale of values is all wrong,

So far, anyhow, this work is not a novel, because it contains none of the passionate and emotional reactions which are at the root of all thought, and which must be conveyed in a novel. This book is all chewed-up newspaper, and chewed-up scientific reports, like a mouse's nest. But perhaps the novel will still come: in Vols. II and III.

For, after all, Mr. Wells is not Mr. Clissold, thank God! And Mr. Wells has given us such brilliant and such very genuine novels that we can only hope the Clissold "angle" will straighten out in Vol. II.

[Review in *Calendar of Modern Letters*, October 1926.]

[58]

Letter to A. W. McLEOD, 9 Feb., 1914
. . . I think Crosland's *Sonnets* are objectionable—he is a nasty person. I think Hilaire Belloc is conceited. Full of that French showing-off which goes down so well in England, and is so smartly shallow. And I have always a greater respect for Mark Rutherford: I *do* think he is jolly good—so thorough, so sound, and so beautiful.

[59]

Letter to A. W. McLEOD, 2 Dec., 1912
. . . I've read the *Revolution in Tanner's Lane*, and find myself fearfully fond of Rutherford. I used to think him dull, but now I see he is so just and plucky and sound—and yes, perhaps I like his dullness—when one lives in a whirl of melodrama, as I seem to do just now, one is glad of a glass of good porter, like Rutherford.

[60]

Letter to J. B. PINKER, 5 Dec., 1914
. . . I am glad of this war. It kicks the pasteboard bottom in of the usual "good" popular novel. People have felt much

more deeply and strongly these last few months, and they are
not going to let themselves be taken in by "serious" works
whose feeling is shallower than that of the official army reports.
Mackenzie was a fool not to know that the times are too serious
to bother about his *Sinister Street* frippery. Folk will either
read sheer rubbish, or something that has in it as much or more
emotional force than the newspaper has in *it* to-day. I am glad
of the war. It sets a slump in trifling. If Lucas reads my novel,
he ought to *know* how good it is, and he ought to respect it.

[61]

Letter to E. M. FORSTER, 20 Sept., 1922
We got here last week from San Francisco—from Sydney—
Found your letter. Yes, I think of you—of your saying to me,
on top of the downs in Sussex—"How do you know I'm not
dead?" Well, you can't be dead, since here's your script. But
think you *did* make a nearly deadly mistake glorifying those
business people in *Howard's End*. Business is no good.

[62]

Letter to MARTIN SECKER, 23 July, 1924
Am reading *Passage to India*. It's good, but makes one wish a
bomb would fall and end everything. Life is more interesting
in its undercurrents than in its obvious; and E. M. does see
people, people and nothing but people: *ad nauseam*.

[63]

Letter to J. M. MURRY, 3 Oct., 1924
. . . I agree Forster doesn't "understand" his Hindu. And
India is to him just negative: because he doesn't go down to the
root to meet it. But the *Passage to India* interested me very much.
At least the repudiation of our white bunk is genuine, sincere,
and pretty thorough, it seems to me. Negative, yes. But King
Charles *must* have his head off. Homage to the headsman.

[64]

Letter to J. M. MURRY, 17 Sept., 1923
   . . . That lady into fox stuff is pretty piffle—just playboy
stuff.*

[65]

FOUR CONTEMPORARY BOOKS

The Station: Athos, Treasures and Men, by Robert Byron;
England and the Octopus, by Clough Williams-Ellis;
Comfortless Memory, by Maurice Baring; *Ashenden,* by
W. Somerset Maugham

ATHOS is an old place, and Mr. Byron is a young man. The
combination for once is really happy. We can imagine ourselves being very bored by a book on ancient Mount Athos and
its ancient monasteries with their ancient rule. Luckily Mr.
Byron belongs to the younger generation, even younger than
the Sitwells, who have shown him the way to be young.
Therefore he is not more than becomingly impressed with
ancientness. He never gapes in front of it. He settles on it like
a butterfly, tastes it, is perfectly honest about the taste, and
flutters on. And it is charming.

We confess that we find this youthful revelation of ancient
Athos charming. It is all in the butterfly manner. But the
butterfly, airy creature, is by no means a fool. And its interest
is wide. It is amusing to watch a spangled beauty settle on the
rose, then on a spat-out cherry-stone, then with a quiver of
sunny attention, upon a bit of horse-droppings in the road. The
butterfly tries them all, with equal concern. It is neither
shocked nor surprised, though sometimes, if thwarted, it is a
little exasperated. But it is still a butterfly, graceful, charming,
and ephemeral. And, of course, the butterfly on its careless,

* *Lady into Fox* by David Garnett, published 1923.

flapping wings is just as immortal as some hooting and utterly learned owl. Which is to say, we are thankful Mr. Byron is no more learned and serious than he is, and his description of Athos is far more vitally convincing than that, for example, of some heavy Gregorovius.

The four young men set out from England with a purpose. The author wants to come into closer contact with the monks and monasteries, which he has already visited; and to write a book about it. He definitely sets out with the intention of writing a book about it. He has no false shame. David, the archæologist, wants to photograph the Byzantine frescoes in the monastery buildings. Mark chases and catches insects. And Reinecker looks at art and old pots. They are four young gentlemen with the echoes of Oxford still in their ears, light and frivolous as butterflies, but with an underneath tenacity of purpose and almost a grim determination *to do something*.

The butterfly and the Sitwellian manner need not deceive us. These young gentlemen are not simply gay. They are grimly in earnest to get something done. They are not young sports amusing themselves. They are young earnests making their mark. They are stoics rather than frivolous, and epicureans truly in the deeper sense, of undergoing suffering in order to achieve a higher pleasure.

For the monasteries of Mount Athos are no Paradise. The food which made the four young men shudder makes us shudder. The vermin in the beds are lurid. The obstinacy and grudging malice of some of the monks, whose one pleasure seems to have been in thwarting and frustrating the innocent desires of the four young men, make our blood boil too. We know exactly what sewage is like, spattering down from above on to leaves and rocks. And the tortures of heat and fatigue are very real indeed.

It is as if the four young men expected to be tormented at every hand's turn. Which is just as well, for tormented they were. Monks apparently have a special gift of tormenting people: though of course some of the monks were charming. But it is chiefly out of the torments of the young butterflies, always humorously and gallantly told, that we get our picture of Athos, its monasteries and its monks. And we are left with no desire at all to visit the holy mountain, unless we could go disembodied, in such state that no flea could bite us, and no stale fish could turn our stomachs.

Then, disembodied, we should like to go and see the unique place, the lovely views, the strange old buildings, the unattractive monks, the paintings, mosaics, frescoes of that isolated little Byzantine world.

For everything artistic is there purely Byzantine. Byzantine is to Mr. Byron what Baroque is to the Sitwells. That is to say, he has a real feeling for it, and finds in it a real kinship with his own war-generation mood. Also, it is his own special elegant stone to sling at the philistine world.

Perhaps, in a long book like this, the unfailing humoresque of the style becomes a little tiring. Perhaps a page or two here and there of honest-to-God simplicity might enhance the high light of the author's facetious impressionism. But then the book might have been undertaken by some honest-to-God professor, and we so infinitely prefer Mr. Byron.

When we leave Mr. Byron we leave the younger generation for the elder; at least as far as style and manner goes. Mr. Williams-Ellis has chosen a thankless subject: *England and the Octopus:* the Octopus being the millions of little streets of mean little houses that are getting England in their grip, and devouring her. It is a depressing theme, and the author rubs it in. We see them all, those millions of beastly little red houses spreading like an eruption over the face of rural England. Look! Look! says Mr. Williams-Ellis, till we want to shout: Oh, shut up! What's the good of our looking! We've looked and got depressed too often. Now leave us alone.

But Mr. Williams-Ellis is honestly in earnest and has an honest sense of responsibility. This is the difference between the attitude of the younger and the older generations. The younger generation can't take anything very seriously, and refuses to feel responsible for humanity. The younger generation says in effect: I didn't make the world. I'm not responsible. All I can do is to make my own little mark and depart. But the elder generation still feels responsible for all humanity.

And Mr. Williams-Ellis feels splendidly responsible for poor old England: the face of her, at least. As he says: You can be put in prison for uttering a few mere swear-words to a policeman, but you can disfigure the loveliest features of the English countryside, and probably be called a public benefactor. And he wants to alter all that.

And he's quite right. His little book is excellent: sincere, honest, and even passionate, the well-written, humorous book of a man who knows what he's writing about. Everybody ought to read it, whether we know all about it beforehand or not. Because in a question like this, of the utter and hopeless disfigurement of the English countryside by modern industrial encroachment, the point is not whether we can do anything about it or not, all in a hurry. The point is, that we should all become acutely conscious of what is happening, and of what has happened; and as soon as we are really awake to this, we can begin to arrange things differently.

Mr. Williams-Ellis makes us conscious. He wakes up our age to our own immediate surroundings. He makes us able to look intelligently at the place we live in, at our own street, our own post office or pub or bank or petrol pump-station. And when we begin to look around us critically and intelligently, it is great fun. It is like analysing a bad picture and seeing how it could be turned into a good picture.

Mr. Williams-Ellis's six questions which should be asked of every building ought to be printed on a card and distributed to every individual in the nation. Because, as a nation, it is our intuitive faculty for seeing beauty and ugliness which is lying dead in us. As a nation we are dying of ugliness.

Let us open our eyes, or let Mr. Williams-Ellis open them for us, to houses, streets, railways, railings, paint, trees, roofs, petrol-pumps, advertisements, tea-shops, factory-chimneys, let us open our eyes and see them as they are, beautiful or ugly, mean and despicable, or grandiose, or pleasant. People who live in mean, despicable surroundings become mean and despicable. The chief thing is to become properly conscious of our environment.

But if some of the elder generation really take things seriously, some others only pretend. And this *pretending* to take things seriously is a vice, a real vice, and the young know it.

Mr. Baring's book *Comfortless Memory* is, thank heaven, only a little book, but it is sheer pretence of taking seriously things which its own author can never for a moment consider serious. That is, it is faked seriousness, which is utterly boring. I don't know when Mr. Baring wrote this slight novel. But he ought to have published it at least twenty years ago, when faked seriousness was more in the vogue. Mr. Byron, the young author, says that progress is the appreciation of Reality. Mr. Baring, the elderly author, offers us a piece of portentous unreality larded with Goethe, Dante, Heine, hopelessly out of date, and about as exciting as stale restaurant cake.

A dull, stuffy elderly author makes faked love to a bewitching but slightly damaged lady who has "lived" with a man she wasn't married to!! She is an enigmatic lady: very! For she falls in love, violently, virginally, deeply, passionately and exclusively, with the comfortably married stuffy elderly author. The stuffy elderly author himself tells us so, much to his own satisfaction. And the lovely, alluring, enigmatic, experienced lady actually expires, in her riding-habit, out of sheer love for the comfortably married elderly author. The elderly author assures us of it. If it were not quite so stale it would be funny.

Mr. Somerset Maugham is even more depressing. His Mr. Ashenden is also an elderly author, who becomes an agent in the British Secret Service during the War. An agent in the Secret Service is a sort of spy. Spying is a dirty business, and Secret Service altogether is a world of under-dogs, a world in which the meanest passions are given play.

And this is Mr. Maugham's, or at least Mr. Ashenden's world. Mr. Ashenden is an elderly author, so he takes life seriously, and takes his fellow-men seriously, with a seriousness already a little out of date. He has a sense of responsibility towards humanity. It would be much better if he hadn't. For Mr. Ashenden's sense of responsibility oddly enough is inverted. He is almost passionately concerned with proving that all men and all women are either dirty dogs or imbeciles. If they are clever men or women, they are crooks, spies, police-agents, and tricksters "making good", living in the best hotels because they know that in a humble hotel they'll be utterly *déclassé*, and showing off their base cleverness, and being dirty dogs, from Ashenden himself, and his mighty clever colonel, and the distinguished diplomat, down to the mean French porters.

If, on the other hand, you get a decent, straight individual, especially an individual capable of feeling love for another,

then you are made to see that such a person is a despicable fool,
encompassing his own destruction. So the American dies for
his dirty washing, the Hindu dies for a blowsy woman who
wants her wrist-watch back, the Greek merchant is murdered
by mistake, and so on. It is better to be a live dirty dog than
a dead lion, says Mr. Ashenden. Perhaps it is, to Mr. Ashenden.
But these stories, being "serious", are faked. Mr. Maugham
is a splendid observer. He can bring before us persons and
places most excellently. But as soon as the excellently observed
characters have to move, it is a fake. Mr. Maugham gives
them a humorous shove or two. We find they are nothing but
puppets, instruments of the author's pet prejudice. The
author's pet prejudice being "humour", it would be hard to
find a bunch of more ill-humoured stories, in which the
humour has gone more rancid.

[Review in *Vogue* (London), 20 July, 1928.]

[66]

Letter to A. HUXLEY, 27 March, 1928
 ... I got yesterday two copies of *Scrutinies*—the book with my
Galsworthy essay in it. Some of 'em hit fairly straight: but
Edwin Muir, real Scotchy, is overpowered by Bennett's gold
watch-chain. I'd like to write an essay on Bennett—sort of
pig in clover.

[67]

Letter to A. HUXLEY, Nov., 1927
Many thanks for *Proper Studies*. I have read 70 pages, with a
little astonishment that you are so serious and professorial.
You are not your grandfather's *Enkel* for nothing—that funny
dry-mindedness and underneath social morality. But you'll say
I'm an introvert, and no fit judge. Though I think to make
people introverts and extraverts is bunk—the words apply,
obviously, to the *direction* of the consciousness or the attention,
and not to anything in the individual essence. You are an
extravert by inheritance far more than *in esse*. You'd have

made a much better introvert, had you been allowed. "Did she fall or was she pushed"—Not that I care very much whether people are intro or extra or anything else, so long as they're a bit *simpatico*. But, my dear, don't be dry and formal and exposition all that—What's the odds! I just read Darwin's *Beagle* again—he dried himself—and *tant de bruit pour des insectes!*—But I like the book.

[68]

Letter to A. HUXLEY, Oct., 1928

I have read *Point Counter Point* with a heart sinking through my boot-soles and a rising admiration. I do think you've shown the truth, perhaps the last truth, about you and your generation, with really fine courage. It seems to me it would take ten times the courage to write *P. Counter P.* that it took to write *Lady C.*: and if the public knew *what* it was reading, it would throw a hundred stones at you, to one at me. I do think that art has to reveal the palpitating moment or the state of man as it is. And I think you do that, terribly. But what a moment! and what a state! if you can only palpitate to murder, suicide, and rape, in their various degrees—and you state plainly that it is so—*caro*, however are we going to live through the days? Preparing still another murder, suicide, and rape? But it becomes of a phantasmal boredom and produces ultimately inertia, inertia, inertia and final atrophy of the feelings. Till, I suppose, comes a final super-war, and murder, suicide, rape sweeps away the vast bulk of mankind. It is as you say—intellectual appreciation does not amount to so much, it's what you thrill to. And if murder, suicide, rape is what you thrill to, and nothing else, then it's your destiny—you can't change it *mentally*. You live by what you thrill to, and there's the end of it. Still for all that it's a *perverse* courage which makes the man accept the slow suicide of inertia and sterility: the perverseness of a perverse child.—It's amazing how men are like that. —— —— is exactly the same inside, murder, suicide, rape—with a desire to *be* raped very strong—same thing really—just like you—only he doesn't face it, and gilds his perverseness. It makes me feel ill, I've had more hemorrhage

here and been in bed this week. *Sporca miseria*. If I don find
some solid spot to climb out of, in this bog, I'm done. I can't
stand murder, suicide, rape—especially rape: and especially
being raped. Why do men only thrill to a woman who'll rape
them? All I want to do to your Lucy is smack her across the
mouth, your Rampion is the most boring character in the book
—a gas-bag. Your attempt at intellectual sympathy!—It's all
rather disgusting, and I feel like a badger that has its hole on
Wimbledon Common and trying not to be caught. Well, *caro*,
I feel like saying good-bye to you—but one will have to go on
saying good-bye for years.

[69]

Letter to LADY OTTOLINE MORRELL, 5 Feb, 1929
    Aldous and Maria were here for ten days or so—neither of
them very well, run down. Aldous with liver, and Maria going
very thin and not eating enough. I think the *Counter-Point*
book sort of got between them—she found it hard to forgive
the death of the child—which one can well understand. But,
as I say, there's more than one self to everybody, and the
Aldous that writes those novels is only one little Aldous amongst
others—probably much nicer—that don't write novels—I mean
it's only one of his little selves that writes the book and makes
the child die, it's not *all* himself. No, I don't like his books:
even if I admire a sort of desperate courage of repulsion and
repudiation in them. But again, I feel only half a man writes
the books—a sort of precocious adolescent. There is surely
much more of a man in the actual Aldous.

[70]

Letter to A. *and* M. HUXLEY, July, 1927
    . . . *Proust* too much water-jelly—I can't read him. *Faux
Monnayeurs* was interesting as a revelation of the modern state
of mind—but it's done to shock and surprise, *pour épater*—and
fanfarons de vice!—not real.

[71]

Letter to A. HUXLEY, 27 March, 1928

. . . Your ideas of the grand perverts is excellent. You might begin with a Roman—and go on to St. Francis—Michael Angelo and Leonardo — Goethe or Kant — Jean-Jacques Rousseau or Louis Quatorze. Byron—Baudelaire—Wilde— Proust: they all did the same thing, or tried to: to kick off, or to intellectualise and so utterly falsify the phallic consciousness, which is the basic consciousness, and the thing we mean, in the best sense, by common sense. I think *Wilhelm Meister* is amazing as a book of peculiar immorality, the perversity of intellectual-ised sex, and the utter incapacity for any *development* of contact with any other human being, which is peculiarly bourgeois and Goethian. Goethe *began* millions of intimacies, and never got beyond the how-do-you-do stage, then fell off into his own boundless ego. He perverted himself into perfection and God-likeness. But do do a book of the grand orthodox perverts. Back of all of them lies ineffable conceit.

[72]

Letter to A. *and* M. HUXLEY, 15 Aug., 1928

. . . I had a copy of *Transition*, that Paris magazine—the Amer. number. My God, what a clumsy *olla putrida* James Joyce is! Nothing but old fags and cabbage-stumps of quotations from the Bible and the rest, stewed in the juice of deliberate, journalistic dirty-mindedness—what old and hard-worked staleness, masquerading as the all-new! Gertrude Stein is more amusing—and some of the Americans quite good. But for prize *jejune pap*, take the letters from Frenchmen at the end —the sheer rinsings of baby's napkins. How feeble the Frenchy mind has become!

[73]

Letter to HARRY CROSBY, 6 Sept., 1928
. . . Some of the things in *Transition* I found really good and amusing. But James Joyce bores me stiff—too terribly would-be and done-on-purpose, utterly without spontaneity or real life. Gertrude Stein amuses me for a while, but soon palls. Some of the other things, *not* the most ambitious, made me laugh. But the feeblest of all feebles were the sayings of the French wise men at the end, about America. Really the French are crumbling to sheer puerile inanity. They have the minds of domestic cats.

[74]

HADRIAN THE SEVENTH

BY BARON CORVO

IN *Hadrian the Seventh*, Frederick Baron Corvo falls in, head over heels, in deadly earnest. A man must keep his earnestness nimble, to escape ridicule. The so-called Baron Corvo by no means escapes. He reaches heights, or depths, of sublime ridiculousness.

It doesn't kill the book, however. Neither ridicule nor dead earnest kills it. It is extraordinarily alive, even though it has been buried for twenty years. Up it rises to confront us. And, great test, it does not "date" as do Huysmans's books, or Wilde's or the rest of them. Only a first-rate book escapes its date.

Frederick Rolfe was a fantastic figure of the nineties, the nineties of the *Yellow Book*, Oscar Wilde, Aubrey Beardsley, Simeon Solomon, and all the host of the godly. The whole decade is now a little ridiculous, ridiculous decadence as well as ridiculous pietism. They said of Rolfe that he was certainly possessed of a devil. At least his devil is still alive, it hasn't turned into a sort of gollywog, like the bulk of the nineties' devils.

Rolfe was one of the Catholic converts of the period, very intense. But if ever a man was a Protestant in all his being, this one was. The acuteness of his protest drove him, like a crazy serpent, into the bosom of the Roman Catholic Church.

He seems to have been a serpent of serpents in the bosom of all the nineties. That in itself endears him to one. The way everyone dropped him with a shudder is almost fascinating.

He died about 1912, when he was already forgotten: an outcast and in a sense a wastrel.

We can well afford to remember him again: he was not nothing, as so many of the estimables were. He was a gentleman of education and culture, pining, for the show's sake, to be a priest. The Church shook him out of her bosom before he could take orders. So he wrote himself Fr. Rolfe. It would do for Frederick, and if you thought it meant Father Rolfe, good old you!

But then his other passion, for medieval royalism, overcame him, and he was Baron Corvo when he signed his name. Lord Rook, Lord Raven, the bird was the same as Fr. Rolfe.

Hadrian the Seventh is, as far as his connexion with the Church was concerned, largely an autobiography of Frederick Rolfe. It is the story of a young English convert, George Arthur Rose (Rose for Rolfe), who has had bitter experience with the priests and clergy, and years of frustration and disappointment, till he arrives at about the age of forty, a highly-bred, highly-sensitive, super-æsthetic man, ascetic out of æstheticism, athletic the same, religious the same. He is to himself beautiful, with a slim, clean-muscled grace, much given to cold baths, white-faced with a healthy pallor, and pure, that is sexually chaste, because of his almost morbid repugnance for women. He had no desires to conquer or to purify. Women were physically repulsive to him, and therefore chastity cost him nothing, the Church would be a kind of asylum.

The priests and clergy, however, turned him down, or dropped him like the proverbial snake in the bosom, and inflamed him against them, so that he was burned through and through with white, ceaseless anger. His anger had become so complete as to be pure: it really was demonish. But it was all nervous and imaginative, an imaginative, sublimated hate, of a creature born crippled in its affective organism.

The first part of the book, describing the lonely man in a London lodging, alone save for his little cat, whose feline qualities of aloofness and self-sufficiency he so much admires, fixes the tone at once. And in the whole of literature I know nothing that resembles those amazing chapters, when the bishop and the archbishop come to him, and when he is ordained and makes his confession. Then the description of the election of the new pope, the cardinals shut up in the Vatican, the failure of the Way of Scrutiny and the Way of Access, the fantastic choice, by the Way of Compromise, of George Arthur Rose, is too extraordinary and daring ever to be forgotten.

From being a rejected aspirant to the priesthood, George Arthur Rose, the man in the London lodgings, finds himself suddenly not only consecrated, but elected head of all the Catholic Church. He becomes Pope Hadrian the Seventh.

Then the real fantasy and failure begins. George Arthur Rose, triple-crowned and in the chair of Peter, is still very much Frederick Rolfe, and perfectly consistent. He is the same man, but now he has it all his own way: a White Pope, pure, scrupulous, chaste, living on two dollars a day, an æsthetic idealist, and really, a super-Protestant. He has the British instinct of authority, which is now gloriously gratified. But he has no inward *power*, power to make true change in the world. Once he is on the throne of high power, we realise his futility.

He is, like most modern men, especially reformers and idealists, through and through a Protestant. Which means, his life is a changeless fervour of protest. He can't help it. Everything he comes into contact with he must criticise, with all his nerves, and react from. Fine, subtle, sensitive, and almost egomaniac, he can accept nothing but the momentary thrill of æsthetic appreciation. His life-flow is like a stream washing against a false world, and ebbing itself out in a marsh and a hopeless bog.

So it is with George Arthur Rose, become Pope Hadrian the Seventh, while he is still in a state of pure protest, he is vivid and extraordinary. But once he is given full opportunity to do as he

SELECTED LITERARY CRITICISM

wishes, and his *raison d'être* as a Protestant is thereby taken
away, he becomes futile, and lapses into the ridiculous.

He can criticise men, exceedingly well: hence his knack of
authority. But the moment he has to build men into a new
form, construct something out of men by making a new unity
among them, swarming them upon himself as bees upon a
queen, he is ridiculous and powerless, a fraud.

It is extraordinary how *blind* he is, with all his keen insight.
He no more "gets" his cardinals than we get the men on Mars.
He can criticise them, and analyse them, and reject or condone
them. But the real old Adam that is in them, the old male
instinct for *power*, this, to him, does not exist.

In actual life, of course, the cardinals would drop a Hadrian
down the oubliette, in ten minutes, and without any difficulty
at all, once he was inside the Vatican. And Hadrian would be
utterly flabbergasted, and call it villainy.

And what's the good of being Pope, if you've nothing but
protest and æsthetics up your sleeve? Just like the reformers
who are excellent, while fighting authority. But once authority
disappears, they fall into nothingness. So with Hadrian the
Seventh. As Pope, he is a fraud. His critical insight makes him
a politician of the League of Nations sort, on a vast and curious
scale. His medievalism makes him a truly comical royalist.
But as a *man*, a real power in the world, he does not exist.

Hadrian unwinding the antimacassar is a sentimental farce.
Hadrian persecuted to the point of suicide by a blowsy lodging-
house keeper is a bathetic farce. Hadrian and the Socialist
"with gorgonzola teeth" is puerile beyond words. It is all
amazing, that a man with so much insight and fineness, on the
one hand, should be so helpless and just purely ridiculous, when
it comes to actualities.

He simply has no conception of what it is to be a natural or
honestly animal man, with the repose and the power that goes
with the honest animal in man. His attempt to appreciate his
Cardinal Ragna—probably meant for Rampolla—is funny. It
is as funny as would be an attempt on the part of the late
President Wilson to appreciate Hernán Cortés, or even
Theodore Roosevelt, supposing they were put face to face.

The time has come for stripping: cries Hadrian. Strip then, if
there are falsities to throw away. But if you go on and on and

on peeling the onion down, you'll be left with blank nothing between your hands, at last. And this is Hadrian's plight. He is assassinated in the streets of Rome by a Socialist, and dies supported by three Majesties, sublimely absurd. And there is nothing to it. Hadrian has stripped himself and everything else till nothing is left but absurd conceit, expiring in the arms of the Majesties.

Lord! be to me a Saviour, not a judge! is Hadrian's prayer: when he is not affectedly praying in Greek. But why should such a white streak of blamelessness as Hadrian need saving so badly? Saved from what? If he has done his best, why mind being judged—at least by Jesus, who in this sense is any man's peer?

The brave man asks for justice: the rabble cries for favours! says some old writer. Why does Hadrian, in spite of all his protest, go in with the rabble?

It is a problem. The book remains a clear and definite book of our epoch, not to be swept aside. If it is the book of a demon, as the contemporaries said, it is the book of a man-demon, not of a mere *poseur.* And if some of it is caviare, at least it came out of the belly of a live fish.

[Review in *Adelplhi,* December 1925.]

[75]

THE DRAGON OF THE APOCALYPSE

By FREDERICK CARTER

IT is some years now since Frederick Carter first sent me the manuscript of his *Dragon of the Apocalypse.* I remember it arrived when I was staying in Mexico, in Chapala. The village postmaster sent for me to the post office: Will the honourable Señor please come to the post office. I went, on a blazing April morning, there in the northern tropics. The postmaster, a dark, fat Mexican with moustaches, was most polite: but also rather mysterious. There was a packet—did I know there was a packet? No, I didn't. Well, after a great deal of suspicious courtesy, the packet was produced; the rather battered typescript of the *Dragon*, together with some of Carter's line-engravings, mainly astrological, which went with it. The postmaster handled them cautiously. What was it? What was it? It was a book, I said, the manuscript of a book, in English. Ah, but what sort of a book? What was the book about? I tried to explain, in my hesitating Spanish, what the *Dragon* was about, with its line-drawings. I didn't get far. The postmaster looked darker and darker, more uneasy. At last he suggested, was it *magic?* I held my breath. It seemed like the Inquisition again. Then I tried to accommodate him. No, I said, it was not magic, but the *history* of magic. It was the history of what magicians had thought, in the past, and these were the designs they had used. Ah! The postman was relieved. The history of magic! A scholastic work! And these were the designs they had used! He fingered them gingerly, but fascinated.

And I walked home at last, under the blazing sun, with the bulky package under my arm. And then, in the cool of the patio, I read the beginning of the first *Dragon*.

The book was not then what it is now. Then, it was nearly all astrology, and very little argument. It was confused: it was, in a sense, a chaos. And it hadn't very much to do with St. John's *Revelation*. But that didn't matter to me. I was very often smothered in words. And then would come a page, or a chapter, that would release my imagination and give me a whole great sky to move in. For the first time I strode forth into the grand fields of the sky. And it was a real experience, for which I have been always grateful. And always the sensation comes back to me, of the dark shade on the veranda in Mexico, and the sudden release into the great sky of the old world, the sky of the zodiac.

I have read books of astronomy which made me dizzy with the sense of illimitable space. But the heart melts and dies—it is the disembodied mind alone which follows on through this horrible hollow void of space, where lonely stars hang in awful isolation. And this is not a release. It is a strange thing, but when science extends space *ad infinitum*, and we get the terrible sense of limitlessness, we have at the same time a secret sense of imprisonment. Three-dimensional space is homogeneous, and no matter *how* big it is, it is a kind of prison. No matter how vast the range of space, there is no release.

Why then, this sense of release, of marvellous release, in reading the *Dragon*? I don't know. But anyhow, the *whole* imagination is released, not a part only. In astronomical space, one can only *move*, one cannot be. In the astrological heavens, that is to say, the ancient zodiacal heavens, the whole man is set free, once the imagination crosses the border. The whole man, bodily and spiritual, walks in the magnificent fields of the stars, and the stars have names, and the feet tread splendidly upon— we know not what, but the heavens, instead of untreadable space.

It is an experience. To enter the astronomical sky of space is a great sensational experience. To enter the astrological sky of the zodiac and the living, roving planets is another experience, another *kind* of experience; it is truly imaginative, and to me, more valuable. It is not a mere extension of what we know: an extension that becomes awful, then appalling. It is the entry into another world, another kind of world, measured by another dimension. And we find some prisoned self in us coming forth to live in this world.

Now it is ridiculous for us to deny any experience. I well remember my first real experience of space, reading a book of modern astronomy. It was rather awful, and since then I rather hate the mere suggestion of illimitable space.

But I also remember very vividly my first experience of the astrological heavens, reading Frederick Carter's *Dragon*: the sense of being the Macrocosm, the great sky with its meaningful stars and its profoundly meaningful motions, its wonderful bodily vastness, not empty, but all alive and doing. And I value this experience more. For the sense of astronomical space merely paralyses me. But the sense of the living astrological heavens gives me an extension of my being, I become big and glittering and vast with a sumptuous vastness. I am the Macrocosm, and it is wonderful. And since I am not afraid to feel my own nothingness in front of the vast void of astronomical space, neither am I afraid to feel my own splendidness in the zodiacal heavens.

The *Dragon* as it exists now is no longer the *Dragon* which I read in Mexico. It has been made more—more argumentative, shall we say. Give me the old manuscript and let me write an introduction to that! I urge. But: No, says Carter. It isn't *sound*.

Sound what? He means his old astrological theory of the Apocalypse was not sound, as it was exposed in the old manuscript. But who cares? We do not care, vitally, about theories of the Apocalypse: what the Apocalypse means. What we care about is the release of the imagination. A real release of the imagination renews our strength and our vitality, makes us feel stronger and happier. Scholastic works don't release the imagination: at the best, they satisfy the intellect, and leave the body an unleavened lump. But when I get the release into the zodiacal cosmos my very feet feel lighter and stronger, my very knees are glad.

What does the Apocalypse matter, unless in so far as it gives us imaginative release into another vital world? After all, what meaning *has* the Apocalypse? For the ordinary reader, not much. For the ordinary student and biblical student, it means a prophetic vision of the martyrdom of the Christian Church, the Second Advent, the destruction of worldly power, particularly the power of the great Roman Empire, and then the institution of the Millennium, the rule of the risen Martyrs of Christendom for the space of one thousand years: after which, the end of everything, the last Judgment, and souls in heaven; all earth, moon and sun being wiped out, all stars and all space. The New Jerusalem, and Finis!

This is all very fine, but we know it pretty well by now, so it offers no imaginative release to most people. It is the orthodox interpretation of the Apocalypse, and probably it is the true superficial meaning, or the final intentional meaning of the work. But what of it? It is a bore. Of all the stale buns, the New Jerusalem is one of the stalest. At the best, it was only invented for the Aunties of this world.

Yet when we read Revelation, we feel at once there are meanings behind meanings. The visions that we have known since childhood are not so easily exhausted by the orthodox commentators. And the phrases that have haunted us all our life, like: And I saw heaven opened, and behold! A white horse!—these are not explained quite away by orthodox explanations. When all is explained and expounded and commented upon, still there remains a curious fitful, half-spurious and half-splendid wonder in the work. Sometimes the great figures loom up marvellous. Sometimes there is a strange sense of incomprehensible drama. Sometimes the figures have a life of their own, inexplicable, which cannot be explained away or exhausted.

And gradually we realise that we are in the world of symbol as well as of allegory. Gradually we realise the book has no one meaning. It has meanings. Not meaning *within* meaning: but rather, meaning against meaning. No doubt the last writer left the Apocalypse as a sort of complete Christian allegory, a Pilgrim's Progress to the Judgment Day and the New Jerusalem: and the orthodox critics can explain the allegory fairly satisfactorily. But the Apocalypse is a compound work. It is no doubt the work of different men, of different generations and even different centuries.

So that we don't have to look for a *meaning*, as we can look for a meaning in an allegory like *Pilgrim's Progress*, or even like Dante. John of Patmos didn't *compose* the Apocalypse. The Apocalypse is the work of no one man. The Apocalypse began probably two centuries before Christ, as some small book, perhaps, of Pagan ritual, or some small pagan-Jewish Apocalypse written in symbols. It was written over by other Jewish apocalyptists, and finally came down to John of Patmos. He turned it more or less, rather less than more, into a Christian allegory. And later scribes trimmed up his work.

So the ultimate intentional, Christian meaning of the book is, in a sense, only plastered over. The great images incorporated are like the magnificent Greek pillars plastered into the Christian Church in Sicily: they are not merely allegorical figures: they are symbols, they belong to a bigger age than that of John of Patmos. And as symbols they defy John's superficial allegorical meaning. You can't give a great symbol a "meaning", any more than you can give a cat a "meaning". Symbols are organic units of consciousness with a life of their own, and you can never explain them away, because their value is dynamic, emotional, belonging to the sense—consciousness of the body and soul, and not simply mental. An allegorical image has a *meaning*. Mr. Facing-both-ways has a meaning. But I defy you to lay your finger on the full meaning of Janus, who is a symbol.

It is necessary for us to realise very definitely the difference between allegory and symbol. Allegory is narrative description using, as a rule, images to express certain definite qualities. Each image means something, and is a term in the argument and nearly always for a moral or didactic purpose, for under the narrative of an allegory lies a didactic argument, usually moral. Myth likewise is descriptive narrative using images. But myth is never an argument, it never has a didactic nor a moral purpose, you can draw no conclusion from it. Myth is an attempt to narrate a whole human experience, of which the purpose is too deep, going too deep in the blood and soul, for mental explanation or description. We *can* expound the myth of Chronos very easily. We can explain it, we can even draw the moral conclusion. But we only look a little silly. The myth of Chronos lives on beyond explanation, for it describes a profound experience of the human body and soul, an experience which is never exhausted and never will be exhausted, for it is being felt and suffered now, and it will be felt and suffered while man remains man. You may explain the myths away: but it only means you go on suffering blindly, stupidly, "in the unconscious," instead of healthily and with the imaginative comprehension playing upon the suffering.

And the images of myth are symbols. They don't "mean something". They stand for units of human *feeling*, human experience. A complex of emotional experience is a symbol. And the power of the symbol is to arouse the deep emotional self, and the dynamic self, beyond comprehension. Many ages of accumulated experience still throb within a symbol. And we throb in response. It takes centuries to create a really significant symbol: even the symbol of the Cross, or of the horseshoe, or the horns. No man can invent symbols. He can invent an emblem, made up of images: or metaphors: or images: but not symbols. Some images, in the course of many generations of men, become symbols, embedded in the soul and ready to start alive when touched, carried on in the human consciousness for centuries. And again, when men become unresponsive and half dead, symbols die.

Now the Apocalypse has many splendid old symbols, to make us throb. And symbols suggest schemes of symbols. So the Apocalypse, with its symbols, suggests schemes of symbols, deep underneath its Christian, allegorical surface meaning of the Church of Christ.

And one of the chief schemes of symbols which the Apocalypse will suggest to any man who has a feeling for symbols, as contrasted with the orthodox feeling for allegory, is the astrological scheme. Again and again the symbols of the Apocalypse are astrological, the movement is star-movement, and these suggest an astrological scheme. Whether it is worth while to work out the astrological scheme from the impure text of the Apocalypse depends on the man who finds it worth while. Whether the scheme *can* be worked out remains for us to judge. In all probability there was once an astrological scheme there.

But what is certain is that the astrological symbols and suggestions are still there, they give us the lead. And the lead leads us sometimes out into a great imaginative world where we feel free and delighted. At least, that is my experience. So what does it matter whether the astrological scheme can be restored intact or not? Who cares about explaining the Apocalypse, either allegorically or astrologically or historically or any other way? All one cares about is the lead, the lead that the symbolic figures give us, and their dramatic movement: the lead, and where it will lead us to. If it leads to a release of the imagination into some new sort of world, then let us be thankful, for that is what we want. It matters so little to us who care more about life than about scholarship, what is correct or what is not correct. What does "correct" mean, anyhow? *Sanahorias* is the Spanish for carrots: I hope I am correct. But what are carrots correct for?

What the ass wants is carrots; not the idea of carrots, nor thought-forms of carrots, but carrots. The Spanish ass doesn't even know that he is eating *sanahorias*. He just eats and feels blissfully full of carrot. Now does *he* have more of the carrot, who eats it, or do I, who know that in Spanish it is called a *sanahoria* (I hope I am correct) and in botany it belongs to the *umbelliferæ?*

We are full of the wind of thought-forms, and starved for a good carrot. I don't care *what* a man sets out to prove, so long as he will interest me and carry me away. I don't in the least care whether he proves his point or not, so long as he has given me a real imaginative experience by the way, and not another

set of bloated thought-forms. We are starved to death, fed on
the eternal sodom-apples of thought-forms. What we want is
complete imaginative experience, which goes through the whole
soul and body. Even at the expense of reason we want imaginative experience. For reason is certainly not the final judge
of life.

Though, if we pause to think about it, we shall realise that
it is not Reason herself whom we have to defy, it is her myrmi-
dons, our accepted ideas and thought-forms. Reason can adjust
herself to almost anything, if we will only free her from her
crinoline and powdered wig, with which she was invested in the
eighteenth and nineteenth centuries. Reason is a supple
nymph, and slippery as a fish by nature. She had as leave give
her kiss to an absurdity any day, as to syllogistic truth. The
absurdity may turn out truer.

So we need not feel ashamed of flirting with the zodiac. The
zodiac is well worth flirting with. But not in the rather silly
modern way of horoscopy and telling your fortune by the stars.
Telling your fortune by the stars, or trying to get a tip from the
stables, before a horse-race. You want to know what horse to
put your money on. Horoscopy is just the same. They want
their "fortune" told, never their misfortune.

Surely one of the greatest imaginative experiences the
human race has ever had was the Chaldean experience of the
stars, including the sun and moon. Sometimes it seems it must
have been greater experience than any God-experience. For
God is only a great imaginative experience. And sometimes it
seems as if the experience of the living heavens, with a living
yet not human sun, and brilliant living stars in *live* space must
have been the most magnificent of all experiences, greater than
any Jehovah or Baal, Buddha or Jesus. It may seem an
absurdity to talk of *live* space. But is it? While we are warm
and well and "unconscious" of our bodies, are we not all the
time ultimately conscious of our bodies in the same way, as live
or living space? And is not this the reason why void space so
terrifies us?

I would like to know the stars again as the Chaldeans knew
them, two thousand years before Christ. I would like to be able
to put my ego into the sun, and my personality into the moon,
and my character into the planets, and live the life of the

heavens, as the early Chaldeans did. The human consciousness is really homogeneous. There is no complete forgetting, even in death. So that somewhere within us the old experience of the Euphrates, Mesopotamia between the rivers, lives still. And in my Mesopotamian self I long for the sun again, and the moon and stars, for the Chaldean sun and the Chaldean stars. I long for them terribly. Because *our* sun and *our* moon are only thought-forms to us, balls of gas, dead globes of extinct volcanoes, things we *know* but never feel by experience. By *experience*, we should feel the sun as the savages feel him, we should "know" him as the Chaldeans knew him, in a terrific embrace. But our experience of the sun is dead, we are cut off. All we have now is the thought-form of the sun. He is a blazing ball of gas, he has spots occasionally, from some sort of indigestion, and he makes you brown and healthy if you let him. The first two "facts" we should never have known if men with telescopes, called astronomers, hadn't told us. It is obvious, they are mere thought-forms. The third "fact", about being brown and healthy, we believe because the doctors have told us it is so. As a matter of fact, many neurotic people become more and more neurotic, the browner and "healthier" they become by sun-baking. The sun can rot as well as ripen. So the third fact is also a thought-form.

And that is all we have, poor things, of the sun. Two or three cheap and inadequate thought-forms. Where, for us, is the great and royal sun of the Chaldeans? Where even, for us, is the sun of the Old Testament, coming forth like a strong man to run a race? We have lost the sun. We have lost the sun, and we have found a few miserable thought-forms. A ball of blazing gas! With spots! He browns you!

To be sure, we are not the first to lose the sun. The Babylonians themselves began the losing of him. The great and living heavens of the Chaldeans deteriorated already in Belshazzar's day to the fortune-telling disc of the night skies. But that was man's fault, not the heavens'. Man always deteriorates. And when he deteriorates he always becomes inordinately concerned about his "fortune" and his fate. While life itself is fascinating, fortune is completely uninteresting, and the idea of fate does not enter. When men become poor in life then they become anxious about their fortune and frightened about their fate. By the time of Jesus, men had become so anxious about their fortunes and so frightened about their fates, that they put up the grand declaration that life was one long misery and you couldn't expect your fortune till you got to Heaven; that is, till after you were dead. This was accepted by all men, and has been the creed till our day, Buddha and Jesus alike. It has provided us with a vast amount of thought-forms, and landed us in a sort of living death.

So now we want the sun again. Not the spotted ball of gas that browns you like a joint of meat, but the living sun, and the living moon of the old Chaldean days. Think of the moon, think of Artemis and Cybele, think of the white wonder of the skies, so rounded, so velvety, moving so serene; and then think of the pock-marked horror of the scientific photographs of the moon!

But when we have seen the pock-marked face of the moon in scientific photographs, need that be the end of the moon for us? Even rationally? I think not. It is a great blow: but the imagination can recover from it. Even if we have to believe the pock-marked photograph, even if we believe in the cold and snow and utter deadness of the moon—which we *don't* quite believe—the moon is not therefore a dead nothing. The moon is a white strange world, great, white, soft-seeming globe in the night sky, and what she actually communicates to me across space I shall never fully know. But the moon that pulls the tides, and the moon that controls the menstrual periods of women, and the moon that touches the lunatics, she is not the mere dead lump of the astronomist. The moon is the great moon still, she gives forth her soft and feline influences, she sways us still, and asks for sympathy back again. In her so-called deadness there is enormous potency still, and power even over our lives. The Moon! Artemis! the great goddess of the splendid past of men! Are you going to tell me she is a dead lump?

She is not dead. But maybe we are dead, half-dead little modern worms stuffing our damp carcasses with thought-forms that have no sensual reality. When we describe the moon as dead, we are describing the deadness in ourselves. When we find space so hideously void, we are describing our own unbearable emptiness. Do we imagine that we, poor worms with spectacles and telescopes and thought-forms, are really more conscious, more vitally aware of the universe than the men in the past were, who called the moon Artemis, or Cybele, or Astarte? Do we imagine that we really, livingly know the moon better than they knew her? That our knowledge of the moon is more real, more "sound"? Let us disabuse ourselves. We know the moon in terms of our own telescopes and our own deadness. We know everything in terms of our own deadness.

But the moon is Artemis still, and a dangerous goddess she is, as she always was. She throws her cold contempt on you as she passes over the sky, poor, mean little worm of a man who thinks she is nothing but a dead lump. She throws back the cold white vitriol of her angry contempt on to your mean, tense nerves, nervous man, and she is corroding you away. Don't think you can escape the moon, any more than you can escape breathing. She is on the air you breathe. She is active within the atom. Her sting is part of the activity of the electron.

Do you think you can put the universe apart, a dead lump here, a ball of gas there, a bit of fume somewhere else? How puerile it is, as if the universe were the back yard of some human chemical works! How gibbering man becomes, when he is really clever, and thinks he is giving the ultimate and final description of the universe! Can't he see that he is merely describing himself, and that the self he is describing is merely one of the more dead and dreary states that man can exist in? When man changes his state of being, he needs an entirely different description of the universe, and so the universe changes its nature to him entirely. Just as the nature of our universe is entirely different from the nature of the Chaldean Cosmos. The Chaldeans described the Cosmos as they found it: Magnificent. We describe the universe as we find it: mostly void, littered with a certain number of dead moons and unborn stars, like the back yard of a chemical works.

Is our description true? Not for a single moment, once you change your state of mind: or your state of soul. It is true for our present deadened state of mind. Our state of mind is becoming unbearable. We shall have to change it. And when we have changed it, we shall change our description of the universe entirely. We shall not call the moon Artemis, but the new name will be nearer to Artemis than to a dead lump or an extinct globe. We shall not get back the Chaldean vision of the living heavens. But the heavens will come to life again for us, and the vision will express also the new men that we are.

And so the value of these studies in the Apocalypse. They wake the imagination and give us at moments a new universe to live in. We may think it is the old cosmos of the Babylonians, but it isn't. We can never recover an old vision, once it has been supplanted. But what we can do is to discover a new vision in harmony with the memories of old, far-off, far, far-off experience that lie within us. So long as we are not deadened or drossy, memories of Chaldean experience still live within us, at great depth, and can vivify our impulses in a new direction, once we awaken them.

Therefore we ought to be grateful for a book like this of the *Dragon*. What does it matter if it is confused? What does it matter if it repeats itself? What does it matter if in parts it is not very interesting, when in other parts it is intensely so, when it suddenly opens doors and lets out the spirit into a new world, even if it is a very old world! I admit that I cannot see eye to eye with Mr. Carter about the Apocalypse itself. I cannot, myself, feel that old John of Patmos spent his time on his island lying on his back and gazing at the resplendent heavens; then afterwards writing a book in which all the magnificent cosmic and starry drama is deliberately wrapped up in Jewish-Christian moral threats and vengeances, sometimes rather vulgar.

But that, no doubt, is due to our different approach to the book. I was brought up on the Bible, and seem to have it in my bones. From early childhood I have been familiar with Apocalyptic language and Apocalyptic image: not because I spent my time reading Revelation, but because I was sent to Sunday School and to Chapel, to Band of Hope and to Christian Endeavour, and was always having the Bible read at me or to me. I did not even listen attentively. But language has a power of echoing and re-echoing in my unconscious mind. I can wake up in the night and "hear" things being said—or hear a piece of music—to which I had paid no attention during the day. The very sound itself registers. And so the sound of Revelation had registered in me very early, and I was as used to: "I was in the Spirit on the Lord's day, and heard behind me a great voice, as of a trumpet, saying: I am Alpha and the Omega"—as I was to a nursery rhyme like "Little Bo-Peep"! I didn't know the meaning, but then children so often prefer sound to sense. "Alleluia: for the Lord God omnipotent reigneth." The Apocalypse is full of sounding phrases, beloved by the uneducated in the chapels for their true liturgical powers. "And he treadeth the winepress of the fierceness and wrath of Almighty God."

No, for me the Apocalypse is altogether too full of fierce feeling, fierce and moral, to be a grand disguised star-myth. And yet it has intimate connexion with star-myths and the movement of the astrological heavens: a sort of submerged star-meaning. And nothing delights me more than to escape from the all-too-moral chapel meaning of the book, to another wider, older, more magnificent meaning. In fact, one of the real joys of middle age is in coming back to the Bible, reading a new translation, such as Moffatt's, reading the modern research and modern criticism of some Old Testament books, and of the Gospels, and getting a whole new conception of the Scriptures altogether. Modern research has been able to put the Bible back into its living connexions, and it is splendid: no longer the Jewish-moral book and a stick to beat an immoral dog, but a fascinating account of the adventure of the Jewish—or Hebrew or Israelite nation, among the great old civilised nations of the past, Egypt, Assyria, Babylon and Persia: then on into the Hellenic world, the Seleucids, and the Romans, Pompey and Antony. Reading the Bible in a new translation, with modern notes and comments, is more fascinating than reading Homer, for the adventure goes even deeper into time and into the soul, and continues through the centuries, and moves from Egypt to Ur and to Nineveh, from Sheba to Tarshish and Athens and Rome. It is the very quick of ancient history.

And the Apocalypse, the last and presumably the latest of the books of the Bible, also comes to life with a great new life, once we look at its symbols and take the lead that they offer us. The next leads most easily into the great chaotic Hellenic world of the first century: Hellenic, not Roman. But the symbols lead much further back.

They lead Frederick Carter back to Chaldea and to Persia, chiefly, for his skies are the late Chaldean, and his mystery is chiefly Mithraic. Hints, we have only hints from the outside. But the rest is within us, and if we can take a hint, it is extraordinary how far and into what fascinating worlds the hints can lead us. The orthodox critics will say: Fantasy! Nothing but fantasy! But then, thank God for fantasy, if it enhances our life.

And even so, the "reproach" is not quite just. The Apocalypse has an old, submerged astrological meaning, and probably even an old astrological scheme. The hints are too obvious and too splendid: like the ruins of an old temple incorporated in a Christian chapel. Is it any more fantastic to try to reconstruct the embedded temple, than to insist that the embedded images and columns are mere rubble in the Christian building, and have no meaning? It is as fantastic to deny meaning when meaning is there, as it is to invent meaning when there is none. And it is much duller. For the invented meaning may still have a life of its own.

[Published entitled simply "Introduction" in *London Mercury*, July 1930. For details of the connection between Lawrence and Frederick Carter's work on the *Apocalypse*, see introduction to *Phoenix*, pp. xviii–xix.]

[76]

From

STUDY OF THOMAS HARDY*

THIS is supposed to be a book about the people in Thomas Hardy's novels. But if one wrote everything they give rise to, it would fill the Judgment Book.

One thing about them is that none of the heroes and heroines care very much for money, or immediate self-pre-

* Lawrence wrote to J. B. Pinker on 5 September, 1914: "What a miserable world. What colossal idiocy, this war. Out of sheer rage I've begun my book about Thomas Hardy. It will be about anything but Thomas Hardy, I am afraid—queer stuff—but not bad."
In fact less than half the *Study* has any direct reference to Hardy: only the relevant parts are reprinted here. A small part of the other material is given on pp. 67–71. None of the *Study* was published in Lawrence's lifetime; it appeared complete for the first time in *Phoenix*.

servation, and all of them are struggling hard to come into being. What exactly the struggle into being consists in, is the question. But most obviously, from the Wessex novels, the first and chiefest factor is the struggle into love and the struggle with love: by love, meaning the love of a man for a woman and a woman for a man. The *via media* to being, for man or woman, is love, and love alone. Having achieved and accomplished love, then the man passes into the unknown. He has become himself, his tale is told. Of anything that is complete there is no more tale to tell. The tale is about becoming complete, or about the failure to become complete.

It is urged against Thomas Hardy's characters that they do unreasonable things—quite, quite unreasonable things. They are always going off unexpectedly and doing something that nobody would do. That is quite true, and the charge is amusing. These people of Wessex are alway bursting suddenly out of bud and taking a wild flight into flower, always shooting suddenly out of a tight convention, a tight, hide-bound cabbage state into something quite madly personal. It would be amusing to count the number of special marriage licenses taken out in Hardy's books. Nowhere, except perhaps in Jude, is there the slightest development of personal action in the characters: it is all explosive. Jude, however, does see more or less what he is doing, and acts from choice. He is more consecutive. The rest explode out of the convention. They are people each with a real, vital, potential self, even the apparently wishy-washy heroines of the earlier books, and this self suddenly bursts the shell of manner and convention and commonplace opinion, and acts independently, absurdly, without mental knowledge or acquiescence.

And from such an outburst the tragedy usually develops. For there does exist, after all, the great self-preservation scheme, and in it we must all live. Now to live in it after bursting out of it was the problem these Wessex people found themselves faced with. And they never solved the problem, none of them except the comically, insufficiently treated Ethelberta.

This because they must subscribe to the system in themselves. From the more immediate claims of self-preservation they could free themselves: from money, from ambition for social success. None of the heroes or heroines of Hardy cared much for these things. But there is the greater idea of self-preservation, which is formulated in the State, in the whole modelling of the community. And from this idea, the heroes and heroines of Wessex, like the heroes and heroines of almost anywhere else, could not free themselves. In the long run, the State, the Community, the established form of life remained, remained intact and impregnable, the individual, trying to break forth from it, died of fear, of exhaustion, or of exposure to attacks from all sides, like men who have left the walled city to live outside in the precarious open.

This is the tragedy of Hardy, always the same: the tragedy of those who, more or less pioneers, have died in the wilderness, whither they had escaped for free action, after having left the walled security, and the comparative imprisonment, of the established convention. This is the theme of novel after novel: remain quite within the convention, and you are good, safe, and happy in the long run, though you never have the vivid pang of sympathy on your side: or, on the other hand, be passionate, individual, wilful, you will find the security of the convention a walled prison, you will escape, and you will die, either of your own lack of strength to bear the isolation and the exposure, or by direct revenge from the community, or from both. This is the tragedy, and only this: it is nothing more metaphysical than the division of a man against himself in such a way: first, that he is a member of the community, and must, upon his honour, in no way move to disintegrate the community, either in its moral or its practical form; second, that the convention of the community is a prison to his natural, individual desire, a desire that compels him, whether he feel justified or not, to break the bounds of the community, lands him outside the pale, there to stand alone, and say: "I was right, my desire was real and inevitable; if I was to be myself I must fulfil it, convention or no convention," or else, there to stand alone, doubting, and saying: "Was I right, was I wrong? If I was wrong, oh, let me die!"—in which case he courts death.

The growth and the development of this tragedy, the deeper and deeper realisation of this division and this problem, the coming towards some conclusion, is the one theme of the Wessex novels.

And therefore the books must be taken chronologically, to reveal the development and to advance towards the conclusion.

1. *Desperate Remedies.*

Springrove, the dull hero, fast within convention, dare not tell Cytherea that he is already engaged, and thus prepares the complication. Manston, represented as fleshily passionate, breaks the convention and commits murder, which is very extreme, under compulsion of his desire for Cytherea. He is aided by the darkly passionate, lawless Miss Aldclyffe. He and Miss Aldclyffe meet death, and Springrove and Cytherea are united to happiness and success.

2. *Under the Greenwood Tree.*

After a brief excursion from the beaten track in the pursuit of social ambition and satisfaction of the imagination, figured by the Clergyman, Fancy, the little school-mistress, returns to Dick, renounces imagination, and settles down to steady, solid, physically satisfactory married life, and all is as it should be. But Fancy will carry in her heart all her life many unopened buds that will die unflowered: and Dick will probably have a bad time of it.

3. *A Pair of Blue Eyes.*

Elfride breaks down in her attempt to jump the first little hedge of convention, when she comes back after running away with Stephen. She cannot stand even a little alone. Knight, his conventional ideas backed up by selfish instinct, cannot endure Elfride when he thinks she is not virgin, though now she loves him beyond bounds. She submits to him, and owns the conventional idea entirely right, even whilst she is innocent. An aristocrat walks off with her whilst the two men hesitate, and she, poor innocent victim of passion not vital enough to overthrow the most banal conventional ideas, lies in a bright coffin, while the three confirmed lovers mourn, and say how great the tragedy is.

4. *Far from the Madding Crowd.*

The unruly Bathsheba, though almost pledged to Farmer Boldwood, a ravingly passionate, middle-aged bachelor pretendant, who has suddenly started in mad pursuit of some unreal conception of woman, personified in Bathsheba, lightly runs off and marries Sergeant Troy, an illegitimate aristocrat, unscrupulous and yet sensitive in taking his pleasures. She

loves Troy, he does not love her. All the time she is loved
faithfully and persistently by the good Gabriel, who is like a
dog that watches the bone and bides the time. Sergeant Troy
treats Bathsheba badly, never loves her, though he is the only
man in the book who knows anything about her. Her pride
helps her to recover. Troy is killed by Boldwood; exit the
unscrupulous, but discriminative, almost cynical young soldier
and the mad, middle-aged pursuer of the *fata Morgana*; enter
the good, steady Gabriel, who marries Bathsheba because he
will make her a good husband, and the flower of imaginative
first love is dead for her with Troy's scorn of her.

    5. *The Hand of Ethelberta.*

    Ethelberta, a woman of character and of brilliant parts, sets
out in pursuit of social success, finds that Julius, the only man
she is inclined to love, is too small for her, hands him over to
the good little Picotee, and she herself, sacrificing almost
cynically what is called her heart, marries the old scoundrelly
Lord Mountclerc, runs him and his estates and governs well,
a sound, strong pillar of established society, now she has nipped
off the bud of her heart. Moral: it is easier for the butler's
daughter to marry a lord than to find a husband with her love,
if she be an exceptional woman.

    The Hand of Ethelberta is the one almost cynical comedy. It
marks the zenith of a certain feeling in the Wessex novels, the
zenith of the feeling that the best thing to do is to kick out the
craving for "Love" and substitute common sense, leaving sentiment to the minor characters.

    This novel is a shrug of the shoulders, and a last taunt to
hope, it is the end of the happy endings, except where sanity
and a little cynicism again appear in *The Trumpet-Major*, to
bless where they despise. It is the hard, resistant, ironical
announcement of personal failure, resistant and half-grinning.
It gives way to violent, angry passions and real tragedy, real
killing of beloved people, self-killing. Till now, only Elfride
among the beloved, has been killed; the good men have
always come out on top.

    6. *The Return of the Native.*

    This is the first tragic and important novel. Eustacia, dark,
wild, passionate, quite conscious of her desires and inheriting
no tradition which would make her ashamed of them, since she

is of a novelistic Italian birth, loves, first, the unstable Wildeve, who does not satisfy her, then casts him aside for the newly returned Clym, whom she marries. What does she want? She does not know, but it is evidently some form of self-realisation; she wants to be herself, to attain herself. But she does not know how, by what means, so romantic imagination says: Paris and the *beau monde*. As if that would have stayed her unsatisfaction.

Clym has found out the vanity of Paris and the *beau monde*. What, then, does he want? He does not know; his imagination tells him he wants to serve the moral system of the community, since the material system is despicable. He wants to teach little Egdon boys in school. There is as much vanity in this, easily, as in Eustacia's Paris. For what is the moral system but the ratified form of the material system? What is Clym's altruism but a deep, very subtle cowardice, that makes him shirk his own being whilst apparently acting nobly; which makes him choose to improve mankind rather than to struggle at the quick of himself into being. He is not able to undertake his own soul, so he will take a commission for society to enlighten the souls of others. It is subtle equivocation. Thus both Eustacia and he sidetrack from themselves, and each leaves the other unconvinced, unsatisfied, unrealised. Eustacia, because she moves outside the convention, must die; Clym, because he identified himself with the community, is transferred from Paris to preaching. He had never become an integral man, because when faced with the demand to produce himself, he remained under cover of the community and excused by his altruism.

His remorse over his mother is adulterated with sentiment; it is exaggerated by the push of tradition behind it. Even in this he does not ring true. He is always according to pattern, producing his feelings more or less on demand, according to the accepted standard. Practically never is he able to act or even feel in his original self; he is always according to the convention. His punishment is his final loss of all his original self: he is left preaching, out of sheer emptiness.

Thomasin and Venn have nothing in them turbulent enough to push them to the bounds of the convention. There is always room for them inside. They are genuine people, and they get the prize within the walls.

Wildeve, shifty and unhappy, attracted always from outside

and never driven from within, can neither stand with nor without the established system. He cares nothing for it, because he is unstable, has no positive being. He is an eternal assumption.

The other victim, Clym's mother, is the crashing-down of one of the old, rigid pillars of the system. The pressure on her is too great. She is weakened from the inside also, for her nature is non-conventional; it cannot own the bounds.

So, in this book, all the exceptional people, those with strong feelings and unusual characters, are reduced; only those remain who are steady and genuine, if commonplace. Let a man will for himself, and he is destroyed. He must will according to the established system.

The real sense of tragedy is got from the setting. What is the great, tragic power in the book? It is Egdon Heath. And who are the real spirits of the Heath? First, Eustacia, then Clym's mother, then Wildeve. The natives have little or nothing in common with the place.

What is the real stuff of tragedy in the book? It is the Heath. It is the primitive, primal earth, where the instinctive life heaves up. There, in the deep, rude stirring of the instincts, there was the reality that worked the tragedy. Close to the body of things, there can be heard the stir that makes us and destroys us. The Heath heaved with raw instinct. Egdon, whose dark soil was strong and crude and organic as the body of a beast. Out of the body of this crude earth are born Eustacia, Wildeve, Mistress Yeobright, Clym, and all the others. They are one year's accidental crop. What matters if some are drowned or dead, and others preaching or married: what matter, any more than the withering heath, the reddening berries, the seedy furze, and the dead fern of one autumn of Egdon? The Heath persists. Its body is strong and fecund, it will bear many more crops beside this. Here is the sombre, latent power that will go on producing, no matter what happens to the product. Here is the deep, black source from whence all these little contents of lives are drawn. And the contents of the small lives are spilled and wasted. There is savage satisfaction in it: for so much more remains to come, such a black, powerful fecundity is working there that what does it matter?

Three people die and are taken back into the Heath; they

mingle their strong earth again with its powerful soil, having been broken off at their stem. It is very good. Not Egdon is futile, sending forth life on the powerful heave of passion. It cannot be futile, for it is eternal. What is futile is the purpose of man.

Man has a purpose which he has divorced from the passionate purpose that issued him out of the earth into being. The Heath threw forth its shaggy heather and furze and fern, clean into being. It threw forth Eustacia and Wildeve and Mistress Yeobright and Clym, but to what purpose? Eustacia thought she wanted the hats and bonnets of Paris. Perhaps she was right. The heavy, strong soil of Egdon, breeding original native beings, is under Paris as well as under Wessex, and Eustacia sought herself in the gay city. She thought life there, in Paris, would be tropical, and all her energy and passion out of Egdon would there come into handsome flower. And if Paris real had been Paris as she imagined it, no doubt she was right, and her instinct was soundly expressed. But Paris real was not Eustacia's imagined Paris. Where was her imagined Paris, the place where her powerful nature could come to blossom? Beside some strong-passioned, unconfined man, her mate.

Which mate Clym might have been. He was born out of passionate Egdon to live as a passionate being whose strong feelings moved him ever further into being. But quite early his life became narrowed down to a small purpose: he must of necessity go into business, and submit his whole being, body and soul as well as mind, to the business and to the greater system it represented. His feelings, that should have produced the man, were suppressed and contained, he worked according to a system imposed from without. The dark struggle of Egdon, a struggle into being as the furze struggles into flower, went on in him, but could not burst the enclosure of the idea, the system which contained him. Impotent to *be*, he must transform himself, and live in an abstraction, in a generalisation, he must identify himself with the system. He must live as Man or Humanity, or as the Community, or as Society, or as Civilisation. "An inner strenuousness was preying on his outer symmetry, and they rated his look as singular. . . . His countenance was overlaid with legible meanings. Without being thought-worn, he yet had certain marks derived from a perception of his surroundings, such as are not infrequently found on man at the end of the four or five years of endeavour which follow the close of placid pupilage. He already showed that thought is a disease of the flesh, and indirectly bore evidence that ideal physical beauty is incompatible with emotional development and a full recognition of the coil of things. Mental luminousness must be fed with the oil of life, even if there is already a physical seed for it; and the pitiful sight of two demands on one supply was just showing itself here."

But did the face of Clym show that thought is a disease of flesh, or merely that in his case a dis-ease, an un-ease, of flesh produced thought? One does not catch thought like a fever: one produces it. If it be in any way a disease of flesh, it is rather the rash that indicates the disease than the disease itself. The "inner strenuousness" of Clym's nature was not fighting against his physical symmetry, but against the limits imposed on his physical movement. By nature, as a passionate, violent product of Egdon, he should have loved and suffered in flesh and in soul from love, long before this age. He should have lived and moved and had his being, whereas he had only his business, and afterwards his inactivity. His years of pupilage were past, "he was one of whom something original was expected," yet he continued in pupilage. For he produced nothing original in being or in act, and certainly no original thought. None of his ideas were original. Even he himself was not original. He was over-taught, had become an echo. His life had been arrested, and his activity turned into repetition. Far from being emotionally developed, he was emotionally undeveloped, almost entirely. Only his mental faculties were developed. And, hid, his emotions were obliged to work according to the label he put upon them: a ready-made label.

Yet he remained for all that an original, the force of life was in him, however much he frustrated and suppressed its natural movement. "As is usual with bright natures, the deity that lies ignominiously chained within an ephemeral human carcass shone out of him like a ray." But was the deity chained within his ephemeral human carcass, or within his limited human consciousness? Was it his blood, which rose dark and potent out of Egdon, which hampered and confined the diety, or was it his mind, that house built of extraneous knowledge and guarded by his will, which formed the prison?

He came back to Egdon—what for? To reunite himself with the strong, free flow of life that rose out of Egdon as from a source? No—"to preach to the Egdon eremites that they might rise to a serene comprehensiveness without going through the process of enriching themselves." As if the Egdon eremites had not already far more serene comprehensiveness than ever he had himself, rooted as they were in the soil of all things, and living from the root! What did it matter how they enriched themselves, so long as they kept this strong, deep root in the primal soil, so long as their instincts moved out to action and to expression? The system was big enough for them, and had no power over their instincts. They should have taught him rather than he them.

And Egdon made him marry Eustacia. Here was action and life, here was a move into being on his part. But as soon as he got her, she became an idea to him, she had to fit in his system of ideas. According to his way of living, he knew her already, she was labelled and classed and fixed down. He had got into this way of living, and he could not get out of it. He had identified himself with the system, and he could not extricate himself. He did not know that Eustacia had her being beyond his. He did not know that she existed untouched by his system and his mind, where no system had sway and where no consciousness had risen to the surface. He did not know that she was Egdon, the powerful, eternal origin seething with production. He thought he knew. Egdon to him was the tract of common land, producing familiar rough herbage, and having some few unenlightened inhabitants. So he skated over heaven and hell, and having made a map of the surface, thought he knew all. But underneath and among his mapped world, the eternal powerful fecundity worked on heedless of him and his arrogance. His preaching, his superficiality made no difference. What did it matter if he had calculated a moral chart from the surface of life? Could that affect life, any more than a chart of the heavens affects the stars, affects the whole stellar universe which exists beyond our knowledge? Could the sound of his words affect the working of the body of Egdon, where in the unfathomable womb was begot and conceived all that would ever come forth? Did not his own heart beat far removed and immune from his thinking and talking? Had he been able to put even his own heart's mysterious resonance upon his map, from which he charted the course of lives in his moral system? And how much more completely, then, had he left out, in utter ignorance, the dark, powerful source whence all things rise into being, whence they will always continue to rise, to struggle forward to further being? A little of the static surface he could see, and map out. Then he thought his map was the thing itself. How blind he was, how utterly blind to the tremendous movement carrying and producing the surface. He did not know that the greater part of every life is underground, like roots in the dark in contact with the beyond. He preached, thinking lives could be moved like hen-houses from here to there. His blindness indeed brought on the calamity. But what matter if Eustacia or Wildeve or Mrs. Yeobright died: what matter if he himself became a mere rattle of repetitive words— what did it matter? It was regrettable; no more. Egdon, the primal impulsive body, would go on producing all that was to be produced, eternally, though the will of man should destroy the blossom yet in bud, over and over again. At last he must learn what it is to be at one, in his mind and will, with the primal impulses that rise in him. Till then, let him perish or preach. The great reality on which the little tragedies enact themselves cannot be detracted from. The will and words which militate against it are the only vanity.

This is a constant revelation in Hardy's novels: that there exists a great background, vital and vivid, which matters more than the people who move upon it. Against the background of dark, passionate Egdon, of the leafy, sappy passion and sentiment of the woodlands, of the unfathomed stars, is drawn the lesser scheme of lives: *The Return of the Native*, *The Woodlanders*, or *Two on a Tower*. Upon the vast, incomprehensible pattern of some primal morality greater than ever the human mind can grasp, is drawn the little, pathetic pattern of man's moral life and struggle, pathetic, almost ridiculous. The little fold of law and order, the little walled city within which man has to defend himself from the waste enormity of nature, becomes always too small, and the pioneers venturing out with the code of the walled city upon them, die in the bonds of that code, free and yet unfree, preaching the walled city and looking to the waste.

This is the wonder of Hardy's novels, and gives them their beauty. The vast, unexplored morality of life itself, what we call the immorality of nature, surrounds us in its eternal incomprehensibility, and in its midst goes on the little human morality play, with its queer frame of morality and its mechanised movement; seriously, portentously, till some one of the protagonists chances to look out of the charmed circle, weary of the stage, to look into the wilderness raging round. Then he is lost, his little drama falls to pieces, or becomes mere repetition, but the stupendous theatre outside goes on enacting its own incomprehensible drama, untouched. There is this quality in almost all Hardy's work, and this is the magnificent irony it all contains, the challenge, the contempt. Not the deliberate ironies, little tales of widows or widowers, contain the irony of human life as we live it in our self-aggrandised gravity, but the big novels, *The Return of the Native*, and the others.

And this is the quality Hardy shares with the great writers, Shakespeare or Sophocles or Tolstoi, this setting behind the small action of his protagonists the terrific action of unfathomed nature; setting a smaller system of morality, the one grasped and formulated by the human consciousness within the vast, uncomprehended and incomprehensible morality of nature or of life itself, surpassing human consciousness. The difference is, that whereas in Shakespeare or Sophocles the greater, uncomprehended morality, or fate, is actively transgressed and gives active punishment, in Hardy and Tolstoi the lesser, human morality, the mechanical system is actively transgressed, and holds, and punishes the protagonist, whilst the greater morality is only passively, negatively transgressed, it is represented merely as being present in background, in scenery, not taking any active part, having no direct connexion with the protagonist. Œdipus, Hamlet, Macbeth set themselves up against, or find themselves set up against, the unfathomed moral forces of nature, and out of this unfathomed force comes their death. Whereas Anna Karenina, Eustacia, Tess, Sue, and Jude find themselves up against the established system of human government and morality, they cannot detach themselves, and are brought down. Their real tragedy is that they are unfaithful

to the greater unwritten morality, which would have bidden
Anna Karenina be patient and wait until she, by virtue of
greater right, could take what she needed from society; would
have bidden Vronsky detach himself from the system, become
an individual, creating a new colony of morality with Anna;
would have bidden Eustacia fight Clym for his own soul, and
Tess take and claim her Angel, since she had the greater light;
would have bidden Jude and Sue endure for very honour's
sake, since one must bide by the best that one has known, and
not succumb to the lesser good.

Had Œdipus, Hamlet, Macbeth been weaker, less full of real,
potent life, they would have made no tragedy; they would have
comprehended and contrived some arrangement of their affairs,
sheltering in the human morality from the great stress and
attack of the unknown morality. But being, as they are, men
to the fullest capacity, when they find themselves, daggers
drawn, with the very forces of life itself, they can only fight till
they themselves are killed, since the morality of life, the greater
morality, is eternally unalterable and invincible. It can be
dodged for some time, but not opposed. On the other hand,
Anna, Eustacia, Tess or Sue—what was there in their position
that was necessarily tragic? Necessarily painful it was, but
they were not at war with God, only with Society. Yet they
were all cowed by the mere judgment of man upon them, and
all the while by their own souls they were right. And the
judgment of man killed them, not the judgment of their own
souls or the judgment of Eternal God.

Which is the weakness of modern tragedy, where transgression
against the social code is made to bring destruction, as though
the social code worked our irrevocable fate. Like Clym, the
map appears to us more real than the land. Shortsighted
almost to blindness, we pore over the chart, map out journeys,
and confirm them: and we cannot see life itself giving us the
lie the whole time.

*   *   *   *   *

Looking over the Hardy novels, it is interesting to see which
of the heroes one would call a distinct individuality, more or
less achieved, which an unaccomplished potential individuality, and which an impure, unindividualised life embedded

in the matrix, either achieving its own lower degree of distinc- .
tion, or not achieving it.

In *Desperate Remedies* there are scarcely any people at all,
particularly when the plot is working. The tiresome part
about Hardy is that, so often, he will neither write a morality
play nor a novel. The people of the first book, as far as the plot
is concerned, are not people: they are the heroine, faultless
and white; the hero, with a small spot on his whiteness; the
villainess, red and black, but more red than black; the villain,
black and red; the Murderer, aided by the Adulteress, obtains
power over the Virgin, who, rescued at the last moment by the
Virgin Knight, evades the evil clutch. Then the Murderer,
overtaken by vengeance, is put to death, whilst Divine Justice
descends upon the Adulteress. Then the Virgin unites with the
Virgin Knight, and receives Divine Blessing.

That is a morality play, and if the morality were vigorous and
original, all well and good. But, between-whiles, we see that
the Virgin is being played by a nice, rather ordinary girl.

In *The Laodicean*, there is all the way through a *prédilection
d'artiste* for the aristocrat, and all the way through a moral
condemnation of him, a substituting the middle- or lower-class
personage with bourgeois virtues into his place. This was the
root of Hardy's pessimism. Not until he comes to Tess and
Jude does he ever sympathise with the aristocrat—unless it be
in *The Mayor of Casterbridge*, and then he sympathises only to
slay. He always, always represents them the same, as having
some vital weakness, some radical ineffectuality. From first to
last it is the same.

Miss Aldclyffe and Manston, Elfride and the sickly lord she
married, Troy and Farmer Boldwood, Eustacia Vye and
Wildeve, de Stancy in *The Laodicean*, Lady Constantine in *Two
on a Tower*, the Mayor of Casterbridge and Lucetta, Mrs.
Charmond and Dr. Fitzpiers in *The Woodlanders*, Tess and Alec
d'Urberville, and, though different, Jude. There is also the
blond, passionate, yielding man: Sergeant Troy, Wildeve,
and, in spirit, Jude.

These are all, in their way, the aristocrat-characters of
Hardy. They must every one die, every single one.

Why has Hardy this *prédilection d'artiste* for the aristocrat, and
why, at the same time, this moral antagonism to him?

It is fairly obvious in *The Laodicean*, a book where, the spirit being small, the complaint is narrow. The heroine, the daughter of a famous railway engineer, lives in the castle of the old de Stancys. She sighs, wishing she were of the de Stancy line: the tombs and portraits have a spell over her. "But," says the hero to her, "have you forgotten you father's line of ancestry: Archimedes, Newcomen, Watt, Tylford, Stephenson?" —"But I have a *prédilection d'artiste* for ancestors of the other sort," sighs Paula. And the hero despairs of impressing her with the list of his architect ancestors: Phidias, Ictinus and Callicrates, Chersiphron, Vitruvius, Wilars of Cambray, William of Wykeham. He deplores her marked preference for an "animal pedigree".

But what is this "animal pedigree"? If a family pedigree of her ancestors, working-men and burghers, had been kept, Paula would not have gloried in it, animal though it were. Hers was a *prédilection d'artiste*.

And this because the aristocrat alone has occupied a position where he could afford to *be*, to be himself, to create himself, to live as himself. That is his eternal fascination. This is why the preference for him is a *prédilection d'artiste*. The preference for the architect line would be a *prédilection de savant*, the preference for the engineer pedigree would be a *prédilection d'économiste*.

The *prédilection d'artiste*—Hardy has it strongly, and it is rooted deeply in every imaginative human being. The glory of mankind has been to produce lives, to produce vivid, independent, individual men, not buildings or engineering works or even art, not even the public good. The glory of mankind is not in a host of secure, comfortable, law-abiding citizens, but in the few more fine, clear lives, beings, individuals, distinct, detached, single as may be from the public.

And these the artist of all time has chosen. Why, then, must the aristocrat always be condemned to death, in Hardy? Has the community come to consciousness in him, as in the French Revolutionaries, determined to destroy all that is not the average? Certainly in the Wessex novels, all but the average people die. But why? Is there the germ of death in these more single, distinguished people, or has the artist himself a bourgeois taint, a jealous vindictiveness that will now take revenge, now that the community, the average, has gained power over the aristocrat, the exception?

It is evident that both is true. Starting with the bourgeois morality, Hardy makes every exceptional person a villain, all exceptional or strong individual traits he holds up as weaknesses or wicked faults. So in *Desperate Remedies, Under the Greenwood Tree, Far from the Madding Crowd, The Hand of Ethelberta, The Return of the Native* (but in *The Trumpet-Major* there is an ironical dig in the ribs to this civic communal morality), *The Laodicean, Two on a Tower, The Mayor of Casterbridge,* and *Tess,* in steadily weakening degree. The blackest villain is Manston, the next, perhaps, Troy, the next Eustacia, and Wildeve, always becoming less villainous and more human. The first show of real sympathy, nearly conquering the bourgeois or commune morality, is for Eustacia, whilst the dark villain is becoming merely a weak, pitiable person in Dr. Fitzpiers. In *The Mayor of Casterbridge* the dark villain is already almost the hero. There is a lapse in the maudlin, weak but not wicked Dr. Fitzpiers, duly condemned, Alec d'Urberville is not unlikeable, and Jude is a complete tragic hero, at once the old Virgin Knight and Dark Villain. The condemnation gradually shifts over from the dark villain to the blond bourgeois virgin hero, from Alec d'Urberville to Angel Clare, till in Jude they are united and loved, though the preponderance is of a dark villain, now dark, beloved, passionate hero. The condemnation shifts over at last from the dark villain to the white virgin, the bourgeois in soul: from Arabella to Sue. Infinitely more subtle and sad is the condemnation at the end, but there it is: the virgin knight is hated with intensity, yet still loved; the white virgin, the beloved, is the arch-sinner against life at last, and the last note of hatred is against her.

It is a complete and devastating shift-over, it is a complete *volte-face* of moralities. Black does not become white, but it takes white's place as good; white remains white, but it is found bad. The old, communal morality is like a leprosy, a white sickness: the old, anti-social, individualist morality is alone on the side of life and health.

But yet, the aristocrat must die, all the way through: even Jude. Was the germ of death in him at the start? Or was he merely at outs with his times, the times of the Average in triumph? Would Manston, Troy, Farmer Boldwood, Eustacia, de Stancy, Henchard, Alec d'Urberville, Jude have been real heroes in heroic times, without tragedy? It seems as if Manston, Boldwood, Eustacia, Henchard, Alec d'Urberville, and almost Jude, might have been. In an heroic age they might have lived and more or less triumphed. But Troy, Wildeve, de Stancy, Fitzpiers, and Jude have something fatal in them. There is a rottenness at the core of them. The failure, the misfortune, or the tragedy, whichever it may be, was inherent in them: as if was in Elfride, Lady Constantine, Marty South in *The Woodlanders*, and Tess. They have all passionate natures, and in them all failure is inherent.

So that we have, of men, the noble Lord in *A Pair of Blue Eyes*, Sergeant Troy, Wildeve, de Stancy, Fitzpiers, and Jude, all passionate, aristocratic males, doomed by their very being, to tragedy, or to misfortune in the end.

Of the same class among women are Elfride, Lady Constantine, Marty South, and Tess, all aristocratic, passionate, yet necessarily unfortunate females.

We have also, of men, Manston, Farmer Boldwood, Henchard, Alec d'Urberville, and perhaps Jude, all passionate, aristocratic males, who fell before the weight of the average, the lawful crowd, but who, in more primitive times, would have formed romantic rather than tragic figures.

Of women in the same class are Miss Aldclyffe, Eustacia, Lucetta, Mrs. Charmond.

The third class, of bourgeois or average hero, whose purpose is to live and have his being in the community, contains the successful hero of *Desperate Remedies*, the unsuccessful but not very much injured two heroes of *A Pair of Blue Eyes*, the successful Gabriel Oak, the unsuccessful, left-preaching Clym, the unsuccessful but not very much injured astronomer of *Two on a Tower*, the successful Scotchman of Casterbridge, the unsuccessful and expired Giles Winterborne of *The Woodlanders*, the archtype, Angel Clare, and perhaps a little of Jude.

The companion women to these men are: the heroine of *Desperate Remedies*, Bathsheba, Thomasin, Paula, Henchard's daughter, Grace in *The Woodlanders*, and Sue.

This, then, is the moral conclusion drawn from the novels:

1. The physical individual is in the end an inferior thing

which must fall before the community: Manston, Henchard, etc.

2. The physical and spiritual individualist is a fine thing which must fall because of its own isolation, because it is a sport, not in the true line of life: Jude, Tess, Lady Constantine.

3. The physical individualist and spiritual bourgeois or communist is a thing, finally, of ugly, undeveloped, non-distinguished or perverted physical instinct, and must fall physically. Sue, Angel Clare, Clym, Knight. It remains, however, fitted into the community.

4. The undistinguished, bourgeois or average being with average or civic virtues usually succeeds in the end. If he fails, he is left practically uninjured. If he expire during probation, he has flowers on his grave.

By individualist is meant, not a selfish or greedy person, anxious to satisfy appetites, but a man of distinct being, who must act in his own particular way to fulfil his own individual nature. He is a man who, being beyond the average, chooses to rule his own life to his own completion, and as such is an aristocrat.

The artist always has a predilection for him. But Hardy, like Tolstoi, is forced in the issue always to stand with the community in condemnation of the aristocrat. He cannot help himself, but must stand with the average against the exception, he must, in his ultimate judgment, represent the interests of humanity, or the community as a whole, and rule out the individual interest.

To do this, however, he must go against himself. His private sympathy is always with the individual against the community: as is the case with the artist. Therefore he will create a more or less blameless individual and, making him seek his own fulfil-ment, his highest aim, will show him destroyed by the com-munity, or by that in himself which represents the community, or by some close embodiment of the civic idea. Hence the pessimism. To do this, however, he must select his individual with a definite weakness, a certain coldness of temper, inelas-tic, a certain inevitable and inconquerable adhesion to the community.

This is obvious in Troy, Clym, Tess, and Jude. They have naturally distinct individuality but, as it were, a weak life-flow, so that they cannot break away from the old adhesion, they cannot separate themselves from the mass which bore them, they cannot detach themselves from the common. Therefore they are pathetic rather than tragic figures. They have not the necessary strength: the question of their unfortunate end is begged in the beginning.

Whereas Œdipus or Agamemnon or Clytemnestra or Orestes, or Macbeth or Hamlet or Lear, these are destroyed by their own conflicting passions. Out of greed for adventure, a desire to be off, Agamemnon sacrifices Iphigenia: moreover he has his love-affairs outside Troy: and this brings on him death from the mother of his daughter, and from his pledged wife. Which is the working of the natural law. Hamlet, a later Orestes, is commanded by the Erinyes of his father to kill his mother and his uncle: but his maternal filial feeling tears him. It is almost the same tragedy as Orestes, without any goddess or god to grant peace.

In these plays, conventional morality is transcended. The action is between the great, single, individual forces in the nature of Man, not between the dictates of the community and the original passion. The Commandment says: "Thou shalt not kill." But doubtless Macbeth had killed many a man who was in his way. Certainly Hamlet suffered no qualms about killing the old man behind the curtain. Why should he? But when Macbeth killed Duncan, he divided himself in twain, into two hostile parts. It was all in his own soul and blood: it was nothing outside himself: as it was, really, with Clym, Troy, Tess, Jude. Troy would probably have been faithful to his little unfortunate person, had she been a lady, and had he not felt himself cut off from society in his very being, whilst all the time he cleaved to it. Tess allowed herself to be condemned, and asked for punishment from Angel Clare. Why? She had done nothing particularly, or at least irrevocably, unnatural, were her life young and strong. But she sided with the community's condemnation of her. And almost the bitterest, most pathetic, deepest part of Jude's misfortune was his failure to obtain admission to Oxford, his failure to gain his place and standing in the world's knowledge, in the world's work.

There is a lack of sternness, there is a hesitating betwixt life and public opinion, which diminishes the Wessex novels from the rank of pure tragedy. It is not so much the eternal, immutable laws of being which are transgressed, it is not that vital life-forces are set in conflict with each other, bringing almost inevitable tragedy—yet not necessarily death, as we see in the most splendid Æschylus. It is, in Wessex, that the individual succumbs to what is in its shallowest, public opinion, in its deepest, the human compact by which we live together, to form a community.

* * * * *

Most fascinating in all artists is this antinomy between Law and Love, between the Flesh and the Spirit, between the Father and the Son.

For the moralist it is easy. He can insist on that aspect of the Law or Love which is in the immediate line of development for his age, and he can sternly and severely exclude or suppress all the rest.

So that all morality is of temporary value, useful to its times. But Art must give a deeper satisfaction. It must give fair play all round.

Yet every work of art adheres to some system of morality. But if it be really a work of art, it must contain the essential criticism on the morality to which it adheres. And hence the antinomy, hence the conflict necessary to every tragic conception.

The degree to which the system of morality, or the metaphysic, of any work of art is submitted to criticism within the work of art makes the lasting value and satisfaction of that work. Æschylus, having caught the oriental idea of Love, correcting the tremendous Greek conception of the Law with this new idea, produces the intoxicating satisfaction of the Orestean trilogy. The Law, and Love, they are here the Two-in-One in all their magnificence. But Euripides, with his aspiration towards Love, Love the supreme, and his almost hatred of the Law, Law the Triumphant but Base Closer of Doom, is less satisfactory, because of the very fact that he holds Love always Supreme, and yet must endure the chagrin of seeing Love perpetually transgressed and overthrown. So he makes his tragedy: the higher thing eternally pulled down by the lower. And this unfairness in the use of terms, higher and lower, but above all, the unfairness of showing Love always violated and suffering, never supreme and triumphant, makes us disbelieve Euripides in the end. For we have to bring in pity, we must admit that Love is at a fundamental disadvantage before the Law, and cannot therefore ever hold its own. Which is weak philosophy.

If Æschylus has a metaphysic to his art, this metaphysic is that Love and Law are Two, eternally in conflict, and eternally being reconciled. This is the tragic significance of Æschylus.

But the metaphysic of Euripides is that the Law and Love are two eternally in conflict, and unequally matched, so that Love must always be borne down. In Love a man shall only suffer. There is also a Reconciliation, otherwise Euripides were not so great. But there is always the unfair matching, this disposition insisted on, which at last leaves one cold and unbelieving.

The moments of pure satisfaction come in the choruses, in the pure lyrics, when Love is put into true relations with the Law, apart from knowledge, transcending knowledge, transcending the metaphysic, where the aspiration to Love meets the acknowledgment of the Law in a consummate marriage, for the moment.

Where Euripides adheres to his metaphysic, he is unsatisfactory. Where he transcends his metaphysic, he gives that supreme equilibrium wherein we know satisfaction.

The adherence to a metaphysic does not necessarily give artistic form. Indeed the over-strong adherence to a metaphysic usually destroys any possibility of artistic form. Artistic form is a revelation of the two principles of Love and the Law in a state of conflict and yet reconciled: pure motion struggling against and yet reconciled with the Spirit: active force meeting and overcoming and yet not overcoming inertia. It is the conjunction of the two which makes form. And since the two must always meet under fresh conditions, form must always be different. Each work of art has its own form, which has no relation to any other form. When a young painter studies an old master, he studies, not the form, that is an abstraction which does not exist: he studies maybe the method of the old great artist: but he studies chiefly to understand how the old great artist suffered in himself the conflict of Love and Law, and brought them to a reconciliation. Apart from artistic method, it is not Art that the young man is studying, but the State of Soul of the great old artist, so that he, the young artist, may understand his own soul and gain a reconciliation between the aspiration and the resistant.

It is most wonderful in poetry, this sense of conflict contained within a reconciliation:

> Hail to thee, blithe Spirit!
> Bird thou never wert,
> That from heaven or near it
> Pourest thy full heart
> In profuse strains of unpremeditated art.

Shelley wishes to say, the skylark is a pure, untrammelled spirit, a pure motion. But the very "Bird thou never wert" admits that the skylark *is* in very fact a bird, a concrete, momentary thing. If the line ran, "Bird thou never art," that would spoil it all. Shelley wishes to say, the song is poured out of heaven: but "or near it", he admits. There is the perfect relation between heaven and earth. And the last line is the tumbling sound of a lark's singing, the real Two-in-One.

The very adherence to rhyme and regular rhythm is a concession to the Law, a concession to the body, to the being and requirements of the body. They are an admission of the living, positive inertia which is the other half of life, other than the pure will to motion. In this consummation, they are the resistance and response of the Bride in the arms of the Bridegroom. And according as the Bride and Bridegroom come closer together, so is the response and resistance more fine, indistinguishable, so much the more, in this act of consummation, is the movement that of Two-in-One, indistinguishable each from the other, and not the movement of two brought together clumsily.

So that in Swinburne, where almost all is concession to the body, so that the poetry becomes almost a sensation and not an experience or a consummation, justifying Spinoza's "*Amor est titillatio, concomitante idea causa externae,*" we find continual adherence to the body, to the Rose, to the Flesh, the physical in everything, in the sea, in the marshes; there is an overbalance in the favour of Supreme Law; Love is not Love, but passion, part of the Law; there is no Love, there is only

Supreme Law. And the poet sings the Supreme Law to gain rebalance in himself, for he hovers always on the edge of death, of Not-Being, he is always out of reach of the Law, bodiless, in the faintness of Love that has triumphed and denied the Law, in the dread of an over-developed, over-sensitive soul which exists always on the point of dissolution from the body.

But he is not divided against himself. It is the novelists and dramatists who have the hardest task in reconciling their metaphysic, their theory of being and knowing, with their living sense of being. Because a novel is a microcosm, and because man in viewing the universe must view it in the light of theory, therefore every novel must have the background or the structural skeleton of some theory of being, some metaphysic. But the metaphysic must always subserve the artistic purpose beyond the artist's conscious aim. Otherwise the novel becomes a treatise.

And the danger is, that a man shall make himself a metaphysic to excuse or cover his own faults or failure. Indeed, a sense of fault or failure is the usual cause of a man's making himself a metaphysic, to justify himself.

Then, having made himself a metaphysic of self-justification, or a metaphysic of self-denial, the novelist proceeds to apply the world to this, instead of applying this to the world.

Tolstoi is a flagrant example of this. Probably because of profligacy in his youth, because he had disgusted himself in his own flesh, by excess or by prostitution, therefore Tolstoi, in his metaphysic, renounced the flesh altogether, later on, when he had tried and had failed to achieve complete marriage in the flesh. But above all things, Tolstoi was a child of the Law, he belonged to the Father. He had a marvellous sensuous understanding, and very little clarity of mind.

So that, in his metaphysic, he had to deny himself, his own being, in order to escape his own disgust of what he had done to himself, and to escape admission of his own failure.

Which made all the later part of his life a crying falsity and shame. Reading the reminiscences of Tolstoi, one can only feel shame at the way Tolstoi denied all that was great in him, with vehement cowardice. He degraded himself infinitely, he perjured himself far more than did Peter when he denied Christ. Peter repented. But Tolstoi denied the Father, and propagated a great system of his recusancy, elaborating his own weakness, blaspheming his own strength. "What difficulty is there in writing about how an officer fell in love with a married woman?" he used to say of his *Anna Karenina*; "there's no difficulty in it, and, above all, no good in it."

Because he was mouthpiece to the Father in uttering the law of passion, he said there was no difficulty in it, because it came naturally to him. Christ might just as easily have said, there was no difficulty in the Parable of the Sower, and no good in it, either, because it flowed out of him without effort.

And Thomas Hardy's metaphysic is something like Tolstoi's. "There is no reconciliation between Love and the Law," says Hardy. "The spirit of Love must always succumb before the blind, stupid, but overwhelming power of the Law."

Already as early as *The Return of the Native* he has come to this theory, in order to explain his own sense of failure. But before that time, from the very start, he has had an overweening theoretic antagonism to the Law. "That which is physical, of the body, is weak, despicable, bad," he said at the very start. He represented his fleshy heroes as villains, but very weak and maundering villains. At its worst, the Law is a weak, craven sensuality: at its best, it is a passive inertia. It is the gap in the armour, it is the hole in the foundation.

Such a metaphysic is almost silly. If it were not that man is much stronger in feeling than in thought, the Wessex novels would be sheer rubbish, as they are already in parts. *The Well-Beloved* is sheer rubbish, fatuity, as is a good deal of *The Dynasts* conception.

But it is not as a metaphysician that one must consider Hardy. He makes a poor show there. For nothing in his work is so pitiable as his clumsy efforts to push events into line with his theory of being, and to make calamity fall on those who represent the principle of Love. He does it exceedingly badly, and owing to this effort his form is execrable in the extreme.

His feeling, his instinct, his sensuous understanding is, however, apart from his metaphysic, very great and deep, deeper than that, perhaps, of any other English novelist. Putting aside his metaphysic, which must always obtrude when he thinks of people, and turning to the earth, to landscape, then he is true to himself.

Always he must start from the earth, from the great source of the Law, and his people move in his landscape almost insignificantly, somewhat like tame animals wandering in the wild. The earth is the manifestation of the Father, of the Creator, Who made us in the Law. God still speaks aloud in His Works, as to Job, so to Hardy, surpassing human conception and the human law. "Dost thou know the balancings of the clouds, the wondrous works of him which is perfect in knowledge? How thy garments are warm, when he quieteth the earth by the south wind? Hast thou with him spread out the sky, which is strong?"

This is the true attitude of Hardy—"With God is terrible majesty." The theory of knowledge, the metaphysic of the man, is much smaller than the man himself. So with Tolstoi.

"Knowest thou the time when the wild goats of the rock bring forth? Or canst thou mark when the hinds do calve? Canst thou number the months that they fulfil? Or knowest thou the time when they bring forth? They bow themselves, they bring forth their young ones, they cast out their sorrows. Their young ones are good in liking, they grow up with corn; they go forth, and return not unto them."

There is a good deal of this in Hardy. But in Hardy there is more than the concept of Job, protesting his integrity. Job says in the end: "Therefore have I uttered that I understood not; things too wonderful for me, which I knew not.

"I have heard of thee by hearing of the ear; but now mine eye seeth thee.

"Wherefore I abhor myself, and repent in dust and ashes."

But Jude ends where Job began, cursing the day and the services of his birth, and in so much cursing the act of the Lord, "Who made him in the womb."

It is the same cry all through Hardy, this curse upon the birth in the flesh, and this unconscious adherence to the flesh. The instincts, the bodily passions are strong and sudden in all Hardy's men. They are too strong and sudden. They fling Jude into the arms of Arabella, years after he has known Sue, and against his own will.

For every man comprises male and female in his being, the male always struggling for predominance. A woman likewise consists in male and female, with female predominant.

And a man who is strongly male tends to deny, to refute the female in him. A real "man" takes no heed for his body, which is the more female part of him. He considers himself only as an instrument, to be used in the service of some idea.

The true female, on the other hand, will eternally hold herself superior to any idea, will hold full life in the body to be the real happiness. The male exists in doing, the female in being. The male lives in the satisfaction of some purpose achieved, the female in the satisfaction of some purpose contained.

In Æschylus, in the *Eumenides*, there is Apollo, Loxias, the Sun God, the prophet, the male: there are the Erinyes, daughters of primeval Mother Night, representing here the female risen in retribution for some crime against the flesh; and there is Pallas, unbegotten daughter of Zeus, who is as the Holy Spirit in the Christian religion, the spirit of wisdom.

Orestes is bidden by the male god, Apollo, to avenge the murder of his father, Agamemnon, by his mother: that is, the male, murdered by the female, must be avenged by the male. But Orestes is child of his mother. He is in himself female. So that in himself the conscience, the madness, the violated part of his own self, his own body, drives him to the Furies. On the male side, he is right; on the female, wrong. But peace is given at last by Pallas, the Arbitrator, the spirit of wisdom.

And although Æschylus in his consciousness makes the Furies hideous, and Apollo supreme, yet, in his own self and in very fact, he makes the Furies wonderful and noble, with their tremendous hymns, and makes Apollo a trivial, sixth-form braggart and ranter. Clytemnestra also, wherever she appears, is wonderful and noble. Her sin is the sin of pride: she was the first to be injured. Agamemnon is a feeble thing beside her.

So Æschylus adheres still to the Law, to Right, to the Creator who created man in His Own Image, and in His Law. What he has learned of Love, he does not yet quite believe.

Hardy has the same belief in the Law, but in conceipt of his own understanding, which cannot understand the Law, he says that the Law is nothing, a blind confusion.

And in conceipt of understanding, he deprecates and destroys both women and men who would represent the old primeval Law, the great Law of the Womb, the primeval Female principle. The Female shall not exist. Where it appears, it is a criminal tendency, to be stamped out.

This in Manston, Troy, Boldwood, Eustacia, Wildeve, Henchard, Tess, Jude, everybody. The women approved of are not Female in any real sense. They are passive subjects to the male, the re-echo from the male. As in the Christian religion, the Virgin worship is no real Female worship, but worship of the Female as she is passive and subjected to the male. Hence the sadness of Botticelli's Virgins.

Thus Tess sets out, not as any positive thing, containing all purpose, but as the acquiescent complement to the male. The female in her has become inert. Then Alec d'Urberville comes along, and possesses her. From the man who takes her Tess expects her own consummation, the singling out of herself, the addition of the male complement. She is of an old line, and has the aristocratic quality of respect for the other being. She does not see the other person as an extension of herself, existing in a universe of which she is the centre and pivot. She knows that other people are outside her. Therein she is an aristocrat. And out of this attitude to the other person came her passivity. It is not the same as the passive quality in the other little heroines, such as the girl in *The Woodlanders*, who is passive because she is small.

Tess is passive out of self-acceptance, a true aristocratic quality, amounting almost to self-indifference. She knows she is herself incontrovertibly, and she knows that other people are not herself. This is a very rare quality, even in a woman. And in a civilisation so unequal, it is almost a weakness.

Tess never tries to alter or to change anybody, neither to alter nor to change nor to divert. What another person decides, that is his decision. She respects utterly the other's right to be. She is herself always.

But the others do not respect her right to be. Alec d'Urberville sees her as the embodied fulfilment of his own desire: something, that is, belonging to him. She cannot, in his conception, exist apart from him nor have any being apart from his being. For she is the embodiment of his desire.

This is very natural and common in men, this attitude to the world. But in Alec d'Urberville it applies only to the woman of his desire. He cares only for her. Such a man adheres to the female like a parasite.

It is a male quality to resolve a purpose to its fulfilment. It is the male quality, to seek the motive power in the female, and to convey this to a fulfilment; to receive some impulse into his senses, and to transmit it into expression.

Alec d'Urberville does not do this. He is male enough, in his way; but only physically male. He is constitutionally an enemy of the principle of self-subordination, which principle is inherent in every man. It is this principle which makes a man, a true male, see his job through, at no matter what cost. A man is strictly only himself when he is fulfilling some purpose he has conceived: so that the principle is not of self-subordination, but of continuity, of development. Only when insisted on, as in Christianity, does it become self-sacrifice. And this resistance to self-sacrifice on Alec d'Urberville's part does not make him an individualist, an egoist, but rather a non-individual, an incomplete, almost a fragmentary thing.

There seems to be in d'Urberville an inherent antagonism to any progression in himself. Yet he seeks with all his power for the source of stimulus in woman. He takes the deep impulse from the female. In this he is exceptional. No ordinary man could really have betrayed Tess. Even if she had had an illegitimate child to another man, to Angel Clare, for example, it would not have shattered her as did her connexion with Alec d'Urberville. For Alec d'Urberville could reach some of the real sources of the female in a woman, and draw from them. Troy could also do this. And, as a woman instinctively knows, such men are rare. Therefore they have a power over a woman. They draw from the depth of her being.

And what they draw, they betray. With a natural male, what he draws from the source of the female, the impulse he receives from the source he transmits through his own being into utterance, motion, action, expression. But Troy and Alec d'Urberville, what they received they knew only as gratification in the senses; some perverse will prevented them from submitting to it, from becoming instrumental to it.

Which was why Tess was shattered by Alec d'Urberville, and why she murdered him in the end. The murder is badly done, altogether the book is botched, owing to the way of thinking in the author, owing to the weak yet obstinate theory of being. Nevertheless, the murder is true, the whole book is true, in its conception.

Angel Clare has the very opposite qualities to those of Alec d'Urberville. To the latter, the female in himself is the only part of himself he will acknowledge: the body, the senses, that which he shares with the female, which the female shares with him. To Angel Clare, the female in himself is detestable, the body, the senses, that which he will share with a woman, is held degraded. What he wants really is to receive the female impulse other than through the body. But his thinking has made him criticise Christianity, his deeper instinct has forbidden him to deny his body any further, a deadlock in his own being, which denies him any purpose, so that he must take to hand, labour out of sheer impotence to resolve himself, drives him unwillingly to woman. But he must see her only as the Female Principle, he cannot bear to see her as the Woman in the Body. Her he thinks degraded. To marry her, to have a physical marriage with her, he must overcome all his ascetic revulsion, he must, in his own mind, put off his own divinity, his pure maleness, his singleness, his pure completeness, and descend to the heated welter of the flesh. It is objectionable to him. Yet his body, his life, is too strong for him.

Who is he, that he shall be pure male, and deny the existence of the female? This is the question the Creator asks of him. Is then the male the exclusive whole of life?—is he even the higher or supreme part of life? Angel Clare thinks so: as Christ thought.

Yet it is not so, as even Angel Clare must find out. Life, that is Two-in-One, Male and Female. Nor is either part greater than the other.

It is not Angel Clare's fault that he cannot come to Tess when he finds that she has, in his words, been defiled. It is the result of generations of ultra-Christian training, which had left in him an inherent aversion to the female, and to all in himself which pertained to the female. What he, in his Christian sense, conceived of as Woman, was only the servant and attendant and administering spirit to the male. He had no idea that there was such a thing as positive Woman, as the Female, another great living Principle counterbalancing his own male principle. He conceived of the world as consisting of the One, the Male Principle.

Which conception was already gendered in Botticelli, whence the melancholy of the Virgin. Which conception reached its fullest in Turner's pictures, which were utterly bodiless; and also in the great scientists or thinkers of the last generation, even Darwin and Spencer and Huxley. For these last conceived of evolution, of one spirit or principle starting at the far end of time, and lonelily traversing Time. But there is not one principle, there are two, travelling always to meet, each step of each one lessening the distance between the two of them. And Space, which so frightened Herbert Spencer, is as a Bride to us. And the cry of Man does not ring out into the Void. It rings out to Woman, whom we know not.

This Tess knew, unconsciously. An aristocrat she was, developed through generations to the belief in her own self-establishment. She could help, but she could not be helped. She could give, but she could not receive. She could attend to the wants of the other person, but no other person, save another aristocrat—and there is scarcely such a thing as another aristocrat—could attend to her wants, her deepest wants.

So it is the aristocrat alone who has any real and vital sense of "the neighbour", of the other person; who has the habit of submerging himself, putting himself entirely away before the other person: because he expects to receive nothing from the other person. So that now he has lost much of his initiative force, and exists almost isolated, detached, and without the surging ego of the ordinary man, because he has controlled his nature according to the other man, to exclude him.

And Tess, despising herself in the flesh, despising the deep Female she was, because Alec d'Urberville had betrayed her very source, loved Angel Clare, who also despised and hated the flesh. She did not hate d'Urberville. What a man did, he did, and if he did it to her, it was her look-out. She did not conceive of him as having any human duty towards her.

The same with Angel Clare as with Alec d'Urberville. She was very grateful to him for saving her from her despair of contamination, and from her bewildered isolation. But when he accused her, she could not plead or answer. For she had no right to his goodness. She stood alone.

The female was strong in her. She was herself. But she was out of place, utterly out of her element and her times. Hence her utter bewilderment. This is the reason why she was so overcome. She was outwearied from the start, in her spirit. For it is only by receiving from all our fellows that we are kept fresh and vital. Tess was herself, female, intrinsically a woman.

The female in her was indomitable, unchangeable, she was utterly constant to herself. But she was, by long breeding, intact from mankind. Though Alec d'Urberville was of no kin to her, yet, in the book, he has always a quality of kinship. It was as if only a kinsman, an aristocrat, could approach her. And this to her undoing. Angel Clare would never have reached her. She would have abandoned herself to him, but he would never have reached her. It needed a physical aristocrat. She would have lived with her husband, Clare, in a state of abandon to him, like a coma. Alec d'Urberville forced her to realise him, and to realise herself. He came close to her, as Clare could never have done. So she murdered him. For she was herself.

And just as the aristocratic principle had isolated Tess, it had isolated Alec d'Urberville. For though Hardy consciously made the younger betrayer a plebeian and an imposter, unconsciously, with the supreme justice of the artist, he made him the same as de Stancy, a true aristocrat, or as Fitzpiers, or Troy. He did not give him the tiredness, the touch of exhaustion necessary, in Hardy's mind, to an aristocrat. But he gave him the intrinsic qualities.

With the men as with the women of old descent: they have nothing to do with mankind in general, they are exceedingly personal. For many generations they have been accustomed to regard their own desires as their own supreme laws. They have not been bound by the conventional morality: this they have transcended, being a code unto themselves. The other person has been always present to their imagination, in the spectacular sense. He has always existed to them. But he has always existed as something other than themselves.

Hence the inevitable isolation, detachment of the aristocrat. His one aim, during centuries, has been to keep himself detached. At last he finds himself, by his very nature, cut off. Then either he must go his own way, or he must struggle towards reunion with the mass of mankind. Either he must be an incomplete individualist, like de Stancy, or like the famous Russian nobles, he must become a wild humanitarian and reformer.

For as all the governing power has gradually been taken from the nobleman, and as, by tradition, by inherent inclination, he does not occupy himself with profession other than government, how shall he use that power which is in him and which comes into him?

He is, by virtue of breed and long training, a perfect instrument. He knows, as every pure-bred thing knows, that his root and source is in his female. He seeks the motive power in the woman. And, having taken it, has nothing to do with it, can find, in this democratic, plebeian age, no means by which to transfer it into action, expression, utterance. So there is a continual gnawing of unsatisfaction, a constant seeking of another woman, still another woman. For each time the impulse comes fresh, everything seems all right.

It may be, also, that in the aristocrat a certain weariness makes him purposeless, vicious, like a form of death. But that is not necessary. One feels that in Manston, and Troy, and Fitzpiers, and Alec d'Urberville, there is good stuff gone wrong. Just as in Angel Clare, there is good stuff gone wrong in the other direction.

There can never be one extreme of wrong, without the other extreme. If there had never been the extravagant Puritan idea, that the Female Principle was to be denied, cast out by man from his soul, that only the Male Principle, of Abstraction, of Good, of Public Good, of the Community, embodied in "Thou shalt love they neighbour as thyself," really existed, there would never have been produced the extreme Cavalier type, which says that only the Female Principle endures in man, that all the Abstraction, the Good, the Public Elevation, the Community, was a grovelling cowardice, and that man lived by enjoyment, through his senses, enjoyment which ended in his senses. Or perhaps better, if the extreme Cavalier type had never been produced, we should not have had the Puritan, the extreme correction.

The one extreme produces the other. It is inevitable for Angel Clare and for Alec d'Urberville mutually to destroy the woman they both loved. Each does her the extreme of wrong, so she is destroyed.

The book is handled with very uncertain skill, botched and bungled. But it contains the elements of the greatest tragedy: Alec d'Urberville, who has killed the male in himself, as Clytemnestra symbolically for Orestes killed Agamemnon; Angel Clare, who has killed the female in himself, as Orestes killed Clytemnestra: and Tess, the Woman, the Life, destroyed by a mechanical fate, in the communal law.

There is no reconciliation. Tess, Angel Clare, Alec d'Urberville, they are all as good as dead. For Angel Clare, though still apparently alive, is in reality no more than a mouth, a piece of paper, like Clym left preaching.

There is no reconciliation, only death. And so Hardy really states his case, which is not his consciously stated metaphysic, by any means, but a statement how man has gone wrong and brought death on himself: how man has violated the Law, how he has supererogated himself, gone so far in his male conceit as to supersede the Creator, and win death as a reward. Indeed, the works of supererogation of our male assiduity help us to a better salvation.

Jude is only Tess turned round about. Instead of the heroine containing the two principles, male and female, at strife within her one being, it is Jude who contains them both, whilst the two women with him take the place of the two men to Tess. Arabella is Alec d'Urberville, Sue is Angel Clare. These represent the same pair of principles.

But, first, let it be said again that Hardy is a bad artist. Because he must condemn Alec d'Urberville, according to his own personal creed, therefore he shows him a vulgar intriguer of coarse lasses, and as ridiculous convert to evangelism. But Alec d'Urberville, by the artist's account, is neither of these. It is, in actual life, a rare man who seeks and seeks among women for one of such character and intrinsic female being as Tess. The ordinary sensualist avoids such characters. They implicate him too deeply. An ordinary sensualist would have been much too common, much too afraid, to turn to Tess. In a way, d'Urberville was her mate. And his subsequent passion for her is in its way noble enough. But whatever his passion, as a male, he must be a betrayer, even if he had been the most faithful husband on earth. He betrayed the female in a woman, by taking her, and by responding with no male impulse from himself. He roused her, but never satisfied her. He could never satisfy her. It was like a soul-disease in him: he was, in the strict though not the technical sense, impotent. But he must have wanted, later on, not to be so. But he could not help himself. He was spiritually impotent in love.

Arabella was the same. She, like d'Urberville, was converted by an evangelical preacher. It is significant in both of them. They were not just shallow, as Hardy would have made them out.

He is, however, more contemptuous in his personal attitude to the woman than to the man. He insists that she is a pig-killer's daughter; he insists that she drag Jude into pig-killing; he lays stress on her false tail of hair. That is not the point at all. This is only Hardy's bad art. He himself, as an artist, manages in the whole picture of Arabella almost to make insignificant in her these pig-sticking, false-hair crudities. But he must have his personal revenge on her for her coarseness, which offends him, because he is something of an Angel Clare.

The pig-sticking and so forth are not so important in the real picture. As for the false tail of hair, few women dared have been so open and natural about it. Few women, indeed, dared have made Jude marry them. It may have been a case with Arabella of "fools rush in". But she was not such a fool. And her motives are explained in the book. Life is not, in the actual, such a simple affair of getting a fellow and getting married. It is, even for Arabella, an affair on which she places her all. No barmaid marries anybody, the first man she can lay hands on. She cannot. It must be a personal thing to her. And no ordinary woman would want Jude. Moreover, no ordinary woman could have laid her hands on Jude.

It is an absurd fallacy this, that a small man wants a woman bigger and finer than he is himself. A man is as big as his real desires. Let a man, seeing with his eyes a woman of force and being, want her for his own, then that man is intrinsically an equal of that woman. And the same with a woman.

A coarse, shallow woman does not want to marry a sensitive, deep-feeling man. She feels no desire for him, she is not drawn to him, but repelled, knowing he will contemn her. She wants a man to correspond to herself: that is, if she is a young woman looking for a mate, as Arabella was.

What an old, jaded, yet still unsatisfied woman or man wants is another matter. Yet not even one of these will take a young creature of real character, superior in force. Instinct and fear prevent it.

Arabella was, under all her disguise of pig-fat and false hair, and vulgar speech, in character somewhat an aristocrat. She was, like Eustacia, amazingly lawless, even splendidly so. She believed in herself and she was not altered by any outside opinion of herself. Her fault was pride. She thought herself the centre of life, that all which existed belonged to her in so far as she wanted it.

In this she was something like Job. His attitude was "I am strong and rich, and, also, I am a good man." He gave out of his own sense of bounty, and felt no indebtedness. Arabella was almost the same. She felt also strong and abundant, arrogant in her hold on life. She needed a complement; and the nearest thing to her satisfaction was Jude. For as she, intrinsically, was a strong female, by far overpowering her Annies and her friends, so was he a strong male.

The difference between them was not so much a difference of quality, or degree, as a difference of form. Jude, like Tess, wanted full consummation. Arabella, like Alec d'Urberville, had that in her which resisted full consummation, wanted only to enjoy herself in contact with the male. She would have no transmission.

There are two attitudes to love. A man in love with a woman says either: "I, the man, the male, am the supreme, I am the one, and the woman is administered unto me, and this is her highest function, to be administered unto me." This was the conscious attitude of the Greeks. But their unconscious attitude was the reverse: they were in truth afraid of the female principle, their vaunt was empty, they went in deep, inner dread of her. So did the Jews, so do the Italians. But after the Renaissance, there was a change. Then began conscious Woman-reverence, and a lack of instinctive reverence, rather only an instinctive pity. It is according to the balance between the Male and Female principles.

The other attitude of a man in love, besides this of "she is administered unto my maleness", is, "She is the unknown, the undiscovered, into which I plunge to discovery, losing myself." And what we call real love has always this latter attitude. The first attitude, which belongs to passion, makes a man feel proud, splendid. It is a powerful stimulant to him, the female administered to him. He feels full of blood, he walks the earth like a Lord. And it is to this state Nietzsche aspires in his *Wille zur Macht.* It is this the passionate nations crave.

And under all this there is, naturally, the sense of fear, transition, and the sadness of mortality. For, the female being herself an independent force, may she not withdraw, and leave a man empty, like ash, as one sees a Jew or an Italian so often?

This first attitude, too, of male pride receiving the female administration may, and often does, contain the corresponding intense fear and reverence of the female, as of the unknown. So that, starting from the male assertion, there came in the old days the full consummation; as often there comes the full consummation now.

But not always. The man may retain all the while the sense of himself, the primary male, receiving gratification. This constant reaction upon himself at length dulls his senses and his sensibility, and makes him mechanical, automatic. He grows gradually incapable of receiving any gratification from the female, and becomes a *roué*, only automatically alive, and frantic with the knowledge thereof.

It is the tendency of the Parisian—or has been—to take this attitude to love, and to intercourse. The woman knows herself all the while as the primary female receiving administration of the male. So she becomes hard and external, and inwardly jaded, tired out. It is the tendency of English women to take this attitude also. And it is this attitude of love, more than anything else, which devitalises a race, and makes it barren.

It is an attitude natural enough to start with. Every young man must think that it is the highest honour he can do to a woman, to receive from her her female administration to his male being, whilst he meanwhile gives her the gratification of himself. But intimacy usually corrects this, love, or use, or marriage: a married man ceases to think of himself as the primary male: hence often his dullness. Unfortunately, he also fails in many cases to realise the gladness of a man in contact with the unknown in the female, which gives him a sense of richness and oneness with all life, as if, by being part of life, he were infinitely rich. Which is different from the sense of power, of dominating life. The *Wille zur Macht* is a spurious feeling.

For a man who dares to look upon, and to venture within the unknown of the female, losing himself, like a man who gives himself to the sea, or a man who enters a primeval, virgin forest, feels, when he returns, the utmost gladness of singing. This is certainly the gladness of a male bird in his singing, the amazing joy of return from the adventure into the unknown, rich with addition to his soul, rich with the knowledge of the utterly illimitable depth and breadth of the unknown; the ever-yielding extent of the unacquired, the unattained; the inexhaustible riches lain under unknown skies over unknown seas, all the magnificence that *is*, and yet which is unknown to any of us. And the knowledge of the reality with which it awaits me, the male, the knowledge of the calling and struggling of all the unknown, illimitable Female towards me, unembraced as yet, towards those men who will endlessly follow me, who will endlessly struggle after me, beyond me, further into this calling, unrealised vastness, nearer to the outstretched, eager, advancing unknown in the woman.

It is for this sense of All the magnificence that is unknown to me, of All that which stretches forth arms and breast to the Inexhaustible Embrace of all the ages, towards me, whose arms are outstretched, for this moment's embrace which gives me the inkling of the Inexhaustible Embrace that every man must and does yearn. And whether he be a *roué*, and vicious, or young and virgin, this is the bottom of every man's desire, for the embrace, for the advancing into the unknown, for the landing on the shore of the undiscovered half of the world, where the wealth of the female lies before us.

What is true of men is so of women. If we turn our faces west, towards nightfall and the unknown within the dark embrace of a wife, they turn their faces east, towards the sunrise and the brilliant, bewildering, active embrace of a husband. And as we are dazed with the unknown in her, so is she dazed with the unknown in us. It is so. And we throw up our joy to heaven like towers and spires and fountains and leaping flowers, so glad we are.

But always, we are divided within ourselves. Is it not that I am wonderful? Is it not a gratification for me when a stranger shall land on my shores and enjoy what he finds there? Shall I not also enjoy it? Shall I not enjoy the strange motion of the stranger, like a pleasant sensation of silk and warmth against me, stirring unknown fibres? Shall I not take this enjoyment without venturing out in dangerous waters, losing myself, perhaps destroying myself seeking the unknown? Shall I not stay at home, and by feeling the swift, soft airs blow out of the unknown upon my body, shall I not have rich pleasure of myself?

And, because they were afraid of the unknown, and because they wanted to retain the full-veined gratification of self-pleasure, men have kept their women tightly in bondage. But when the men were no longer afraid of the unknown, when they deemed it exhausted, they said, "There are no women; there are only daughters of men"—as we say now, as the Greeks tried to say. Hence the "Virgin" conception of woman, the passionless, passive conception, progressing from Fielding's Amelia to Dickens's Agnes, and on to Hardy's Sue.

Whereas Arabella in *Jude the Obscure* has what one might call the selfish instinct for love, Jude himself has the other, the unselfish. She sees in him a male who can gratify her. She takes him, and is gratified by him. Which makes a man of him. He becomes a grown, independent man in the arms of Arabella, conscious of having met, and satisfied, the female demand in him. This makes a man of any youth. He is proven unto himself as a male being, initiated into the freedom of life.

But Arabella refused his purpose. She refused to combine with him in one purpose. Just like Alec d'Urberville, she had from the outset an antagonism to the submission to any change in herself, to any development. She had the will to remain where she was, static, and to receive and exhaust all impulse she received from the male, in her senses. Whereas in a normal woman, impulse received from the male drives her on to a sense of joy and wonder and glad freedom in touch with the unknown of which she is made aware, so that she exists on the edge of the unknown half in rapture. Which is the state the writers wish to portray in "Amelia" and "Agnes", but particularly in the former; which Reynolds wishes to portray in his pictures of women.

To all this Arabella was antagonistic. It seems like a perversion in her, as if she played havoc with the stuff she was made of, as Alec d'Urberville did. Nevertheless she remained always unswervable female, she never truckled to the male idea, but was self-responsible, without fear. It is easier to imagine such a woman, out of one's desires, than to find her in real life. For, where a half-criminal type, a reckless, dare-devil type resembling her, may be found on the outskirts of society, yet these are not Arabella. Which criminal type, or reckless, low woman, would want to marry Jude? Arabella wanted Jude. And it is evident she was not too coarse for him, since she made no show of refinement from the first. The female in her, reckless and unconstrained, was strong enough to draw him after her, as her male, right to the end. Which other woman could have done this? At least let acknowledgment be made to her great female force of character. Her coarseness seems to me exaggerated to make the moralist's case good against her.

Jude could never hate her. She did a great deal for the true making of him, for making him a grown man. She gave him to himself.

And there was danger at the outset that he should never become a man, but that he should remain incorporated, smothered out under his idea of learning. He was somewhat in Angel Clare's position. Not that generations of particular training had made him almost rigid and paralysed to the female: but that his whole passion was concentrated away from woman to reinforce in him the male impulse towards extending the consciousness. His family was a difficult family to marry. And this because, whilst the men were physically vital, with a passion towards the female from which no moral training had restrained them, like a plant tied to a stick and diverted, they had at the same time an inherent complete contempt of the female, valuing only that which was male. So that they were strongly divided against themselves, with no external hold, such as a moral system, to grip to.

It would have been possible for Jude, monkish, passionate, medieval, belonging to woman yet striving away from her, refusing to know her, to have gone on denying one side of his nature, adhering to his idea of learning, till he had stultified the physical impulse of his being and perverted it entirely. Arabella brought him to himself, gave him himself, made him free, sound as a physical male.

That she would not, or could not, combine her life with him for the fulfilment of a purpose was their misfortune. But at any rate, his purpose of becoming an Oxford don was a cut-and-dried purpose which had no connexion with his living body, and for which probably no woman could have united with him.

No doubt Arabella hated his books, and hated his whole attitude to study. What had he, a passionate, emotional nature, to do with learning for learning's sake, with mere academics? Any woman must know it was ridiculous. But he persisted with the tenacity of all perverseness. And she, in this something of an aristocrat, like Tess, feeling that she had no right to him, no right to receive anything from him, except his sex, in which she felt she gave and did not receive, for she conceived of herself as the primary female, as that which, in taking the male, conferred on him his greatest boon, she left him alone. Her attitude was, that he would find all he desired in coming to her. She was occupied with herself. It was not that she wanted *him*. She wanted to have the sensation of herself in contact with him. His being she refused. She allowed only her own being.

Therefore she scarcely troubled him, when he earned little money and took no notice of her. He did not refuse to take notice of her because he hated her, or was deceived by her, or disappointed in her. He was not. He refused to consider her seriously because he adhered with all his pertinacity to the idea of study, from which he excluded her.

Which she saw and knew, and allowed. She would not force him to notice her, or to consider her seriously. She would compel him to nothing. She had had a certain satisfaction of him, which would be no more if she stayed for ever. For she was non-developing. When she knew him in her senses she knew the end of him, as far as she was concerned. That was all.

So she just went her way. He did not blame her. He scarcely missed her. He returned to his books.

Really, he had lost nothing by his marriage with Arabella:

neither innocence nor belief nor hope. He had indeed gained his manhood. She left him the stronger and completer.

And now he would concentrate all on his male idea, of arresting himself, of becoming himself a non-developing quality, an academic mechanism. That was his obsession. That was his craving: to have nothing to do with his own life. This was the same as Tess when she turned to Angel Clare. She wanted life merely in the secondary, outside form, in the consciousness.

It was another form of the disease, or decay of old family, which possessed Alec d'Urberville; a different form, but closely related. D'Urberville wanted to arrest all his activity in his senses. Jude Fawley wanted to arrest all his activity in his mind. Each of them wanted to become an impersonal force working automatically. Each of them wanted to deny, or escape the responsibility and trouble of living as a complete person, a full individual.

And neither was able to bring it off. Jude's real desire was, not to live in the body. He wanted to exist only in his mentality. He was as if bored, or *blasé*, in the body, just like Tess. This seems to be the result of coming of an old family, that had been long conscious, long self-conscious, specialised, separate, exhausted.

This drove him to Sue. She was his kinswoman, as d'Urberville was kinsman to Tess. She was like himself in her being and her desire. Like Jude, she wanted to live partially, in the consciousness, in the mind only. She wanted no experience in the senses, she wished only to know.

She belonged, with Tess, to the old woman-type of witch or prophetess, which adhered to the male principle, and destroyed the female. But in the true prophetess, in Cassandra, for example, the denial of the female cost a strong and almost maddening effect. But in Sue it was done before she was born.

She was born with the vital female atrophied in her: she was almost male. Her *will* was male. It was wrong for Jude to take her physically, it was a violation of her. She was not the virgin type, but the witch type, which has no sex. Why should she be forced into intercourse that was not natural to her?

It was not natural for her to have children. It is inevitable that her children die. It is not natural for Tess nor for Angel

Clare to have children, nor for Arabella nor for Alec d'Urberville. Because none of these wished to give of themselves to the
lover, none of them wished to mate: they only wanted their own
experience. For Jude alone it was natural to have children,
and this in spite of himself.

Sue wished to identify herself utterly with the male principle.
That which was female in her she wanted to consume within the
male force, to consume it in the fire of understanding, of giving
utterance. Whereas an ordinary woman knows that she
contains all understanding, that she is the unutterable which
man must for ever continue to try to utter, Sue felt that all must
be uttered, must be given to the male, that, in truth, only Male
existed, that everything was the Word, and the Word was
everything.

Sue is the production of the long selection by man of the
woman in whom the female is subordinated to the male
principle. A long line of Amelias and Agneses, those women
who submitted to the man-idea, flattered the man, and bored
him, the Gretchens and the Turgenev heroines, those who have
betrayed the female and who therefore only seem to exist to be
betrayed by their men, these have produced at length a Sue,
the pure thing. And as soon as she is produced she is execrated.

What Cassandra and Aspasia became to the Greeks, Sue has
become to the northern civilisation. But the Greeks never
pitied Woman. They did not show her that highest impertinence—not even Euripides.

But Sue is scarcely a woman at all, though she is feminine
enough. Cassandra submitted to Apollo, and gave him the
Word of affiance, brought forth prophecy to him, not children.
She received the embrace of the spirit, He breathed His Grace
upon her: and she conceived and brought forth a prophecy.
It was still a marriage. Not the marriage of the Virgin with
the Spirit, but the marriage of the female spirit with the male
spirit, bodiless.

With Sue, however, the marriage was no marriage, but a
submission, a service, a slavery. Her female spirit did not wed
with the male spirit: she could not prophesy. Her spirit
submitted to the male spirit, owned the priority of the male
spirit, wished to become the male spirit. That which was
female in her, resistant, gave her only her critical faculty.

When she sought out the physical quality in the Greeks, that was her effort to make even the unknowable physique a part of knowledge, to contain the body within the mind.

One of the supremest products of our civilisation is Sue, and a product that well frightens us. It is quite natural that, with all her mental alertness, she married Phillotson without ever considering the physical quality of marriage. Deep instinct made her avoid the consideration. And the duality of her nature made her extremely liable to self-destruction. The suppressed, atrophied female in her, like a potent fury, was always there, suggesting to her to make the fatal mistake. She contained always the rarest, most deadly anarchy in her own being.

It needed that she should have some place in society where the clarity of her mental being, which was in itself a form of death, could shine out without attracting any desire for her body. She needed a refinement on Angel Clare. For she herself was a more specialised, more highly civilised product on the female side, than Angel Clare on the male. Yet the atrophied female in her would still want the bodily male.

She attracted to herself Jude. His experience with Arabella had for the time being diverted his attention altogether from the female. His attitude was that of service to the pure male spirit. But the physical male in him, that which knew and belonged to the female, was potent, and roused the female in Sue as much as she wanted it roused, so much that it was a stimulant to her, making her mind the brighter.

It was a cruelly difficult position. She must, by the constitution of her nature, remain quite physically intact, for the female was atrophied in her, to the enlargement of the male activity. Yet she wanted some quickening for this atrophied female. She wanted even kisses. That the new rousing might give her a sense of life. But she could only *live* in the mind.

Then, where could she find a man who would be able to feed her with his male vitality, through kisses, proximity, without demanding the female return? For she was such that she could only receive quickening from a strong male, for she was herself no small thing. Could she then find a man, a strong, passionate male, who would devote himself entirely to the production of the mind in her, to the production of male activity, or of female activity critical to the male?

She could only receive the highest stimulus, which she must inevitably seek, from a man who put her in constant jeopardy. Her essentiality rested upon her remaining intact. Any suggestion of the physical was utter confusion to her. Her principle was the ultra-Christian principle—of living entirely according to the Spirit, to the One, male spirit, which knows, and utters, and shines, but exists beyond feeling, beyond joy or sorrow, or pain, exists only in Knowing. In tune with this, she was herself. Let her, however, be turned under the influence of the other dark, silent, strong principle, of the female, and she would break like a fine instrument under discord.

Yet, to live at all in tune with the male spirit, she must receive the male stimulus from a man. Otherwise she was as an instrument without a player. She must feel the hands of a man upon her, she must be infused with his male vitality, or she was not alive.

Here then was her difficulty: to find a man whose vitality could infuse her and make her live, and who would not, at the same time, demand of her a return, the return of the female impulse into him. What man could receive this drainage, receiving nothing back again? He must either die, or revolt.

One man had died. She knew it well enough. She knew her own fatality. She knew she drained the vital, male stimulus out of a man, producing in him only knowledge of the mind, only mental clarity: which man must always strive to attain, but which is not life in him, rather the product of life.

Just as Alec d'Urberville, on the other hand, drained the female vitality out of a woman, and gave her only sensation, only experience in the senses, a sense of herself, nothing to the soul or spirit, thereby exhausting her.

Now Jude, after Arabella, and following his own *idée fixe*, wanted this mental clarity, this knowing, above all. What he contained in himself, of male and female impulse, he wanted to bring forth, to draw into his mind, to resolve into understanding, as a plant resolves that which it contains into flower.

This Sue could do for him. By creating a vacuum, she could cause the vivid flow which clarified him. By rousing him, by drawing from him his turgid vitality, made thick and heavy and physical with Arabella, she could bring into consciousness that which he contained. For he was heavy and full of unrealised life, clogged with untransmuted knowledge, with accretion of his senses. His whole life had been till now an indrawing, ingestion. Arabella had been a vital experience for him, received into his blood. And how was he to bring out all this fulness into knowledge or utterance? For all the time he was being roused to new physical desire, new life-experience, new sense-enrichening, and he could not perform his male function of transmitting this into expression, or action. The particular form his flowering should take, he could not find. So he hunted and studied, to find the call, the appeal which should call out of him that which was in him.

And great was his transport when the appeal came from Sue. She wanted, at first, only his words. That of him which could come to her through speech, through his consciousness, her mind, like a bottomless gulf, cried out for. She wanted satisfaction through the mind, and cried out for him to satisfy her through the mind.

Great, then, was his joy at giving himself out to her. He gave, for it was more blessed to give than to receive. He gave, and she received some satisfaction. But where she was not satisfied, there he must try still to satisfy her. He struggled to bring it all forth. She was, as himself, asking himself what he was. And he strove to answer, in a transport.

And he answered in a great measure. He singled himself out from the old matrix of the accepted idea, he produced an individual flower of his own.

It was for this he loved Sue. She did for him quickly what he would have done for himself slowly, through study. By patient, diligent study, he would have used up the surplus of that turgid energy in him, and would, by long contact with old truth, have arrived at the form of truth which was in him. What he indeed wanted to get from study was, not a store of learning, nor the vanity of education, a sort of superiority of educational wealth, though this also gave him pleasure. He wanted, through familiarity with the true thinkers and poets, particularly with the classic and theological thinkers, because of their comparative sensuousness, to find conscious expression for that which he held in his blood. And to do this, it was necessary for him to resolve and to reduce his blood, to overcome the female sensuousness in himself, to transmute his

sensuous being into another state, a state of clarity, of consciousness. Slowly, laboriously, struggling with the Greek and
the Latin, he would have burned down his thick blood as
fuel, and have come to the true light of himself. This Sue did for him. In marriage, each party fulfils a dual
function with regard to the other: exhaustive and enrichening.
The female at the same time exhausts and invigorates the male,
the male at the same time exhausts and invigorates the female.
The exhaustion and invigoration are both temporary and
relative. The male, making the effort to penetrate into the
female, exhausts himself and invigorates her. But that which,
at the end, he discovers and carries off from her, some seed of
being, enrichens him and exhausts her. Arabella, in taking
Jude, accepted very little from him. She absorbed very little of
his strength and vitality into herself. For she only wanted to
be aware of herself in contact with him, she did not want him
to penetrate into her very being, till he moved her to her very
depths, till she loosened to him some of her very self for his
enrichening. She was intrinsically impotent, as was Alec
d'Urberville.

So that in her Jude went very little further in Knowledge, or
in Self-Knowledge. He took only the first steps: of knowing
himself sexually, as a sexual male. That is only the first, the
first necessary, but rudimentary, step.

When he came to Sue, he found her physically impotent, but
spiritually potent. That was what he wanted. Of Knowledge
in the blood he had a rich enough store: more than he knew
what to do with. He wished for the further step, of reduction,
of essentialising into Knowledge. Which Sue gave to him.

So that his experience with Arabella, plus his first experience
of trembling intimacy and incandescent realisation with Sue
made one complete marriage: that is, the two women added
together made One Bride.

When Jude had exhausted his surplus self, in spiritual
intimacy with Sue, when he had gained through her all the
wonderful understanding she could evoke in him, when he was
clarified to himself, then his marriage with Sue was over. Jude's
marriage with Sue was over before he knew her physically. She
had, physically, nothing to give him.

Which, in her deepest instinct, she knew. She made no

mistake in marrying Phillotson. She acted according to the pure logic of her nature. Phillotson was a man who wanted no marriage whatsoever with the female. Sexually, he wanted her as an instrument through which he obtained relief, and some gratification: but, really, relief. Spiritually, he wanted her as a thing to be wondered over and delighted in, but quite separately from himself. He knew quite well he could never marry her. He was a human being as near to mechanical function as a human being can be. The whole process of digestion, masticating, swallowing, digesting, excretion, is a sort of super-mechanical process. And Phillotson was like this. He was an organ, a function-fulfilling organ, he had no separate existence. He could not create a single new movement or thought or expression. Everything he did was a repetition of what had been. All his study was a study of what had been. It was a mechanical, functional process. He was a true, if small, form of the *Savant*. He could understand only the functional laws of living, but these he understood honestly. He was true to himself, he was not overcome by any cant or sentimentalising. So that in this he was splendid. But it is a cruel thing for a complete, or a spiritual, individuality to be submitted to a functional organism.

The Widow Edlin said that there are some men no woman of any feeling could touch, and Phillotson was one of them. If the Widow knew this, why was Sue's instinct so short?

But Mrs. Edlin was a full human being, creating life in a new form through her personality. She must have known Sue's deficiency. It was natural for Sue to read and to turn again to:

> Thou hast conquered, O pale Galilean!
> The world has grown grey from Thy breath.

In her the pale Galilean had indeed triumphed. Her body was as insentient as hoar-frost. She knew well enough that she was not alive in the ordinary human sense. She did not, like an ordinary woman, receive all she knew through her senses, her instincts, but through her consciousness. The pale Galilean had a pure disciple in her: in her He was fulfilled. For the senses, the body, did not exist in her; she existed as a consciousness. And this is so much so, that she was almost an

Apostate. She turned to look at Venus and Apollo. As if she could know either Venus or Apollo, save as ideas. Nor Venus nor Aphrodite had anything to do with her, but only Pallas and Christ.

She was unhappy every moment of her life, poor Sue, with the knowledge of her own non-existence within life. She felt all the time the ghastly sickness of dissolution upon her, she was as a void unto herself.

So she married Phillotson, the only man she could, in reality, marry. To him she could be a wife: she could give him the sexual relief he wanted of her, and supply him with the transcendence which was a pleasure to him; it was hers to seal him with the seal which made an honourable human being of him. For he felt, deep within himself, something a reptile feels. And she was his guarantee, his crown.

Why does a snake horrify us, or even a newt? Why was Phillotson like a newt? What is it, in our life or in our feeling, to which a newt corresponds? Is it that life has the two sides, of growth and of decay, symbolised most acutely in our bodies by the semen and the excreta? Is it that the newt, the reptile, belong to the putrescent activity of life; the bird, the fish to the growth activity? Is it that the newt and the reptile are suggested to us through those sensations connected with excretion? And was Phillotson more or less connected with the decay activity of life? Was it his function to reorganise the life-excreta of the ages? At any rate, one can honour him, for he was true to himself.

Sue married Phillotson according to her true instinct. But being almost pure Christian, in the sense of having no physical life, she had turned to the Greeks, and with her mind was an Aphrodite-worshipper. In craving for the highest form of that which she lacked, she worshipped Aphrodite. There are two sets of Aphrodite-worshippers: daughters of Aphrodite and the almost neutral daughters of Mary of Bethany. Sue was, oh, cruelly far from being a daughter of Aphrodite. She was the furthest alien from Aphrodite. She might excuse herself through her Venus Urania—but it was hopeless.

Therefore, when she left Phillotson, in whose marriage she consummated her own crucifixion, to go to Jude, she was deserting the God of her being for the God of her hopeless want.

How much could she become a living, physical woman? But she would get away from Phillotson.

She went to Jude to continue the spiritual marriage, bodiless. That was all very well, if he had been satisfied. If he had been satisfied, they might have lived in this spiritual intimacy, without physical contact, for the rest of their lives, so strong was her true instinct for herself.

He, however, was not satisfied. He reached the point where he was clarified, where he had reduced from his blood into his consciousness all that was uncompounded before. He had become himself as far as he could, he had fulfilled himself. All that he had gathered in his youth, all that he had gathered from Arabella, was assimilated now, fused and transformed into one clear Jude.

Now he wants that which is necessary for him if he is to go on. He wants, at its lowest, the physical, sexual relief. For continually baulked sexual desire, or necessity, makes a man unable to live freely, scotches him, stultifies him. And where a man is roused to the fullest pitch, as Jude was roused by Sue, then the principal connexion becomes a necessity, if only for relief. Anything else is a violation.

Sue ran away to escape physical connexion with Phillotson, only to find herself in the arms of Jude. But Jude wanted of her more than Phillotson wanted. This was what terrified her to the bottom of her nature. Whereas Phillotson always only wanted sexual relief of her, Jude wanted the consummation of marriage. He wanted that deepest experience, that penetrating far into the unknown and undiscovered which lies in the body and blood of man and woman, during life. He wanted to receive from her the quickening, the primitive seed and impulse which should start him to a new birth. And for this he must go back deep into the primal, unshown, unknown life of the blood, the thick source-stream of life in her.

And she was terrified lest he should find her out, that it was wanting in her. This was her deepest dread, to see him inevitably disappointed in her. She could not bear to be put into the balance, wherein she knew she would be found wanting.

For she knew in herself that she was cut off from the source and origin of life. For her, the way back was lost irrevocably. And when Jude came to her, wanting to retrace with her the course right back to the springs and the welling-out, she was more afraid than of death. For she could not. She was like a flower broken off from the tree, that lives a while in water, and even puts forth. So Sue lived sustained and nourished by the rarefied life of books and art, and by the inflow from the man. But, owing to centuries and centuries of weaning away from the body of life, centuries of insisting upon the supremacy and bodilessness of Love, centuries of striving to escape the conditions of being and of striving to attain the condition of Knowledge, centuries of pure Christianity, she had gone too far. She had climbed and climbed to be near the stars. And now, at last, on the topmost pinnacle, exposed to all the horrors and the magnificence of space, she could not go back. Her strength had fallen from her. Up at that great height, with scarcely any foothold, but only space, space all round her, rising up to her from beneath, she was like a thing suspended, supported almost at the point of extinction by the density of the medium. Her body was lost to her, fallen away, gone. She existed there as a point of consciousness, no more, like one swooned at a great height, held up at the tip of a fine pinnacle that drove upwards into nothingness.

Jude rose to that height with her. But he did not die as she died. Beneath him the foothold was more, he did not swoon. There came a time when he wanted to go back, down to earth. But she was fastened like Andromeda.

Perhaps, if Jude had not known Arabella, Sue might have persuaded him that he too was bodiless, only a point of consciousness. But she was too late; another had been before her and given her the lie.

Arabella was never so jealous of Sue as Sue of Arabella. How shall the saint that tips the pinnacle, Saint Simon Stylites thrust on the highest needle that pricks the heavens, be envied by the man who walks the horizontal earth? But Sue was cruelly anguished with jealousy of Arabella. It was only this, this knowledge that Jude wanted Arabella, which made Sue give him access to her own body.

When she did that, she died. The Sue that had been till then, the glimmering, pale, star-like Sue, died and was revoked on the night when Arabella called at their house at Aldbrickham, and Jude went out in his slippers to look for her, and did not find her, but came back to Sue, who in her anguish gave him then the access to her body. Till that day, Sue had been, in her will and in her very self, true to one motion, to Love, to Knowledge, to the Light, to the upward motion. Phillotson had not altered this. When she had suffered him, she had said: "He does not touch me; I am beyond him."

But now she must give her body to Jude. At that moment her light began to go out, all she had lived for and by began to turn into a falseness, Sue began to nullify herself.

She could never become physical. She could never return down to earth. But there, lying bound at the pinnacle-tip, she had to pretend she was lying on the horizontal earth, prostrate with a man.

It was a profanation and a pollution, worse than the pollution of Cassandra or of the Vestals. Sue had her own form: to break this form was to destroy her. Her destruction began only when she said to Jude, "I give in."

As for Jude, he dragged his body after his consciousness. His instinct could never have made him actually desire physical connexion with Sue. He was roused by an appeal made through his consciousness. This appeal automatically roused his senses. His consciousness desired Sue. So his senses were forced to follow his consciousness.

But he must have felt, in knowing her, the *frisson* of sacrilege, something like the Frenchman who lay with a corpse. Her body, the body of a Vestal, was swooned into that state of bloodless ecstasy wherein it was dead to the senses. Or it was the body of an insane woman, whose senses are directed from the disordered mind, whose mind is not subjected to the senses.

But Jude was physically undeveloped. Altogether he was medieval. His senses were vigorous but not delicate. He never realised what it meant to *him*, his taking Sue. He thought he was satisfied.

But if it was death to her, or profanation, or pollution, or breaking, it was unnatural to him, blasphemy. How could he, a living, loving man, warm and productive, take with his body the moonlit cold body of a woman who did not live to him, and did not want him? It was monstrous, and it sent him mad.

She knew it was wrong, she knew it should never be. But what else could she do? Jude loved her now with his will. To have left him to Arabella would have been to destroy him. To have shared him with Arabella would have been possible to Sue, but impossible to him, for he had the strong, purist idea that a man's body should follow and be subordinate to his spirit, his senses should be subordinate to and subsequent to his mind. Which idea is utterly false.

So Jude and Sue are damned, partly by their very being, but chiefly by their incapacity to accept the conditions of their own and each other's being. If Jude could have known that he did not want Sue physically, and then have made his choice, they might not have wasted their lives. But he could not know.

If he could have known, after a while, after he had taken her many times, that it was wrong, still they might have made a life. He must have known that, after taking Sue, he was depressed as she was depressed. He must have known worse than that. He must have felt the devastating sense of the unlivingness of life, things must have ceased to exist for him, when he rose from taking Sue, and he must have felt that he walked in a ghastly blank, confronted just by space, void.

But he would acknowledge nothing of what he felt. He must feel according to his idea and his will. Nevertheless, they were too truthful ever to marry. A man as real and personal as Jude cannot, from his deeper religious sense, marry a woman unless indeed he can marry her, unless with her he can find or approach the real consummation of marriage. And Sue and Jude could not lie to themselves, in their last and deepest feelings. They knew it was no marriage; they knew it was wrong, all along; they knew they were sinning against life, in forcing a physical marriage between themselves.

How many people, man and woman, live together, in England, and have children, and are never, never asked whether they have been through the marriage ceremony together? Why then should Jude and Sue have been brought to task? Only because of their own uneasy sense of wrong, of sin, which they communicated to other people. And this wrong or sin was not against the community, but against their own being, against life. Which is why they were, the pair of them, instinctively disliked.

They never knew happiness, actual, sure-footed happiness,

not for a moment. That was incompatible with Sue's nature. But what they knew was a very delightful but poignant and unhealthy condition of lightened consciousness. They reacted on each other to stimulate the consciousness. So that, when they went to the flower-show, her sense of the roses, and Jude's sense of the roses, would be most, most poignant. There is always this pathos, this poignancy, this trembling on the verge of pain and tears, in their happiness.

"Happy?" he murmured. She nodded.

The roses, how the roses glowed for them! The flowers had more being than either he or she. But as their ecstasy over things sank a little, they felt, the pair of them, as if they themselves were wanting in real body, as if they were too unsubstantial, too thin and evanescent in substance, as if the other solid people might jostle right through them, two wandering shades as they were.

This they felt themselves. Hence their uncertainty in contact with other people, hence their abnormal sensitiveness. But they had their own form of happiness, nevertheless, this trembling on the verge of ecstasy, when, the senses strongly roused to the service of the consciousness, the things they contemplated took flaming being, became flaming symbols of their own emotions to them.

So that the real marriage of Jude and Sue was in the roses. Then, in the third state, in the spirit, these two beings met upon the roses and in the roses were symbolised in consummation. The rose is the symbol of marriage-consummation in its beauty. To them it is more than a symbol, it is a fact, a flaming experience.

They went home tremblingly glad. And then the horror when, because of Jude's unsatisfaction, he must take Sue sexually. The flaming experience became a falsity, or an *ignis fatuus* leading them on.

They exhausted their lives, he in the consciousness, she in the body. She was glad to have children, to prove she was a woman. But in her it was a perversity to wish to prove she was a woman. She was no woman. And her children, the proof thereof, vanished like hoar-frost from her.

It was not the stone-masonry that exhausted him and weakened him and made him ill. It was this continuous feeding of his consciousness from his senses, this continuous state of incandescence of the consciousness, when his body, his vital tissues, the very protoplasm in him, was being slowly consumed away. For he had no life in the body. Every time he went to Sue, physically, his inner experience must have been a shock back from life and from the form of outgoing, like that of a man who lies with a corpse. He had no life in the senses: he had no inflow from the source to make up for the enormous wastage. So he gradually became exhausted, burned more and more away, till he was frail as an ember.

And she, her body also suffered. But it was in the mind that she had had her being, and it was in the mind she paid her price. She tried and tried to receive and to satisfy Jude physically. She bore him children, she gave herself to the life of the body.

But as she was formed she was formed, and there was no altering it. She needed all the life that belonged to her, and more, for the supplying of her mind, since such a mind as hers is found only, healthily, in a person of powerful vitality. For the mind, in a common person, is created out of the surplus vitality, or out of the remainder after all the sensuous life has been fulfilled.

She needed all the life that belonged to her, for her mind. It was her form. To disturb that arrangement was to make her into somebody else, not herself. Therefore, when she became a physical wife and a mother, she forswore her own being. She abjured her own mind, she denied it, took her faith, her belief, her very living away from it.

It is most probable she lived chiefly in her children. They were her guarantee as a physical woman, the being to which she now laid claim. She had forsaken the ideal of an independent mind.

She would love her children with anguish, afraid always for their safety, never certain of their stable existence, never assured of their real reality. When they were out of her sight, she would be uneasy, uneasy almost as if they did not exist. There would be a gnawing at her till they came back. She would not be satisfied till she had them crushed on her breast. And even then, she would not be sure, she would not be sure. She could not be sure, in life, of anything. She could only be sure, in the old days, of what she saw with her mind. Of that she was absolutely sure.

Meanwhile Jude became exhausted in vitality, bewildered, aimless, lost, pathetically non-productive.

Again one can see what instinct, what feeling it was which made Arabella's boy bring about the death of the children and of himself. He, sensitive, so bodiless, so selfless as to be a sort of automaton, is very badly suggested, exaggerated, but one can see what is meant. And he feels, as any child will feel, as many children feel to-day, that they are really anachronisms, accidents, fatal accidents, unreal, false notes in their mothers' lives, that, according to her, they have no being: that, if they have being, then she has not. So he takes away all the children.

And then Sue ceases to be: she strikes the line through her own existence, cancels herself. There exists no more Sue Fawley. She cancels herself. She wishes to cease to exist, as a person, she wishes to be absorbed away, so that she is no longer self-responsible.

For she denied and forsook and broke her own real form, her own independent, cool-lighted mind-life. And now her children are not only dead, but self-slain, those pledges of the physical life for which she abandoned the other.

She has a passion to expiate, to expiate, to expiate. Her children should never have been born: her instinct always knew this. Now their dead bodies drive her mad with a sense of blasphemy. And she blasphemed the Holy Spirit, which told her she is guilty of their birth and their death, of the horrible nothing which they are. She is even guilty of their little, palpitating sufferings and joys of mortal life, now made nothing. She cannot bear it—who could? And she wants to expiate, doubly expiate. Her mind, which she set up in her conceit, and then forswore, she must stamp it out of existence, as one stamps out fire. She would never again think or decide for herself. The world, the past, should have written every decision for her. The last act of her intellect was the utter renunciation of her mind and the embracing of utter ortho-doxy, where every belief, every thought, every decision was made ready for her, so that she did not exist self-responsible. And then her loathed body, which had committed the crime of bearing dead children, which had come to life only to spread nihilism like a pestilence, that too should be scourged out of existence. She chose the bitterest penalty in going back to Phillotson.

There was no more Sue. Body, soul, and spirit, she annihilated herself. All that remained of her was the will by which she annihilated herself. That remained fixed, a locked centre of self-hatred, life-hatred so utter that it had no hope of death. It knew that life is life, and there is no death for life.

Jude was too exhausted himself to save her. He says of her she was not worth a man's love. But that was not the point. It was not a question of her worth. It was a question of her being. If he had said she was not capable of receiving a man's love as he wished to bestow it, he might have spoken nearer the truth. But she practically told him this. She made it plain to him what she wanted, what she could take. But he overrode her. She tried hard to abide by her own form. But he forced her. He had no case against her, unless she made the great appeal for him, that he should flow to her, whilst at the same time she could not take him completely, body and spirit both.

She asked for what he could not give—what perhaps no man can give: passionate love without physical desire. She had no blame for him: she had no love for him. Self-love triumphed in her when she first knew him. She almost deliberately asked for more, far more, than she intended to give. Self-hatred triumphed in the end. So it had to be.

As for Jude, he had been dying slowly, but much quicker than she, since the first night she took him. It was best to get it done quickly in the end.

And this tragedy is the result of over-development of one principle of human life at the expense of the other; an over-balancing; a laying of all the stress on the Male, the Love, the Spirit, the Mind, the Consciousness; a denying, a blaspheming against the Female, the Law, the Soul, the Senses, the Feelings. But she is developed to the very extreme, she scarcely lives in the body at all. Being of the feminine gender, she is yet no woman at all, nor male; she is almost neuter. He is nearer the balance, nearer the centre, nearer the wholeness. But the whole human effort, towards pure life in the spirit, towards becoming pure Sue, drags him along; he identifies himself with this effort, destroys himself and her in his adherence to this identification.

But why, in casting off one or another form of religion, has man ceased to be religious altogether? Why will he not recognise Sue and Jude, as Cassandra was recognised long ago, and Achilles, and the Vestals, and the nuns, and the monks? Why must being be denied altogether?

Sue had a being, special and beautiful. Why must not Jude recognise it in all its speciality? Why must man be so utterly irreverent, that he approaches each being as if it were no-being? Why must it be assumed that Sue is an "ordinary" woman—as if such a thing existed? Why must she feel ashamed if she is specialised? And why must Jude, owing to the conception he is brought up in, force her to act as if she were his "ordinary" abstraction, a woman?

She was not a woman. She was Sue Bridehead, something very particular. Why was there no place for her? Cassandra had the Temple of Apollo. Why are we so foul that we have no reverence for that which we are and for that which is amongst us? If we had reverence for our life, our life would take at once religious form. But as it is, in our filthy irreverence, it remains a disgusting slough, where each one of us goes so thoroughly disguised in dirt that we are all alike and indistinguishable.

If we had reverence for what we are, our life would take real form, and Sue would have a place, as Cassandra had a place; she would have a place which does not yet exist, because we are all so vulgar, we have nothing.

*   *   *   *   *

It seems as if the history of humanity were divided into two epochs: the Epoch of the Law and the Epoch of Love. It seems as though humanity, during the time of its activity on earth, has made two great efforts: the effort to appreciate the Law and the effort to overcome the Law in Love. And in both efforts it has succeeded. It has reached and proved the Two Complementary Absolutes, the Absolute of the Father, of the Law, of Nature, and the Absolute of the Son, of Love, of Knowledge. What remains is to reconcile the two.

In the beginning, Man said: "What am I, and whence is this world around me, and why is it as it is?" Then he proceeded to explore and to personify and to deify the Natural Law, which he called Father. And having reached the point where he conceived of the Natural Law in its purity, he had finished his journey, and was arrested.

But he found that he could not remain at rest. He must still go on. Then there was to discover by what principle he must proceed further than the Law. And he received an inkling of Love. All over the world the same, the second great epoch started with the incipient conception of Love, and continued until the principle of Love was conceived in all its purity. Then man was again at an end, in a *cul-de-sac*.

The Law it is by which we exist. It was the Father, the Law-Maker, Who said: "Let there be Light": it was He Who breathed life into the handful of dust and made man. "Thus have I made man, in mine own image. I have ordered his outgoing and his incoming, and have cast the line whereby he shall walk." So said the Father. And man went out and came in according to the ordering of the Lord; he walked by the line of the Lord and did not deviate. Till the path was worn barren, and man knew all the way, and the end seemed to have drawn nigh.

Then he said: "I will leave the path. I will go out as the Lord hath not ordained, and come in when my hour is fulfilled. For it is written, a man shall eat and drink with the Lord: but I will neither eat nor drink, I will go hungry, yet I will not die. It is written, a man shall take himself a wife and beget him seed unto the glory of God. But I will not take me a wife, nor beget seed, but I will know no woman. Yet will I not die. And it is written, a man shall save his body from harm, and preserve his flesh from hurt, for he is made in the image and likeness of the Father. But I will deliver up my body to hurt, and give my flesh unto the dust, yet will I not die, but live. For man does not live by bread alone, nor by the common law of the Father. Beyond this common law, I am I. When my body is destroyed and my bones have perished, then I am I. Yes, not until my body is consumed and my bones have mingled with the dust, not until then am I whole, not until then do I live. But I die in Christ, and rise again. And when I am risen again, I live in the

spirit. Neither hunger nor cold can lay hold on me, nor desire
lay hands on me. When I am risen again, then I shall *know*.
Then I shall live in the ineffable bliss of knowledge. When the
sun goes forth in the morning, I shall know the glory of God,
who passes the sun from His left hand to His right, in the peace
of His Understanding. As the night comes in her divers
shadows, I know the peace that passeth all understanding. For
God knoweth. Neither does He Will nor Command nor desire
nor act, but exists perfect in the peace of knowledge."

If a man must live still and act in the body, then let his
action be to the recognising of the life in other bodies. Each
man is to himself the Natural Law. He can only conceive of
the Natural Law as he knows it in himself. The hardest thing
for any man to do is for him to recognise and to know that the
natural law of his neighbour is other than, and maybe even
hostile to, his own natural law, and yet is true. This hard
lesson Christ tried to instil in the doctrine of the other cheek.
Orestes could not conceive that it was the natural law of
Clytemnestra's nature that she should murder Agamemnon for
sacrificing her daughter, and for leaving herself abandoned in
the pride of her womanhood, unmated because he wanted the
pleasure of war, and for his unfaithfulness to her with other
women; Clytemnestra could not understand that Orestes
should want to kill her for fulfilling the law of her own nature.
The law of the mother's nature was other than the law of the
son's nature. This they could neither of them see: hence the
killing. This Christianity would teach them: to recognise and
to admit the law of the other person, outside and different
from the law of one's own being. It is the hardest lesson of
love. And the lesson of love learnt, there must be learned the
next lesson, of reconciliation between different, maybe hostile,
things. That is the final lesson. Christianity ends in submission,
in recognising and submitting to the law of the other person.
"Thou shalt love they enemy."

Therefore, since by the law man must act or move, let his
motion be the utterance of the God of Peace, of the perfect,
unutterable Peace of Knowledge.

And man has striven this way, to utter the Universal Peace of
God. And, striving on, he has passed beyond the limits of

utterance, and has reached once more the silence of the beginning.

After Sue, after Dostoievsky's *Idiot*, after Turner's latest pictures, after the symbolist poetry of Mallarmé and the others, after the music of Debussy, there is no further possible utterance of the peace that passeth all understanding, the peace of God which is Perfect Knowledge. There is only silence beyond this.

Just as after Plato, after Dante, after Raphael, there was no further utterance of the Absoluteness of the Law, of the Immutability of the Divine Conception.

So that, as the great pause came over Greece, and over Italy, after the Renaissance, when the Law had been uttered in its absoluteness, there comes over us now, over England and Russia and France, the pause of finality, now we have seen the purity of Knowledge, the great, white, uninterrupted Light, infinite and eternal.

But that is not the end. The two great conceptions, of Law and of Knowledge or Love, are not diverse and accidental, but complementary. They are, in a way, contradictions each of the other. But they are complementary. They are the Fixed Absolute, the Geometric Absolute, and they are the radiant Absolute, the Unthinkable Absolute of pure, free motion. They are the perfect Stability, and they are the perfect Mobility. They are the fixed condition of our being, and they are the transcendent condition of knowledge in us. They are our Soul, and our Spirit, they are our Feelings, and our Mind. They are our Body and our Brain. They are Two-in-One.

And everything that has ever been produced has been produced by the combined activity of the two, in humanity, by the combined activity of soul and spirit. When the two are acting together, then Life is produced, then Life, or Utterance, Something, is *created*. And nothing is or can be created save by combined effort of the two principles, Law and Love.

All through the medieval times, Law and Love were striving together to give the perfect expression to the Law, to arrive at the perfect conception of the Law. All through the rise of the Greek nation, to its culmination, the Law and Love were working in that nation to attain the perfect expression of the Law. They were driven by the Unknown Desire, the Holy

Spirit, the Unknown and Unexpressed. But the Holy Spirit is the Reconciler and the Originator. Him we do not know.

The greatest of all Utterance of the Law has given expression to the Law as it is in relation to Love, both ruled by the Holy Spirit. Such is the Book of Job, such Æschylus in the Trilogy, such, more or less, is Dante, such is Botticelli. Those who gave expression to the Law after these suppressed the contact, and achieved an abstraction. Plato, Raphael.

The greatest utterance of Love has given expression to Love as it is in relation to the Law: so Rembrandt, Shakespeare, Shelley, Wordsworth, Goethe, Tolstoi. But beyond these there have been Turner, who suppressed the context of the Law; also there have been Dostoievsky, Hardy, Flaubert. These have shown Love in conflict with the Law, and only Death the resultant, no Reconciliation. So that humanity does not continue for long to accept the conclusions of these writers, nor even of Euripides and Shakespeare always. These great tragic writers endure by reason of the truth of the conflict they describe, because of its completeness, Law, Love, and Reconciliation, all active. But with regard to their conclusions, they leave the soul finally unsatisfied, unbelieving.

Now the aim of man remains to recognise and seek out the Holy Spirit, the Reconciler, the Originator, He who drives the twin principles of Law and of Love across the ages.

Now it remains for us to know the Law and to know the Love, and further to seek out the Reconciliation. It is time for us to build our temples to the Holy Spirit, and to raise our altars to the Holy Ghost, the Supreme, Who is beyond us but is with us.

We know of the Law, and we know of Love, and to that little we know of each of these we have given our full expression. But have not completed one perfect utterance, not one. Small as is the circle of our knowledge, we are not able to cast it complete. In Æschylus's *Eumenides*, Apollo is foolish, Athena mechanical. In Shakespeare's *Hamlet* the conclusion is all foolish. If we had conceived each party in his proper force, if Apollo had been equally potent with the Furies and no Pallas had appeared to settle the question merely by dropping a pebble, how would Æschylus have solved his riddle? He could not work out the solution he knew must come, so he forced it.

And so it has always been, always: either a wrong conclusion, or one forced by the artist, as if he put his thumb in the scale to equalise a balance which he could not make level. Now it remains for us to seek the true balance, to give each party, Apollo and the Furies, Love and the Law, his due, and so to seek the Reconciler.

Now the principle of the Law is found strongest in Woman, and the principle of Love in Man. In every creature, the mobility, the law of change, is found exemplified in the male; the stability, the conservatism is found in the female. In woman man finds his root and establishment. In man woman finds her exfoliation and florescence. The woman grows downwards, like a root, towards the centre and the darkness and the origin. The man grows upwards, like the stalk, towards discovery and light and utterance.

Man and Woman are, roughly, the embodiment of Love and the Law: they are the two complementary parts. In the body they are most alike, in genitals they are almost one. Starting from the connexion, almost unification, of the genitals, and travelling towards the feelings and the mind, there becomes ever a greater difference and a finer distinction between the two, male and female, till at last, at the other closing in the circle, in pure utterance, the two are really one again, so that any pure utterance is a perfect unity, the two as one, united by the Holy Spirit.

We start from one side or the other, from the female side or the male, but what we want is always the perfect union of the two. That is the Law of the Holy Spirit, the law of Consummate Marriage. That every living thing seeks, individually and collectively. Every man starts with his deepest desire, a desire for consummation of marriage between himself and the female, a desire for completeness, that completeness of being which will give completeness of satisfaction and completeness of utterance. No man can as yet find perfect consummation of marriage between himself and the Bride, be the bride either Woman or an Idea, but he can approximate to it, and every generation can get a little nearer.

But it needs that a man shall first know in reverence and submit to the Natural Law of his own individual being: that he shall also know that he is but contained within the great

Natural Law, that he is but a Child of God, and no God himself: that he shall then poignantly and personally recognise that the law of another man's nature is different from the law of his own nature, that it may be even hostile to him, and yet is part of the great Law of God, to be admitted: this is the Christian action of "loving thy neighbour", and of dying to be born again: lastly, that a man shall know that between his law and the law of his neighbour there is an affinity, that all is contained in one, through the Holy Spirit.

It needs that a man shall know the natural law of his own being, then that he shall seek out the law of the female, with which to join himself as complement. He must know that he is half, and the woman is the other half: that they are two, but that they are two-in-one.

He must with reverence submit to the law of himself: and he must with suffering and joy know and submit to the law of the woman: and he must know that they two together are one within the Great Law, reconciled within the Great Peace. Out of this final knowledge shall come his supreme art. There shall be the art which recognises and utters his own law; there shall be the art which recognises his own and also the law of the woman, his neighbour, utters the glad embraces and the struggle between them, and the submission of one; there shall be the art which knows the struggle between the two conflicting laws, and knows the final reconciliation, where both are equal, two in one, complete. This is the supreme art, which yet remains to be done. Some men have attempted it, and left us the results of efforts. But it remains to be fully done.

But when the two clasp hands, a moment, male and female, clasp hands and are one, the poppy, the gay poppy flies into flower again; and when the two fling their arms about each other, the moonlight runs and clashes against the shadow; and when the two toss back their hair, all the larks break out singing; and when they kiss on the mouth, a lovely human utterance is heard again—and so it is.

PART FIVE

Continentals

[77]

Letter to LADY OTTOLINE MORRELL, June 1915
. . . I have been reading Dostoievsky's *Idiot*. I don't like
Dostoievsky. He is again like the rat, slithering along in hate,
in the shadows, and, in order to belong to the light, professing
love, all love. But his nose is sharp with hate, his running is
shadowy and rat-like, he is a will fixed and gripped like a trap.
He is not nice.

[78]

Letter to LADY OTTOLINE MORRELL, 1 Feb., 1916
. . . I send you also Petronius. He startled me at first, but I
liked him. He is a gentleman, when all is said. I have taken a
great dislike to Dostoievsky in the *Possessed*. It seems so sensational, and such a degrading of the pure mind, somehow.
It seems as though the pure mind, the true reason, which surely
is noble, were made trampled and filthy under the hoofs of
secret, perverse, undirect sensuality. Petronius is straight and
above-board. Whatever he does, he doesn't try to degrade and
dirty the pure mind in him. But Dostoievsky, mixing God and
Sadism, he is foul.

[79]

Letter to J. M. MURRY and KATHERINE MANSFIELD, 17 Feb.,
1916
. . . I've just read *The Possessed*. I find I've gone off Dostoievsky, and could write about him in very cold blood. I

didn't care for *The Possessed*: nobody was possessed enough really to interest me. They bore me, these squirming sorts of people: they teem like insects.

I'll write you some "notes" on Dostoievsky—you can translate them into your own language, if they interest you.

1. He has a fixed will, a mania to be infinite, to be God.
2. Within this will, his activity is twofold:
   (*a*) To be self-less, a pure Christian, to live in the outer whole, the social whole, the self-less whole, the universal consciousness.
   (*b*) To be a pure, absolute self, all-devouring and all-consuming.

That is the main statement about him.

His desire to achieve the sensual, all-devouring consummation comes out in Dmitri Karamazov, and Rogozhin, and, not so clearly, in Stavrogin.

His desire for the spiritual, turn-the-other-cheek consummation, comes out in the Idiot himself, in Alyosha, partly in Stavrogin.

There is the third type, which represents pure unemotional *will*: this is the third Karamazov brother, and Pyotr Stepanovitch, and the young secretary man at whose house the Idiot at first lodges—he who is going to marry the young woman— Gavril, is [that] his name?

The whole point of Dostoievsky lies in the fact of his fixed will that the individual ego, the achieved I, the conscious entity, shall be infinite, God-like, and absolved from all relation, i.e. free.

I like *The Idiot* best. The Idiot is showing the last stage of Christianity, of becoming purely self-less, of becoming disseminated out into a pure, absolved consciousness. This is the Christian ecstasy, when I become so transcendently superconscious that I am bodiless, that the universe is my consciousness. This is the little Idiot prince. It is the ecstasy of being devoured in the body, like the Christian lamb, and of transcendence in the consciousness, the spirit.

Karamazov is concerned with the last stages—not nearly so far gone—of sensuality, of unconscious experience purely within the self. I reach such a pitch of dark sensual ecstasy that I seem to be, I myself, the universal night that has swallowed everything. I become universal, the universal devouring darkness. This is Dmitri Karamazov. This was Dostoievsky's real desire, to obtain this sensual ecstasy of universality. This is why Father Zossima bowed to Dmitri—Zossima is pure Christian, self-less, universal in the social whole. Dead, he stinks.

He was sadish because his *will* was fixed on the social virtues, because he felt himself *wrong* in his sensual seekings. Therefore he was cruel, he tortured himself and others, and *goûtait* the tortures.

The Christian ecstasy leads to imbecility (*The Idiot*). The sensual ecstasy leads to universal murder: for mind, the acme of sensual ecstasy, lies in *devouring* the other, even in the pleasures of love; it is a devouring, like a tiger drinking blood. But the full sensual ecstasy is never reached except by Rogozhin in murdering Nastasya. It is nipped in the last stages by the *will*, the social will. When the police stripped Dmitri Karamazov naked, they killed in him the quick of his being, his lust for the sensual ecstasy.

The men who represent the will, the pure mental, social, rational, absolved will, Ivan Karamazov, and Pyotr Stepanovitch, and Gavril, they represent the last stages of our social development, the human being become mechanical, absolved from all relation. When Stepan talks with the devil, the devil is a decayed *social* gentleman—only that. The mechanical social forms and aspirations and ideals, I suppose, are the devil.

The women are not important. They are the mere echoes and objectives of the men. They *desire* the sensual ecstasy, all of them, even the cripple in *The Possessed* ("My hawk, my eagle," she says to Stavrogin). They have the opposite wild love for purity, selflessness, extreme Christianity. And they are *all* ultimately bound to the social convention—all the "great" women, that is. The cripple in *The Possessed*, and Nastasya Filipovna, and Dmitri Karamazov's woman, these desire only the sensual ecstasy: but all the while they *admit* themselves the inferior of the other Christian ecstasy: which is the social ecstasy.

They are great parables, the novels, but false art. They are only parables. All the people are *fallen angels*—even the dirtiest scrubs. This I cannot stomach. People are not fallen angels, they are merely people. But Dostoievsky used them all

as theological or religious units, they are all terms of divinity,
like Christ's "Sower went forth to sow", and Bunyan's *Pilgrim's
Progress*. They are bad art, false truth.

[8]

Letter to J. M. MURRY, 28 Aug., 1916

Thank you very much for your book on Dostoievsky, which
has just come. I have only just looked in it here and there—and
read the epilogue. I wonder how much you or anybody else is
ready to face out the old life, and so transcend it. An epoch of
the human mind may have come to the end in Dostoievsky: but
humanity is capable of going on a very long way further yet, in
a state of mindlessness—curse it. And you've got the cart
before the horse. It isn't the being that must follow the mind,
but the mind must follow the being. And if only the cursed
cowardly world had the courage to follow its own being with its
mind, if it only had the courage to know what its unknown *is*,
its own desires and its own activities, it might get beyond to the
new secret. But the trick is, when you draw somewhere near
the "brink of the revelation", to dig your head in the sand like
the disgusting ostrich, and see the revelation there. Meanwhile,
with their head in the sand of pleasing visions and secrets and
revelations, they kick and squirm with their behinds, most
disgustingly. I don't blame humanity for having no mind, I
blame it for putting its mind in a box and using it as a nice little
self-gratifying instrument. You've got to know, and know
everything, before you "transcend" into the "unknown". But
Dostoievsky, like the rest, can nicely stick his head between the
feet of Christ, and waggle his behind in the air. And though
the behind-wagglings are a revelation, I don't think much even
of the feet of Christ as a bluff for the cowards to hide their eyes
against.

[81]

THE GRAND INQUISITOR

By F. M. Dostoievsky

It is a strange experience, to examine one's reaction to a book over a period of years. I remember when I first read *The Brothers Karamazov*, in 1913, how fascinated yet unconvinced it left me. And I remember Middleton Murry* saying to me: "Of course the whole clue to Dostoievsky is in that Grand Inquisitor story." And I remember saying: "Why? It seems to me just rubbish."

And it was true. The story seemed to me just a piece of showing off: a display of cynical-satanical pose which was simply irritating. The cynical-satanical pose always irritated me, and I could see nothing else in that black-a-vised Grand Inquisitor talking at Jesus at such length. I just felt it was all pose; he didn't really mean what he said; he was just showing off in blasphemy.

Since then I have read *The Brothers Karamazov* twice, and each time found it more depressing because, alas, more drearily true to life. At first it had been lurid romance. Now I read *The Grand Inquisitor* once more, and my heart sinks right through my shoes. I still see a trifle of cynical-satanical showing off. But under that I hear the final and unanswerable criticism of Christ. And it is a deadly, devastating summing up, unanswerable because borne out by the long experience of humanity. It is reality versus illusion, and the illusion was Jesus', while time itself retorts with the reality.

If there is any question: Who is the grand Inquisitor?—then surely we must say it is Ivan himself. And Ivan is the thinking mind of the human being in rebellion, thinking the whole thing out to the bitter end. As such he is, of course, identical with the Russian revolutionary of the thinking type. He is also, of course, Dostoievsky himself, in his thoughtful, as apart from

* Before this preface was published in *The Grand Inquisitor* the name of Katherine Mansfield was substituted for that of Middleton Murry.

his passional and inspirational self. Dostoievsky half hated Ivan. Yet, after all, Ivan is the greatest of the three brothers, pivotal. The passionate Dmitri and the inspired Alyosha are, at last, only offsets to Ivan.

And we cannot doubt that the Inquisitor speaks Dostoievsky's own final opinion about Jesus. The opinion is, baldly, this: Jesus, you are inadequate. Men must correct you. And Jesus in the end gives the kiss of acquiescence to the Inquisitor, as Alyosha does to Ivan. The two inspired ones recognise the inadequacy of their inspiration: the thoughtful one has to accept the responsibility of a complete adjustment.

We may agree with Dostoievsky or not, but we have to admit that his criticism of Jesus is the final criticism, based on the experience of two thousand years (he says fifteen hundred) and on a profound insight into the nature of mankind. Man can but be true to his own nature. No inspiration whatsoever will ever get him permanently beyond his limits.

And what are the limits? It is Dostoievsky's first profound question. What are the limits to the nature, not of Man in the abstract, but of men, mere men, everyday men?

The limits are, says the Grand Inquisitor, three. Mankind in the bulk can never be "free", because man on the whole makes three grand demands on life, and cannot endure unless these demands are satisfied.

1. He demands bread, and not merely as foodstuff, but as a miracle, given from the hand of God.
2. He demands mystery, the sense of the miraculous in life.
3. He demands somebody to bow down to, and somebody before whom all men shall bow down.

These three demands, for miracle, mystery and authority, prevent men from being "free". They are man's "weakness". Only a few men, the elect, are capable of abstaining from the absolute demand for bread, for miracle, mystery, and authority. These are the strong, and they must be as gods, to be able to be Christians fulfilling all the Christ-demand. The rest, the millions and millions of men throughout time, they are as babes or children or geese, they are too weak, "impotent, vicious, worthless and rebellious" even to be able to share out the earthly bread, if it is left to them.

This, then, is the Grand Inquisitor's summing up of the

nature of mankind. The inadequacy of Jesus lies in the fact that Christianity is too difficult for men, the vast mass of men. It could only be realised by the few "saints" or heroes. For the rest, man is like a horse harnessed to a load he cannot possibly pull. "Hadst Thou respected him less, Thou wouldst have demanded less of him, and that would be nearer to love, for his burden would be lighter."

Christianity, then, is the ideal, but it is impossible. It is impossible because it makes demands greater than the nature of man can bear. And therefore, to get a livable, working scheme, some of the elect, such as the Grand Inquisitor himself, have turned round to "him", that other great Spirit, Satan, and have established Church and State on "him". For the Grand Inquisitor finds that to be able to live at all, mankind must be loved more tolerantly and more contemptuously than Jesus loved it, loved, for all that, more truly, since it is loved for itself, for what it is, and not for what it ought to be. Jesus loved mankind for what it ought to be, free and limitless. The Grand Inquisitor loves it for what it is, with all its limitations. And he contends his is the kinder love. And yet he says it is Satan. And Satan, he says at the beginning, means annihilation, and not-being.

As always in Dostoievsky, the amazing perspicacity is mixed with ugly perversity. Nothing is pure. His wild love for Jesus is mixed with perverse and poisonous hate of Jesus: his moral hostility to the devil is mixed with secret worship of the devil. Dostoievsky is always perverse, always impure, always an evil thinker and a marvellous seer.

Is it true that mankind demands, and will always demand, miracle, mystery, and authority? Surely it is true. To-day, man gets his sense of the miraculous from science and machinery, radio, aeroplanes, vast ships, zeppelins, poison gas, artificial silk: these things nourish man's sense of the miraculous as magic did in the past. But now, man is master of the mystery, there are no occult powers. The same with mystery: medicine, biological experiment, strange feats of the psychic people, spiritualists, Christian scientists—it is all mystery. And as for authority, Russia destroyed the Tsar to have Lenin and the present mechanical despotism, Italy has the rationalised despotism of Mussolini, and England is longing for a despot.

Dostoievsky's diagnosis of human nature is simple and unanswerable. We have to submit, and agree that men are like that. Even over the question of sharing the bread, we have to agree that man is too weak, or vicious, or something, to be able to do it. He has to hand the common bread over to some absolute authority, Tsar or Lenin, to be shared out. And yet the mass of men are *incapable* of looking on bread as a mere means of sustenance, by which man sustains himself for the purpose of true living, true life being the "heavenly bread". It seems a strange thing that men, the mass of men, cannot understand that *life* is the great reality, that true living fills us with vivid life, "the heavenly bread," and earthly bread merely supports this. No, men cannot understand, never have understood that simple fact. They cannot see the distinction between bread, or property, money, and vivid life. They think that property and money are the same thing as vivid life. Only the few, the potential heroes or the "elect", can see the simple distinction. The mass *cannot* see it, and will never see it.

Dostoievsky was perhaps the first to realise this devastating truth, which Christ had not seen. A truth it is, none the less, and once recognised it will change the course of history. All that remains is for the elect to take charge of the bread—the property, the money—and then give it back to the masses as if it were really the gift of life. In this way, mankind might live happily, as the Inquisitor suggests. Otherwise, with the masses making the terrible mad mistake that money is life, and that therefore no one shall control the money, men shall be "free" to get what they can, we are brought to a condition of competitive insanity and ultimate suicide.

So far, well and good, Dostoievsky's diagnosis stands. But is it then to betray Christ and turn over to Satan if the elect should at last realise that instead of refusing Satan's three offers, the heroic Christian must now accept them? Jesus refused the three offers out of pride and fear: he wanted to be greater than these, and "above" them. But we now realise, no man, not even Jesus, is really "above" miracle, mystery, and authority. The one thing that Jesus is truly above, is the confusion between money and life. Money is not life, says Jesus, therefore you can ignore it and leave it to the devil.

Money is not life, it is true. But ignoring money and leaving it to the devil means handing over the great mass of men to the devil, for the mass of men *cannot* distinguish between money and life. It is hard to believe: certainly Jesus didn't believe it: and yet, as Dostoievsky and the Inquisitor point out, it is so.

Well, and what then? Must we therefore go over to the devil? After all, the whole of Christianity is not contained in the rejection of the three temptations. The essence of Christianity is a love of mankind. If a love of mankind entails accepting the bitter limitation of the mass of men, their inability to distinguish between money and life, then accept the limitation, and have done with it. Then take over from the devil the money (or bread), the miracle, and the sword of Cæsar, and, for the love of mankind, give back to men the bread, with its wonder, and give them the miracle, the marvellous, and give them, in a hierarchy, someone, some men, in higher and higher degrees, to bow down to. Let them bow down, let them bow down *en masse*, for the mass, who do not understand the difference between money and life, should always bow down to the elect, who do.

And is that serving the devil? It is certainly not serving the spirit of annihilation and not-being. It is serving the great wholeness of mankind, and in that respect, it is Christianity. Anyhow, it is the service of Almighty God, who made men what they are, limited and unlimited.

Where Dostoievsky is perverse is in his making the old, old, wise governor of men a Grand Inquisitor. The recognition of the weakness of man has been a common trait in all great, wise rulers of people, from the Pharaohs and Darius through the great patient Popes of the early Church right down to the present day. They have known the weakness of men, and felt a certain tenderness. This is the spirit of all great government. But it was not the spirit of the Spanish Inquisition. The Spanish Inquisition in 1500 was a newfangled thing, peculiar to Spain, with her curious death-lust and her bullying, and, strictly, a Spanish-political instrument, not Catholic at all, but rabidly national. The Spanish Inquisition actually was diabolic. It could not have produced a Grand Inquisitor who put Dostoeivsky's sad questions to Jesus. And the man who put those sad questions to Jesus could not possibly have been a Spanish Inquisitor. He could not possibly have burnt a hundred people in an *auto-da-fé*. He would have been too wise and far-seeing.

So that, in this respect, Dostoievsky showed his epileptic and slightly criminal perversity. The man who feels a certain tenderness for mankind in its weakness or limitation is not therefore diabolic. The man who realises that Jesus asked too much of the mass of men, in asking them to choose between earthly and heavenly bread, and to judge between good and evil, is not therefore satanic. Think how difficult it is to know the difference between good and evil! Why, sometimes it is evil to be good. And how is the ordinary man to understand that? He can't. The extraordinary men have to understand it for him. And is that going over to the devil? Or think of the difficulty in choosing between the earthly and heavenly bread. Lenin, surely a pure soul, rose to great power simply to give men—what? The earthly bread. And what was the result? Not only did they lose the heavenly bread, but even the earthly bread disappeared out of wheat-producing Russia. It is most strange. And all the socialists and the generous thinkers of to-day, what are they striving for? The same: to share out more evenly the earthly bread. Even *they*, who are practising Christianity *par excellence*, cannot properly choose between the heavenly and earthly bread. For the poor, they choose the earthly bread, and once more the heavenly bread is lost: and once more, as soon as it is really chosen, the earthly bread begins to disappear. It is a great mystery. But to-day, the most passionate believers in Christ believe that all you have to do is to struggle to give earthly bread (good houses, good sanitation, etc.) to the poor, and that is in itself the heavenly bread. But it isn't. Especially for the poor, it isn't. It is for them the loss of heavenly bread. And the poor are the vast majority. Poor things, how everybody hates them to-day! For benevolence is a form of hate.

What then is the heavenly bread? Every generation must answer for itself. But the heavenly bread is life, is living. Whatever makes life vivid and delightful is the heavenly bread. And the earthly bread must come as a by-product of the heavenly bread. The vast mass will never understand this. Yet it is the essential truth of Christianity, and of life itself. The few will understand. Let them take the responsibility.

Again, the Inquisitor says that it is a weakness in men, that they must have miracle, mystery and authority. But is it? Are they not bound up in our emotions, always and for ever, these three demands of miracle, mystery, and authority? If Jesus cast aside miracle in the Temptation, still there is miracle again in the Gospels. And if Jesus refused the earthly bread, still he said: "In my Father's house are many mansions." And for authority: "Why call ye me Lord, Lord, and do not the things which I say?"

The thing Jesus was trying to do was to supplant physical emotion by moral emotion. So that earthly bread becomes, in a sense, immoral, as it is to many refined people to-day. The Inquisitor sees that this is the mistake. The earthly bread must in itself be the miracle, and be bound up with the miracle.

And here, surely, he is right. Since man began to think and to feel vividly, seed-time and harvest have been the two great sacred periods of miracle, rebirth, and rejoicing. Easter and harvest-home are festivals of the earthly bread, and they are festivals which go to the roots of the soul. For it is the earthly bread as a miracle, a yearly miracle. All the old religions saw it: the Catholic still sees it, by the Mediterranean. And this is not weakness. This is *truth*. The rapture of the Easter kiss, in old Russia, is intimately bound up with the springing of the seed and the first footstep of the new earthly bread. It is the rapture of the Easter kiss which makes the bread worth eating. It is the absence of the Easter kiss which makes the Bolshevist bread barren, dead. They eat dead bread, now.

The earthly bread is leavened with the heavenly bread. The heavenly bread is life, is contact, and is consciousness. In sowing the seed man has his contact with earth, with sun and rain: and he *must not* break the contact. In the awareness of the springing of the corn he has his ever-renewed consciousness of miracle, wonder, and mystery: the wonder of creation, pro-creation, and re-creation, following the mystery of death and the cold grave. It is the grief of Holy Week and the delight of Easter Sunday. And man must not, must not lose this supreme state of consciousness out of himself, or he has lost the best part of him. Again, the reaping and the harvest are another contact, with earth and sun, a rich touch of the cosmos, a living stream of activity, and then the contact with harvesters, and the joy of harvest-home. All this is life, life, it is the heavenly bread which we eat in the course of getting the earthly bread. Work is, or should be, our heavenly bread of activity, contact and consciousness. All work that it not this, is anathema. True, the work is hard; there is the sweat of the brow. But what of it? In decent proportion, this is life. The sweat of the brow is the heavenly butter.

I think the older Egyptians understood this, in the course of their long and marvellous history. I think that probably, for thousands of years, the masses of the Egyptians were happy, in the hierarchy of the State.

Miracle and mystery run together, they merge. Then there is the third thing, authority. The word is bad: a policeman has authority, and no one bows down to him. The Inquisitor means: "that which men bow down to". Well, they bowed down to Cæsar, and they bowed down to Jesus. They will bow down, first, as the Inquisitor saw, to the one who has the power to control the bread.

The bread, the earthly bread, while it is being reaped and grown, it is life. But once it is harvested and stored, it becomes a commodity, it becomes riches. And then it becomes a danger. For men think, if they only possessed the hoard, they need not work; which means, really, they need not live. And that is the real blasphemy. For while we live we must live, we must not wither or rot inert.

So that ultimately men bow down to the man, or group of men, who can and dare take over the hoard, the store of bread, the riches, to distribute it among the people again. The lords, the givers of bread. How profound Dostoievsky is when he says that the people will forget that it is their own bread which is being given back to them. While they keep their own bread, it is not much better than stone to them—inert possessions. But given back to them from the great Giver, it is divine once more, it has the quality of miracle to make it taste well in the mouth and in the belly.

Men bow down to the lord of bread, first and foremost. For, by knowing the difference between earthly and heavenly bread, he is able calmly to distribute the earthly bread, and to give it, for the commonalty, the heavenly taste which they can never give it. That is why, in a democracy, the earthly bread loses its taste,

the salt loses its savour, and there is no one to bow down to.
It is not man's weakness that he needs someone to bow down
to. It is his nature, and his strength, for it puts him into touch
with far, far greater life than if he stood alone. All life bows
to the sun. But the sun is very far away to the common man.
It needs someone to bring it to him. It needs a lord: what the
Christians call one of the elect, to bring the sun to the common
man, and put the sun in his heart. The sight of a true lord, a
noble, a nature-hero puts the sun into the heart of the ordinary
man, who is no hero, and therefore cannot know the sun direct.

This is one of the real mysteries. As the Inquisitor says, the
mystery of the elect is one of the inexplicable mysteries of
Christianity, just as the lord, the natural lord among men, is
one of the inexplicable mysteries of humanity throughout time.
We must accept the mystery, that's all.

But to do so is not diabolic.

And Ivan need not have been so tragic and satanic. He had
made a discovery about men, which was due to be made. It
was the rediscovery of a fact which was known universally
almost till the end of the eighteenth century, when the illusion
of the perfectibility of men, of all men, took hold of the
imagination of the civilised nations. It was an illusion. And
Ivan has to make a restatement of the old truth, that most men
cannot choose between good and evil, because it is so extremely
difficult to know which is which, especially in crucial cases:
and that most men *cannot* see the difference between life-values
and money-values: they can only see money-values; even nice
simple people who *live* by the life-values, kind and natural,
yet can only estimate value in terms of money. So let the
specially gifted few make the decision between good and evil,
and establish the life-values against the money-values. And
let the many accept the decision, with gratitude, and bow down
to the few, in the hierarchy. What is there diabolical or satanic
in that? Jesus kisses the Inquisitor: Thank you, you are right,
wise old man! Alyosha kisses Ivan: Thank you, brother, you
are right, you take a burden off me! So why should Dostoievsky
drag in Inquisitors and *autos-da-fé*, and Ivan wind up so morbidly suicidal? Let them be glad they've found the truth again.

[Preface to *The Grand Inquisitor*, translated by S. S. Koteliansky, London,
1930.]

[82]

Letter to CATHERINE CARSWELL, 2 Dec., 1916
. . . Oh, don't think I would belittle the Russians. They
have meant an enormous amount to me; Turgenev, Tolstoi,
Dostoievsky—mattered almost more than anything, and I
thought them the greatest writers of all time. And now, with
something of a shock, I realise a certain crudity and thick,
uncivilised, insensitive stupidity about them, I realise how
much finer and purer and more ultimate our own stuff is.

[83]

Letter to RHYS DAVIES, 25 Dec., 1928
. . . Tell your man Tchekhov is a second-rate writer and a
willy wet-leg.

[84]

ALL THINGS ARE POSSIBLE

BY LEO SHESTOV

IN his paragraph on The Russian Spirit, Shestov gives us the
real clue to Russian literature. European culture is a rootless
thing in the Russians. With us, it is our very blood and bones,
the very nerve and root of our psyche. We think in a certain
fashion, we feel in a certain fashion, because our whole substance is of this fashion. Our speech and feeling are organically
inevitable to us.

With the Russians it is different. They have only been
inoculated with the virus of European culture and ethic. The
virus works in them like a disease. And the inflammation and
irritation comes forth as literature. The bubbling and fizzing
is almost chemical, not organic. It is an organism seething as

it accepts and masters the strange virus. What the Russian is struggling with, crying out against, is not life itself: it is only European culture which has been introduced into his psyche, and which hurts him. The tragedy is not so much a real soul tragedy, as a surgical one. Russian art, Russian literature after all does not stand on the same footing as European and Greek or Egyptian art. It is not spontaneous utterance. It is not the flowering of a race. It is a surgical outcry, horrifying, or marvellous, lacerating at first; but when we get used to it, not really so profound, not really ultimate, a little extraneous.

What is valuable is the evidence against European culture, implied in the novelists, here at last expressed. Since Peter the Great Russia has been accepting Europe, and seething Europe down in a curious process of catabolism. Russia has been expressing nothing inherently Russian. Russia's modern Christianity even was not Russian. Her genuine Christianity, Byzantine and Asiatic, is incomprehensible to us. So with her true philosophy. What she has actually uttered is her own unwilling, fantastic reproduction of European truths. What she has really to utter the coming centuries will hear. For Russia will certainly inherit the future. What we already call the greatness of Russia is only her pre-natal struggling.

It seems as if she had at last absorbed and overcome the virus of old Europe. Soon her new, healthy body will begin to act in its own reality, imitative no more, protesting no more, crying no more, but full and sound and lusty in itself. Real Russia is born. She will laugh at us before long. Meanwhile she goes through the last stages of reaction against us, kicking away from the old womb of Europe.

In Shestov one of the last kicks is given. True, he seems to be only reactionary and destructive. But he can find a little amusement at last in tweaking the European nose, so he is fairly free. European idealism is anathema. But more than this, it is a little comical. We feel the new independence in his new, half-amused indifference.

He is only tweaking the nose of European idealism. He is preaching nothing: so he protests time and again. He absolutely refutes any imputation of a central idea. He is so afraid lest it should turn out to be another hateful hedge-stake of an ideal.

"Everything is possible"—this is his really central cry. It is not nihilism. It is only a shaking free of the human psyche from old bonds. The positive central idea is that the human psyche, or soul, really believes in itself, and in nothing else.

Dress this up in a little comely language, and we have a real ideal, that will last us for a new, long epoch. The human soul itself is the source and well-head of creative activity. In the unconscious human soul the creative prompting issues first into the universe. Open the consciousness to this prompting, away with all your old sluice-gates, locks, dams, channels. No ideal on earth is anything more than an obstruction, in the end, to the creative issue of the spontaneous soul. Away with all ideals. Let each individual act spontaneously from the for ever incalculable prompting of the creative well-head within him. There is no universal law. Each being is, at his purest, a law unto himself, single, unique, a Godhead, a fountain from the unknown.

This is the ideal which Shestov refuses positively to state, because he is afraid it may prove in the end a trap to catch his own spirit. So it may. But it is none the less a real, living ideal for the moment, the very salvation. When it becomes ancient, and like the old lion who lay in his cave and whined, devours all its servants, then it can be dispatched. Meanwhile it is a really liberating word.

Shestov's style is puzzling at first. Having found the "ands" and "buts" and "becauses" and "therefores" hampered him, he clips them all off deliberately and even spitefully, so that his thought is like a man with no buttons on his clothes, ludicrously hitching along all undone. One must be amused, not irritated. Where the armholes were a bit tight, Shestov cuts a slit. It is baffling, but really rather piquant. The real conjunction, the real unification lies in the reader's own amusement, not in the author's unbroken logic.

[Preface to *All Things are Possible*, translated by S. S. Koteliansky, London, 1920.]

[85]

SOLITARIA

By V. V. Rozanov

We are told on the wrapper of this book that Prince Mirsky
considered Rozanov "one of the greatest Russians of modern
times . . . Rozanov is the greatest revelation of the Russian
mind yet to be shown to the West."

We become diffident, confronted with these superlatives.
And when we have read E. Gollerbach's long "Critico-Biographical Study", forty-three pages, we are suspicious still, in
spite of the occasionally profound and striking quotations from
Solitaria and from the same author's *Fallen Leaves*. But there we
are; we've got another of these morbidly introspective Russians,
morbidly wallowing in adoration of Jesus, then getting up and
spitting in His beard, or in His back hair, at least; characters
such as Dostoievsky has familiarised us with, and of whom we
are tired. Of these self-divided, *gamin*-religious Russians who
are so absorbedly concerned with their own dirty linen and
their own piebald souls we have had a little more than enough.
The contradictions in them are not so very mysterious, or
edifying, after all. They have a spurting, *gamin* hatred of
civilisation, of Europe, of Christianity, of governments, and of
everything else, in their moments of energy; and in their
inevitable relapses into weakness, they make the inevitable
recantation; they whine, they humiliate themselves, they seek
unspeakable humiliation for themselves, and call it Christ-like,
and then with the left hand commit some dirty little crime or
meanness, and call it the mysterious complexity of the human
soul. It's all masturbation, half-baked, and one gets tired of it.
One gets tired of being told that Dostoievsky's *Legend of the
Grand Inquisitor* "is the most profound declaration which ever
was made about man and life". As far as I'm concerned, in
proportion as a man gets more profoundly and personally
interested in himself, so does my interest in him wane. The
more Dostoievsky gets worked up about the tragic nature of

the human soul, the more I lose interest. I have read the *Grand Inquisitor* three times, and never can remember what it's really about. This I make as a confession, not as a vaunt. It always seems to me, as the Germans say, *mehr Schrei wie Wert.*

And in Rozanov one fears one has got a pup out of the Dostoievsky kennel. *Solitaria* is a sort of philosophical work, about a hundred pages, of a kind not uncommon in Russia, consisting in fragmentary jottings of thoughts which occurred to the author, mostly during the years 1910 and 1911, apparently, and scribbled down where they came, in a cab, in the train, in the w.c., on the sole of a bathing-slipper. But the thought that came in a cab might just as well have come in the w.c. or "examining my coins", so what's the odds? If Rozanov wanted to give the physical context to the thought, he'd have to create the scene. "In a cab," or "examining my coins" means nothing.

Then we get a whole lot of bits, some of them interesting, some not; many of them to be classified under the heading of: To Jesus or not to Jesus! if we may profanely parody Hamlet's To be or not to be. But it is the Russian's own parody. Then you get a lot of self-conscious personal bits: "The only *masculine* thing about you—is your trousers": which was said to Rozanov by a girl; though, as it isn't particularly true, there was no point in his repeating it. However, he has that "self-probing" nature we have become acquainted with. "Teaching is form, and I am formless. In teaching there must be order and a system, and I am systemless and even disorderly. There is duty—and to me any duty at the bottom of my heart always seemed comical, and on any duty, at the bottom of my heart, I always wanted to play a trick (except tragic duty). . . ."

Here we have the pup of the Dostoievsky kennel, a so-called nihilist: in reality, a Mary-Mary-quite-contrary. It is largely tiresome contrariness, even if it is spontaneous and not self-induced.

And, of course, in Mary-Mary-quite-contrary we have the ever-recurrent whimper: *I* want to be good! I *am* good: Oh, I am *so* good, I'm better than anybody! I love Jesus and all the saints, and above all, the blessed Virgin! Oh, how I love purity!—and so forth. Then they give a loud *crepitus ventris* as a punctuation.

Dostoievsky has accustomed us to it, and we are hard-boiled. Poor Voltaire, if he recanted, he only recanted once, when his strength had left him, and he was neither here nor there. But these Russians are for ever on their death-beds, and neither here nor there.

Rozanov's talk about "lovely faces and dear souls" of children, and "for two years I have been 'in Easter', in the pealing of bells", truly "arrayed in white raiment", just makes me feel more hard-boiled than ever. It's a cold egg.

Yet, in *Solitaria* there are occasional profound things. "I am not such a scoundrel yet as to think about morals"—"Try to crucify the Sun, and you will see which is God"—and many others. But to me, self-conscious personal revelations, touched with the guttersnipe and the actor, are not very interesting. One has lived too long.

So that I come to the end of Gollerbach's "Critico-Biographical Study" sick of the self-fingering sort of sloppiness, and I have very much the same feeling at the end of *Solitaria*, though occasionally Rozanov hits the nail on the head and makes it jump.

Then come twenty pages extracted from Rozanov's *The Apocalypse of Our Times*, and at once the style changes, at once you have a real thing to deal with. The *Apocalypse* must be a far more important book than *Solitaria*, and we wish to heaven we had been given it instead. Now at last we see Rozanov as a real thinker, and "the greatest revelation of the Russian mind yet to be shown to the West".

Rozanov had a real man in him, and it is true, what he says of himself, that he did not feel in himself that touch of the criminal which Dostoievsky felt in *himself*. Rozanov was not a criminal. Somewhere, he was integral, and grave, and a seer, a true one, not a *gamin*. We see it all in his *Apocalypse*. He is not really a Dostoievskian. That's only his Russianitis.

The book is an attack on Christianity, and as far as we are given to see there is no canting or recanting in it. It is passionate, and suddenly valid. It is not jibing or criticism or pulling to pieces. It is a real passion. Rozanov has more or less recovered the genuine pagan vision, the phallic vision, and with those eyes he looks, in amazement and consternation, on the mess of Christianity.

For the first time we get what we have got from no Russian, neither Tolstoi nor Dostoievsky nor any of them, a real, positive view on life. It is as if the pagan Russian had wakened up in Rozanov, a kind of Rip van Winkle, and was just staggering at what he saw. His background is the vast old pagan background, the phallic. And in front of this, the tortured complexity of Christian civilisation—what else can we call it?—is a kind of phantasmagoria to him.

He is the first Russian, as far as I am concerned, who has ever said anything to me. And his vision is full of passion, vivid, valid. He is the first to see that immortality is in the vividness of life, not in the loss of life. The butterfly becomes a whole revelation to him: and to us.

When Rozanov is wholly awake, and a new man, a risen man, the living and resurrected pagan, then he is a great man and a great seer, and perhaps, as he says himself, the first Russian to emerge. Speaking of Tolstoi and Leontiev and Dostoievsky, Rozanov says: "I speak straight out what they dared not even suspect. I speak because after all I am more of a thinker than they. That is all." . . . "But the problem (in the case of Leontiev and Dostoievsky) is and was about anti-Christianity, about the victory over the very essence of Christianity, over that terrible avitalism. Whereas from him, from the phallus everything flows."

When Rozanov is in this mood, and in this vision, he is not dual, nor divided against himself. He is one complete thing. His vision and his passion are positive, non-tragical.

Then again he starts to Russianise, and he comes in two. When he becomes aware of himself, and personal, he is often ridiculous, sometimes pathetic, sometimes a bore, and almost always "dual". Oh, how they love to be dual, and divided against themselves, these Dostoievskian Russians! It is as good as a pose: always a Mary-Mary-quite-contrary business. "The great horror of the human soul consists in this, that while thinking of the Madonna it at the same times does not cease thinking of Sodom and of its sins; and the still greater horror is that even in the very midst of Sodom it does not forget the Madonna, it yearns for Sodom and the Madonna, and this at one and the same time, without any discord."

The answer to that is, that Sodom and Madonna-ism are

two halves of the same movement, the mere tick-tack of lust and asceticism, pietism and pornography. If you're not pious, you won't be pornographical, and *vice versa*. If there are no saints, there'll be no sinners. If there were no ascetics, there'd be no lewd people. If you divide the human psyche into two halves, one half will be white, the other black. It's the division itself which is pernicious. The swing to one extreme causes the swing to the other. The swing towards Immaculate Madonnaism inevitably causes the swing back to the whore of prostitution, then back again to the Madonna, and so *ad infinitum*. But you can't blame the soul for this. All you have to blame is the craven, cretin human intelligence, which is always seeking to get away from its own centre.

But Rozanov, when he isn't Russianising, is the first Russian really to see it, and to recover, if unstably, the old human wholeness.

So that this book is extremely interesting, and really important. We get impatient with the Russianising. And yet, with Gollerbach's Introduction and the letters at the end, we do get to know all we want to know about Rozanov, personally. It is not of vast importance, what he was personally. If he behaved perversely, he was never, like Dostoievsky, inwardly perverse, and when he says he was not "born rightly", he is only yelping like a Dostoievsky pup.

It is the voice of the new man in him, not the Dostoievsky whelp, that means something. And it means a great deal. We shall wait for a full translation of *The Apocalypse of Our Times*, and of *Oriental Motifs*. Rozanov matters, for the future.

[Review in *Calendar of Modern Letters*, July 1927.]

[86]

FALLEN LEAVES

By V. V. Rozanov

Rozanov is now acquiring something of a European reputation. There is a translation in French, and one promised in

German, and the advanced young writers in Paris and Berlin talk of him as one of the true lights. Perhaps *Solitaria* is more popular than *Fallen Leaves*: but then, perhaps it is a little more sensational: *Fallen Leaves* is not sensational: it is on the whole quiet and sad, and truly Russian.

The book was written, apparently, round about 1912: and the author died a few years later. So that, from the western point of view, Rozanov seems like the last of the Russians. Post-revolution Russians are something different.

Rozanov is the last of the Russians, after Tchekhov. It is the true Russian voice, become very plaintive now. Artzybashev, Gorky, Merejkovski are his contemporaries, but they are all three a little bit off the tradition. But Rozanov is right on it. His first wife had been Dostoievsky's mistress: and somehow his literary spirit showed the same kind of connexion: a Dostoeivskian flicker that steadied and became a legal and orthodox light, yet always, of course, suspect. For Rozanov had been a real and perverse liar before he reformed and became a pious, yet suspected conservative. Perhaps he was a liar to the end: who knows? Yet *Solitaria* and *Fallen Leaves* are not lies, not so much lies as many more esteemed books.

The *Fallen Leaves* are just fragments of thought jotted down anywhere and anyhow. As to the importance of the where or how, perhaps it *is* important to keep throwing the reader out into the world, by means of the: At night: At work: In the tram: In the w.c.—which is sometimes printed after the reflections. Perhaps, to avoid any appearance of systematisation, or even of philosophic abstraction, these little *addenda* are useful. Anyhow, it is Russian, and deliberate, done with the intention of keeping the reader—or Rozanov himself—in contact with the *moment*, the actual time and place. Rozanov says that with *Solitaria* he introduced a new *tone* into literature, the tone of manuscript, a manuscript being unique and personal, coming from the individual alone direct to the reader. And "the secret (bordering on madness) that I am talking to myself: so constantly and attentively and *passionately*, that apart from this I practically hear nothing"—this is the secret of his newness, and of his book.

The description is just: and fortunately, on the whole, Rozanov talks sincerely to himself; he really does, on the whole,

refrain from performing in front of himself. Of course he is
self-conscious: he knows it and accepts it and tries to make it a
stark-naked self-consciousness, between himself and himself as
between himself and God. "Lord, preserve in me that chastity
of the writer: not to look in the glass." From a professional liar
it is a true and sincere prayer. "I am coquetting like a girl
before the whole world, hence my constant agitation." "A
writer must suppress the writer in himself (authorship,
literariness)."

He is constantly expressing his hatred of literature, as if it
poisoned life for him, as if he felt he did not live, he was only
literary. "The *most happy* moments of life I remember were
those when I saw (heard) people in a state of happiness. Stakha
and A.P.P.-va, 'My Friend's' story of her first love and marriage
(the culminating point of my life). From this I conclude that I
was born a contemplator, not an actor. I came into the world
in order to *see*, and not to *accomplish*." There is his trouble, that
he felt he was always looking on at life, rather than partaking
in it. And he felt this as a humiliation: and in his earlier days,
it had made him act up, as the Americans say. He had acted
up as if he were a real actor on life's stage. But it was too
theatrical: his "lying", his "evil" were too much acted up. A
liar and an evil bird he no doubt was, because the lies and the
acting up to evil, whether they are "pose" or spontaneous, have
a vile effect. But he never got any real satisfaction even out of
that. He never felt he had really been evil. He had only acted
up, like all the Stavrogins, or Ivan Karamazovs of Dostoeivsky.
Always acting up, trying to *act* feelings because you haven't
really got any. That was the condition of the Russians at the
end: even Tchekhov. Being terribly emotional, terribly full of
feeling, terribly good and pathetic or terribly evil and shocking,
just to *make* yourself have feelings, when you have none. This
was very Russian—and is very modern. A great deal of the
world is like it to-day.

Rozanov left off "acting up" and became quiet and decent,
except, perhaps, for little bouts of hysteria, when he would be
perfectly vicious towards a friend, or make a small splash of
"sin". As far as a man who *has* no real fount of emotion can
love he loved his second wife, "My Friend". He tried very,
very hard to love her, and no doubt he succeeded. But there

was always the taint of pity, and she, poor thing, must have been terribly emotionally overwrought, as a woman is with an emotional husband who has no real virile emotion or compassion, only "pity". "European civilisation will perish through compassion," he says: but then goes on to say, profoundly, that it is not compassion but pseudo-compassion, with an element of perversity in it. This is very Dostoievskian: and this pseudo-compassion tainted even Rozanov's love for his wife. There is somewhere an element of mockery. And oh, how Rozanov himself would have liked to escape it, and just to feel simple affection. But he couldn't. " 'To-day' was completely absent in Dostoievsky," he writes. Which is a very succinct way of saying that Dostoievsky never had any immediate feelings, only "projected" ones, which are bound to destroy the immediate object, the actual "to-day", the very body which is "to-day". So poor Rozanov saw his wife dying under his eyes with a paralysis due to a disease of the brain. She was his "to-day", and he could not help, somewhere, jeering at her. But he suffered, and suffered deeply. At the end, one feels his suffering *was* real: his grief over his wife *was* real. So he had gained that much reality: he really grieved for her, and that was love. It was a great achievement, after all, for the most difficult thing in the world is to achieve real feeling, especially real sympathy, when the sympathetic centres seem, from the very start, as in Rozanov, dead. But Rozanov knew his own nullity, and tried very hard to come through to real honest feeling. And in his measure, he succeeded. After all the Dostoievskian hideous "impurity" he did achieve a certain final purity, or genuineness, or true individuality, towards the end. Even at the beginning of *Fallen Leaves* he is often sentimental and false, repulsive.

And one cannot help feeling a compassion for the Russians of the old regime. They were such healthy barbarians in Peter the Great's time. Then the whole accumulation of western ideas, ideals, and inventions was poured in a mass into their hot and undeveloped consciousness, and worked like wild yeast. It produced a century of literature, from Pushkin to Rozanov, and then the wild working of this foreign leaven had ruined, for the time being, the very constitution of the Russian psyche. It was as if they had taken too violent a drug, or been injected with too strong a vaccine. The affective and effective centres collapsed, the control went all wrong, the energy died down in a rush, the nation fell, for the time being completely ruined. Too sudden civilisation always kills. It kills the South Sea Islanders: it killed the Russians, more slowly, and perhaps even more effectually. Once the idea and the ideal become too strong for the spontaneous emotion in the individual, the civilising influence ceases to be civilising and becomes very harmful, like powerful drugs which ruin the balance and destroy the control of the organism.

Rozanov knew this well. What he says about revolution and democracy leaves nothing to be said. And what he says of "officialdom" is equally final. I believe Tolstoi would be absolutely amazed if he could come back and see the Russia of to-day. I believe Rozanov would feel no surprise. He knew the inevitability of it. His attitude to the Jews is extraordinary, and shows uncanny penetration. And his sort of "conservatism", which would be Fascism to-day, was only a hopeless attempt to draw back from the way things were going.

But the disaster was inside himself already; there was no drawing back. Extraordinary is his note on his "dreaminess". "At times I am aware of something monstrous in myself. And that monstrous thing is my dreaminess. Then nothing can penetrate the circle traced by it.

"I am all stone.

"And a stone is a monster.

"For one must love and be aflame.

"From that dreaminess have come all my misfortunes in life (my former work in the Civil Service), the mistake of my whole proceedings (only when 'out of myself' was I attentive to My Friend [his wife]—and her pains), and also my sins.

"In my dreaminess I could do nothing.

"And on the other hand I could do anything ['sin'].

"Afterwards I was sorry: but it was too late. Dreaminess has devoured me, and everything round me."

There is the clue to the whole man's life: this "dreaminess" when he is like stone, insentient, and can do nothing, yet can do "anything". Over this dreaminess he has no control, nor over the stoniness. But what seemed to him dreaminess and stoniness seemed to others, from his actions, vicious malice and depravity. So that's that. It is one way of being damned. And there we have the last word of the Russian, before the great *débâcle*. Anyone who understands in the least Rozanov's state of soul, in which, apparently, he was born, born with this awful insentient stoniness somewhere in him, must sympathise deeply with his real suffering and his real struggle to get back a positive self, a feeling self: to overcome the "dreaminess", to dissolve the stone. How much, and how little, he succeeded we may judge from this book: and from his harping on the beauty of procreation and fecundity: and from his strange and self-revealing statements concerning Weininger. Rozanov is modern, terribly modern. And if he does not put the fear of God into us, he puts a real fear of destiny, or of doom: and of "civilisation" which does not come from within, but which is poured over the mind, by "education".

[Review in *Everyman*, 23 January, 1930.]

[87]

Letter to NELLY MORRISON, 1 Sept., 1921
. . . I tried Casanova, but he smells. One can be immoral if one likes, but one must not be a creeping, itching, fingering, inferior being, led on chiefly by a dirty sniffing kind of curiosity, without pride or clearness of soul. For me, a man must have pride, good natural inward pride. Without that, cleverness only stinks. But I will treat the battered volumes as gingerly as such *crotte* deserves.

[88]

THE GOOD MAN

THERE is something depressing about French eighteenth-century literature, especially that of the latter half of the century. All those sprightly memoirs and risky stories and senti-mental effusions constitute, perhaps, the dreariest body of literature we know, once we do know it. The French are essentially critics of life, rather than creators of life. And when the life itself runs rather thin, as it did in the eighteenth century, and the criticism rattles all the faster, it just leaves one feeling wretched.

England during the eighteenth century was far more alive. The sentimentalism of Sterne laughs at itself, is full of teasing self-mockery. But French sentimentalism of the same period is wholesale and like stale fish. It is difficult, even if one rises on one's hind legs and feels "superior", like a highbrow in an East End music-hall, to be amused by Restif de la Bretonne. One just sits in amazement that these clever French can be such stale fish of sentimentalism and prurience.

The Duc de Lauzun belongs to what one might call the fag-end period. He was born in 1747, and was twenty-seven years old when Louis XV died. Belonging to the high nobility, and to a family prominent at court, he escapes the crass sentimentalism of the "humbler" writers, but he also escapes what bit of genuine new feeling they had. He is far more manly than a Jean Jacques, but he is still less of a man in himself.

French eighteenth-century literature is so puzzling to the *emotions*, that one has to try to locate some spot of firm feeling inside oneself, from which one can survey the morass. And since the essential problem of the eighteenth century was the problem of *morality*, since the new homunculus produced in that period was the *homme de bien*, the "good man", who, of course, included the "man of feeling", we have to go inside ourselves and discover what we really feel about the "goodness", or morality, of the eighteenth century.

Because there is no doubt about it, the "good man" of to-day was produced in the chemical retorts of the brain and emotional centres of people like Rousseau and Diderot. It took him, this "good man", a hundred years to grow to his full stature. Now, after a century and a half, we have him in his dotage, and find he was a robot.

And there is no doubt about it, it was the writing of this new little "good man", the new *homme de bien*, in the human consciousness, which was the essential cause of the French revolution. The new little homunculus was soon ready to come out of the womb of consciousness on to the stage of life. Once on the stage, he soon grew up, and soon grew into a kind of Woodrow

Wilson dotage. But be that as it may, it was the kicking of this new little monster, to get out of the womb of time, which caused the collapse of the old show.

The new little monster, the new "good man", was perfectly reasonable and perfectly irreligious. Religion knows the great passions. The *homme de bien*, the "good man", performs the robot trick of isolating himself from the great passions. For the passion of life he substitutes the reasonable social virtues. You must be honest in your material dealings, you must be kind to the poor, and you must have "feelings" for your fellow-man and for nature. Nature with a capital. There is nothing to *worship*. Such a thing as worship is nonsense. But you may get a "feeling" out of anything.

In order to get nice "feelings" out of things, you must of course be quite "free", you mustn't be interfered with. And to be "free", you must incur the enmity of no man, you must be "good". And when everybody is "good" and "free", then we shall all have nice feelings about everything.

This is the gist of the idea of the "good man", chemically evolved by emotional alchemists such as Rousseau. Like every other homunculus, this little "good man" soon grows into a slight deformity, then into a monster, then into a grinning vast idiot. This monster produced our great industrial civilisation, and the huge thing, gone idiot, is now grinning at us and showing its teeth.

We are all, really, pretty "good". We are all extraordinarily "free". What other freedom can we imagine, than what we've got? So then, we ought all to have amazingly nice feelings about everything.

The last phase of the bluff is to pretend that we *do* all have nice feelings about everything, if we are nice people. It is the last grin of the huge grinning sentimentalism which the Rousseau-ists invented. But really, it's getting harder and harder to keep up the grin.

As a matter of fact, far from having nice feelings about everything, we have nice feelings about practically nothing. We get less and less our share of nice feelings. More and more we get horrid feelings, which we have to suppress hard. Or, if we don't admit it, then we must admit that we get less and less feelings of any sort. Our capacity for feeling anything is going numb, more and more numb, till we feel we shall soon reach zero, and pure insanity.

This is the horrid end of the "good man" homunculus.

Now the "good man" is all right as far as he goes. One must be honest in one's dealings, and one does feel kindly towards the poor man—unless he's one of the objectionable sort. If I turn myself into a swindler, and am a brute to every beggar, I shall only be a "not good man" instead of a "good man". It's just the same species, really. Immorality is no new ground. There's nothing original in it. Whoever invents morality invents, tacitly, immorality. And the immoral, unconventional people are only the frayed skirt-tails of the conventional people.

The trouble about the "good man" is that he's only one-hundredth part of a man. The eighteenth century, like a vile Shylock, carved a pound of flesh from the human psyche, conjured with it like a cunning alchemist, set it smirking, called it a "good man"—and lo! we all began to reduce ourselves to this little monstrosity. What's the matter with us, is that we are bound up like a China-girl's foot, that has got to cease developing and turn into a "lily". We are absolutely bound up tight in the bandages of a few ideas, and tight shoes are nothing to it.

When Oscar Wilde said that it was nonsense to assert that art imitates nature, because nature always imitates art, this was absolutely true of human nature. The thing called "spontaneous human nature" does not exist, and never did. Human nature is always made to some pattern or other. The wild Australian aborigines are absolutely bound up tight, tighter than a China-girl's foot, in their few savage conventions. They are bound up tighter than we are. But the length of the ideal bondage doesn't matter. Once you begin to feel it pressing, it'll press tighter and tighter, till either you burst it, or collapse inside it, or go deranged. And the conventional and ideal and emotional bandage presses as tight upon the free American girl as the equivalent bandage presses upon the Australian black girl in her tribe. An elephant bandaged up tight, so that he can only move his eyes, is no better off than a bandaged-up mouse. Perhaps worse off. The mouse has more chance to nibble a way out.

And this we must finally recognise. No man has "feelings of his own". The feelings of all men in the civilised world to-day are practically all alike. Men *can* only feel the feelings they know how to feel. The feelings they don't know how to feel, they don't feel. This is true of all men, and all women, and all children.

It is true, children do have lots of unrecognised feelings. But an unrecognized feeling, if it forces itself into any recognition, is only recognised as "nervousness" or "irritability". There are certain feelings we recognise, but as we grow up, every single disturbance in the psyche, or in the soul, is transmitted into one of the recognised feeling-patterns, or else left in that margin called "nervousness".

This is our true bondage. This is the agony of our human existence, that we can only feel things in conventional feeling-patterns. Because when these feeling-patterns become inadequate, when they will no longer body forth the workings of the yeasty soul, then we are in torture. It is like a deaf-mute trying to speak. Something is inadequate in the expression-apparatus, and we hear strange howlings. So are we now howling inarticulate, because what is yeastily working in us has no voice and no language. We are like deaf-mutes, or like the China-girl's foot.

Now the eighteenth century did let out a little extra length of bandage for the bound-up feet. But oh! it was a short length! We soon grew up to its capacity, and the pressure again became intolerable, horrible, unbearable: as it is today.

We compare England to-day with France of 1780. We sort of half expect revolutions of the same sort. But we have little grounds for the comparison and the expectation. It is true our feelings are going dead, we have to work hard to get any feeling out of ourselves: which is true of the Louis XV and more so of the Louis XVI people like the Duc de Lauzun. But at the same time, we know quite well that if all our heads were chopped off, and the working classes were left to themselves, with a clear field, nothing would have happened, really. Bolshevist Russia, one feels, and feels with bitter regret, is nothing new on the face of the earth. It is only a sort of America. And no matter how many revolutions take place, all we can hope for is different sorts of America. And since America is *chose connue*, since America is known to us, in our imaginative souls, with dreary finality, what's the odds? America has no new feelings: less even than England: only disruption of old feelings. America is bandaged more tightly even than Europe in the bandages of old ideas and ideals. Her feelings are even more fixed to pattern: or merely devolutionary. Her art forms are even more lifeless.

So what's the point in a revolution? Where's the homunculus? Where is the new baby of a new conception of life? Who feels him kicking in the womb of time?

Nobody! Nobody! Not even the Socialists and Bolshevists themselves. Not the Buddhists, nor the Christian Scientists, nor the scientists, nor the Christians. Nobody! So far, there is no new baby. And therefore, there is no revolution. Because a revolution is really the birth of a new baby, a new idea, a new feeling, a new way of feeling, a new feeling-pattern. It is the birth of a new man. "For I will put a new song into your mouth."

There is no new song. There is no new man. There is no new baby.

And therefore, I repeat, there is no revolution.

You who want a revolution, beget and conceive the new baby in your bodies: and not a homunculus robot like Rousseau's.

But you who are afraid of a revolution, realise that there will be no revolution, just as there will be no pangs of parturition if there is no baby to be born.

Instead, however, you may get that which is not revolution. You may, and you will, get a *débâcle*. *Après moi le déluge* was premature. The French revolution was only a bit of a brief inundation. The real deluge lies just ahead of us.

There is no choice about it. You can't keep the *status quo*, because the homunculus robot, the "good man", is dead. We killed him rather hastily and with hideous brutality, in the great war that was to save democracy. He is dead, and you can't keep him from decaying. You can't keep him from decomposition. You cannot.

Neither can you expect a revolution, because there is no new baby in the womb of our society. Russia is a collapse, not a revolution.

All that remains, since it's Louis XV's Deluge which is louring, rather belated: all that remains is to be a Noah, and build an ark. An ark, an ark, my kingdom for an ark! An ark of the covenant, into which also the animals shall go in two by two, for there's one more river to cross!

[First published, posthumously, in *Phoenix*.]

[89]

THOMAS MANN

THOMAS MANN is perhaps the most famous of German novelists now writing. He, and his elder brother, Heinrich Mann, with Jakob Wassermann, are acclaimed the three artists in fiction of present-day Germany.

But Germany is now undergoing that craving for form in fiction, that passionate desire for the mastery of the medium of narrative, that will of the writer to be greater than and undisputed lord over the stuff he writes, which is figured to the world in Gustave Flaubert.

Thomas Mann is over middle age*, and has written three or four books: *Buddenbrooks*, a novel of the patrician life of Lübeck; *Tristan*, a collection of six *Novellen*; *Königliche Hoheit*, an unreal Court romance; various stories, and lastly, *Der Tod in Venedig*. The author himself is the son of a Lübeck *Patrizier*.

It is as an artist rather than as a story-teller that Germany worships Thomas Mann. And yet it seems to me, this craving for form is the outcome, not of artistic conscience, but of a certain attitude to life. For form is not a personal thing like style. It is impersonal like logic. And just as the school of Alexander Pope was logical in its expressions, so it seems the school of Flaubert is, as it were, logical in its æsthetic form. "Nothing outside the definite line of the book," is a maxim. But can the human mind fix absolutely the definite line of a book, any more than it can fix absolutely any definite line of action for a living being?

Thomas Mann, however, is personal, almost painfully so, in his subject-matter. In "Tonio Kröger", the long *Novelle* at the end of the *Tristan* volume, he paints a detailed portrait of himself as a youth and younger man, a careful analysis. And

*Mann was actually just 38 when this article was first published—ten years older than Lawrence.

he expresses at some length the misery of being an artist. "Literature is not a calling, it is a curse." Then he says to the Russian painter girl: "There is no artist anywhere but longs again, my love, for the common life." But any young artist might say that. It is because the stress of life in a young man, but particularly in an artist, is very strong, and has as yet found no outlet, so that it rages inside him in *Sturm und Drang*. But the condition is the same, only more tragic, in the Thomas Mann of fifty-three. He has never found any outlet for himself, save his art. He has never given himself to anything but his art. This is all well and good, if his art absorbs and satisfies him, as it has done some great men, like Corot. But then there are the other artists, the more human, like Shakespeare and Goethe, who must give themselves to life as well as to art. And if these were afraid, or despised life, then with their surplus they would ferment and become rotten. Which is what ails Thomas Mann. He is physically ailing, no doubt. But his complaint is deeper: it is of the soul.

And out of this soul-ailment, this unbelief, he makes his particular art, which he describes, in "Tonio Kröger", as "*Wählerisch, erlesen, kostbar, fein, reizbar gegen das Banale, und aufs höchste empfindlich in Fragen des Taktes und Geschmacks*". He is a disciple, in method, of the Flaubert who wrote: "I worked sixteen hours yesterday, to-day the whole day, and have at last finished one page." In writing of the *Leitmotiv* and its influence, he says: "Now this method alone is sufficient to explain my slowness. It is the result neither of anxiety nor indigence, but of an overpowering sense of responsibility for the choice of every word, the coining of every phrase . . . a responsibility that longs for perfect freshness, and which, after two hours' work, prefers not to undertake an important sentence. For which sentence is important, and which not? Can one know beforehand whether a sentence, or part of a sentence may not be called upon to appear again as *Motiv*, peg, symbol, citation or connexion? And a sentence which must be heard twice must be fashioned accordingly. It must—I do not speak of beauty—possess a certain high level, and symbolic suggestion, which will make it worthy to sound again in any epic future. So every point becomes a standing ground, every adjective a decision, and it is clear that such work is not to be produced off-hand."

This, then, is the method. The man himself was always delicate in constitution. "The doctors said he was too weak to go to school, and must work at home." I quote from Aschenbach, in *Der Tod in Venedig*. "When he fell, at the age of fifty-three, one of his closest observers said of him: 'Aschenbach has always lived like this'—and he gripped his fist hard clenched; 'never like this'—and he let his open hand lie easily on the arm of the chair."

He forced himself to write, and kept himself to the work. Speaking of one of his works, he says: "It was pardonable, yea, it showed plainly the victory of his morality, that the uninitiated reader supposed the book to have come of a solid strength and one long breath; whereas it was the result of small daily efforts and hundreds of single inspirations."

And he gives the sum of his experience in the belief: "*dass beinahe alles Grosse, was dastehe, als ein Trotzdem dastehe, trotz Kummer und Qual, Armut, Verlassenheit, Körperschwäche, Laster, Leidenschaft und tausend hemmnischen Zustände gekommen sei.*" And then comes the final revelation, difficult to translate. He is speaking of life as it is written into his books:

"For endurance of one's fate, grace in suffering, does not only mean passivity, but is an active work, a positive triumph, and the Sebastian figure is the most beautiful symbol, if not of all art, yet of the art in question. If one looked into this portrayed world and saw the elegant self-control that hides from the eyes of the world to the last moment the inner undermining, the biological decay; saw the yellow ugliness which, sensuously at a disadvantage, could blow its choking heat of desire to a pure flame, and even rise to sovereignty in the kingdom of beauty; saw the pale impotence which draws out of the glowing depths of its intellect sufficient strength to subdue a whole vigorous people, bring them to the foot of the Cross, to the feet of impotence; saw the amiable bearing in the empty and severe service of Form; saw the quickly enervating longing and art of the born swindler: if one saw such a fate as this, and all the rest it implied, then one would be forced to doubt whether there were in reality any other heroism than that of weakness. Which heroism, in any case, is more of our time than this?"

Perhaps it is better to give the story of *Der Tod in Venedig*, from which the above is taken, and to whose hero it applies.

Gustav von Aschenbach, a fine, famous author, over fifty years of age, coming to the end of a long walk one afternoon, sees as he is approaching a burying-place, near Munich, a man standing between the chimeric figures of the gateway. This man in the gate of the cemetery is almost the *Motiv* of the story. By him, Aschenbach is infected with a desire to travel. He examines himself minutely, in a way almost painful in its frankness, and one sees the whole soul of this author of fifty-three. And it seems, the artist has absorbed the man, and yet the man is there, like an exhausted organism on which a parasite has fed itself strong. Then begins a kind of Holbein *Totentanz*. The story is quite natural in appearance, and yet there is the gruesome sense of symbolism throughout. The man near the burying-ground has suggested travel—but whither? Aschenbach sets off to a watering-place on the Austrian coast of the Adriatic, seeking some adventure, some passionate adventure, to which his sick soul and unhealthy body have been kindled. But finding himself on the Adriatic, he knows it is not thither that his desire draws him, and he takes ship for Venice. It is all real, and yet with a curious sinister unreality, like decay, the "biological decay". On board there is a man who reminds one of the man in the gateway, though there is no connexion. And then, among a crowd of young Poles who are crossing, is a ghastly fellow, whom Aschenbach sees is an old man dressed up as young, who capers unsuspected among the youths, drinks hilariously with them, and falls hideously drunk at last on the deck, reaching to the author, and slobbering about *"dem allerliebsten, dem schönsten Liebchen"*. Suddenly the upper plate of his false teeth falls on his underlip.

Aschenbach takes a gondola to the Lido, and again the gondolier reminds one of the man in the cemetery gateway. He is, moreover, one who will make no concession, and, in spite of Aschenbach's demand to be taken back to St. Mark's, rows him in his black craft to the Lido, talking to himself softly all the while. Then he goes without payment.

The author stays in a fashionable hotel on the Lido. The adventure is coming, there by the pallid sea. As Aschenbach comes down into the hall of the hotel, he sees a beautiful Polish boy of about fourteen, with honey-coloured curls clustering round his pale face, standing with his sisters and their governess.

Aschenbach loves the boy—but almost as a symbol. In him he loves life and youth and beauty, as Hyacinth in the Greek myth. This, I suppose, is blowing the choking heat to pure flame, and raising it to the kingdom of beauty. He follows the boy, watches him all day long on the beach, fascinated by beauty concrete before him. It is still the *Künstler* and his abstraction: but there is also the "yellow ugliness, sensuously at a disadvantage", of the elderly man below it all. But the picture of the writer watching the folk on the beach gleams and lives with a curious, gold-phosphorescent light, touched with the brightness of Greek myth, and yet a modern seashore with folks on the sands, and a half-threatening, diseased sky.

Aschenbach, watching the boy in the hotel lift, finds him delicate, almost ill, and the thought that he may not live long fills the elderly writer with a sense of peace. It eases him to think the boy should die.

Then the writer suffers from the effect of the *sirocco*, and intends to depart immediately from Venice. But at the station he finds with joy that his luggage has gone wrong, and he goes straight back to the hotel. There, when he sees Tadzio again, he knows why he could not leave Venice.

There is a month of hot weather, when Aschenbach follows Tadzio about, and begins to receive a look, loving, from over the lad's shoulder. It is wonderful, the heat, the unwholesomeness, the passion in Venice. One evening comes a street singer, smelling of carbolic acid, and sings beneath the veranda of the hotel. And this time, in gruesome symbolism, it is the man from the burying-ground distinctly.

The rumour is, that the black cholera is in Venice. An atmosphere of secret plague hangs over the city of canals and palaces. Aschenbach verifies the report at the English bureau, but cannot bring himself to go away from Tadzio, nor yet to warn the Polish family. The secretly pest-smitten days go by. Aschenbach follows the boy through the stinking streets of the town and loses him. And on the day of the departure of the Polish family, the famous author dies of the plague.

It is absolutely, almost intentionally, unwholesome. The man is sick, body and soul. He portrays himself as he is, with wonderful skill and art, portrays his sickness. And since any genuine portrait is valuable, this book has its place. It portrays one man, one atmosphere, one sick vision. It claims to do no more. And we have to allow it. But we know it is unwholesome—it does not strike me as being morbid for all that, it is too well done—and we give it its place as such.

Thomas Mann seems to me the last sick sufferer from the complaint of Flaubert. The latter stood away from life as from a leprosy. And Thomas Mann, like Flaubert, feels vaguely that he has in him something finer than ever physical life revealed. Physical life is a disordered corruption, against which he can fight with only one weapon, his fine æsthetic sense, his feeling for beauty, for perfection, for a certain fitness which soothes him, and gives him an inner pleasure, however corrupt the stuff of life may be. There he is, after all these years, full of disgusts and loathing of himself as Flaubert was, and Germany is being voiced, or partly so, by him. And so, with real suicidal intention, like Flaubert's, he sits, a last too-sick disciple, reducing himself grain by grain to the statement of his own disgust, patiently, self-destructively, so that his statement at least may be perfect in a world of corruption. But he is so late.

Already I find Thomas Mann, who, as he says, fights so hard against the banal in his work, somewhat banal. His expression may be very fine. But by now what he expresses is stale. I think we have learned our lesson, to be sufficiently aware of the fulsomeness of life. And even while he has a rhythm in style, yet his work has none of the rhythm of a living thing, the rise of a poppy, then the after uplift of the bud, the shedding of the calyx and the spreading wide of the petals, the falling of the flower and the pride of the seed-head. There is an unexpectedness in this such as does not come from their carefully plotted and arranged developments. Even *Madame Bovary* seems to me dead in respect to the living rhythm of the whole work. While it is there in *Macbeth* like life itself.

But Thomas Mann is old—and we are young. Germany does not feel very young to me.

[*Blue Review*, July 1913.]

[90]

MAX HAVELAAR

By E. D. Dekker (Multatuli, pseud.)

Max Havelaar was first published in Holland, nearly seventy years ago, and it created a *furore*. In Germany it was the book of the moment, even in England it had a liberal vogue. And to this day it remains vaguely in the minds of foreigners as the one Dutch classic.

I say vaguely, because many well-read people know nothing about it. Mr. Bernard Shaw, for example, confessed that he had never heard of it. Which is curious, considering the esteem in which it was held by men whom we might call the pre-Fabians, both in England and in America, sixty years ago.

But then *Max Havelaar*, when it appeared, was hailed as a book with a purpose. And the Anglo-Saxon mind loves to hail such books. They are so obviously in the right. The Anglo-Saxon mind also loves to forget completely, in a very short time, any book with a purpose. It is a bore, with its insistency.

So we have forgotten, with our usual completeness, all about *Max Havelaar* and about Multatuli, its author. Even the pseudonym, Multatuli (Latin for: I suffered much, or: I endured much), is to us irritating as it was exciting to our grandfathers. We don't care for poor but noble characters who are aware that they have suffered much. There is too much self-awareness.

On the surface, *Max Havelaar* is a tract or a pamphlet very much in the same line as *Uncle Tom's Cabin*. Instead of "pity the poor negro slave" we have "pity the poor oppressed Javanese"; with the same urgent appeal for legislation, for the government to do something about it. Well, the government did something about negro slaves, and *Uncle Tom's Cabin* fell out of date. The Netherlands government is also said to have done something in Java for the poor Javanese, on the strength of Multatuli's book. So that *Max Havelaar* became a back number.

So far so good. If by writing tract-novels you can move governments to improve matters, then write tract-novels by all means. If the government, however, plays up, and does its bit, then the tract-novel has served its purpose, and descends from the stage like a political orator who has made his point.

This is all in the course of nature. And because this is the course of nature, many educated Hollanders to-day become impatient when they hear educated Germans or English or Americans referring to *Max Havelaar* as "the one Dutch classic". So Americans would feel if they heard *Uncle Tom's Cabin* referred to as "the one American classic". *Uncle Tom* is a back number in the English-speaking world, and *Max Havelaar* is, to the Dutch-speaking world, another.

If you ask a Hollander for a really good Dutch novelist he refers you to the man who wrote: *Old People and the Things that Pass*, (Louis Couperus)—or else to somebody you know nothing about.

As regards the Dutch somebody I know nothing about, I am speechless. But as regards *Old People and the Things that Pass* I still think *Max Havelaar* a far more real book. And since *Old People* etc. is quite a good contemporary novel, one needs to find out why *Max Havelaar* is better.

I have not tried to read *Uncle Tom's Cabin* since I was a boy, and wept. I will try again, when I come across a copy. But I am afraid it will pall. I know I shan't weep.

Then why doesn't *Max Havelaar* pall? Why can one still read every word of it? As far as composition goes, it is the greatest mess possible. How the reviewers of to-day would tear it across and throw it in the w.p.b! But the reviewers of to-day, like the clergy, feel that they must justify God to man, and when they find they can't do it, when the book or the Almighty seems really unjustifiable, in the sight of common men, they apply the w.p.b.

It is surely the mistake of modern criticism, to conceive the public, the man in the street, as the real god, who must be served and flattered by every book that appears, even if it were the Bible. To my thinking, the critic, like a good beadle, should rap the public on the knuckles and make it attend

during divine service. And any good book is divine service.
The critic, having dated *Max Havelaar* a back number, hits
him on the head if he dares look up, and says: Down! Revere
the awesome modernity of the holy public!

I say: Not at all! The thing in *Max* that the public once
loved, the tract, is really a back number. But there is so very
little of the tract, actually, and what there is, the author has
retracted so comically, as he went, that the reader can grin as
he goes.

It was a stroke of cunning journalism on Multatuli's part
(Dostoievsky also made such strokes of cunning journalism) to
put his book through on its face value as a tract. What
Multatuli really wanted was to get his book over. He wanted to
be heard. He wanted to be read. *I want to be heard. I will be
heard!* he vociferates on the last pages. He himself must have
laughed in his sleeve as he vociferated. But the public gaped
and fell for it.

He was the passionate missionary for the poor Javanese!
Because he knew missionaries were, and are, listened to! And
the Javanese were a good stick with which to beat the dog.
The successful public being the dog. Which dog he longed to
beat. To give it the trouncing of its life!

He did it, in missionary guise, in *Max Havelaar*. The book
isn't really a tract, it is a satire. Multatuli isn't really a preacher,
he's a satirical humorist. Straight on in the life of Jean Paul
Richter the same bitter almost mad-dog aversion from humanity
that appeared in Jean Paul, appears again in Multatuli, as it
appears in the later Mark Twain. Dostoievsky was somewhat
the same, but in him the missionary had swallowed the mad dog
of revulsion, so that the howls of derision are all ventrilo-
quistic undertone.

Max Havelaar isn't a tract or a pamphlet, it is a satire. The
satire on the Dutch bourgeois, in Drystubble, is final. The
coffee-broker is reduced to his ultimate nothingness, in pure
humour. It is the reduction of the prosperous business man in
America and England to-day, just the same, essentially the
same: and it is a death-stroke.

Similarly, the Java part of the book is a satire on colonial
administration, and on government altogether. It is quite
direct and straightforward satire, so it is wholesome. Multatuli

never quite falls down the fathomless well of his own revulsion, as Dostoievsky did, to become a lily-mouthed missionary rumbling with ventral howls of derision and dementia. At his worst, Multatuli is irritatingly sentimental, harping on pity when he is inspired by hate. Maybe he deceives himself. But never for long.

His sympathy with the Javanese is also genuine enough; there was a man in him whose bowels of compassion were moved. Whereas a great nervous genius like Dostoievsky never felt a moment of real physical sympathy in his life. But with Multatuli, the sympathy for the Javanese is rather an excuse for hating the Dutch authorities still further. It is the sympathy of a man preoccupied with other feelings.

We see this in the famous idyll of Saïdyah and Adinda, once the most beloved and most quoted part of the book. We see how it bored the author to write it, after the first few pages. He *tells* us it bored him. It bored him to write sympathetically. He was by nature a satirical humorist, and it was far more exciting for him to be attacking the Dutch officials than sympathising with the Javanese.

This is again obvious in his partiality for the old Native Prince, the Regent. It is obvious that all the *actual* oppression of the poor Javanese came from the Javanese themselves, the native princes. It isn't the Dutch officials who steal Saidyah's buffalo: it is the princely Javanese. The oppression has been going on, Havelaar himself says it, *since the beginning of time*. Not since the coming of the Dutch. Indeed, it is the Oriental idea that the prince shall oppress his humble subjects. So why blame the Dutch officials so absolutely? Why not take the old native Regent by the beard?

But no! Multatuli, Max Havelaar, swims with pity for the poor and oppressed, but only because he hates the powers-that-be so intensely. He doesn't hate the powers because he loves the oppressed. The boot is on the other leg. The chick of pity comes out of the egg of hate. It is perhaps always so, with pity. But here we have to distinguish compassion from pity.

Surely, when Saïdyah sets off into the world, or is defended by the buffalo, it is compassion Multatuli feels for him, not pity. But the end is pity only.

The bird of hate hatches the chick of pity. The great dynamic force in Multatuli is as it was, really, in Jean Paul and in Swift and Gogol and in Mark Twain, hate, a passionate, honourable hate. It is honourable to hate Drystubble, and Multatuli hated him. It is honourable to hate cowardly officialdom, and Multatuli hated that. Sometimes, it is even honourable, and necessary, to hate society, as Swift did, or to hate mankind altogether, as often Voltaire did.

For man tends to deteriorate into that which Drystubble was, and the Governor-General and Slimering, something hateful, which must be destroyed. Then in comes Multatuli, like Jack and the Beanstalk, to fight the giant.

And when Jack fights the giant, he *must* have recourse to a trick. David thought of a sling and stone. Multatuli took a sort of missionary disguise. The gross public accepted the disguise, and David's stone went home. *À la guerre comme à la guerre.*

When there are no more Drystubbles, no more Governor-Generals or Slimerings, then *Max Havelaar* will be out of date. The book is a pill rather than a comfit. The jam of pity was put on to get the pill down. Our fathers and grandfathers licked the jam off. We can still go on taking the pill, for the social constipation is as bad as ever.

[Preface to *Max Havelaar*, translated by W. Siebenhaar, New York, 1927.]

[91]

MASTRO-DON GESUALDO

By Giovanni Verga

It seems curious that modern Italian literature has made so little impression on the European consciousness. A hundred years ago, when Manzoni's *I Promessi Sposi* came out, it met with European applause. Along with Sir Walter Scott and Byron, Manzoni stood for "Romance" to all Europe. Yet where is Manzoni now, even compared to Scott and Byron? Actually, I mean. Nominally, *I Promessi Sposi* is a classic; in fact, it is usually considered *the* classic Italian novel. It is set in all "literature courses". But who reads it? Even in Italy, who reads it? And yet, to my thinking, it is one of the best and most interesting novels ever written: surely a greater book than *Ivanhoe* or *Paul et Virginie* or *Werther*. Why then does nobody read it? Why is it found boring? When I gave a good English translation to the late Katharine Mansfield, she said, to my astonishment: I couldn't read it. Too long and boring.

It is the same with Giovanni Verga. After Manzoni, he is Italy's accepted greatest novelist. Yet nobody takes any notice of him. He is, as far as anybody knows his name, just the man who wrote the libretto to *Cavalleria Rusticana*. Whereas, as a matter of fact, Verga's story *Cavalleria Rusticana* is as much superior to Mascagni's rather cheap music as wine is superior to sugar-water. Verga is one of the greatest masters of the short story. In the volume *Novelle Rusticane* and in the volume entitled *Cavalleria Rusticana* are some of the best short stories ever written. They are sometimes as short and as poignant as Tchekhov. I prefer them to Tchekhov. Yet nobody reads them. They are "too depressing". They don't depress me half as much as Tchekhov does. I don't understand the popular taste.

Verga wrote a number of novels, of different sorts: very different. He was born about 1850, and died, I believe, at the beginning of 1921. So he is a modern. At the same time, he is a classic. And at the same time, again, he is old-fashioned.

The earlier novels are rather of the French type of the seventies—Octave Feuillet, with a touch of Gyp. There is the depressing story of the Sicilian young man who made a Neapolitan marriage, and on the last page gives his wife a much-belated slap across the face. There is the gruesome book, *Tigre Reale*, of the Russian countess—or princess, whatever it is—who comes to Florence and gets fallen in love with by the young Sicilian, with all the subsequent horrid affair: the weird woman dying of consumption, the man weirdly infatuated, in the suicidal South-Italian fashion. It is a bit in the manner of Matilda Serao. And though unpleasant, it is impressive.

Verga himself was a Sicilian, from one of the lonely agricultural villages in the south of the island. He was a gentleman—but not a rich one, presumably: with some means. As a young man, he went to Naples, then he worked at journalism in Milan and Florence. And finally he retired to Catania, to an exclusive, aristocratic old age. He was a shortish, broad man with a big red moustache. He never married.

His fame rests on his two long Sicilian novels, *I Malavoglia* and *Mastro-don Gesualdo*, also on the books of short pieces, *Cavalleria Rusticana*, *Novelle Rusticane*, and *Vagabondaggio*. These are all placed in Sicily, as is the short novel, *Storia di Una Capinera*. Of this last little book, one of the leading literary young Italians in Rome said to me the other day: Ah, yes, Verga! *Some* of his things! But a thing like *Storia di Una Capinera*, now, is ridiculous.

But why? It is rather sentimental, maybe. But it is no more sentimental than *Tess*. And the sentimentality seems to me to belong to the Sicilian characters in the book, it is true to type, quite as much so as the sentimentality of a book like Dickens's *Christmas Carol*, or George Eliot's *Silas Marner*, both of which works are "ridiculous", if you like, without thereby being wiped out of existence.

The trouble with Verga, as with all Italians, is that he never seems quite to know where he is. When one reads Manzoni, one wonders if he is not more "Gothic" or Germanic, than Italian. And Verga, in the same way, seems to have a borrowed outlook on life: but this time, borrowed from the French. With d'Annunzio the same, it is hard to believe he is really being himself. He gives one the impression of "acting up". Pirandello goes on with the game to-day. The Italians are always that way: always acting up to somebody else's vision of life. Men like Hardy, Meredith, Dickens, they are just as sentimental and false as the Italians, in their own way. It only happens to be our own brand of falseness and sentimentality.

And yet, perhaps, one can't help feeling that Hardy, Meredith, Dickens, and Maupassant and even people like the Goncourts and Paul Bourget, false in part though they be, are still looking on life with their own eyes. Whereas the Italians give one the impression that they are always borrowing somebody else's eyes to see with, and then letting loose a lot of emotion into a borrowed vision.

This is the trouble with Verga. But on the other hand, everything he does has a weird quality of Verga in it, quite distinct and like nothing else. And yet, perhaps the gross vision of the man is not quite his own. All his movements are his own. But his main motive is borrowed.

This is the unsatisfactory part about all Italian literature, as far as I know it.

The main motive, the gross vision of all the nineteenth-century literature, is what we may call the emotional-democratic vision or motive. It seems to me that since 1860, or even 1830, the Italians have always borrowed their ideals of democracy from the northern nations, and poured great emotion into them, without ever being really grafted by them. Some of the most wonderful martyrs for democracy have been Neapolitan men of birth and breeding. But none the less, it seems a mistake: an attempt to live by somebody else's lights.

Verga's first Sicilian novel, *I Malavoglia*, is of this sort. It was considered his greatest work. It is a great book. But it is *parti pris*. It is one-sided. And therefore it dates. There is too much, too much of the tragic fate of the poor, in it. There is a sort of wallowing in tragedy: the tragedy of the humble. It belongs to a date when the "humble" were almost the most fashionable thing. And the Malavoglia family are most humbly humble. Sicilians of the sea-coast, fishers, small traders—their humble tragedy is so piled on, it becomes almost disastrous. The book was published in America under the title of *The House by the Medlar Tree*, and can still be obtained. It is a great book, a great picture of poor life in Sicily, on the coast just north of Catania. But it is rather overdone on the pitiful side. Like the woebegone pictures by Bastien Lepage. Nevertheless, it is essentially a true picture, and different from anything else in literature. In most books of the period—even in *Madame Bovary*, to say nothing of Balzac's earlier *Lys dans la Vallée*— one has to take off about twenty per cent of the tragedy. One does it in Dickens, one does it in Hawthorne, one does it all the time, with all the great writers. Then why not with Verga? Just knock off about twenty per cent of the tragedy in *I Malavoglia*, and see what a great book remains. Most books that live, live in spite of the author's laying it on thick. Think of *Wuthering Heights*. It is quite as impossible to an Italian as even *I Malavoglia* is to us. But it is a great book.

The trouble with realism—and Verga was a realist—is that the writer, when he is a truly exceptional man like Flaubert or like Verga, tries to read his own sense of tragedy into people much smaller than himself. I think it is a final criticism against

Madame Bovary that people such as Emma Bovary and her husband Charles simply are too insignificant to carry the full weight of Gustave Flaubert's sense of tragedy. Emma and Charles Bovary are a couple of little people. Gustave Flaubert is not a little person. But, because he is a realist and does not believe in "heroes", Flaubert insists on pouring his own deep and bitter tragic consciousness into the little skins of the country doctor and his uneasy wife. The result is a discrepancy. *Madame Bovary* is a great book and a very wonderful picture of life. But we cannot help resenting the fact that the great tragic soul of Gustave Flaubert is, so to speak, given only the rather commonplace bodies of Emma and Charles Bovary. There's a misfit. And to get over the misfit, you have to let in all sorts of seams of pity. Seams of pity, which won't be hidden.

The tragic soul of Shakespeare borrows the bodies of kings and princes—not out of snobbism, but out of natural affinity. You can't put a great soul into a commonplace person. Commonplace persons have commonplace souls. Not all the noble sympathy of Flaubert or Verga for Bovarys and Malavoglias can prevent the said Bovarys and Malavoglias from being commonplace persons. They were deliberately chosen because they *were* commonplace, and not heroic. The authors insisted on the treasure of the humble. But they had to lend the humble by far the best part of their own treasure, before the said humble could show any treasure at all.

So, if *I Malavoglia* dates, so does *Madame Bovary*. They belong to the emotional-democratic, treasure-of-the-humble period of the nineteenth century. The period is just rather out of fashion. We still feel the impact of the treasure-of-the-humble too much. When the emotion will have quite gone out of us, we can accept *Madame Bovary* and *I Malavoglia* in the same free spirit with the same detachment as that in which we accept Dickens or Richardson.

Mastro-don Gesualdo, however, is not nearly so much treasure-of-the-humble as *I Malavoglia*. Here, Verga is not dealing with the disaster of poverty, and calling it tragedy. On the contrary, he is a little bored by poverty. He must have a hero who wins out, and makes his pile, and then succumbs under the pile.

Mastro-don Gesualdo started life as a barefoot peasant brat, not a don at all. He becomes very rich. But all he gets of it is a great tumour of bitterness inside, which kills him.

Verga must have known, in actual life, the prototype of Gesualdo. We see him in the marvellous realistic story in *Cavalleria Rusticana*, of a fat little peasant who has become enormously rich, grinding his labourers, and now is diseased and must die. This little fellow is quite unheroic. He has the indomitable greedy will, but nothing else of Gesualdo's rather attractive character.

Gesualdo is attractive, and, in a sense, heroic. But still he is not allowed to emerge in the old heroic sense, with swagger and nobility and head-and-shoulders taller than anything else. He is allowed to have exceptional qualities, and above all, exceptional force. But these things do not make a hero of a man. A hero must be a hero by grace of God, and must have an inkling of the same. Even the old Paladin heroes had a great idea of themselves as exemplars. And Hamlet had the same. "O cursed spite that ever I was born to set it right." Hamlet didn't succeed in setting anything right, but he felt that way. And so all heroes must feel.

But Gesualdo, and Jude, and Emma Bovary are not allowed to feel any of these feelings. As far as *destiny* goes, they felt no more than anybody else. And this is because they belong to the realistic world.

Gesualdo is just an ordinary man with extraordinary energy. That, of course, is the intention. But he is a Sicilian. And here lies the difficulty. Because the realistic-democratic age has dodged the dilemma of having no heroes by having every man his own hero. This is reached by what we call subjective intensity, and in this subjectively-intense every-man-his-own-hero business the Russians have carried us to the greatest lengths. The merest scrub of a pickpocket is so phenomenally aware of his own soul, that we are made to bow down before the imaginary coruscations that go on inside him. That is almost the whole of Russian literature: the phenomenal coruscations of the souls of quite commonplace people.

Of course your soul will coruscate, if you think it does. That's why the Russians are so popular. No matter how much of a shabby animal you may be, you can learn from Dostoievsky and Tchekhov, etc., how to have the most tender, unique, coruscating soul on earth. And so you may be most vastly important to yourself. Which is the private aim of all men. The hero had it openly. The commonplace person has it inside himself, though outwardly he says: Of course I'm no better than anybody else! His very asserting it shows he doesn't think it for a second. Every character in Dostoievsky or Tchekhov thinks himself *inwardly* a nonesuch, absolutely unique.

And here you get the blank opposite, in the Sicilians. The Sicilians simply don't have any subjective idea of themselves, or any souls. Except, of course, that funny little *alter ego* of a soul which can be prayed out of purgatory into paradise, and is just as objective as possible.

The Sicilian, in our sense of the word, doesn't have any soul. He just hasn't got our sort of subjective consciousness, the soulful idea of himself. Souls, to him, are little naked people uncomfortably hopping on hot bricks, and being allowed at last to go up to a garden where there is music and flowers and sanctimonious society, Paradise. Jesus is a man who was crucified by a lot of foreigners and villains, and who can help you against the villainous lot nowadays: as well as against witches and the rest.

The self-tortured Jesus, the self-tortured Hamlet, simply does not exist. Why should a man torture himself? Gesualdo would ask in amazement. Aren't there scoundrels enough in the world to torture him?

Of course, I am speaking of the Sicilians of Verga's day, fifty and sixty years ago, before the great emigration to America, and the great return, with dollars and bits of self-aware souls: at least politically self-aware.

So that in *Mastro-don Gesualdo* you have the very antithesis of what you get in *The Brothers Karamazov*. Anything more un-Russian than Verga it would be hard to imagine: save Homer. Yet Verga has the same sort of pity as the Russians. And, with the Russians, he is a realist. He won't have heroes, nor appeals to gods above nor below.

The Sicilians of to-day are supposed to be the nearest thing to the classic Greeks that is left to us: that is, they are the nearest descendants on earth. In Greece to-day there are no Greeks. The nearest thing is the Sicilian, the eastern and south-eastern Sicilian.

And if you come to think of it, Gesualdo Motta might really be a Greek in modern setting, except that he is not intellectual. But this many Greeks were not. And he has the energy, the quickness, the vividness of the Greek, the same vivid passion for wealth, the same ambition, the same lack of scruples, the same queer openness, without ever really openly committing himself. He is not a bit furtive, like an Italian. He is astute instead, far too astute and Greek to let himself be led by the nose. Yet he has a certain frankness, far more than an Italian. And far less fear than an Italian. His boldness and his queer sort of daring are Sicilian rather than Italian, so is his independent manliness.

He is Greek above all in not having any soul or any lofty ideals. The Greeks were far more bent on making an audacious, splendid impression than on fulfilling some noble purpose. They loved the splendid look of a thing, the splendid ring of words. Even tragedy was to them a grand gesture, rather than something to mope over. Peak and pine they would not, and unless some Fury pursued them to punish them for their sins, they cared not a straw for sins: their own or anyone else's.

As for being burdened with souls, they were not such fools.

But alas, ours is the day of souls, when soul pays, and when having a soul is as important to the young as solitaire to a valetudinarian. If you don't have feelings about your soul, what sort of person can you be?

And Gesualdo didn't have feelings about his soul. He was remorselessly and relentlessly objective, like all people that belong to the sun. In the sun, men are objective, in the mist and snow, subjective. Subjectivity is largely a question of the thickness of your overcoat.

When you get to Ceylon, you realise that, to the swarthy Cingalese, even Buddhism is a purely objective affair. And we have managed to spiritualise it to such a subjective pitch.

Then you have the setting to the hero. The south-Sicilian setting to *Mastro-don Gesualdo* is perhaps nearer to the true medieval than anything else in modern literature, even barring the Sardinian medievalism of Grazia Deledda. You have the Sicily of the Bourbons, the Sicily of the Kingdom of Naples. The island is incredibly poor and incredibly backward. There are practically no roads for wheeled vehicles, and consequently no wheeled vehicles, neither carts nor carriages, outside the towns. Everything is packed on asses or mules, man travels on horseback or on foot, or, if sick, in a mule-litter. The land is held by the great landowners, the peasants are almost serfs. It is as wild, as poor, and in the ducal houses of Palermo even as splendid and ostentatious as Russia.

Yet how different from Russia! Instead of the wild openness of the north, you have the shut-in, guarded watchfulness of the old Mediterranean. For centuries, the people of the Mediterranean have lived on their guard, intensely on their guard, on the watch, wary, always wary, and holding aloof. So it is even to-day, in the villages: aloof, holding aloof, each individual inwardly holding aloof from the others; and this in spite of the returned "Americans".

How utterly different it is from Russia, where the people are always—in the books—expanding to one another, and pouring out tea and their souls to one another all night long. In Sicily, by nightfall, nearly every man is barricaded inside his own house. Save in the hot summer, when the night is more or less turned into day.

It all seems, to some people, dark and squalid and brutal and boring. There is no soul, no enlightenment at all. There is not one single enlightened person. If there had been, he would have departed long ago. He could not have stayed.

And for people who seek enlightenment, oh, how boring! But if you have any physical feeling for life, apart from nervous feelings such as the Russians have, nerves, nerves—if you have any appreciation for the southern way of life, then what a strange, deep fascination there is in *Mastro-don Gesualdo*! Perhaps the deepest nostalgia I have ever felt has been for Sicily, reading Verga. Not for England or anywhere else—for Sicily, the beautiful, that which goes deepest into the blood. It is so clear, so beautiful, so like the physical beauty of the Greek.

Yet the lives of the people all seem so squalid, so pottering, so despicable: like a crawling of beetles. And then, the moment you get outside the grey and squalid walls of the village, how wonderful in the sun, with the land lying apart. And isolated, the people too have some of the old Greek singleness, carelessness, dauntlessness. It is only when they bunch together as citizens that they are squalid. In the countryside, they are portentous and subtle, like the wanderers in the Odyssey. And their relations are all curious and immediate, objective. They are so little aware of themselves, and so much aware of their own effects.

It all depends what you are looking for. Gesualdo's lifelong love-affair with Diodata is, according to our ideas, quite impossible. He puts no value on sentiment at all: or almost none: again a real Greek. Yet there is a strange forlorn beauty in it, impersonal, a bit like Rachel or Rebecca. It is of the old, old world, when man is aware of his own belongings, acutely, but only very dimly aware of his own feelings. And feelings you are not aware of, you don't have.

Gesualdo seems so potent, so full of potency. Yet nothing emerges, and he never says anything. It is the very reverse of the Russian, who talks and talks, out of impotence.

And you have a wretched, realistic kind of tragedy for the end. And you feel, perhaps the book was all about nothing, and Gesualdo wasn't worth the labour of Verga.

But that is because we are spiritual snobs, and think, because a man can fume with "To be or not to be", therefore he is a person to be taken account of. Poor Gesualdo had never heard of: To be or not to be, and he wouldn't have taken any notice if he had. He lived blindly, with the impetuosity of blood and muscles, sagacity and will, and he never woke up to himself. Whether he would have been any the better for waking up to himself, who knows!

[First published, posthumously, in *Phoenix*.]

[92]

CAVALLERIA RUSTICANA

By GIOVANNI VERGA

Cavalleria Rusticana is in many ways the most interesting of the Verga books. The volume of short stories under this title appeared in 1880, when the author was forty years old, and when he had just "retired" from the world.

The Verga family owned land around Vizzini, a biggish village in southern Sicily; and here, in and around Vizzini, the tragedies of Turiddu and La Lupa and Jeli take place. But it was only in middle life that the drama of peasant passion really made an impression on Giovanni Verga. His earlier imagination, naturally, went out into the great world.

The family of the future author lived chiefly at Catania, the seaport of east Sicily, under Etna. And Catania was really Verga's home town, just as Vizzini was his home village.

But as a young man of twenty he already wanted to depart into the bigger world of "the Continent", as the Sicilians called the mainland of Italy. It was the Italy of 1860, the Italy of Garibaldi, and the new era. Verga seems to have taken little interest in politics. He had no doubt the southern idea of himself as a gentleman and an aristocrat, beyond politics. And he had the ancient southern thirst for show, for lustre, for glory, a desire to figure grandly among the first society of the world. His nature was proud and unmixable. At the same time, he had the southern passionate yearning for tenderness and generosity. And so he ventured into the world, without much money; and, in true southern fashion, he was dazzled. To the end of his days he was dazzled by elegant ladies in elegant equipages: one sees it, amusingly, in all his books.

He was a handsome man, by instinct haughty and reserved: because, partly, he was passionate and emotional, and did not choose to give himself away. A true provincial, he had to try to enter the *beau monde*. He lived by journalism, more or less: certainly the Vizzini lands would not keep him in affluence. But still, in his comparative poverty, he must enter the *beau monde*.

He did so: and apparently with a certain success. And for nearly twenty years he lived in Milan, in Florence, in Naples, writing, and imagining he was fulfilling his thirst for glory by having love-affairs with elegant ladies: most elegant ladies, as he assures us.

To this period belong the curiously unequal novels of the city world: *Eva*, *Tigre Reale*, *Eros*. They are interesting, alive, bitter, somewhat unhealthy, smelling of the seventies and of the Paris of the Goncourts, and, in some curious way, abortive. The man had not found himself. He was in his wrong element, fooling himself and being fooled by show, in a true Italian fashion. Then, towards the age of forty, came the recoil, and the *Cavalleria Rusticana* volume is the first book of the recoil. It was a recoil away from the *beau monde* and the "Continent", back to Sicily, to Catania, to the peasants. Verga never married: but he was deeply attached to his own family. He lived in Catania, with his sister. His brother, or brother-in-law, who had looked after the Vizzini property, was ill. So for the first time in his life Giovanni Verga had to undertake the responsibility for the family estate and fortune. He had to go to Vizzini and more or less manage the farm work—at least keep an eye on it. He said he hated the job, that he had no capacity for business, and so on. But we may be sure he managed very well. And certainly from this experience he gained his real fortune, his genuine sympathy with peasant life, instead of his spurious sympathy with elegant ladies. His great books all followed: *Cavalleria Rusticana* and *Mastro-don Gesualdo* and the *Novelle Rusticane* ("Little Novels of Sicily") and most of the sketches have their scenes laid in or around Vizzini.

So that *Cavalleria Rusticana* marks a turning-point in the man's life. Verga still looks back to the city elegance, and makes such a sour face over it, it is really funny. The sketch he calls "Fantasticheria" ("Caprice") and the last story in the book, "Il Come, il Quando, et il Perché" ("The How, When, and Wherefore") both deal with the elegant little lady herself. The sketch "Caprice" we may take as autobiographical—the story not entirely so. But we have enough data to go on.

The elegant little lady is the same, pretty, spoilt, impulsive emotional, but without passion. The lover, Polidori, is only half-sketched. But evidently he is a passionate man who *thinks* he can play at love and then is mortified to his very soul because he finds it is only a game. The tone of mortification is amusingly evident both in the sketch and in the story. Verga is profoundly and everlastingly offended with the little lady, with all little ladies, for not taking him absolutely seriously as an amorous male, when all the time he doesn't quite take himself seriously, and doesn't take the little lady seriously at all.

Nevertheless, the moment of sheer roused passion is serious in the man: and apparently not so in the woman. Each time the moment comes, it involves the whole nature of the man and does not involve the whole nature of the woman: she still clings to her social safeguards. It is the difference between a passionate nature and an emotional nature. But then the man goes out deliberately to make love to the emotional elegant woman who is truly social and not passionate. So he has only himself to blame if his passionate nose is out of joint.

It is most obviously out of joint. His little picture of the elegant little lady jingling her scent-bottle and gazing in nervous anxiety for the train from Catania which will carry her away from Aci-Trezza and her too-intense lover, back to her light, gay, secure world on the mainland is one of the most amusingly biting things in the literature of love. How glad she must have been to get away from him! And how bored she must have been by his preaching the virtues of the humble poor, holding them up before her to make her feel small. We may be sure she doesn't feel small, only nervous and irritable. For apparently she had no deep warmth or generosity of nature.

So Verga recoiled to the humble poor, as we see in his "Caprice" sketch. Like a southerner, what he did he did wholesale. Floods of savage and tragic pity he poured upon the humble fisher-folk of Aci-Trezza, whether they asked for it or not—partly to spite the elegant little lady. And this particular flood spreads over the whole of his long novel concerning the fisher-folk of Aci-Trezza: *I Malavoglia*. It is a great novel, in spite of the pity: but always in spite of it.

In *Cavalleria Rusticana*, however, Verga had not yet come to the point of letting loose his pity. He is still too much and too profoundly offended, as a passionate male. He recoils savagely away from the sophistications of the city life of elegant little ladies, to the peasants in their most crude and simple, almost brute-like aspect.

When one reads, one after the other, the stories of Turiddu, La Lupa, Jeli, Brothpot, Rosso Malpelo, one after the other, stories of crude killing, it seems almost too much, too crude, too violent, too much a question of mere brutes.

As a matter of fact, the judgment is unjust. Turiddu is not a brute: neither is Alfio. Both are men of sensitive and even honourable nature. Turiddu knows he is wrong, and would even let himself be killed, he says, but for the thought of his old

mother. The elegant Maria and her Erminia are never so
sensitive and direct in expressing themselves; not so frankly
warm-hearted.

As for Jeli, who could call him a brute? or Nanni? or Brothpot?
They are perhaps not brutal enough. They are too gentle and
forbearing, too delicately naïve. And so grosser natures trespass
on them unpardonably; and the revenge flashes out.

His contemporaries abused Verga for being a realist of the
Zola school. The charge is unjust. The base of the charge
against Zola is that he made his people too often merely
physical-functional arrangements, physically and materially
functioning without any "higher" nature. The charge against
Zola is often justifiable. It is completely justifiable against the
earlier d'Annunzio. In fact, the Italian tends on the one hand
to be this creature of physical-functional activity and nothing
else, spasmodically sensual and materialist; hence the violent
Italian outcry against the portrayal of such creatures, and
d'Annunzio's speedy transition to neurotic Virgins of the Rocks
and ultra-refinements.

But Verga's people are always people in the purest sense of
the word. They are not intellectual, but then neither was
Hector nor Ulysses intellectual. Verga, in his recoil, mis-
trusted everything that smelled of sophistication. He had a
passion for the most naïve, the most unsophisticated manifestation of human nature. He was not seeking the brute, the
animal man, the so-called cave-man. Far from it. He knew
already too well that the brute and the cave-man lie quite near
under the skin of the ordinary successful man of the world.
There you have the predatory cave-man of vulgar imagination,
thinly hidden under expensive cloth.

What Verga's soul yearned for was the purely naïve human
being, in contrast to the sophisticated. It seems as if Sicily, in
some way, under all her amazing forms of sophistication and
corruption, still preserves some flower of pure human candour:
the same thing that fascinated Theocritus. Theocritus was an
Alexandrine courtier, singing from all his "musk and insolence"
of the pure idyllic Sicilian shepherds. Verga is the Theocritus of
the nineteenth century, born among the Sicilian shepherds, and
speaking of them in prose more sadly than Theocritus, yet with
some of the same eternal Sicilian dawn-freshness in his vision.

It is almost bitter to think that Rosso Malpelo must often have looked along the coast and seen the rocks that the Cyclops flung at Ulysses; and that Jeli must some time or other have looked to the yellow temple-ruins of Girgenti.

Verga was fascinated, after his mortification in the *beau monde*, by pure naïveté and by the spontaneous passion of life, that spurts beyond all convention or even law. Yet as we read, one after the other, of these betrayed husbands killing the co-respondents, it seems a little mechanical. Alfio, Jeli, Brothpot, Gramigna ending their life in prison: it seems a bit futile and hopeless, mechanical again.

The fault is partly Verga's own, the fault of his own obsession. He felt himself in some way deeply mortified, insulted in his ultimate sexual or male self, and he enacted over and over again the drama of revenge. We think to ourselves, ah, how stupid of Alfio, of Jeli, of Brothpot, to have to go killing a man and getting themselves shut up in prison for life, merely because the man had committed adultery with their wives. Was it worth it? Was the wife worth one year of prison, to a man, let alone a lifetime?

We ask the question with our reason, and with our reason we answer No! Not for a moment was any of these women worth it. Nowadays we have learnt more sense, and we let her go her way. So the stories are too old-fashioned.

And again, it was not for love of their wives that Jeli and Alfio and Brothpot killed the other man. It was because people talked. It was because of the fiction of "honour". We have got beyond all that.

We are so much more reasonable. All our life is so much more reasoned and reasonable. *Nous avons changé tout cela.*

And yet, as the years go by, one wonders if mankind is so radically changed. One wonders whether reason, sweet reason, has really changed us, or merely delayed or diverted our reactions. Are Alfio and Jeli and Gramigna utterly out of date, a thing superseded for ever? Or are they eternal?

Is man a sweet and reasonable creature? Or is he, basically, a passional phenomenon? Is man a phenomenon on the face of the earth, or a rational consciousness? Is human behaviour to be reasonable, throughout the future, reasoned and rational?— or will it always display itself in strange and violent phenomena?

Judging from all experience, past and present, one can only decide that human behaviour is ultimately one of the natural phenomena, beyond all reason. Part of the phenomenon, for the time being, is human reason, the control of reason, and the power of the Word. But the Word and the reason are themselves only part of the coruscating phenomenon of human existence; they are, so to speak, one rosy shower from the rocket, which gives way almost instantly to the red shower of ruin or the green shower of despair.

Man is a phenomenon on the face of the earth. But the phenomena have their laws. One of the laws of the phenomenon called a human being is that, hurt this being mortally at its sexual root, and it will recoil ultimately into some form of killing. The recoil may be prompt, or delay by years or even by generations. But it will come. We may take it as a law.

We may take it as another law that the very deepest quick of a man's nature is his own pride and self-respect. The human being, weird phenomenon, may be patient for years and years under insult, insult to his very quick, his pride in his own natural being. But at last, O phenomenon, killing will come of it. All bloody revolutions are the result of the long, slow, accumulated insult to the quick of pride in the mass of men.

A third law is that the naïve or innocent core in a man is always his vital core, and infinitely more important than his intellect or his reason. It is only from his core of unconscious naïveté that the human being is ultimately a responsible and dependable being. Break this human core of naïveté—and the evil of the world all the time tries to break it, in Jeli, in Rosso Malpelo, in Brothpot, in all these Verga characters—and you get either a violent reaction, or, as is usual nowadays, a merely rational creature whose core of spontaneous life is dead. Now the rational creature, who is merely rational, by some cruel trick of fate remains rational only for one or two generations at best. Then he is quite mad. It is one of the terrible qualities of the reason that it has no life of its own, and unless continually kept nourished or modified by the naïve life in man and woman, it becomes a purely parasitic and destructive thing. Make any human being a really rational being, and you have made him a parasitic and destructive force. Make any people mainly rational in their life, and their inner activity will be the activity of destruction. The more the populations of the world become only rational in their consciousness, the swifter they bring about their destruction pure and simple.

Verga, like every great artist, had sensed this. What he bewails really, as the tragedy of tragedies, in this book, is the ugly trespass of the sophisticated greedy ones upon the naïve life of the true human being: the death of the naïve, pure being—or his lifelong imprisonment—and the triumph or the killing of the sophisticated greedy ones.

This is the tragedy of tragedies in all time, but particularly in our epoch: the killing off of the naïve innocent life in all of us, by which alone we can continue to live, and the ugly triumph of the sophisticated greedy.

It may be urged that Verga commits the Tolstoian fallacy, of repudiating the educated world and exalting the peasant. But this is not the case. Verga is very much the gentleman, exclusively so, to the end of his days. He did not dream of putting on a peasant's smock, or following the plough. What Tolstoi somewhat perversely worshipped in the peasants was poverty itself, and humility, and what Tolstoi perversely hated was instinctive pride or spontaneous passion. Tolstoi has a perverse pleasure in making the later Vronsky abject and pitiable: because Tolstoi so meanly envied the healthy passionate male in the young Vronsky. Tolstoi cut off his own nose to spite his face. He envied the reckless passionate male with a carking envy, because he must have felt himself in some way wanting in comparison. So he exalts the peasant: not because the peasant may be a more natural and spontaneous creature than the city man or the guardsman, but just because the peasant is poverty-striken and humble. This is malice, the envy of weakness and deformity.

We know now that the peasant is no better than anybody else; no better than a prince or a selfish young army officer or a governor or a merchant. In fact, in the mass, the peasant is worse than any of these. The peasant mass is the ugliest of all human masses, most greedily selfish and brutal of all. Which Tolstoi, leaning down from the gold bar of heaven, will have had opportunity to observe. If we have to trust to a *mass*, then better trust the upper or middle-class mass, all masses being odious.

But Verga by no means exalts the peasants as a class: nor does he believe in their poverty and humility. Verga's peasants are certainly not Christ-like, whatever else they are. They are most normally ugly and low, the bulk of them. And individuals are sensitive and simple.

Verga turns to the peasants only to seek for a certain something which, as a healthy artist, he worshipped. Even Tolstoi, as a healthy artist, worshipped it the same. It was only as a moralist and a personal being that Tolstoi was perverse. As a true artist, he worshipped, as Verga did, every manifestation of pure, spontaneous, passionate life, life kindled to vividness. As a perverse moralist with a sense of some subtle deficiency in himself, Tolstoi tries to insult and to damp out the vividness of life. Imagine any great artist making the vulgar social condemnation of Anna and Vronsky figure as divine punishment! Where now is the society that turned its back on Vronsky and Anna? Where is it? And what is its condemnation worth, to-day?

Verga turned to the peasants to find, *in individuals*, the vivid spontaneity of sensitive passionate life, non-moral and non-didactic. He found it always *defeated*. He found the vulgar and the greedy always destroying the sensitive and the passionate. The vulgar and the greedy are themselves usually peasants: Verga was far too sane to put an aureole round the whole class. Still more are the women greedy and egoistic. But even so, Turiddu and Jeli and Rosso Malpelo and Nanni and Gramigna and Brothpot are not humble. They have no saint-like, self-sacrificial qualities. They are only naïve, passionate, and natural. They are "defeated" not because there is any glory or sanctification in defeat; there is no martyrdom about it. They are defeated because they are too unsuspicious, not sufficiently armed and ready to do battle with the greedy and the sophisticated. When they do strike, they destroy themselves too. So the real tragedy is that they are not sufficiently conscious and developed to defend their own naïve sensitiveness against the inroads of the greedy and the vulgar. The greedy and the vulgar win all the time: which, alas, is only too true, in Sicily as everywhere else. But Giovanni Verga certainly doesn't help them, by preaching humility. He does show them the knife of revenge at their throat.

And these stories, instead of being out of date, just because the manners depicted are more or less obsolete, even in Sicily, which is a good deal Americanised and "cleaned up", as the reformers would say; instead of being out of date, they are dynamically perhaps the most up to date of stories. The Tchekhovian after-influenza effect of inertia and will-lessness is wearing off, all over Europe. We realise we've had about enough of being null. And if Tchekhov represents the human being driven into an extremity of self-consciousness and faintly-wriggling inertia, Verga represents him as waking suddenly from inaction into the stroke of revenge. We shall see which of the two visions is more deeply true to life.

"Cavalleria Rusticana" and "La Lupa" have always been hailed as masterpieces of brevity and gems of literary form. Masterpieces they are, but one is now a little sceptical of their form. After the enormous diffusiveness of Victor Hugo, it was perhaps necessary to make the artist more self-critical and self-effacing. But any wholesale creed in art is dangerous. Hugo's romanticism, which consisted in letting himself go, in an orgy of effusive self-conceit, was not much worse than the next creed the French invented for the artist, of self-effacement. Self-effacement is quite as self-conscious, and perhaps even more conceited than letting oneself go. Maupassant's self-effacement becomes more blatant than Hugo's self-effusion. As for the perfection of form achieved—Mérimée achieved the highest, in his dull stories like "Mateo Falcone" and "L'Enlèvement de la Redoute". But they are hopelessly literary, fabricated. So is most of Maupassant. And if *Madame Bovary* has form, it is a pretty flat form.

But Verga was caught up by the grand idea of self-effacement in art. Anything more confused, more silly, really, than the pages prefacing the excellent story "Gramigna's Lover" would be hard to find, from the pen of a great writer. The moment Verga starts talking theories, our interest wilts immediately. The theories were none of his own: just borrowed from the literary smarties of Paris. And poor Verga looks a sad sight in Paris ready-mades. And when he starts putting his theories into practice, and effacing himself, one is far more aware of his interference than when he just goes ahead. Naturally! Because self-effacement is, of course, self-conscious, and any form of emotional self-consciousness hinders a first-rate artist: though it may help the second-rate.

Therefore in "Cavalleria Rusticana" and in "La Lupa" we are just a bit too much aware of the author and his scissors. He has clipped too many away. The transitions are too abrupt. All is over in a gasp: whereas a story like "La Lupa" covers at least several years of time.

As a matter of fact, we need more looseness. We need an apparent formlessness, definite form is mechanical. We need more easy transition from mood to mood and from deed to deed. A great deal of the meaning of life and of art lies in the apparently dull spaces, the pauses, the unimportant passages. They are truly passages, the places of passing over.

So that Verga's deliberate missing-out of transition passages is, it seems to me, often a defect. And for this reason a story like "La Lupa" loses a great deal of its life. It may be a masterpiece of concision, but it is hardly a masterpiece of narration. It is so short, our acquaintance with Nanni and Maricchia is so fleeting, we forget them almost at once. "Jeli" makes a far more profound impression, so does "Rosso Malpelo". These seem to me the finest stories in the book, and among the finest stories ever written. Rosso Malpelo is an extreme of the human consciousness, subtle and appalling as anything done by the Russians, and at the same time substantial, not introspective vapours. You will never forget him.

And it needed a deeper genius to write "Rosso Malpelo" than to write "Cavalleria Rusticana" or "La Lupa". But the literary smarties, being so smart, have always praised the latter two above the others.

This business of missing out transition passages is quite deliberate on Verga's part. It is perhaps most evident in this volume, because it is here that Verga practises it for the first time. It was a new dodge, and he handled it badly. The sliding-over of the change from Jeli's boyhood to his young manhood is surely too deliberately confusing!

But Verga had a double motive. First was the Frenchy idea of self-effacement, which, however, didn't go very deep, as Verga was too much of a true southerner to know quite what it meant. But the second motive was more dynamic. It was connected with Verga's whole recoil from the sophisticated

world, and it effected a revolution in his style. Instinctively he
had come to hate the tyranny of a persistently logical sequence,
or even a persistently chronological sequence. Time and the
syllogism both seemed to represent the sophisticated falsehood
and a sort of bullying, to him.

He tells us himself how he came across his new style:

"I had published several of my first novels. They went well:
I was preparing others. One day, I don't know how, there came
into my hands a sort of broadside, a halfpenny sheet, sufficiently
ungrammatical and disconnected, in which a sea-captain
succinctly relates all the vicissitudes through which his sailing-
ship has passed. Seaman's language, short, without an unnecessary phrase. It struck me, and I read it again; it was what
I was looking for, without definitely knowing it. Sometimes,
you know, just a sign, an indication is enough. It is a revelation. . . ."

This passage explains all we need to know about Verga's
style, which is perhaps at its most extreme in this volume. He
was trying to follow the workings of the unsophisticated mind,
and trying to reproduce the pattern.

Now the emotional mind, if we may be allowed to say so, is
not logical. It is a psychological fact, that when we are thinking
emotionally or passionately, thinking and feeling at the same
time, we do not think rationally: and therefore, and therefore,
and therefore. Instead, the mind makes curious swoops and
circles. It touches the point of pain or interest, then sweeps
away again in a cycle, coils round and approaches again the
point of pain or interest. There is a curious spiral rhythm, and
the mind approaches again and again the point of concern,
repeats itself, goes back, destroys the time-sequence entirely, so
that time ceases to exist, as the mind stoops to the quarry, then
leaves it without striking, soars, hovers, turns, swoops, stoops
again, still does not strike, yet is nearer, nearer, reels away again,
wheels off into the air, even forgets, quite forgets, yet again turns,
bends, circles slowly, swoops and stoops again, until at last
there is the closing-in, and the clutch of a decision or a resolve.

This activity of the mind is strictly timeless, and illogical.
Afterwards you can deduce the logical sequence and the time
sequence, as historians do from the past. But in the happening,
the logical and the time sequence do not exist.

Verga tried to convey this in his style. It gives at first the sense of jumble and incoherence. The beginning of the story "Brothpot" is a good example of this breathless muddle of the peasant mind. When one is used to it, it is amusing, and a new movement in deliberate consciousness: though the humorists have used the form before. But at first it may be annoying. Once he starts definitely narrating, however, Verga drops the "muddled" method, and seeks only to be concise, often too concise, too abrupt in the transition. And in the matter of punctuation he is, perhaps deliberately, a puzzle, aiming at the same muddled swift effect of the emotional mind in its movements. He is doing, as a great artist, what men like James Joyce do only out of contrariness and desire for a sensation. The emotional mind, however apparently muddled, has its own rhythm, its own commas and colons and full-stops. They are not always as we should expect them, but they are there, indicating that other rhythm.

Everybody knows, of course, that Verga made a dramatised version of "Cavalleria Rusticana", and that this dramatised version is the libretto of the ever-popular little opera of the same name. So that Mascagni's rather feeble music has gone to immortalise a man like Verga, whose only *popular* claim to fame is that he wrote the aforesaid libretto. But that is fame's fault, not Verga's.

[Introduction to Lawrence's translation of *Cavalleria Rusticana*, London, 1928.]

[93]

THE MOTHER

BY GRAZIA DELEDDA

GRAZIA DELEDDA is already one of the elder living writers of Italy, and though her work does not take on quite so rapidly as the novels of Fogazzaro, or even d'Annunzio, that peculiarly obscuring nebulousness of the past-which-is-only-just-gone-by, still, the dimness has touched it. It is curious that fifteen or twenty years ago should seem so much more remote than fifty or eighty years ago. But perhaps it is organically necessary to us that our feelings should die, temporarily, towards that strange intermediate period which lies between present actuality and the revived past. We can hardly bear to recall the emotions of twenty or fifteen years ago, hardly at all, whereas we respond again quite vividly to the emotions of Jane Austen or Dickens, nearer a hundred years ago. There, the past is safely and finally past. The past of fifteen years ago is still yeastily working in us.

It takes a really good writer to make us overcome our repugnance to the just-gone-by emotions. Even d'Annunzio's novels are hardly readable at present: Matilda Serao's still less so. But we can still read Grazia Deledda with genuine interest.

The reason is that, though she is not a first-class genius, she belongs to more than just her own day. She does more than reproduce the temporary psychological condition of her period. She has a background, and she deals with something more fundamental than sophisticated feeling. She does not penetrate, as a great genius does, the very sources of human passion and motive. She stays far short of that. But what she does do is to create the passionate complex of a primitive populace.

To do this, one must have an isolated populace: just as Thomas Hardy isolates Wessex. Grazia Deledda has an island to herself, her own island of Sardinia, that she loves so deeply: especially the more northerly, mountainous part of Sardinia.

Still Sardinia is one of the wildest, remotest parts of Europe, with a strange people and a mysterious past of its own. There is still an old mystery in the air, over the forest slopes of Mount Gennargentu, as there is over some old Druid places, the mystery of an unevolved people. The war, of course, partly gutted Sardinia, as it gutted everywhere. But the island is still a good deal off the map, on the face of the earth.

An island of rigid conventions, the rigid conventions of barbarism, and at the same time the fierce violence of the instinctive passions. A savage tradition of chastity, with a savage lust of the flesh. A barbaric overlordship of the gentry, with a fierce indomitableness of the servile classes. A lack of public opinion, a lack of belonging to any other part of the world, a lack of mental awakening, which makes inland Sardinia almost as savage as Benin, and makes Sardinian singing as wonderful and almost as wild as any on earth. It is the human instinct still uncontaminated. The money-sway still did not govern central Sardinia, in the days of Grazia Deledda's books, twenty, a dozen years ago, before the war. Instead, there was a savage kind of aristocracy and feudalism, and a rule of ancient instinct, instinct with the definite but indescribable tang of the aboriginal people of the island, not absorbed into the world: instinct often at war with the Italian Government; a determined, savage individualism often breaking with the law, or driven into brigandage: but human, of the great human mystery.

It is this old Sardinia, at last being brought to heel, which is the real theme of Grazia Deledda's books. She is fascinated by her island and its folks, more than by the problems of the human psyche. And therefore this book, *The Mother*, is perhaps one of the least typical of her novels, one of the most "Continental". Because here, she has a definite universal theme: the consecrated priest and the woman. But she keeps on forgetting her theme. She becomes more interested in the death of the old hunter, in the doings of the boy Antiochus, in the exorcising of the spirit from the little girl possessed. She is herself somewhat bored by the priest's hesitations; she shows herself suddenly impatient, a pagan sceptical of the virtues of chastity, even in consecrated priests; she is touched, yet annoyed, by the pathetic, tiresome old mother who made her son a priest out of ambition, and who simply expires in the terror of a public exposure: and, in short, she makes a bit of a mess of the book, because she started a problem she didn't quite dare to solve. She shirks the issue atrociously. But neither will the modern spirit solve the problem by killing off the fierce instincts that made the problem. As for Grazia Deledda, first she started by sympathising with the mother, and then must sympathise savagely with the young woman, and then can't make up her mind. She kills off the old mother in disgust at the old woman's triumph, so leaving the priest and the young woman hanging in space. As a sort of problem-story, it is disappointing. No doubt, if the priest had gone off with the woman, as he first intended, then all the authoress's sympathy would have fallen to the old abandoned mother. As it is, the sympathy falls between two stools, and the title *La Madre* is not really justified. The mother turns out not to be the heroine.

But the interest of the book lies, not in plot or characterisation, but in the presentation of sheer instinctive life. The love of the priest for the woman is sheer instinctive passion, pure and undefiled by sentiment. As such it is worthy of respect, for in other books on this theme the instinct is swamped and extinguished in sentiment. Here, however, the instinct of direct sex is so strong and so vivid, that only the other blind instinct of mother-obedience, the child-instinct, can overcome it. All the priest's education and Christianity are really mere snuff of the candle. The old, wild instinct of a mother's ambition for her son defeats the other wild instinct of sexual mating. An old woman who has never had any sex-life—and it is astonishing, in barbaric half-civilisation, how many people are denied a sex-life—she succeeds, by her old barbaric maternal power over her son, in finally killing his sex-life too. It is the suicide of semi-barbaric natures under the sway of a dimly comprehended Christianity, and falsely conceived ambition.

The old, blind life of instinct, and chiefly frustrated instinct and the rage thereof, as it is seen in the Sardinian hinterland, this is Grazia Deledda's absorption. The desire of the boy Antiochus to be a priest is an instinct: perhaps an instinctive recoil from his mother's grim priapism. The dying man escapes from the village, back to the rocks, instinctively needing to die in the wilds. The feeling of Agnes, the woman who loves the priest, is sheer female instinctive passion, something as in Emily Brontë. It too has the ferocity of frustrated instinct, and is bare and stark, lacking any of the graces of sentiment. This saves it from "dating" as d'Annunzio's passions date. Sardinia is by no means a land for Romeos and Juliets, nor even Virgins of the Rocks. It is rather the land of *Wuthering Heights*.

The book, of course, loses a good deal in translation, as is inevitable. In the mouths of the simple people, Italian is a purely instinctive language, with the rhythm of instinctive rather than mental processes. There are also many instinct-words with meanings never clearly mentally defined. In fact, nothing is brought to real mental clearness, everything goes by in a stream of more or less vague, more or less realised, feeling, with a natural mist or glow of sensation over everything, that counts more than the actual words said; and which, alas, it is almost impossible to reproduce in the more cut-and-dried northern languages, where every word has its fixed value and meaning, like so much coinage. A language can be killed by over-precision, killed especially as an effective medium for the conveyance of instinctive passion and instinctive emotion. One feels this, reading a translation from the Italian. And though Grazia Deledda is not masterly as Giovanni Verga is, yet, in Italian at least, she can put us into the mood and rhythm of Sardinia, like a true artist, an artist whose work is sound and enduring.

[Preface to *The Mother* translated by M. G. Steegmann, London, 1928.]

PART SIX

Americans

[94]

THE SPIRIT OF PLACE

WE like to think of the old fashioned American classics as children's books. Just childishness, on our part. The old American art-speech contains an alien quality, which belongs to the American continent and to nowhere else. But, of course, so long as we insist on reading the books as children's tales, we miss all that.

One wonders what the proper highbrow Romans of the third and fourth or later centuries read into the strange utterances of Lucretius or Apuleius or Tertullian, Augustine or Athanasius. The uncanny voice of Iberian Spain, the weirdness of old Carthage, the passion of Libya and North Africa; you may bet the proper old Romans never heard these at all. They read old Latin inference over the top of it, as we read old European inference over the top of Poe or Hawthorne.

It is hard to hear a new voice, as hard as it is to listen to an unknown language. We just don't listen. There is a new voice in the old American classics. The world has declined to hear it, and has babbled about children's stories.

Why?—Out of fear. The world fears a new experience more than it fears anything. Because a new experience displaces so many old experiences. And it is like trying to use muscles that have perhaps never been used, or that have been going stiff for ages. It hurts horribly.

The world doesn't fear a new idea. It can pigeon-hole any idea. But it can't pigeon-hole a real new experience. It can only dodge. The world is a great dodger, and the Americans the greatest. Because they dodge their own very selves.

There is a new feeling in the old American books, far more

than there is in the modern American books, which are pretty empty of any feeling, and proud of it. There is a "different" feeling in the old American classics. It is the shifting over from the old psyche to something new, a displacement. And displacements hurt. This hurts. So we try to tie it up, like a cut finger. Put a rag round it.

It is a cut too. Cutting away the old emotions and consciousness. Don't ask what is left.

Art-speech is the only truth. An artist is usually a damned liar, but his art, if it be art, will tell you the truth of his day. And that is all that matters. Away with eternal truth. Truth lives from day to day, and the marvellous Plato of yesterday is chiefly bosh to-day.

The old American artists were hopeless liars. But they were artists, in spite of themselves. Which is more than you can say of most living practitioners.

And you can please yourself, when you read *The Scarlet Letter*, whether you accept what that sugary, blue-eyed little darling of a Hawthorne has to say for himself, false as all darlings are, or whether you read the impeccable truth of his art-speech.

The curious thing about art-speech is that it prevaricates so terribly, I mean it tells such lies. I suppose because we always all the time tell ourselves lies. And out of a pattern of lies art weaves the truth. Like Dostoievsky posing as a sort of Jesus, but most truthfully revealing himself all the while as a little horror.

Truly art is a sort of subterfuge. But thank God for it, we can see through the subterfuge if we choose. Art has two great functions. First, it provides an emotional experience. And then, if we have the courage of our own feelings, it becomes a mine of practical truth. We have had the feelings *ad nauseam*. But we've never dared dig the actual truth out of them, the truth that concerns us, whether it concerns our grandchildren or not.

The artist usually sets out—or used to—to point a moral and adorn a tale. The tale, however, points the other way, as a rule. Two blankly opposing morals, the artist's and the tale's. Never trust the artist. Trust the tale. The proper function of a critic is to save the tale from the artist who created it.

Now we know our business in these studies; saving the
American tale from the American artist.

Let us look at this American artist first. How did he ever
get to America, to start with? Why isn't he a European still,
like his father before him?

Now listen to me, don't listen to him. He'll tell you the lie
you expect. Which is partly your fault for expecting it.

He didn't come in search of freedom of worship. England
had more freedom of worship in the year 1700 than America
had. Won by Englishmen who wanted freedom, and so stopped
at home and fought for it. And got it. Freedom of worship?
Read the history of New England during the first century of
its existence.

Freedom anyhow? The land of the free! This the land of the
free! Why, if I say anything that displeases them, the free
mob will lynch me, and that's my freedom. Free? Why I
have never been in any country where the individual has such
an abject fear of his fellow-countrymen. Because, as I say, they
are free to lynch him the moment he shows he is not one of
them.

No, no, if you're so fond of the truth about Queen Victoria,
try a little about yourself.

Those Pilgrim Fathers and their successors never came here
for freedom of worship. What did they set up when they got
here? Freedom, would you call it?

They didn't come for freedom. Or if they did, they sadly
went back on themselves.

All right then, what did they come for? For lots of reasons.
Perhaps least of all in search of freedom of any sort: positive
freedom, that is.

They came largely to get *away*—that most simple of motives.
To get away. Away from what? In the long run, away from
themselves. Away from everything. That's why most people
have come to America, and still do come. To get away from
everything they are and have been.

"Henceforth be masterless."

Which is all very well, but it isn't freedom. Rather the
reverse. A hopeless sort of constraint. It is never freedom
till you find something you really *positively want to be*. And
people in America have always been shouting about the things

they are *not*. Unless, of course, they are millionaires, made or in the making.

And after all there is a positive side to the movement. All that vast flood of human life that has flowed over the Atlantic in ships from Europe to America has not flowed over simply on a tide of revulsion from Europe and from the confinements of the European ways of life. This revulsion was, and still is, I believe, the prime motive in emigration. But there was some cause, even for the revulsion.

It seems as if at times man had a frenzy for getting away from any control of any sort. In Europe the old Christianity was the real master. The Church and the true aristocracy bore the responsibility for the working out of the Christian ideals: a little irregularly, maybe, but responsible nevertheless.

Mastery, kingship, fatherhood had their power destroyed at the time of the Renaissance.

And it was precisely at this moment that the great drift over the Atlantic started. What were men drifting away from? The old authority of Europe? Were they breaking the bonds of authority, and escaping to a new more absolute unrestrainedness? Maybe. But there was more to it.

Liberty is all very well, but men cannot live without masters. There is always a master. And men either live in glad obedience to the master they believe in, or they live in a frictional opposition to the master they wish to undermine. In America this frictional opposition has been the vital factor. It has given the Yankee his kick. Only the continual influx of more servile Europeans has provided America with an obedient labouring class. The true obedience never outlasting the first generation.

But there sits the old master, over in Europe. Like a parent. Somewhere deep in every American heart lies a rebellion against the old parenthood of Europe. Yet no American feels he has completely escaped its mastery. Hence the slow, smouldering patience of American opposition. The slow, smouldering, corrosive obedience to the old master Europe, the unwilling subject, the unremitting oposition.

Whatever else you are, be masterless.

Ca Ca Caliban
Get a new master, be a new man.

Escaped slaves, we might say, people the republics of Liberia or Haiti. Liberia enough! Are we to look at America in the same way? A vast republic of escaped slaves. When you consider the hordes from eastern Europe, you might well say it: a vast republic of escaped slaves. But one dare not say this of the Pilgrim Fathers, and the great old body of idealist Americans, the modern Americans tortured with thought. A vast republic of escaped slaves. Look out, America! And a minority of earnest, self-tortured people.

The masterless.

> Ca Ca Caliban
> Get a new master, be a new man.

What did the Pilgrim Fathers come for, then, when they came so gruesomely over the black sea? Oh, it was in a black spirit. A black revulsion from Europe, from the old authority of Europe, from kings and bishops and popes. And more. When you look into it, more. They were black, masterful men, they wanted something else. No kings, no bishops maybe. Even no God Almighty. But also, no more of this new "humanity" which followed the Renaissance. None of this new liberty which was to be so pretty in Europe. Something grimmer, by no means free-and-easy.

America has never been easy, and is not easy to-day. Americans have always been at a certain tension. Their liberty is a thing of sheer will, sheer tension: a liberty of THOU SHALT NOT. And it has been so from the first. The land of THOU SHALT NOT. Only the first commandment is: THOU SHALT NOT PRESUME TO BE A MASTER. Hence democracy.

"We are the masterless." That is what the American Eagle shrieks. It's a Hen-Eagle.

The Spaniards refused the post-Renaissance liberty of Europe. And the Spaniards filled most of America. The Yankees, too, refused, refused the post-Renaissance humanism of Europe. First and foremost, they hated masters. But under that, they hated the flowing ease of humour in Europe. At the bottom of the American soul was always a dark suspense, at the bottom of the Spanish-American soul the same. And this dark suspense hated and hates the old European spontaneity, watches it collapse with satisfaction.

Every continent has its own great spirit of place. Every people is polarised in some particular locality, which is home, the homeland. Different places on the face of the earth have different vital effluence, different vibration, different chemical exhalation, different polarity with different stars: call it what you like. But the spirit of place is a great reality. The Nile valley produced not only the corn, but the terrific religions of Egypt. China produces the Chinese, and will go on doing so. The Chinese in San Francisco will in time cease to be Chinese, for America is a great melting-pot.

There was a tremendous polarity in Italy, in the city of Rome. And this seems to have died. For even places die. The Island of Great Britain had a wonderful terrestrial magnetism or polarity of its own, which made the British people. For the moment, this polarity seems to be breaking. Can England die? And what if England dies?

Men are less free than they imagine; ah, far less free. The freest are perhaps least free.

Men are free when they are in a living homeland, not when they are straying and breaking away. Men are free when they are obeying some deep, inward voice of religious belief. Obeying from within. Men are free when they belong to a living, organic, *believing* community, active in fulfilling some unfulfilled, perhaps unrealised purpose. Not when they are escaping to some wild west. The most unfree souls go west, and shout of freedom. Men are freest when they are most unconscious of freedom. The shout is a rattling of chains, always was.

Men are not free when they are doing just what they like. The moment you can do just what you like, there is nothing you care about doing. Men are only free when they are doing what the deepest self likes.

And there is getting down to the deepest self! It takes some diving.

Because the deepest self is way down, and the conscious self is an obstinate monkey. But of one thing we may be sure. If one wants to be free, one has to give up the illusion of doing what one likes, and seek what IT wishes done.

But before you can do what IT likes, you must first break the spell of the old mastery, the old IT.

Perhaps at the Renaissance, when kingship and fatherhood fell, Europe drifted into a very dangerous half-truth: of liberty and equality. Perhaps the men who went to America felt this, and so repudiated the old world altogether. Went one better than Europe. Liberty in America has meant so far the breaking away from *all* dominion. The true liberty will only begin when Americans discover IT, and proceed possibly to fulfil IT. IT being the deepest *whole* self of man, the self in its wholeness, not idealistic halfness.

That's why the Pilgrim Fathers came to America, then; and that's why we come. Driven by IT. We cannot see that invisible winds carry us, as they carry swarms of locusts, that invisible magnetism brings us as it brings the migrating birds to their unforeknown goal. But it is so. We are not the marvellous choosers and deciders we think we are. IT chooses for us, and decides for us. Unless, of course, we are just escaped slaves, vulgarly cocksure of our ready-made destiny. But if we are living people, in touch with the source, IT drives us and decides us. We are free only so long as we obey. When we run counter, and think we will do as we like, we just flee around like Orestes pursued by the Eumenides.

And still, when the great day begins, when Americans have at last discovered America and their own wholeness, still there will be the vast number of escaped slaves to reckon with, those who have no cocksure, ready-made destinies.

Which will win in America, the escaped slaves, or the new whole men?

The real American day hasn't begun yet. Or at least, not yet sunrise. So far it has been the false dawn. That is, in the progressive American consciousness there has been the one dominant desire, to do away with the old thing. Do away with masters, exalt the will of the people. The will of the people being nothing but a figment, the exalting doesn't count for much. So, in the name of the will of the people, get rid of masters. When you have got rid of masters, you are left with this mere phrase of the will of the people. Then you pause and bethink yourself, and try to recover your own wholeness.

So much for the conscious American motive, and for democracy over here. Democracy in America is just the tool with which the old master of Europe, the European spirit, is under-mined. Europe destroyed, potentially, American democracy will evaporate. America will begin.

American consciousness has so far been a false dawn. The negative ideal of democracy. But underneath, and contrary to this open ideal, the first hints and revelations of IT. IT, the American whole soul.

You have got to pull the democratic and idealistic clothes off American utterance, and see what you can of the dusky body of IT underneath.

"Henceforth be masterless."

Henceforth be mastered.

[From *Studies in Classic American Literature*, 1924.]

[95]

FENIMORE COOPER'S WHITE NOVELS

BENJAMIN FRANKLIN had a specious little equation in provi-dential mathematics:

$$Rum + Savage = 0.$$

Awfully nice! You might add up the universe to nought, if you kept on.

Rum plus Savage may equal a dead savage. But is a dead savage nought? Can you make a land virgin by killing off its aborigines?

The Aztec is gone, and the Incas. The Red Indian, the Esquimo, the Patagonian are reduced to negligible numbers.

Où sont les neiges d'antan?

My dear, wherever they are, they will come down again next winter, sure as houses.

Not that the Red Indian will ever possess the broad lands of America. At least I presume not. But his ghost will.

The Red Man died hating the white man. What remnant of him lives, lives hating the white man. Go near the Indians, and you just feel it. As far as we are concerned, the Red Man is subtly and unremittingly diabolic. Even when he doesn't know it. He is dispossessed in life, and unforgiving. He doesn't believe in us and our civilisation, and so is our mystic enemy, for we push him off the face of the earth.

Belief is a mysterious thing. It is the only healer of the soul's wounds. There is no belief in the world.

The Red Man is dead, disbelieving in us. He is dead and unappeased. Do not imagine him happy in his Happy Hunting Ground. No. Only those that die in belief die happy. Those that are pushed out of life in chagrin come back unappeased, for revenge.

A curious thing about the Spirit of Place is the fact that no place exerts its full influence upon a new-comer until the old inhabitant is dead or absorbed. So America. While the Red Indian existed in fairly large numbers, the new colonials were in a great measure immune from the daimon, or demon, of America. The moment the last nuclei of Red life break up in America, then the white men will have to reckon with the full force of the demon of the continent. At present the demon of the place and the unappeased ghosts of the dead Indians act within the unconscious or under-conscious soul of the white American, causing the great American grouch, the Orestes-like frenzy of restlessness in the Yankee soul, the inner malaise which amounts almost to madness, sometimes. The Mexican is macabre and disintegrated in his own way. Up till now, the unexpressed spirit of America has worked covertly in the American, the white American soul. But within the present generation the surviving Red Indians are due to merge in the great white swamp. Then the Daimon of America will work overtly, and we shall see real changes.

There has been all the time, in the white American soul, a dual feeling about the Indian. First was Franklin's feeling, that a wise Providence no doubt intended the extirpation of these savages. Then came Crèvecœur's contradictory feeling about the noble Red Man and the innocent life of the wigwam. Now we hate to subscribe to Benjamin's belief in a Providence that wisely extirpates the Indian to make room for "cultivators of the soul". In Crèvecœur we meet a sentimental desire for the glorification of the savages. Absolutely sentimental. Hector pops over to Paris to enthuse about the wigwam.

The desire to extirpate the Indian. And the contradictory desire to glorify him. Both are rampant still, to-day.

The bulk of the white people who live in contact with the Indian to-day would like to see this Red brother exterminated; not only for the sake of grabbing his land, but because of the silent, invisible, but deadly hostility between the spirit of the two races. The minority of whites intellectualise the Red Man and laud him to the skies. But this minority of whites is mostly a highbrow minority with a big grouch against its own whiteness. So there you are.

I doubt if there is possible any real reconciliation, in the flesh, between the white and the red. For instance, a Red Indian girl who is servant in the white man's home, if she is treated with natural consideration, will probably serve well, even happily. She is happy with the new power over the white woman's kitchen. The white world makes her feel prouder, so long as she is free to go back to her own people at the given times. But she is happy because she is playing at being a white woman. There are other Indian women who would never serve the white people, and who would rather die than have a white man for a lover.

In either case, there is no reconciliation. There is no mystic conjunction between the spirit of the two races. The Indian girl who happily serves white people leaves out her own race-consideration, for the time being.

Supposing a white man goes out hunting in the mountains with an Indian. The two will probably get on like brothers. But let the same white man go alone with two Indians, and there will start a most subtle persecution of the unsuspecting white. If they, the Indians, discover that he has a natural fear of steep places, then over every precipice in the country will the trail lead. And so on. Malice! That is the basic feeling in the Indian heart, towards the white. It may even be purely unconscious.

Supposing an Indian loves a white woman, and lives with her. He will probably be very proud of it, for he will be a big man among his own people, especially if the white mistress has money. He will never get over the feeling of pride at dining in a white dining-room and smoking in a white drawing-room. But at the same time he will subtly jeer at his white mistress, try to destroy her white pride. He will submit to her, if he is forced to, with a kind of false, unwilling childishness, and even love her with the same childlike gentleness, sometimes beautiful. But at the bottom of his heart he is gibing, gibing, gibing at her. Not only is it the sex resistance, but the race resistance as well.

There seems to be no reconciliation in the flesh.

That leaves us only expiation, and then reconciliation in the soul. Some strange atonement: expiation and oneing.

Fenimore Cooper has probably done more than any writer to present the Red Man to the white man. But Cooper's presentment is indeed a wish-fulfilment. That is why Fenimore is such a success still.

Modern critics begrudge Cooper his success. I think I resent it a little myself. This popular wish-fulfilment stuff makes it so hard for the real thing to come through, later.

Cooper was a rich American of good family. His father founded Cooperstown, by Lake Champlain. And Fenimore was a gentleman of culture. No denying it.

It is amazing how cultured these Americans of the first half of the eighteenth century were. Most intensely so. Austin Dobson and Andrew Lang are flea-bites in comparison. Volumes of very *raffiné* light verse and finely drawn familiar literature will prove it to anyone who cares to commit himself to these elderly books. The English and French writers of the same period were clumsy and hoydenish, judged by the same standards.

Truly, European decadence was anticipated in America; and American influence passed over to Europe, was assimilated there, and then returned to this land of innocence as something purplish in its modernity and a little wicked. So absurd things are.

Cooper quotes a Frenchman, who says, *"L'Amérique est pourrie avant d'être mûre."* And there is a great deal in it. America was not taught by France—by Baudelaire, for example. Baudelaire learned his lesson from America.

Cooper's novels fall into two classes: his white novels, such as *Homeward Bound, Eve Effingham, The Spy, The Pilot,* and then the *Leatherstocking Series.* Let us look at the white novels first.

The Effinghams are three extremely refined, genteel Americans who are "Homeward Bound" from England to the States.

Their party consist of father, daughter, and uncle, and faithful nurse. The daughter has just finished her education in Europe. She has, indeed, skimmed the cream off Europe. England, France, Italy, and Germany have nothing more to teach her. She is bright and charming, admirable creature; a real modern heroine; intrepid, calm, and self-collected, yet admirably impulsive, always in perfectly good taste; clever and assured in her speech, like a man, but withal charmingly deferential and modest before the stronger sex. It is the perfection of the ideal female. We have learned to shudder at her, but Cooper still admired.

On board is the other type of American, the parvenu, the demagogue, who has "done" Europe and put it in his breeches pocket, in a month. Oh, Septimus Dodge, if a European had drawn you, that European would never have been forgiven by America. But an American drew you, so Americans wisely ignore you.

Septimus is the American self-made man. God had no hand in his make-up. He made himself. He has been to Europe, no doubt seen everything, including the Venus de Milo. "What, is *that* the Venus de Milo?" And he turns his back on the lady. He's seen her. He's got her. She's a fish he has hooked, and he's off to America with her, leaving the scum of a statue standing in the Louvre.

That is one American way of Vandalism. The original Vandals would have given the complacent dame a knock with a battle-axe, and ended her. The insatiable American looks at her. "Is *that* the Venus de Milo?—come on!" And the Venus de Milo stands there like a naked slave in a market-place, whom someone has spat on. Spat on!

I have often thought, hearing American tourists in Europe —in the Bargello in Florence, for example, or in the Piazza di San Marco in Venice—exclaiming, "Isn't that just too cunning!" or else, "Aren't you perfectly crazy about Saint Mark's! Don't you think those cupolas are like the loveliest *turnips* upside down, you know"—as if the beautiful things of Europe were just having their guts pulled out by these American admirers. They admire so wholesale. Sometimes they even seem to grovel. But the golden cupolas of St. Mark's in Venice are turnips upside down in a stale stew, after enough American tourists have looked at them. Turnips upside down in a stale stew. Poor Europe!

And there you are. When a few German bombs fell upon Rheims Cathedral up went a howl of execration. But there are more ways than one of vandalism. I should think the American admiration of five-minutes' tourists has done more to kill the sacredness of old European beauty and aspiration than multitudes of bombs would have done.

But there you are. Europe has got to fall, and peace hath her victories.

Behold then Mr. Septimus Dodge returning to Dodge-town victorious. Not crowned with laurel, it is true, but wreathed in lists of things he has seen and sucked dry. Seen and sucked dry, you know: Venus de Milo, the Rhine, or the Coliseum: swallowed like so many clams, and left the shells.

Now the aristocratic Effinghams, Homeward Bound from Europe to America, are at the mercy of Mr. Dodge: Septimus. He is their compatriot, so they may not disown him. Had they been English, of course, they would never once have let themselves become aware of his existence. But no. They are American democrats, and therefore, if Mr. Dodge marches up and says: "Mr. Effingham? Pleased to meet you, Mr. Effingham"—why, then Mr. Effingham is *forced* to reply: "Pleased to meet you, Mr. Dodge." If he didn't, he would have the terrible hounds of democracy on his heels and at his throat, the moment he landed in the Land of the Free. An Englishman is free to continue unaware of the existence of a fellow-countryman, if the looks of that fellow-countryman are distasteful. But every American citizen is free to force his presence upon you, no matter how unwilling you may be.

Freedom!

The Effinghams detest Mr. Dodge. They abhor him. They loathe and despise him. They have an unmitigated contempt for him. Everything he is, says, and does, seems to them too vulgar, too despicable. Yet they are forced to answer, when he presents himself: "Pleased to meet you, Mr. Dodge."

Freedom!

Mr. Dodge, of Dodge-town, alternately fawns and intrudes, cringes and bullies. And the Effinghams, terribly "superior" in a land of equality, writhe helpless. They would fain snub

Septimus out of existence. But Septimus is not to be snubbed. As a true democrat, he is unsnubbable. As a true democrat, he has right on his side. And right is might.

Right is might. It is the old struggle for power.

Septimus, as a true democrat, is the equal of any man. As a true democrat with a full pocket, he is, by the amount that fills his pocket, so much the superior of the democrats with empty pockets. Because, though all men are born equal and die equal, you will not get anybody to admit that ten dollars equal ten thousand dollars. No, no, there's a difference there, however far you may push equality.

Septimus has the Effinghams on the hip. He has them fast, and they will not escape. What tortures await them at home, in the Land of the Free, at the hands of the hideously affable Dodge, we do not care to disclose. What was the persecution of a haughty Lord or a marauding Baron or an inquisitorial Abbot compared to the persecution of a million Dodges? The proud Effinghams are like men buried naked to the chin in ant-heaps, to be bitten into extinction by a myriad ants. Stoically, as good democrats and idealists, they writhe and endure, without making too much moan.

They writhe and endure. There is no escape. Not from that time to this. No escape. They writhed on the horns of the Dodge dilemma.

Since then Ford has gone one worse.

Through these white novels of Cooper runs the acid of ant-bites, the formic acid of democratic poisoning. The Effinghams feel superior. Cooper felt superior. Mrs. Cooper felt superior too. And bitten.

For they were democrats. They didn't believe in kings, or lords, or masters, or real superiority of any sort. Before God, of course. In the sight of God, of course, all men were equal. This they believed. And therefore, though they *felt* terribly superior to Mr. Dodge, yet, since they were his equals in the sight of God, they could not feel free to say to him: "Mr. Dodge, please go to the devil." They had to say: "Pleased to meet you."

What a lie to tell! Democratic lies.

What a dilemma! To feel so superior. To *know* you are superior. And yet to believe that, in the sight of God, you are equal. Can't help yourself.

Why couldn't they let the Lord Almighty look after the equality, since it seems to happen specifically in His sight, and stick themselves to their own superiority. Why couldn't they?

Somehow they daren't.

They were Americans, idealists. How dare they balance a mere tense feeling against an IDEA and an IDEAL?

Ideally—i.e., in the sight of God, Mr. Dodge was their equal. What a low opinion they held of the Almighty's faculty for discrimination.

But it was so. The IDEAL of EQUALITY.

Pleased to meet you, Mr. Dodge.

We are equal in the sight of God, of course. But er——

Very glad to meet you, Miss Effingham. Did you say—*er*? Well now, I think my bank balance will bear it.

Poor Eve Effingham.

Eve! Think of it. Eve! And birds of paradise. And apples. And Mr. Dodge.

This is where apples of knowledge get you, Miss Eve. You should leave 'em alone.

"Mr. Dodge, you are a hopeless and insufferable inferior."

Why couldn't she say it? She felt it. And she was a heroine.

Alas, she was an American heroine. She was an EDUCATED WOMAN. She KNEW all about IDEALS. She swallowed the IDEAL of EQUALITY with her first mouthful of KNOWLEDGE. Alas for her and that apple of Sodom that looked so rosy. Alas for all her knowing.

Mr. Dodge (in check knickerbockers): Well, feeling a little uncomfortable below the belt, are you, Miss Effingham?

Miss Effingham (with difficulty withdrawing her gaze from the INFINITE OCEAN): Good morning, Mr. Dodge. I was admiring the dark blue distance.

Mr. Dodge: Say, couldn't you admire something a bit nearer.

Think how easy it would have been for her to say "Go away!" or "Leave me, varlet!"—or "Hence base-born knave!" Or just to turn her back on him.

But then he would simply have marched round to the other side of her.

Was she his superior, or wasn't she?

Why surely, intrinsically, she *was*. Intrinsically Fenimore Cooper was the superior of the Dodges of his day. He felt it. But he felt he ought not to feel it. And he never had it out with himself.

That is why one rather gets impatient with him. He feels he is superior, and feels he ought *not* to feel so, and is therefore rather snobbish, and at the same time a little apologetic. Which is surely tiresome.

If a man feels superior, he should have it out with himself. "Do I feel superior because I *am* superior? Or is it just the snobbishness of class, or education, or money?"

Class, education, money won't make a man superior. But if he's just *born* superior, in himself, there it is. Why deny it?

It is a nasty sight to see the Effinghams putting themselves at the mercy of a Dodge, just because of a mere idea or ideal. Fools. They ruin more than they know. Because at the same time they are snobbish.

Septimus at the Court of King Arthur.

Septimus: Hello, Arthur! Pleased to meet you. By the way, what's all that great long sword about?

Arthur: This is Excalibur, the sword of my knighthood and my kingship.

Septimus: That so! We're all equal in the sight of God, you know, Arthur.

Arthur: Yes.

Septimus: Then I guess it's about time I had that yard-and-a-half of Excalibur to play with. Don't you think so? We're equal in the sight of God, and you've had it for quite a while.

Arthur: Yes, I agree. (Hands him Excalibur.)

Septimus (prodding Arthur with Excalibur): Say, Art, which is your fifth rib?

Superiority is a sword. Hand it over to Septimus, and you'll get it back between your ribs.—The whole moral of democracy.

But there you are. Eve Effingham had pinned herself down on the *Contrat Social*, and she was prouder of that pin through her body than of any mortal thing else. Her IDEAL. Her IDEAL of DEMOCRACY.

When America set out to destroy Kings and Lords and Masters, and the whole paraphernalia of European superiority, it pushed a pin right through its own body, and on that pin it still flaps and buzzes and twists in misery. The pin of democratic equality. Freedom.

There'll never be any life in America till you pull the pin out and admit natural inequality. Natural superiority, natural inferiority. Till such time, Americans just buzz round like various sorts of propellers, pinned down by their freedom and equality.

That's why these white novels of Fenimore Cooper are only historically and sardonically interesting. The people are all pinned down by some social pin, and buzzing away in social importance or friction, round and round on the pin. Never real human beings. Always things pinned down, choosing to be pinned down, transfixed by the idea or ideal of equality and democracy, on which they turn loudly and importantly, like propellers propelling. These States. Humanly, it is boring. As a historic phenomenon, it is amazing, ludicrous, and irritating.

If you don't pull the pin out in time, you'll never be able to pull it out. You must turn on it for ever, or bleed to death.

> Naked to the waist was I,
> And deep within my breast did lie,
> Though no man any blood could spy,
> The truncheon of a spear——

Is it already too late?

Oh God, the democratic pin!

Freedom, Equality, Equal Opportunity, Education, Rights of Man.

The pin! The pin!

Well, there buzzes Eve Effingham, snobbishly, impaled. She is a perfect American heroine, and I'm sure she wore the first smartly-tailored "suit" that ever woman wore. I'm sure she spoke several languages. I'm sure she was hopelessly competent. I'm sure she "adored" her husband, and spent masses of his money, and divorced him because he didn't understand Love.

American women in their perfect "suits". American men in their imperfect coats and skirts!

I feel I'm the superior of most men I meet. Not in birth,

because I never had a great-grandfather. Not in money, because I've got none. Not in education, because I'm merely scrappy. And certainly not in beauty or in manly strength.

Well, what then?

Just in myself.

When I'm challenged, I do feel myself superior to most of the men I meet. Just a natural superiority.

But not till there enters an element of challenge.

When I meet another man, and he is just himself—even if he is an ignorant Mexican pitted with smallpox—then there is no question between us of superiority or inferiority. He is a man and I am a man. We are ourselves. There is no question between us.

But let a question arise, let there be a challenge, and then I feel he should do reverence to the gods in me, because they are more than the gods in him. And he should give reverence to the very me, because it is more at one with the gods than is his very self.

If this is conceit, I am sorry. But it's the gods in me that matter. And in other men.

As for me, I am so glad to salute the brave, reckless gods in another man. So glad to meet a man who will abide by his very self.

Ideas! Ideals! All this paper between us. What a weariness.

If only people would meet in their very selves, without wanting to put some idea over one another, or some ideal.

Damn all ideas and all ideals. Damn all the false stress, and the pins.

I am I. Here am I. Where are you?

Ah, there you are! Now, damn the consequences, we have met.

That's my idea of democracy, if you can call it an idea.

[From *Studies in Classic American Literature*, 1924.]

[96]

FENIMORE COOPER'S LEATHERSTOCKING NOVELS

In his Leatherstocking books, Fenimore is off on another track. He is no longer concerned with social white Americans that buzz with pins through them, buzz loudly against every mortal thing except the pin itself. The pin of the Great Ideal.

One gets irritated with Cooper because he never for once snarls at the Great Ideal Pin which transfixes him. No, indeed. Rather he tries to push it through the very heart of the Continent.

But I have loved the Leatherstocking books so dearly. Wish-fulfilment!

Anyhow, one is not supposed to take LOVE seriously, in these books. Eve Effingham, impaled on the social pin, conscious all the time of her own ego and of nothing else, suddenly fluttering in throes of love: no, it makes me sick. LOVE is never LOVE until it has a pin pushed through it and becomes an IDEAL. The ego, turning on a pin, is wildly IN LOVE, always. Because that's the thing to be.

Cooper was a GENTLEMAN, in the worst sense of the word. In the Nineteenth Century sense of the word. A correct, clockwork man.

Not altogether, of course.

The great national Grouch was grinding inside him. Probably he called it COSMIC URGE. Americans usually do: in capital letters.

Best stick to National Grouch. The great American grouch. Cooper had it, gentleman that he was. That is why he flitted round Europe so uneasily. Of course, in Europe he could be, and was, a gentleman to his heart's content.

"In short", he says in one of his letters, "we were at table two counts, one monsignore, an English Lord, an Ambassador, and my humble self."

Were we really!

How nice it must have been to know that one self, at least, was humble.

And he felt the democratic American tomahawk wheeling over his uncomfortable scalp all the time.

The great American grouch.

Two monsters loomed in Cooper's horizon.

Mrs. Cooper	My Work
My Work	My Wife
My Wife	My Work

The Dear Children
My Work ! ! !

There you have the essential keyboard of Cooper's soul.

If there is one thing that annoys me more than a business man and his Business, it is an artist, a writer, painter, musician, and My Work. When an artist says My Work, the flesh goes tired on my bones. When he says My Wife, I want to hit him.

Cooper grizzled about his work. Oh, heaven, he cared so much whether it was good or bad, and what the French thought, and what Mr. Snippy Knowall said, and how Mrs. Cooper took it. The pin, the pin!

But he was truly an artist: then an American: then a gentleman.

And the grouch grouched inside him, through all.

They seem to have been specially fertile in imagining themselves "under the wigwam", do these Americans, just when their knees were comfortably under the mahogany, in Paris, along with the knees of

4 Counts
2 Cardinals
1 Milord
5 Cocottes
1 Humble self

You bet, though, that when the cocottes were being raffled off, Fenimore went home to his Wife.

Wish Fulfilment		Actuality
The Wigwam	vs.	My Hotel
Chingachgook	vs.	My Wife
Natty Bumppo	vs.	My Humble Self

Fenimore, lying in his Louis-Quatorze hotel in Paris, passionately musing about Natty Bumppo and the pathless forest, and mixing his imagination with the Cupids and Butterflies on the painted ceiling, while Mrs. Cooper was struggling with her latest gown in the next room, and the *déjeuner* was with the Countess at eleven. . . .

Men live by lies.

In actuality, Fenimore loved the genteel continent of Europe, and waited gasping for the newspapers to praise his WORK.

In another actuality he loved the tomahawking continent of America, and imagined himself Natty Bumppo.

His actual desire was to be: *Monsieur Fenimore Cooper, le grand écrivain américain.*

His innermost wish was to be: Natty Bumppo.

Now Natty and Fenimore, arm-in-arm, are an odd couple.

You can see Fenimore: blue coat, silver buttons, silver-and-diamond buckle shoes, ruffles.

You see Natty Bumppo: a grizzled, uncouth old renegade, with gaps in his old teeth and a drop on the end of his nose.

But Natty was Fenimore's great wish: his wish-fulfilment.

"It was a matter of course," says Mrs. Cooper, "that he should dwell on the better traits of the picture rather than on the coarser and more revolting, though more common points. Like West, he could see Apollo in the young Mohawk."

The coarser and more revolting, though more common points.

You see now why he depended so absolutely on MY WIFE. She had to look things in the face for him. The coarser and more revolting, and certainly more common points, she had to see.

He himself did so love seeing pretty-pretty, with the thrill of a red scalp now and then.

Fenimore, in his imagination, wanted to be Natty Bumppo, who, I am sure, belched after he had eaten his dinner. At the same time Mr. Cooper was nothing if not a gentleman. So he decided to stay in France and have it all his own way.

In France, Natty would not belch after eating, and Chingachgook could be all the Apollo he liked.

As if ever any Indian was like Apollo. The Indians, with their curious female quality, their archaic figures, with high shoulders and deep, archaic waists, like a sort of woman! And their natural devilishness, their natural insidiousness.

But men see what they want to see: especially if they look from a long distance, across the ocean, for example.

Yet the Leatherstocking books are lovely. Lovely half-lies.

They form a sort of American Odyssey, with Natty Bumppo for Odysseus.

Only, in the original Odyssey, there is plenty of devil, Circes and swine and all. And Ithacus is devil enough to outwit the devils. But Natty is a saint with a gun, and the Indians are gentlemen through and through, though they may take an occasional scalp.

There are five Leatherstocking novels: a *decrescendo* of reality, and a crescendo of beauty.

1. *Pioneers:* A raw frontier-village on Lake Champlain, at the end of the eighteenth century. Must be a picture of Cooper's home, as he knew it when a boy. A very lovely book. Natty Bumppo an old man, an old hunter half civilised.

2. *The Last of the Mohicans:* A historical fight between the British and the French, with Indians on both sides, at a Fort by Lake Champlain. Romantic flight of the British general's two daughters, conducted by the scout, Natty, who is in the prime of life; romantic death of the last of the Delawares.

3. *The Prairie:* A wagon of some huge, sinister Kentuckians trekking west into the unbroken prairie. Prairie Indians, and Natty, an old, old man; he dies seated on a chair on the Rocky Mountains, looking east.

4. *The Pathfinder:* The Great Lakes. Natty, a man of about thirty-five, makes an abortive proposal to a bouncing damsel, daughter of the Sergeant at the Fort.

5. *Deerslayer:* Natty and Hurry Harry, both quite young, are hunting in the virgin wild. They meet two white women. Lake Champlain again.

These are the five Leatherstocking books: Natty Bumppo being Leatherstocking, Pathfinder, Deerslayer, according to his ages.

Now let me put aside my impatience at the unreality of this vision, and accept it as a wish-fulfilment vision, a kind of yearning myth. Because it seems to me that the things in Cooper that make one so savage, when one compares them with actuality, are perhaps, when one considers them as presentations of a deep subjective desire, real in their way, and almost prophetic.

The passionate love for America, for the soil of America, for example. As I say, it is perhaps easier to love America passionately, when you look at it through the wrong end of the telescope, across all the Atlantic water, as Cooper did so often, than when you are right there. When you are actually *in* America, America hurts, because it has a powerful disintegrative influence upon the white psyche. It is full of grinning, unappeased aboriginal demons, too, ghosts, and it persecutes the white men, like some Eumenides, until the white men give up their absolute whiteness. America is tense with latent violence and resistance. The very common sense of white Americans has a tinge of helplessness in it, and deep fear of what might be if they were not common-sensical.

Yet one day the demons of America must be placated, the ghosts must be appeased, the Spirit of Place atoned for. Then the true passionate love for American Soil will appear. As yet, there is too much menace in the landscape.

But probably, one day America will be as beautiful in actuality as it is in Cooper. Not yet, however. When the factories have fallen down again.

And again, this perpetual blood-brother theme of the Leatherstocking novels, Natty and Chingachgook, the Great Serpent. At present it is a sheer myth. The Red Man and the White Man are not blood-brothers: even when they are most friendly. When they are most friendly, it is as a rule the one betraying his race-spirit to the other. In the white man—rather highbrow —who "loves" the Indian, one feels the white man betraying his own race. There is something unproud, underhand in it. Renegade. The same with the Americanised Indian who believes absolutely in the white mode. It is a betrayal. Renegade again.

In the actual flesh, it seems to me the white man and the red man cause a feeling of oppression, the one to the other, no matter what the good will. The red life flows in a different direction from the white life. You can't make two streams that flow in opposite directions meet and mingle soothingly.

Certainly, if Cooper had had to spend his whole life in the backwoods, side by side with a Noble Red Brother, he would have screamed with the oppression of suffocation. He had to have Mrs. Cooper, a straight strong pillar of society, to hang on to. And he had to have the culture of France to turn back to, or he would just have been stifled. The Noble Red Brother would have smothered him and driven him mad.

So that the Natty and Chingachgook myth must remain a myth. It is a wish-fulfilment, an evasion of actuality. As we have said before, the folds of the Great Serpent would have been heavy, very heavy, too heavy, on any white man. Unless the white man were a true renegade, hating himself and his own race spirit, as sometimes happens.

It seems there can be no fusion in the flesh. But the spirit can change. The white man's spirit can never become as the red man's spirit. It doesn't want to. But it can cease to be the opposite and the negative of the red man's spirit. It can open out a new great area of consciousness, in which there is room for the red spirit too.

To open out a new wide area of consciousness means to slough the old consciousness. The old consciousness has become a tight-fitting prison to us, in which we are going rotten.

You can't have a new, easy skin before you have sloughed the old, tight skin.

You can't.

And you just can't, so you may as well leave off pretending.

Now the essential history of the people of the United States seems to me just this: At the Renaissance the old consciousness was becoming a little tight. Europe sloughed her last skin, and started a new, final phase.

But some Europeans recoiled from the last final phase. They wouldn't enter the *cul-de-sac* of post-Renaissance, "liberal" Europe. They came to America.

They came to America for two reasons:

1. To slough the old European consciousness completely.

2. To grow a new skin underneath, a new form. This second is a hidden process.

The two processes go on, of course, simultaneously. The slow forming of the new skin underneath is the slow sloughing of the old skin. And sometimes this immortal serpent feels very happy, feeling a new golden glow of a strangely-patterned skin envelop him: and sometimes he feels very sick, as if his very entrails were being torn out of him, as he wrenches once more at his old skin, to get out of it.

Out! Out! he cries, in all kinds of euphemisms.

He's got to have his new skin on him before ever he can get out.

And he's got to get out before his new skin can ever be his own skin.

So there he is, a torn, divided monster.

The true American, who writhes and writhes like a snake that is long in sloughing.

Sometimes snakes can't slough. They can't burst their old skin. Then they go sick and die inside the old skin, and nobody ever sees the new pattern.

It needs a real desperate recklessness to burst your old skin at last. You simply don't care what happens to you, if you rip yourself in two, so long as you do get out.

It also needs a real belief in the new skin. Otherwise you are likely never to make the effort. Then you gradually sicken and go rotten and die in the old skin.

Now Fenimore stayed very safe inside the old skin: a gentleman, almost a European, as proper as proper can be. And, safe inside the old skin, he *imagined* the gorgeous American pattern of a new skin.

He hated democracy. So he evaded it, and had a nice dream of something beyond democracy. But he belonged to democracy all the while.

Evasion!—Yet even that doesn't make the dream worthless.

Democracy in America was never the same as Liberty in Europe. In Europe Liberty was a great life-throb. But in America Democracy was always something anti-life. The greatest democrats, like Abraham Lincoln, had always a sacrificial, self-murdering note in their voices. American Democracy was a form of self-murder, always. Or of murdering somebody else.

Necessarily. It was a *pis aller*. It was the *pis aller* to European Liberty. It was a cruel form of sloughing. Men murdered themselves into this democracy. Democracy is the utter hardening of the old skin, the old form, the old psyche. It hardens till it is tight and fixed and inorganic. Then it *must* burst, like a chrysalis shell. And out must come the soft grub, or the soft damp butterfly of the American-at-last.

America has gone the *pis aller* of her democracy. Now she must slough even that, chiefly that, indeed.

What did Cooper dream beyond democracy? Why, in his immortal friendship of Chingachgook and Natty Bumppo he dreamed the nucleus of a new society. That is, he dreamed a new human relationship. A stark, stripped human relationship of two men, deeper than the deeps of sex. Deeper than property, deeper than fatherhood, deeper than marriage, deeper than love. So deep that it is loveless. The stark, loveless, wordless unison of two men who have come to the bottom of themselves. This is the new nucleus of a new society, the clue to a new world-epoch. It asks for a great and cruel sloughing first of all. Then it finds a great release into a new world, a new moral, a new landscape.

Natty and the Great Serpent are neither equals nor unequals. Each obeys the other when the moment arrives. And each is stark and dumb in the other's presence, starkly himself, without illusion created. Each is just the crude pillar of a man, the crude living column of his own manhood. And each knows the godhead of this crude column of manhood. A new relationship.

The Leatherstocking novels create the myth of this new relation. And they go backwards, from old age to golden youth. That is the true myth of America. She starts old, old, wrinkled and writhing in an old skin. And there is a gradual sloughing of the old skin, towards a new youth. It is the myth of America.

You start with actuality. *Pioneers* is no doubt Cooperstown, when Cooperstown was in the stage of inception: a village of one wild street of log cabins under the forest hills by Lake Champlain: a village of crude, wild frontiersmen, reacting against civilisation.

Towards this frontier-village in the winter time, a negro slave drives a sledge through the mountains, over deep snow. In the sledge sits a fair damsel, Miss Temple, with her handsome pioneer father, Judge Temple. They hear a shot in the trees.

It is the old hunter and backwoodsman, Natty Bumppo, long and lean and uncouth, with a long rifle and gaps in his teeth.

Judge Temple is "squire" of the village, and he has a ridiculous, commodious "hall" for his residence. It is still the old English form. Miss Temple is a pattern young lady, like Eve Effingham: in fact, she gets a young and very genteel but impoverished Effingham for a husband. The old world holding its own on the edge of the wild. A bit tiresomely too, with rather more prunes and prisms than one can digest. Too romantic.

Against the "hall" and the gentry, the real frontiers-folk, the rebels. The two groups meet at the village inn, and at the frozen church, and at the Christmas sports, and on the ice of the lake, and at the great pigeon shoot. It is a beautiful, resplendent picture of life. Fenimore puts in only the glamour.

Perhaps my taste is childish, but these scenes in *Pioneers* seem to me marvellously beautiful. The raw village street, with wood fires blinking through the unglazed window-chinks, on a winter's night. The inn, with the rough woodsman and the drunken Indian John; the church, with the snowy congregation crowding to the fire. Then the lavish abundance of Christmas cheer, and turkey shooting in the snow. Spring coming, forests all green, maple-sugar taken from the trees: and clouds of pigeons flying from the south, myriads of pigeons, shot in heaps; and night-fishing on the teeming, virgin lake; and deer-hunting.

Pictures! Some of the loveliest, most glamorous pictures in all literature.

Alas, without the cruel iron of reality. It is all real enough. Except that one realises that Fenimore was writing from a safe distance, where he would idealise and have his wish-fulfilment.

Because, when one comes to America, one finds that there is always a certain slightly devilish resistance in the American landscape, and a certain slightly bitter resistance in the white man's heart. Hawthorne gives this. But Cooper glosses it over.

The American landscape has never been at one with the white man. Never. And white men have probably never felt so bitter anywhere, as here in America, where the very landscape, in its very beauty, seems a bit devilish and grinning, opposed to us.

Cooper, however, glosses over this resistance, which in actuality can never quite be glossed over. He *wants* the landscape to be at one with him. So he goes away to Europe and sees it as such. It is a sort of vision.

And, nevertheless, the oneing will surely take place—some day.

The myth is the story of Natty. The old, lean hunter and backwoodsman lives with his friend, the grey-haired Indian John, an old Delaware chief, in a hut within reach of the village. The Delaware is christianised and bears the Christian name of John. He is tribeless and lost. He humiliates his grey hairs in drunkenness, and dies, thankful to be dead, in a forest fire, passing back to the fire whence he derived.

And this is Chingachgook, the splendid Great Serpent of the later novels.

No doubt Cooper, as a boy, knew both Natty and the Indian John. No doubt they fired his imagination even then. When he is a man, crystallised in society and sheltering behind the safe pillar of Mrs. Cooper, these two old fellows become a myth to his soul. He traces himself to a new youth in them.

As for the story: Judge Temple has just been instrumental in passing the wise game laws. But Natty has lived by his gun all his life in the wild woods, and simply childishly cannot understand how he can be poaching on the Judge's land among the pine trees. He shoots a deer in the close season. The Judge is all sympathy, but the law *must* be enforced. Bewildered Natty, an old man of seventy, is put in stocks and in prison. They release him as soon as possible. But the thing was done.

The letter killeth.

Natty's last connexion with his own race is broken. John, the Indian, is dead. The old hunter disappears, lonely and severed, into the forest, away, away from his race.

In the new epoch that is coming, there will be no letter of the Law.

Chronologically, *The Last of the Mohicans* follows *Pioneers*. But in the myth, *The Prairie* comes next.

Cooper of course knew his own America. He travelled west and saw the prairies, and camped with the Indians of the prairie.

The Prairie, like *Pioneers*, bears a good deal the stamp of actuality. It is a strange, splendid book, full of sense of doom. The figures of the great Kentuckian men, with their wolf-women, loom colossal on the vast prairie, as they camp with their wagons. These are different pioneers from Judge Temple. Lurid, brutal, tinged with the sinisterness of crime; these are the gaunt white men who push west, push on and on against the natural opposition of the continent. On towards a doom. Great wings of vengeful doom seem spread over the west, grim against the intruder. You feel them again in Frank Norris's novel, *The Octopus*. While in the West of Bret Harte there is a very devil in the air, and beneath him are sentimental self-conscious people being wicked and goody by evasion.

In *The Prairie* there is a shadow of violence and dark cruelty flickering in the air. It is the aboriginal demon hovering over the core of the continent. It hovers still, and the dread is still there.

Into such a prairie enters the huge figure of Ishmael, ponderous, pariah-like Ishmael and his huge sons and his were-wolf wife. With their wagons they roll on from the frontiers of Kentucky, like Cyclops into the savage wilderness. Day after day they seem to force their way into oblivion. But their force of penetration ebbs. They are brought to a stop. They recoil in the throes of murder and entrench themselves in isolation on a hillock in the midst of the prairie. There they hold out like demi-gods against the elements and the subtle Indian.

The pioneering brute invasion of the West, crime-tinged!

And into this setting, as a sort of minister of peace, enters the old, old hunter Natty, and his suave, horse-riding Sioux Indians. But he seems like a shadow.

The hills rise softly west, to the Rockies. There seems a new peace: or is it only suspense, abstraction, waiting? Is it only a sort of beyond?

Natty lives in these hills, in a village of the suave, horse-riding Sioux. They revere him as an old wise father.

In these hills he dies, sitting in his chair and looking far east, to the forest and great sweet waters, whence he came. He dies gently, in physical peace with the land and the Indians. He is an old, old man.

Cooper could see no further than the foothills where Natty died, beyond the prairie.

The other novels bring us back east.

The Last of the Mohicans is divided between real historical narrative and true "romance". For myself, I prefer the romance. It has a myth meaning, whereas the narrative is chiefly record.

For the first time we get actual women: the dark, handsome Cora and her frail sister, the White Lily. The good old division, the dark sensual woman and the clinging, submissive little blonde, who is so "pure".

These sisters are fugitives through the forest, under the protection of a Major Heyward, a young American officer and Englishman. He is just a "white" man, very good and brave and generous, etc., but limited, most definitely *borné*. He would probably love Cora, if he dared, but he finds it safer to adore the clinging White Lily of a younger sister.

This trio is escorted by Natty, now Leatherstocking, a hunter and scout in the prime of life, accompanied by his inseparable friend Chingachgook, and the Delaware's beautiful son—Adonis rather than Apollo—Uncas, The Last of the Mohicans.

There is also a "wicked" Indian, Magua, handsome and injured incarnation of evil.

Cora is the scarlet flower of womanhood, fierce, passionate offspring of some mysterious union between the British officer and a Creole woman in the West Indies. Cora loves Uncas, Uncas loves Cora. But Magua also desires Cora, violently desires her. A lurid little circle of sensual fire. So Fenimore kills them all off, Cora, Uncas, and Magua, and leaves the White Lily to carry on the race. She will breed plenty of white children to Major Heyward. These tiresome "lilies that fester", of our day.

Evidently Cooper—or the artist in him—has decided that there can be no blood-mixing of the two races, white and red. He kills 'em off.

Beyond all this heart-beating stand the figures of Natty and Chingachgook: the two childless, womanless men, of opposite races. They are the abiding thing. Each of them is alone, and final in his race. And they stand side by side, stark, abstract, beyond emotion, yet eternally together. All the other loves seem frivolous. This is the new great thing, the clue, the inception of a new humanity.

And Natty, what sort of a white man is he? Why, he is a man with a gun. He is a killer, a slayer. Patient and gentle as he is, he is a slayer. Self-effacing, self-forgetting, still he is a killer.

Twice, in the book, he brings an enemy down hurtling in death through the air, downwards. Once it is the beautiful, wicked Magua—shot from a height, and hurtling down ghastly through space, into death.

This is Natty, the white forerunner. A killer. As in *Deerslayer*, he shoots the bird that flies in the high, high sky, so that the bird falls out of the invisible into the visible, dead, he symbolises himself. He will bring the bird of the spirit out of the high air. He is the stoic American killer of the old great life. But he kills, as he says, only to live.

Pathfinder takes us to the Great Lakes, and the glamour and beauty of sailing the great sweet waters. Natty is now called Pathfinder. He is about thirty-five years old, and he falls in love. The damsel is Mabel Dunham, daughter of Sergeant Dunham of the Fort garrison. She is blonde and in all things admirable. No doubt Mrs. Cooper was very much like Mabel.

And Pathfinder doesn't marry her. She won't have him. She wisely prefers a more comfortable Jasper. So Natty goes off to grouch, and to end by thanking his stars. When he had got right clear, and sat by the campfire with Chingachgook, in the forest, didn't he just thank his stars! A lucky escape!

Men of an uncertain age are liable to these infatuations. They aren't always lucky enough to be rejected.

Whatever would poor Mabel have done, had she been Mrs. Bumppo?

Natty had no business marrying. His mission was elsewhere.

The most fascinating Leatherstocking book is the last, *Deerslayer*. Natty is now a fresh youth, called Deerslayer. But the kind of silent prim youth who is never quite young, but reserves himself for different things.

It is a gem of a book. Or a bit of perfect paste. And myself, I like a bit of perfect paste in a perfect setting, so long as I am not fooled by pretence of reality. And the setting of Deerslayer *could* not be more exquisite. Lake Champlain again.

Of course it never rains: it is never cold and muddy and

dreary: no one has wet feet or toothache: no one ever feels filthy, when they can't wash for a week. God knows what the women would really have looked like, for they fled through the wilds without soap, comb, or towel. They breakfasted off a chunk of meat, or nothing, lunched the same, and supped the same.

Yet at every moment they are elegant, perfect ladies, in correct toilet.

Which isn't quite fair. You need only go camping for a week, and you'll see.

But it is a myth, not a realistic tale. Read it as a lovely myth. Lake Glimmerglass.

Deerslayer, the youth with the long rifle, is found in the woods with a big, handsome, blond-bearded backwoodsman called Hurry Harry. Deerslayer seems to have been born under a hemlock tree out of a pine-cone: a young man of the woods. He is silent, simple, philosophic, moralistic, and an unerring shot. His simplicity is the simplicity of age rather than of youth. He is race-old. All his reactions and impulses are fixed, static. Almost he is sexless, so race-old. Yet intelligent, hardy, dauntless.

Hurry Harry is a big blusterer, just the opposite of Deerslayer. Deerslayer keeps the centre of his own consciousness steady and unperturbed. Hurry Harry is one of those floundering people who bluster from one emotion to another, very self-conscious, without any centre to them.

These two young men are making their way to a lovely, smallish lake, Lake Glimmerglass. On this water the Hutter family has established itself. Old Hutter, it is suggested, has a criminal, coarse, buccaneering past, and is a sort of fugitive from justice. But he is a good enough father to his two grown-up girls. The family lives in a log hut "castle", built on piles in the water, and the old man has also constructed an "ark", a sort of house-boat, in which he can take his daughters when he goes on his rounds to trap the beaver.

The two girls are the inevitable dark and light. Judith, dark, fearless, passionate, a little lurid with sin, is the scarlet-and-black blossom. Hetty, the younger, blonde, frail and innocent, is the white lily again. But alas, the lily has begun to fester. She is slightly imbecile.

The two hunters arrive at the lake among the woods just as war has been declared. The Hutters are unaware of the fact. And hostile Indians are on the lake already. So, the story of thrills and perils.

Thomas Hardy's inevitable division of women into dark and fair, sinful and innocent, sensual and pure, is Cooper's division too. It is indicative of the desire in the man. He wants sensuality and sin, and he wants purity and "innocence". If the innocence goes a little rotten, slightly imbecile, bad luck!

Hurry Harry, of course, like a handsome impetuous meat-fly, at once wants Judith, the lurid poppy-blossom. Judith rejects him with scorn.

Judith, the sensual woman, at once wants the quiet, reserved, unmastered Deerslayer. She wants to master him. And Deerslayer is half tempted, but never more than half. He is not going to be mastered. A philosophic old soul, he does not give much for the temptations of sex. Probably he dies virgin.

And he is right of it. Rather than be dragged into a false heat of deliberate sensuality, he will remain alone. His soul is alone, for ever alone. So he will preserve his integrity, and remain alone in the flesh. It is a stoicism which is honest and fearless, and from which Deerslayer never lapses, except when, approaching middle age, he proposes to the buxom Mabel.

He lets his consciousness penetrate in loneliness into the new continent. His contacts are not human. He wrestles with the spirits of the forest and the American wild, as a hermit wrestles with God and Satan. His one meeting is with Chingachgook, and this meeting is silent, reserved, across an unpassable distance.

Hetty, the White Lily, being imbecile, although full of vaporous religion and the dear, good God, "who governs all things by his providence," is hopelessly infatuated with Hurry Harry. Being innocence gone imbecile, like Dostoievsky's Idiot, she longs to give herself to the handsome meat-fly. Of course he doesn't want her.

And so nothing happens: in that direction. Deerslayer goes off to meet Chingachgook, and help him woo an Indian maid. Vicarious.

It is the miserable story of the collapse of the white psyche. The white man's mind and soul are divided between these two things: innocence and lust, the Spirit and Sensuality. Sensuality always carries a stigma, and is therefore more deeply desired, or lusted after. But spirituality alone gives the sense of uplift, exaltation, and "winged life", with the inevitable reaction into sin and spite. So the white man is divided against himself. He plays off one side of himself against the other side, till it is really a tale told by an idiot, and nauseating.

Against this, one is forced to admire the stark, enduring figure of Deerslayer. He is neither spiritual nor sensual. He is a moraliser, but he always tries to moralise from actual experience, not from theory. He says: "Hurt nothing unless you're forced to." Yet he gets his deepest thrill of gratification, perhaps, when he puts a bullet through the heart of a beautiful buck, as its stoops to drink at the lake. Or when he brings the invisible bird fluttering down in death, out of the high blue. "Hurt nothing unless you're forced to." And yet he lives by death, by killing the wild things of the air and earth.

It's not good enough.

But you have there the myth of the essential white America. All the other stuff, the love, the democracy, the floundering into lust, is a sort of by-play. The essential American soul is hard, isolate, stoic, and a killer. It has never yet melted.

Of course, the soul often breaks down into disintegration, and you have lurid sin and Judith, imbecile innocence lusting, in Hetty, and bluster, bragging, and self-conscious strength, in Harry. But there are the disintegration products.

What true myth concerns itself with is not the disintegration product. True myth concerns itself centrally with the onward adventure of the integral soul. And this, for America, is Deerslayer. A man who turns his back on white society. A man who keeps his moral integrity hard and intact. An isolate, almost selfless, stoic, enduring man, who lives by death, by killing, but who is pure white.

This is the very intrinsic-most American. He is at the core of all the other flux and fluff. And when *this* man breaks from his static isolation, and makes a new move, then look out, something will be happening.

[From *Studies in Classic American Literature*, 1924.]

[97]

EDGAR ALLAN POE

POE has no truck with Indians or Nature. He makes no bones about Red Brothers and Wigwams.

He is absolutely concerned with the disintegration-processes of his own psyche. As we have said, the rhythm of American art-activity is dual.

1. A disintegrating and sloughing of the old consciousness.
2. The forming of a new consciousness underneath.

Fenimore Cooper has the two vibrations going on together. Poe has only one, only the disintegrative vibration. This makes him almost more a scientist than an artist.

Moralists have always wondered helplessly why Poe's "morbid" tales need have been written. They need to be written because old things need to die and disintegrate, because the old white psyche has to be gradually broken down before anything else can come to pass.

Man must be stripped even of himself. And it is a painful, sometimes a ghastly process.

Poe has a pretty bitter doom. Doomed to seethe down his soul in a great continuous convulsion of disintegration, and doomed to register the process. And then doomed to be abused for it, when he had performed some of the bitterest tasks of human experience that can be asked of a man. Necessary tasks, too. For the human soul must suffer its own disintegration, *consciously*, if ever it is to survive.

But Poe is rather a scientist than an artist. He is reducing his own self as a scientist reduces a salt in a crucible. It is an almost chemical analysis of the soul and consciousness. Whereas in true art there is always the double rhythm of creating and destroying.

This is why Poe calls his things "tales". They are a concatenation of cause and effect.

His best pieces, however, are not tales. They are more. They are ghastly stories of the human soul in its disruptive throes.

Moreover, they are "love" stories.

Ligeia and *The Fall of the House of Usher* are really love stories.

Love is the mysterious vital attraction which draws things together, closer, closer together. For this reason sex is the actual crisis of love. For in sex the two blood-systems, in the male and female, concentrate and come into contact, the merest film intervening. Yet if the intervening film breaks down, it is death.

So there you are. There is a limit to everything. There is a limit to love.

The central law of all organic life is that each organism is intrinsically isolate and single in itself.

The moment its isolation breaks down, and there comes an actual mixing and confusion, death sets in.

This is true of every individual organism, from man to amœba.

But the secondary law of all organic life is that each organism only lives through contact with other matter, assimilation, and contact with other life, which means assimilation of new vibrations, non-material. Each individual organism is vivified by intimate contact with fellow organisms: up to a certain point.

So man. He breathes the air into him, he swallows food and water. But more than this. He takes into him the life of his fellow men, with whom he comes into contact, and he gives back life to them. This contact draws nearer and nearer, as the intimacy increases. When it is a whole contact, we call it love. Men live by food, but die if they eat too much. Men live by love, but die, or cause death, if they love too much.

There are two loves: sacred and profane, spiritual and sensual.

In sensual love, it is the two blood-systems, the man's and the woman's, which sweep up into pure contact, and *almost* fuse. Almost mingle. Never quite. There is always the finest imaginable wall between the two blood-waves, through which pass unknown vibrations, forces, but through which the blood itself must never break, or it means bleeding.

In spiritual love, the contact is purely nervous. The nerves in the lovers are set vibrating in unison like two instruments. The pitch can rise higher and higher. But carry this too far, and the nerves begin to break, to bleed, as it were, and a form of death sets in.

The trouble about man is that he insists on being master of his own fate, and he insists on *oneness*. For instance, having discovered the ecstasy of spiritual love, he insists that he shall have this all the time, and nothing but this, for this is life. It is what he calls "heightening" life. He wants his nerves to be set vibrating in the intense and exhilarating unison with the nerves of another being, and by this means he acquires an ecstasy of vision, he finds himself in glowing unison with all the universe.

But as a matter of fact this glowing unison is only a temporary thing, because the first law of life is that each organism is isolate in itself, it must return to its own isolation.

Yet man has tried the glow of unison, called love, and he *likes* it. It gives him his highest gratification. He wants it. He wants it all the time. He wants it and he will have it. He doesn't want to return to his own isolation. Or if he must, it is only as a prowling beast returns to its lair to rest and set out again.

This brings us to Edgar Allan Poe. The clue to him lies in the motto he chose for *Ligeia*, a quotation from the mystic Joseph Glanville: "And the will therein lieth, which dieth not. Who knoweth the mysteries of the will, with its vigour? For God is but a great Will pervading all things by nature of its intentness. Man doth not yield himself to the angels, nor unto death utterly, save only through the weakness of his feeble will."

It is a profound saying: and a deadly one.

Because if God is a great will, then the universe is but an instrument.

I don't know what God is. But He is not simply a will. That is too simple. Too anthropomorphic. Because a man wants his own will, and nothing but his will, he needn't say that God is the same will, magnified *ad infinitum*.

For me, there may be one God, but He is nameless and unknowable.

For me, there are also many gods, that come into me and leave me again. And they have very various wills, I must say.

But the point is Poe.

Poe had experienced the ecstasies of extreme spiritual love. And he wanted those ecstasies and nothing but those ecstasies.

He wanted that great gratification, the sense of flowing, the sense of unison, the sense of heightening of life. He had experienced this gratification. He was told on every hand that this ecstasy of spiritual, nervous love was the greatest thing in life, was life itself. And he had tried it for himself, he knew that for him it *was* life itself. So he wanted it. And he *would have* it. He set up his will against the whole of the limitations of nature.

This is a brave man, acting on his own belief, and his own experience. But it is also an arrogant man, and a fool.

Poe was going to get the ecstasy and the heightening, cost what it might. He went on in a frenzy, as characteristic American women nowadays go on in a frenzy, after the very same thing: the heightening, the flow, the ecstasy. Poe tried alcohol, and any drug he could lay his hand on. He also tried any human being he could lay his hands on.

His grand attempt and achievement was with his wife; his cousin, a girl with a singing voice. With her he went in for the intensest flow, the heightening, the prismatic shades of ecstasy. It was the intensest nervous vibration of unison, pressed higher and higher in pitch, till the blood-vessels of the girl broke, and the blood began to flow out loose. It was love. If you call it love.

Love can be terribly obscene.

It is love that causes the neuroticism of the day. It is love that is the prime cause of tuberculosis.

The nerves that vibrate most intensely in spiritual unisons are the sympathetic ganglia of the breast, of the throat, and the hind brain. Drive this vibration over-intensely, and you weaken the sympathetic tissues of the chest—the lungs—or of the throat, or of the lower brain, and the tubercles are given a ripe field.

But Poe drove the vibrations beyond any human pitch of endurance.

Being his cousin, she was more easily keyed to him.

Ligeia is the chief story. Ligeia! A mental-derived name. To him the woman, his wife, was not Lucy. She was Ligeia. No doubt she even preferred it thus.

Ligeia is Poe's love-story, and its very fantasy makes it more truly his own story.

It is a tale of love pushed over a verge. And love pushed to extremes is a battle of wills between the lovers.

Love is become a battle of wills.

Which shall first destroy the other, of the lovers? Which can hold out longest, against the other?

Ligeia is still the old-fashioned woman. Her will is still to submit. She wills to submit to the vampire of her husband's consciousness. Even death.

"In stature she was tall, somewhat slender, and, in her later days, even emaciated. I would in vain attempt to portray the majesty, the quiet ease, of her demeanour, or the incomprehensible lightness and elasticity of her footfall. I was never made aware of her entrance into my closed study save by the dear music of her low, sweet voice, as she placed her marble hand on my shoulder."

Poe has been so praised for his style. But it seems to me a meretricious affair. "Her marble hand" and "the elasticity of her footfall" seem more like chair-springs and mantelpieces than a human creature. She never was quite a human creature to him. She was an instrument from which he got his extremes of sensation. His *machine à plaisir*, as somebody says.

All Poe's style, moreover, has this mechanical quality, as his poetry has a mechanical rhythm. He never sees anything in terms of life, almost always in terms of matter, jewels, marble, etc.,—or in terms of force, scientific. And his cadences are all managed mechanically. This is what is called "having a style".

What he wants to do with Ligeia is to analyse her, till he knows all her component parts, till he has got her all in his consciousness. She is some strange chemical salt which he must analyse out in the test-tubes of his brain, and then—when he's finished the analysis—*E finita la commedia!*

But she won't be quite analysed out. There is something, something he can't get. Writing of her eyes, he says: "They were, I must believe, far larger than the ordinary eyes of our race"—as if anybody would want eyes "far larger" than other folks'. "They were even fuller than the fullest of the gazelle eyes of the tribe of Nourjahad"—which is blarney. "The hue of the orbs was the most brilliant of black and, far over them, hung jetty lashes of great length"—suggests a whip-lash. "The brows, slightly irregular in outline, had the same tint. The *strangeness*, which I found in the eyes, was of a nature distinct from the formation, or the colour, or the brilliancy of the features, and must, after all, be referred to as the *expression*."—Sounds like an anatomist anatomising a cat—"Ah, word of no meaning! behind whose vast latitude of sound we entrench our ignorance of so much of the spiritual. The expression of the eyes of Ligeia! How for long hours have I pondered upon it! How have I, through the whole of a midsummer night, struggled to fathom it! What was it— that something more profound than the well of Democritus —which lay far within the pupils of my beloved? What *was* it? I was possessed with a passion to discover. . . ."

It is easy to see why each man kills the thing he loves. To *know* a living thing is to kill it. You have to kill a thing to know it satisfactorily. For this reason, the desirous consciousness, the SPIRIT, is a vampire.

One should be sufficiently intelligent and interested to know a good deal *about* any person one comes into close contact with. *About* her. Or *about* him.

But to try to *know* any living being is to try to suck the life out of that being.

Above all things, with the woman one loves. Every sacred instinct teaches one that one must leave her unknown. You know your woman darkly, in the blood. To try to *know* her mentally is to try to kill her. Beware, O woman, of the man who wants to *find out what you are*. And, O men, beware a thousand times more of the woman who wants to *know* you, or *get* you, what you are.

It is the temptation of a vampire fiend, is this knowledge.

Man does so horribly want to master the secret of life and of individuality *with his mind*. It is like the analysis of proto- plasm. You can only analyse *dead* protoplasm, and know its constituents. It is a death process.

Keep KNOWLEDGE for the world of matter, force, and func- tion. It has got nothing to do with being.

But Poe wanted to know—wanted to know what was the strangeness in the eyes of Ligeia. She might have told him it was horror at his probing, horror at being vamped by his consciousness.

But she wanted to be vamped. She wanted to be probed by

his consciousness, to be KNOWN. She paid for wanting it, too.

Nowadays it is usually the man who wants to be vamped, to be KNOWN.

Edgar Allan probed and probed. So often he seemed on the verge. But she went over the verge of death before he came over the verge of knowledge. And it is always so.

He decided, therefore, that the clue to the strangeness lay in the mystery of will. "And the will therein lieth, which dieth not. . . ."

Ligeia had a "gigantic volition". . . . "An intensity in thought, action, or speech was possibly, in her, a result, or at least an index" (he really meant indication) "of that gigantic volition which, during our long intercourse, failed to give other and more immediate evidence of its existence."

I should have thought her long submission to him was chief and ample "other evidence".

"Of all the women whom I have ever known, she, the outwardly calm, the ever-placid Ligeia, was the most violently a prey to the tumultuous vultures of stern passion. And of such passion I could form no estimate, save by the miraculous expansion of those eyes which at once so delighted and appalled me—by the almost magical melody, modulation, distinctness, and placidity of her very low voice—and by the fierce energy (rendered doubly effective by contrast with her manner of utterance) of the wild words which she habitually uttered." ·

Poor Poe, he had caught a bird of the same feather as himself. One of those terrible cravers, who crave the further sensation. Crave to madness or death. "Vultures of stern passion" indeed! Condors.

But having recognised that the clue was in her gigantic volition, he should have realised that the process of this loving, this craving, this knowing, was a struggle of wills. But Ligeia, true to the great tradition and mode of womanly love, by her will kept herself submissive, recipient. She is the passive body who is explored and analysed into death. And yet, at times, her great female will must have revolted. "Vultures of stern passion!" With a convulsion of desire she desired his further probing and exploring. To any lengths. But then, "tumultuous vultures of stern passion". She had to fight with herself.

But Ligeia wanted to go on and on with the craving, with the love, with the sensation, with the probing, with the knowing, on and on to the end.

There is no end. There is only the rupture of death. That's where men, and women, are "had". Man is always sold, in his search for final KNOWLEDGE.

"That she loved me I should not have doubted; and I might have been easily aware that, in a bosom such as hers, love would have reigned no ordinary passion. But in death only was I fully impressed with the strength of her affection. For long hours, detaining my hand, would she pour out before me the overflowing of a heart whose more than passionate devotion amounted to idolatry." (Oh, the indecency of all this endless intimate talk!) "How had I deserved to be blessed by such confessions?" (Another man would have felt himself cursed.) "How had I deserved to be cursed with the removal of my beloved in the hour of her making them? But upon this subject I cannot bear to dilate. Let me say only that in Ligeia's more than womanly abandonment to a love, alas! unmerited, all unworthily bestowed, I at length recognised the principle of her longing with so wildly earnest a desire for the life which was fleeing so rapidly away. It is this wild longing—it is this vehement desire for life—*but* for life—that I have no power to portray—no utterance capable of expressing."

Well, that is ghastly enough, in all conscience.

"And from them that have not shall be taken away even that which they have."

"To him that hath life shall be given life, and from him that hath not life shall be taken away even that life which he hath."

Or her either.

These terribly conscious birds, like Poe and his Ligeia, deny the very life that is in them; they want to turn it all into talk, into *knowing*. And so life, which will *not* be known, leaves them.

But poor Ligeia, how could she help it. It was her doom. All the centuries of the SPIRIT, all the years of American rebellion against the Holy Ghost, had done it to her.

She dies, when she would rather do anything than die. And when she dies the clue, which he only lived to grasp, dies with her.

Foiled!

Foiled!

No wonder she shrieks with her last breath.

On the last day Ligeia dictates to her husband a poem. As poems go, it is rather false, meretricious. But put yourself in Ligeia's place, and it is real enough, and ghastly beyond bearing.

> Out, out are all the lights—out all!
>   And over each quivering form
> The curtain, a funeral pall,
>   Comes down with the rush of a storm,
> And the angels, all pallid and wan,
>   Uprising, unveiling, affirm
> That the play is the tragedy, "Man",
> And its hero, the Conqueror Worm.

Which is the American equivalent for a William Blake poem. For Blake, too, was one of these ghastly, obscene "Knowers".

" 'O God!' half shrieked Ligeia, leaping to her feet and extending her arms aloft with a spasmodic movement, as I made an end of these lines. 'O God! O Divine Father!—shall these things be undeviatingly so? Shall this conqueror be not once conquered? Are we not part and parcel in Thee? Who—who knoweth the mysteries of the angels, *nor unto death utterly*, save only through the weakness of his feeble will.' "

So Ligeia dies. And yields to death at least partly. *Anche troppo.*

As for her cry to God—has not God said that those who sin against the Holy Ghost shall not be forgiven?

And the Holy Ghost is within us. It is the thing that prompts us to be real, not to push our own cravings too far, not to submit to stunts and high-falutin, above all, not to be too egoistic and wilful in our conscious self, but to change as the spirit inside us bids us change, and leave off when it bids us leave off, and laugh when we must laugh, particularly at ourselves, for in deadly earnestness there is always something a bit ridiculous. The Holy Ghost bids us never be too deadly in our earnestness, always to laugh in time, at ourselves and everything. Particularly at our sublimities. Everything has its hour of ridicule—everything.

Now Poe and Ligeia, alas, couldn't laugh. They were
frenziedly earnest. And frenziedly they pushed on this vibration of consciousness and unison in consciousness. They sinned
against the Holy Ghost that bids us all laugh and forget, bids
us know our own limits. And they weren't forgiven.

Ligeia needn't blame God. She had only her own will, her
"gigantic volition" to thank, lusting after more consciousness,
more beastly KNOWING.

Ligeia dies. The husband goes to England, vulgarly buys
or rents a gloomy, grand old abbey, puts it into some sort of
repair, and furnishes it with exotic, mysterious, theatrical
splendour. Never anything open and real. This theatrical
"volition" of his. The bad taste of sensationalism.

Then he marries the fair-haired, blue-eyed Lady Rowena
Trevanion, of Tremaine. That is, she would be a sort of
Saxon-Cornish blue-blood damsel. Poor Poe!

"In halls such as these—in a bridal chamber such as this—
I passed, with the Lady of Tremaine, the unhallowed hours
of the first month of our marriage—passed them with but
little disquietude. That my wife dreaded the fierce moodiness
of my temper—that she shunned and loved me but little—I
could not help perceiving, but it gave me rather pleasure than
otherwise. I loathed her with a hatred belonging rather to
a demon than a man. My memory flew back (Oh, with what
intensity of regret!) to Ligeia, the beloved, the august, the
entombed. I revelled in recollections of her purity . . ." etc.,

Now the vampire lust is consciously such.

In the second month of the marriage the Lady Rowena
fell ill. It is the shadow of Ligeia hangs over her. It is the
ghostly Ligeia who pours poison into Rowena's cup. It is
the spirit of Ligeia, leagued with the spirit of the husband, that
now lusts in the slow destruction of Rowena. The two vampires, dead wife and living husband.

For Ligeia has not yielded unto death *utterly*. Her fixed,
frustrated will comes back in vindictiveness. She could not
have her way in life. So she, too, will find victims in life. And
the husband, all the time, only uses Rowena as a living body
on which to wreak his vengeance for his being thwarted with
Ligeia. Thwarted from the final KNOWING her.

And at last from the corpse of Rowena, Ligeia rises. Out

of her death, through the door of a corpse they have destroyed between them, reappears Ligeia, still trying to have her will, to have more love and knowledge, the final gratification which is never final, with her husband.

For it is true, as William James and Conan Doyle and the rest allow, that a spirit can persist in the after-death. Persist by its own volition. But usually, the evil persistence of a thwarted will, returning for vengeance on life. Lemures, vampires.

It is a ghastly story of the assertion of the human will, the will-to-love and the will-to-consciousness, asserted against death itself. The pride of human conceit in KNOWLEDGE.

There are terrible spirits, ghosts, in the air of America.

Eleanora, the next story, is a fantasy revealing the sensational delights of the man in his early marriage with the young and tender bride. They dwelt, he, his cousin and her mother, in the sequestered Valley of Many-coloured Grass, the valley of prismatic sensation, where everything seems spectrum-coloured. They looked down at their *own images* in the River of Silence, and drew the god Eros from that wave: out of their own self-consciousness, that is. This is a description of the life of introspection and of the love which is begotten by the self in the self, the self-made love. The trees are like serpents worshipping the sun. That is, they represent the phallic passion in its poisonous or mental activity. Everything runs to consciousness: serpents worshipping the sun. The embrace of love, which should bring darkness and oblivion, would with these lovers be a daytime thing bringing more heightened consciousness, visions, spectrum-visions, prismatic. The evil thing that daytime love-making is, and all sex-palaver.

In *Berenice* the man must go down to the sepulchre of his beloved and pull out her thirty-two small white teeth, which he carries in a box with him. It is repulsive and gloating. The teeth are the instruments of biting, or resistance, of antagonism. They often become symbols of opposition, little instruments of entities of crushing and destroying. Hence the dragon's teeth in the myth. Hence the man in *Berenice* must take possession of the irreducible part of his mistress. "*Toutes ses dents étaient des idées,*" he says. Then they are little fixed ideas of mordant hate, of which he possesses himself.

The other great story linking up with this group is *The Fall of the House of Usher*. Here the love is between brother and sister. When the self is broken, and the mystery of the recognition of *otherness* fails, then the longing for identification with the beloved becomes a lust. And it is this longing for identification, utter merging, which is at the base of the incest problem. In psycho-analysis almost every trouble in the psyche is traced to an incest-desire. But it won't do. Incest-desire is only one of the modes by which men strive to get their gratification of the intensest vibration of the spiritual nerves, without any resistance. In the family, the natural vibration is most nearly in unison. With a stranger, there is greater resistance. Incest is the getting of gratification and the avoiding of resistance.

The root of all evil is that we all want this spiritual gratification, this flow, this apparent heightening of life, this knowledge, this valley of many-coloured grass, even grass and light prismatically decomposed, giving ecstasy. We want all this *without resistance*. We want it continually. And this is the root of all evil in us.

We ought to pray to be resisted, and resisted to the bitter end. We ought to decide to have done at last with craving.

The motto to *The Fall of the House of Usher* is a couple of lines from Béranger.

> *Son cœur est un luth suspendu;*
> *Sitôt qu'on le touche il résonne.*

We have all the trappings of Poe's rather overdone, vulgar fantasy. "I reined my horse to the precipitous brink of a black and lurid tarn that lay in unruffled lustre by the dwelling, and gazed down—but with a shudder even more thrilling than before—upon the remodelled and inverted images of the grey sedge, and the ghastly tree-stems, and the vacant and eye-like windows." The House of Usher, both dwelling and family, was very old. Minute fungi overspread the exterior of the house, hanging in festoons from the eaves. Gothic archways, a valet of stealthy step, sombre tapestries, ebon black floors, a profusion of tattered and antique furniture, feeble gleams of encrimsoned light through latticed panes, and over all "an air of stern, deep, irredeemable gloom"—this makes up the interior.

The inmates of the house, Roderick and Madeline Usher, are the last remnants of their incomparably ancient and decayed race. Roderick has the same large, luminous eye, the same slightly arched nose of delicate Hebrew model, as charac-terised Ligeia. He is ill with the nervous malady of his family. It is he whose nerves are so strung that they vibrate to the unknown quiverings of the ether. He, too, has lost his self, his living soul, and become a sensitised instrument of the external influences; his nerves are verily like an æolian harp which must vibrate. He lives in "some struggle with the grim phantasm, Fear", for he is only the physical, post-mortem reality of a living being.

It is a question how much, once the true centrality of the self is broken, the instrumental consciousness of man can register. When man becomes selfless, wafting instrumental like a harp in an open window, how much can his elemental con-sciousness express? The blood as it runs has its own sympathies and responses to the material world, quite apart from seeing. And the nerves we know vibrate all the while to unseen presences, unseen forces. So Roderick Usher quivers on the edge of material existence.

It is this mechanical consciousness which gives "the fervid facility of his impromptus". It is the same thing that gives Poe his extraordinary facility in versification. The absence of real central or impulsive being in himself leaves him inordi-nately, mechanically sensitive to sounds and effects, associations of sounds, associations of rhyme, for example—mechanical, facile, having no root in any passion. It is all a secondary, meretricious process. So we get Roderick Usher's poem, The Haunted Palace, with its swift yet mechanical subtleties of rhyme and rhythm, its vulgarity of epithet. It is all a sort of dream-process, where the association between parts is mechanical, accidental as far as passional meaning goes.

Usher thought that all vegetable things had sentience. Surely all material things have a *form* of sentience, even the inorganic: surely they all exist in some subtle and complicated tension of vibration which makes them sensitive to external influence and causes them to have an influence on other external objects, irrespective of contact. It is of this vibration or inorganic consciousness that Poe is master: the sleep-consciousness. Thus Roderick Usher was convinced that his whole surroundings, the stones of the house, the fungi, the water in the tarn, the very reflected image of the whole, was woven into a physical oneness with the family, condensed, as it were, into one atmosphere—the special atmosphere in which alone the Ushers could live. And it was this atmosphere which had moulded the destinies of his family.

But while ever the soul remains alive, it is the moulder and not the moulded. It is the souls of living men that subtly impregnate stones, houses, mountains, continents, and give these their subtlest form. People only become subject to stones after having lost their integral souls.

In the human realm, Roderick had one connection: his sister Madeline. She, too, was dying of a mysterious disorder, nervous, cataleptic. The brother and sister loved each other passionately and exclusively. They were twins, almost identical in looks. It was the same absorbing love between them, this process of unison in nerve-vibration, resulting in more and more extreme exaltation and a sort of consciousness, and a gradual break-down into death. The exquisitely sensitive Roger, vibrating without resistance with his sister Madeline, more and more exquisitely, and gradually devouring her, sucking her life like a vampire in his anguish of extreme love. And she asking to be sucked.

Madeline died and was carried down by her brother into the deep vaults of the house. But she was not dead. Her brother roamed about in incipient madness—a madness of unspeakable terror and guilt. After eight days they were suddenly startled by a clash of metal, then a distinct, hollow, metallic, and clangorous, yet apparently muffled, reverberation. Then Roderick Usher, gibbering, began to express himself: *"We have put her living into the tomb!* Said I not that my senses were acute? I *now* tell you that I heard her first feeble movements in the hollow coffin. I heard them—many, many days ago—yet I dared not—*I dared not speak."*

It is the same old theme of "each man kills the thing he loves". He knew his love had killed her. He knew she died at last, like Ligeia, unwilling and unappeased. So, she rose again upon him. "But then without those doors there *did* stand the lofty and enshrouded figure of the Lady Madeline of Usher. There was blood upon her white robes, and the evidence of some bitter struggle upon every portion of her emaciated frame. For a moment she remained trembling and reeling to and fro upon the threshold, then, with a low moaning cry, fell heavily inward upon the person of her brother, and in her violent and now final death-agonies bore him to the floor a corpse, and a victim to the terrors he had anticipated."

It is lurid and melodramatic, but it is true. It is a ghastly psychological truth of what happens in the last stages of this beloved love, which cannot be separate, cannot be isolate, cannot listen in isolation to the isolate Holy Ghost. For it is the Holy Ghost we must live by. The next era is the era of the Holy Ghost. And the Holy Ghost speaks individually inside each individual: always, for ever a ghost. There is no manifestation to the general world. Each isolate individual listening in isolation to the Holy Ghost within him.

The Ushers, brother and sister, betrayed the Holy Ghost in themselves. They would love, love, love, without resistance. They would love, they would merge, they would be as one thing. So they dragged each other down into death. For the Holy Ghost says you must *not* be as one thing with another being. Each must abide by itself, and correspond only within certain limits.

The best tales all have the same burden. Hate is as inordinate as love, and as slowly consuming, as secret, as underground, as subtle. All this underground vault business in Poe only symbolises that which takes place *beneath* the consciousness. On top, all is fair-spoken. Beneath, there is awful murderous extremity of burying alive. Fortunato, in *The Cask of Amontillado*, is buried alive out of perfect hatred, as the Lady Madeline of Usher is buried alive out of love. The lust of hate is the inordinate desire to consume and unspeakably possess the soul of the hated one, just as the lust of love is the desire to possess, or to be possessed by, the beloved, utterly. But in either case the result is the dissolution of both souls, each losing itself in transgressing its own bounds.

The lust of Montresor is to devour utterly the soul of Fortunato. It would be no use killing him outright. If a man is killed outright his soul remains integral, free to return into the bosom of some beloved, where it can enact itself. In walling-up his enemy in the vault, Montresor seeks to bring about the indescribable capitulation of the man's soul, so that he, the victor, can possess himself of the very being of the vanquished. Perhaps this can actually be done. Perhaps, in the attempt, the victor breaks the bonds of his own identity, and collapses into nothingness, or into the infinite. Becomes a monster.

What holds good for inordinate hate holds good for inordinate love. The motto, *Nemo me impune lacessit*, might just as well be *Nemo me impune amat*.

In *William Wilson* we are given a rather unsubtle account of the attempt of a man to kill his own soul. William Wilson the mechanical, lustful ego succeeds in killing William Wilson the living self. The lustful ego lives on, gradually reducing itself towards the dust of the infinite.

In the *Murders in the Rue Morgue* and *The Gold Bug* we have those mechanical tales where the interest lies in the following out of a subtle chain of cause and effect. The interest is scientific rather than artistic, a study in psychologic reactions.

The fascination of murder itself is curious. Murder is not just killing. Murder is a lust to get at the very quick of life itself, and kill it—hence the stealth and the frequent morbid dismemberment of the corpse, the attempt to get at the very quick of the murdered being, to find the quick and to possess it. It is curious that the two men fascinated by the art of murder, though in different ways, should have been De Quincey and Poe, men so different in ways of life, yet perhaps not so widely different in nature. In each of them is traceable that strange lust for extreme love and extreme hate, possession by mystic violence of the other soul, or violent deathly surrender of the soul in the self: an absence of manly virtue, which stands alone and accepts limits.

Inquisition and torture are akin to murder: the same lust. It is a combat between inquisitor and victim as to whether the inquisitor shall get at the quick of life itself, and pierce it. Pierce the very quick of the soul. The evil will of man tries to do this. The brave soul of man refuses to have the life-quick pierced in him. It is strange: but just as the thwarted will can persist evilly, after death, so can the brave spirit preserve, even through torture and death, the quick of life and truth.

Nowadays society is evil. It finds subtle ways of torture, to destroy the life-quick, to get at the life-quick in a man. Every possible form. And still a man can hold out, if he can laugh and listen to the Holy Ghost.—But society is evil, evil, and love is evil. And evil breeds evil, more and more.

So the mystery goes on. La Bruyère says that all our human unhappiness *viennent de ne pouvoir être seuls*. As long as man lives he will be subject to the yearning of love or the burning of hate, which is only inverted love.

But he is subject to something more than this. If we do not live to eat, we do not live to love either.

We live to stand alone, and listen to the Holy Ghost. The Holy Ghost, who is inside us, and who is many gods. Many gods come and go, some say one thing and some say another, and we have to obey the God of the innermost hour. It is the multiplicity of gods within us make up the Holy Ghost.

But Poe knew only love, love, love, intense vibrations and heightened consciousness. Drugs, women, self-destruction, but anyhow the prismatic ecstasy of heightened consciousness and sense of love, of flow. The human soul in him was beside itself. But it was not lost. He told us plainly how it was, so that we should know.

He was an adventurer into vaults and cellars and horrible underground passages of the human soul. He sounded the horror and the warning of his own doom.

Doomed he was. He died wanting more love, and love killed him. A ghastly disease, love. Poe telling us of his disease: trying even to make his disease fair and attractive. Even succeeding.

Which is the inevitable falseness, duplicity of art, American art in particular.

[From *Studies in Classic American Literature,* 1924]

[98]

NATHANIEL HAWTHORNE AND
THE SCARLET LETTER

NATHANIEL HAWTHORNE writes romance.

And what's romance? Usually, a nice little tale where you have everything As You Like It, where rain never wets your jacket and gnats never bite your nose and it's always daisy-time. *As You Like It* and *Forest Lovers*, etc. *Morte D'Arthur.*

Hawthorne obviously isn't this kind of romanticist: though nobody has muddy boots in *The Scarlet Letter*, either.

But there is more to it. *The Scarlet Letter* isn't a pleasant, pretty romance. It is a sort of parable, an earthly story with a hellish meaning.

All the time there is this split in the American art and art-consciousness. On the top it is as nice as pie, goody-goody and lovey-dovey. Like Hawthorne being such a blue-eyed darling, in life, and Longfellow and the rest such sucking-doves. Hawthorne's wife said she "never saw him in time", which doesn't mean she saw him too late. But always in the "frail effulgence of eternity".

Serpents they were. Look at the inner meaning of their art and see what demons they were.

You *must* look through the surface of American art, and see the inner diabolism of the symbolic meaning. Otherwise it is all mere childishness.

That blue-eyed darling Nathaniel knew disagreeable things in his inner soul. He was careful to send them out in disguise.

Always the same. The deliberate consciousness of Americans so fair and smooth-spoken, and the under-consciousness so devilish. *Destroy! destroy! destroy!* hums the under-consciousness. *Love and produce! Love and produce!* cackles the upper consciousness. And the world hears only the Love-and-produce cackle. Refuses to hear the hum of destruction underneath. Until such time as it will *have* to hear.

The American has got to destroy. It is his destiny. It is

his destiny to destroy the whole corpus of the white psyche, the white consciousness. And he's got to do it secretly. As the growing of a dragon-fly inside a chrysalis or cocoon destroys the larva grub, secretly.

Though many a dragon-fly never gets out of the chrysalis case: dies inside. As America might.

So the secret chrysalis of *The Scarlet Letter*, diabolically destroying the old psyche inside.

Be good! Be good! warbles Nathaniel. *Be good, and never sin! Be sure your sins will find you out.*

So convincingly that his wife never saw him "as in time".

Then listen to the diabolic undertone of *The Scarlet Letter*.

Man ate of the tree of knowledge, and became ashamed of himself.

Do you imagine Adam had never lived with Eve before that apple episode? Yes, he had. As a wild animal with his mate.

It didn't become "sin" till the knowledge-poison entered. That apple of Sodom.

We are divided in ourselves, against ourselves. And that is the meaning of the cross symbol.

In the first place, Adam knew Eve as a wild animal knows its mate, momentaneously, but vitally, in blood-knowledge. Blood-knowledge, not mind-knowledge. Blood-knowledge, that seems utterly to forget, but doesn't. Blood-knowledge, instinct, intuition, all the vast vital flux of knowing that goes on in the dark, antecedent to the mind.

Then came that beastly apple, and the other sort of knowledge started.

Adam began to look at himself. "My hat!" he said. "What's this? My Lord! What the deuce!—And Eve! I wonder about Eve."

Thus starts KNOWING. Which shortly runs to UNDERSTANDING, when the devil gets his own.

When Adam went and took Eve, *after* the apple, he didn't do any more than he had done many a time before, in act. But in consciousness he did something very different. So did Eve. Each of them kept an eye on what they were doing, they watched what was happening to them. They wanted to KNOW. And that was the birth of sin. Not *doing* it, but KNOWING about it. Before the apple, they had shut their eyes and their

minds had gone dark. Now, they peeped and pried and
imagined. They watched themselves. And they felt uncomfortable after. They felt self-conscious. So they said, "The
act is sin. Let's hide. We've sinned."

No wonder the Lord kicked them out of the Garden. Dirty
hypocrites.

The sin was the self-watching, self-consciousness. The sin,
and the doom. Dirty understanding.

Nowadays men do hate the idea of dualism. It's no good,
dual we are. The cross. If we accept the symbol, then,
virtually, we accept the fact. We are divided against ourselves.

For instance, the blood *hates* being KNOWN by the mind. It
feels itself destroyed when it is KNOWN. Hence the profound
instinct of privacy.

And on the other hand, the mind and the spiritual consciousness of man simply *hates* the dark potency of blood-acts: hates
the genuine dark sensual orgasms, which do, for the time being,
actually obliterate the mind and the spiritual consciousness,
plunge them in a suffocating flood of darkness.

You can't get away from this.

Blood-consciousness overwhelms, obliterates, and annuls
mind-consciousness.

Mind-consciousness extinguishes blood-consciousness, and
consumes the blood.

We are all of us conscious in both ways. And the two ways
are antagonistic in us.

They will always remain so.

That is our cross.

The antagonism is so obvious, and so far-reaching, that it
extends to the smallest thing. The cultured, highly-conscious
person of to-day *loathes* any form of physical, "menial" work:
such as washing dishes or sweeping a floor or chopping wood.
This menial work is an insult to the spirit. "When I see men
carrying heavy loads, doing brutal work, it always makes me
want to cry," said a beautiful, cultured woman to me.

"When you say that, it makes me want to beat you," said
I, in reply. "When I see you with your beautiful head ponder-
ing heavy thoughts, I just want to hit you. It outrages me."

My father hated books, hated the sight of anyone reading or
writing.

My mother hated the thought that any of her sons should be condemned to manual labour. Her sons must have something higher than that.

She won. But she died first.

He laughs longest who laughs last.

There is a basic hostility in all of us between the physical and the mental, the blood and the spirit. The mind is "ashamed" of the blood. And the blood is destroyed by the mind, actually. Hence pale-faces.

At present the mind-consciousness and the so-called spirit triumphs. In America supremely. In America, nobody does anything from the blood. Always from the nerves, if not from the mind. The blood is chemically reduced by the nerves, in American activity.

When an Italian labourer labours, his mind and nerves sleep, his blood acts ponderously.

Americans, when they are *doing* things, never seem really to be doing them. They are "busy about" it. They are always busy "about" something. But truly *immersed* in *doing* something, with the deep blood-consciousness active, that they never are.

They *admire* the blood-conscious spontaneity. And they want to get it in their heads. "Live from the body," they shriek. It is their last mental shriek. *Co-ordinate.*

It is a further attempt still to rationalise the body and blood. "Think about such and such a muscle," they say, "and relax there."

And every time you "conquer" the body with the mind (you can say "heal" it, if you like) you cause a deeper, more dangerous complex or tension somewhere else.

Ghastly Americans, with their blood no longer blood. A yellow spiritual fluid.

The Fall.

There have been lots of Falls.

We *fell* into *knowledge* when Eve bit the apple. Self-conscious knowledge. For the first time the mind put up a fight against the blood. Wanting to UNDERSTAND. That is to intellectualise the blood.

The blood must be *shed*, says Jesus.

Shed on the cross of our own divided psyche.

Shed the blood, and you become mind-conscious. Eat the

body and drink the blood, self-cannibalising, and you become extremely conscious, like Americans and some Hindus. Devour yourself, and God knows what a lot you'll know, what a lot you'll be conscious of.

Mind you don't choke yourself.

For a long time men *believed* that they could be perfected through the mind, through the spirit. They believed, passionately. They had their ecstasy in pure consciousness. They *believed* in purity, chastity, and the wings of the spirit.

America soon plucked the bird of the spirit. America soon killed the *belief* in the spirit. But not the practice. The practice continued with a sarcastic vehemence. America, with a perfect inner contempt for the spirit and the consciousness of man, practises the same spirituality and universal love and KNOWING all the time, incessantly, like a drug habit. And inwardly gives not a fig for it. Only for the *sensation*. The pretty-pretty *sensation* of love, loving all the world. And the nice fluttering aeroplane *sensation* of knowing, knowing, knowing. Then the prettiest of all sensations, the sensation of UNDERSTANDING. Oh, what a lot they understand, the darlings! *So* good at the trick, they are. Just a trick of self-conceit.

The Scarlet Letter gives the show away.

You have your pure-pure young parson Dimmesdale.

You have the beautiful Puritan Hester at his feet.

And the first thing she does is to seduce him.

And the first thing he does is to be seduced.

And the second thing they do is to hug their sin in secret, and gloat over it, and try to understand.

Which is the myth of New England.

Deerslayer refused to be seduced by Judith Hutter. At least the Sodom apple of sin didn't fetch him.

But Dimmesdale was seduced gloatingly. Oh, luscious Sin!

He was such a pure young man.

That he had to make a fool of purity.

The American psyche.

Of course, the best part of the game lay in keeping up pure appearances.

The greatest triumph a woman can have, especially an American woman, is the triumph of seducing a man: especially if he is pure.

And he gets the greatest thrill of all, in falling.—"Seduce me, Mrs. Hercules."

And the pair of them share the subtlest delight in keeping up pure appearances, when everybody knows all the while. But the power of pure appearances is something to exult in. All America gives in to it. *Look* pure!

To seduce a man. To have everybody know. To keep up appearances of purity. Pure!

This is the great triumph of woman.

A. The Scarlet Letter. Adulteress! The great Alpha. Alpha! Adulteress! The new Adam and Adama! American!

A. Adulteress! Stitched with gold thread, glittering upon the bosom. The proudest insignia.

Put her upon the scaffold and worship her there. Worship her there. The Woman, the Magna Mater. *A.* Adulteress! Abel!

Abel! Abel! Abel! Admirable!

It becomes a farce.

The fiery heart. *A.* Mary of the Bleeding Heart. Mater Adolerata! *A.* Capital *A.* Adulteress. Glittering with gold thread. Abel! Adultery. Admirable!

It is, perhaps, the most colossal satire ever penned. *The Scarlet Letter.* And by a blue-eyed darling of a Nathaniel.

Not Bumppo, however.

The human spirit, fixed in a lie, adhering to a lie, giving itself perpetually the lie.

All begins with *A.*

Adulteress. Alpha. Abel, Adam. *A.* America.

The Scarlet Letter.

"Had there been a Papist among the crowd of Puritans, he might have seen in this beautiful woman, so picturesque in her attire and mien, and with the infant at her bosom, an object to remind him of the image of Divine Maternity, which so many illustrious painters have vied with one another to represent; something which should remind him, indeed, but only by contrast, of that sacred image of sinless Motherhood, whose infant was to redeem the world."

Whose infant was to redeem the world indeed! It will be a startling redemption the world will get from the American infant.

"Here was a taint of deepest sin in the most sacred quality of human life, working such effect that the world was only the darker for this woman's beauty, and more lost for the infant she had borne."

Just listen to the darling. Isn't he a master of apology?

Of symbols, too.

His pious blame is a chuckle of praise all the while.

Oh, Hester, you are a demon. A man *must* be pure, just that you can seduce him to a fall. Because the greatest thrill in life is to bring down the Sacred Saint with a flop into the mud. Then when you've brought him down, humbly wipe off the mud with you hair, another Magdalen. And then go home and dance a witch's jig of triumph, and stitch yourself a Scarlet Letter with gold thread, as duchesses used to stitch themselves coronets. And then stand meek on the scaffold and fool the world. Who will all be envying you your sin, and beating you because you've stolen an advantage over them.

Hester Prynne is the great nemesis of woman. She is the KNOWING Ligeia risen diabolic from the grave. Having her own back. UNDERSTANDING.

This time it is Mr. Dimmesdale who dies. She lives on and is Abel.

His spiritual love was a lie. And prostituting the woman to his spiritual love, as popular clergymen do, in his preachings and loftiness, was a tall white lie. Which came flop.

We are so pure in spirit. Hi-tiddly-i-ty!

Till she tickled him in the right place, and he fell.

Flop.

Flop goes spiritual love.

But keep up the game. Keep up appearances. Pure are the pure. To the pure all things, etc.

Look out, Mister, for the Female Devotee. Whatever you do, don't let her start tickling you. She knows your weak spot. Mind your Purity.

When Hester Prynne seduced Arthur Dimmesdale it was the beginning of the end. But from the beginning of the end to the end of the end is a hundred years or two.

Mr. Dimmesdale also wasn't at the end of his resources. Previously, he had lived by governing his body, ruling it, in the interests of his spirit. Now he has a good time all by himself torturing his body, whipping it, piercing it with thorns, macerating himself. It's a form of masturbation. He wants to get a mental grip on his body. And since he can't quite manage it with the mind, witness his fall—he will give it what for, with whips. His will shall *lash* his body. And he enjoys his pains. Wallows in them. To the pure all things are pure.

It is the old self-mutilation process, gone rotten. The mind wanting to get its teeth in the blood and flesh. The ego exulting in the tortures of the mutinous flesh. I, the ego, I *will* triumph over my own flesh. Lash! Lash! I am a grand free spirit. *Lash!* I am the master of my soul! *Lash! Lash!* I am the captain of my soul. *Lash!* Hurray! "In the fell clutch of circumstance," etc., etc.

Good-bye Arthur. He depended on women for his Spiritual Devotees, spiritual brides. So, the woman just touched him in his weak spot, his Achilles Heel of the flesh. Look out for the spiritual bride. She's after the weak spot.

It is the battle of wills.

"For the will therein lieth, which dieth not——"

The Scarlet Woman becomes a Sister of Mercy. Didn't she just, in the late war. Oh, Prophet Nathaniel!

Hester urges Dimmesdale to go away with her, to a new country, to a new life. He isn't having any.

He knows there is no new country, no new life on the globe to-day. It is the same old thing, in different degrees, everywhere. *Plus ça change, plus c'est la même chose.*

Hester thinks, with Dimmesdale for her husband, and Pearl for her child, in Australia, maybe, she'd have been perfect.

But she wouldn't. Dimmesdale had already fallen from his integrity as a minister of the Gospel of the Spirit. He had lost his manliness. He didn't see the point of just leaving himself between the hands of a woman and going away to a "new country", to be her thing entirely. She'd only have despised him more, as every woman despises a man who has "fallen" to her; despises him with her tenderest lust.

He stood for nothing any more. So let him stay where he was and dree out his weird.

She had dished him and his spirituality, so he hated her. As Angel Clare was dished, and hated Tess. As Jude in the

end hated Sue: or should have done. The women make fools
of them, the spiritual men. And when, as men, they've gone
flop in their spirituality, they can't pick themselves up whole
any more. So they just crawl, and die detesting the female,
or the females, who made them fall.

The saintly minister gets a bit of his own back, at the last
minute, by making public confession from the very scaffold
where she was exposed. Then he dodges into death. But
he's had a bit of his own back, on everybody.

" 'Shall we not meet again?' whispered she, bending her
face down close to him. 'Shall we not spend our immortal
life together? Surely, surely we have ransomed one another
with all this woe! Thou lookest far into eternity with those
bright dying eyes. Tell me what thou seest!' "

" 'Hush, Hester—hush,' said he, with tremulous solemnity.
'The law we broke!—the sin here so awfully revealed! Let
these alone be in thy thoughts. I fear! I fear!' "

So he dies, throwing the "sin" in her teeth, and escaping
into death.

The law we broke, indeed. You bet!

Whose law?

But it is truly a law, that man must either stick to the belief
he has grounded himself on, and obey the laws of that belief,
or he must admit the belief itself to be inadequate, and prepare
himself for a new thing.

There was no change in belief, either in Hester or in Dimmesdale or in Hawthorne or in America. The same old treacherous
belief, which was really cunning disbelief, in the Spirit, in
Purity, in Selfless Love, and in Pure Consciousness. They
would go on following this belief, for the sake of the sensationalism of it. But they would make a fool of it all the time. Like
Woodrow Wilson, and the rest of modern Believers. The rest
of modern Saviours.

If you meet a Saviour, to-day, be sure he is trying to make
an innermost fool of you. Especially if the saviour be an
UNDERSTANDING WOMAN, offering her love.

Hester lives on, pious as pie, being a public nurse. She
becomes at last an acknowledged saint, Abel of the Scarlet
Letter.

She would, being a woman. She has had her triumph over

the individual man, so she quite loves subscribing to the whole spiritual life of society. She will make herself as false as hell, for society's sake, once she's had her real triumph over Saint Arthur.

Blossoms out into a Sister-of-Mercy Saint.

But it's a long time before she really takes anybody in. People kept on thinking her a witch, which she was.

As a matter of fact, unless a woman is held, by man, safe within the bounds of belief, she becomes inevitably a destructive force. She can't help herself. A woman is almost always vulnerable to pity. She can't bear to see anything *physically* hurt. But let a woman loose from the bounds and restraints of man's fierce belief, in his gods and in himself, and she becomes a gentle devil. She becomes subtly diabolic. The colossal evil of the united spirit of Woman. WOMAN, German woman or American woman, or every other sort of woman, in the last war, was something frightening. As every *man* knows.

Woman becomes a helpless, would-be-loving demon. She is helpless. Her very love is a subtle poison.

Unless a man believes in himself and his gods, *genuinely*: unless he fiercely obeys his own Holy Ghost; his woman will destroy him. Woman is the nemesis of doubting man. She can't help it.

And with Hester, after Ligeia, woman becomes a nemesis to man. She bolsters him up from the outside, she destroys him from the inside. And he dies hating her, as Dimmesdale did.

Dimmesdale's spirituality had gone on too long, too far. It had become a false thing. He found his nemesis in woman. And he was done for.

Woman is a strange and rather terrible phenomenon, to man. When the subconscious soul of woman recoils from its creative union with man, it becomes a destructive force. It exerts, willy-nilly, an invisible destructive influence. The woman herself may be as nice as milk, to all appearance, like Ligeia. But she is sending out waves of silent destruction of the faltering spirit in men, all the same. She doesn't know it. She can't even help it. But she does it. The devil is in her.

The very women who are most busy saving the bodies of men, and saving the children: these women-doctors, these nurses, these educationalists, these public-spirited women, these female saviours: they are all, from the inside, sending out waves of destructive malevolence which eat out the inner life of a man, like a cancer. It is so, it will be so, till men realise it and react to save themselves.

God won't save us. The women are so devilish godly. Men must save themselves in this strait, and by no sugary means either.

A woman can use her sex in sheer malevolence and poison, while she is *behaving* as meek and good as gold. Dear darling, she is really snow-white in her blamelessness. And all the while she is using her sex as a she-devil, for the endless hurt of her man. She doesn't know it. She will never believe it if you tell her. And if you give her a slap in the face for her fiendishness, she will rush to the first magistrate, in indignation. She is so *absolutely* blameless, the she-devil, the dear, dutiful creature.

Give her the great slap, just the same, just when she is being most angelic. Just when she is bearing her cross most meekly.

Oh, woman out of bounds is a devil. But it is man's fault. Woman never *asked*, in the first place, to be cast out of her bit of an Eden of belief and trust. It is man's business to bear the responsibility of belief. If he becomes a spiritual fornicator and liar, like Ligeia's husband and Arthur Dimmesdale, how *can* a woman believe in him? Belief doesn't go by choice. And if a woman doesn't believe in a *man*, she believes, essentially, in nothing. She becomes, willy-nilly, a devil.

A devil she is, and a devil she will be. And most men will succumb to her devilishness.

Hester Prynne was a devil. Even when she was so meekly going round as a sick-nurse. Poor Hester. Part of her wanted to be saved from her own devilishness. And another part wanted to go on and on in devilishness, for revenge. Revenge! REVENGE! It is this that fills the unconscious spirit of woman to-day. Revenge against man, and against the spirit of man, which has betrayed her into unbelief. Even when she is most sweet and a salvationist, she is her most devilish, is woman. She gives her man the sugar-plum of her own submissive sweetness. And when he's taken this sugar-plum in his mouth, a scorpion comes out of it. After he's taken this Eve to his bosom, oh, so loving, she destroys him inch by inch. Woman and her revenge! She will have it, and go on having it, for decades and decades, unless she's stopped. And to stop her you've got to believe in yourself and your gods, your own Holy Ghost, Sir Man; and then you've got to fight her, and never give in. She's a devil. But in the long run she is conquerable. And just a tiny bit of her wants to be conquered. You've got to fight three-quarters of her, in absolute hell, to get at the final quarter of her that wants a release, at last, from the hell of her own revenge. But it's a long last. And not yet.

"She had in her nature a rich, voluptuous, oriental characteristic—a taste for the gorgeously beautiful." This is Hester. This is American. But she repressed her nature in the above direction. She would not even allow herself the luxury of labouring at fine, delicate stitching. Only she dressed her little sin-child Pearl vividly, and the scarlet letter was gorgeously embroidered. Her Hecate and Astarte insignia.

"A voluptuous, oriental characteristic——" That lies waiting in American women. It is probable that the Mormons are the forerunners of the coming real America. It is probable that men will have more than one wife, in the coming America. That you will have again a half-oriental womanhood, and a polygamy.

The grey nurse, Hester. The Hecate, the hell-cat. The slowly-evolving voluptuous female of the new era, with a whole new submissiveness to the dark, phallic principle.

But it takes time. Generation after generation of nurses and political women and salvationists. And in the end, the dark erection of the images of sex-worship once more, and the newly submissive women. That kind of depth. Deep women in that respect. When we have at last broken this insanity of mental-spiritual consciousness. And the women *choose* to experience again the great submission.

"The poor, whom she sought out to be the objects of her bounty, often reviled the hand that was stretched to succour them."

Naturally. The poor hate a salvationist. They smell the devil underneath.

"She was patient—a martyr indeed—but she forbore to pray for her enemies, lest, in spite of her forgiving aspirations, the words of the blessing should stubbornly twist themselves into a curse."

So much honesty, at least. No wonder the old witch-lady Mistress Hibbins claimed her for another witch.

"She grew to have a dread of children; for they had imbibed from their parents a vague idea of something horrible in this dreary woman gliding silently through the town, with never any companion but only one child."

"A vague idea!" Can't you see her "gliding silently"? It's not a question of a vague idea imbibed, but a definite feeling directly received.

"But sometimes, once in many days, or perchance in many months, she felt an eye—a human eye—upon the ignominious brand, that seemed to give a momentary relief, as if half her agony were shared. The next instant, back it all rushed again, with a still deeper throb of pain; for in that brief interval she had sinned again. Had Hester sinned alone?"

Of course not. As for sinning again, she would go on all her life silently, changelessly "sinning". She never repented. Not she. Why should she? She had brought down Arthur Dimmesdale, that too-too snow-white bird, and that was her life-work.

As for sinning again when she met two dark eyes in a crowd, why of course. Somebody who understood as she understood.

I always remember meeting the eyes of a gipsy woman, for one moment, in a crowd, in England. She knew, and I knew. What did we know? I was not able to make out. But we knew.

Probably the same fathomless hate of this spiritual-conscious society in which the outcast woman and I both roamed like meek-looking wolves. Tame wolves waiting to shake off their tameness. Never able to.

And again, that "voluptuous, oriental" characteristic that knows the mystery of the ithyphallic gods. She would not betray the ithyphallic gods to this white, leprous-white society of "lovers". Neither will I, if I can help it. These leprous-white, seducing, spiritual women, who "understand" so much. One has been too often seduced, and "understood". "I can read him like a book," said my first lover of me. The book is in several volumes, dear. And more and more comes back to me the gulf of dark hate and *other* understanding, in the eyes of the gipsy woman. So different from the hateful white light of understanding which floats like scum on the eyes of white, oh, so white English and American women, with their understanding voices and their deep, sad words, and their profound, *good* spirits. Pfui!

Hester was scared only of one result of her sin: Pearl. Pearl, the scarlet letter incarnate. The little girl. When women bear children, they produce either devils or sons with gods in them. And it is an evolutionary process. The devil in Hester produced a purer devil in Pearl. And the devil in Pearl will produce—she married an Italian Count—a piece of purer devilishness still.

And so from hour to hour we ripe and ripe.

And then from hour to hour we rot and rot.

There was that in the child "which often impelled Hester to ask in bitterness of heart, whether it were for good or ill that the poor little creature had been born at all."

For ill, Hester. But don't worry. Ill is as necessary as good. Malevolence is as necessary as benevolence. If you have brought forth, spawned, a young malevolence, be sure there is a rampant falseness in the world against which this malevolence must be turned. Falseness has to be bitten and bitten, till it is bitten to death. Hence Pearl.

Pearl. Her own mother compares her to the demon of plague, or scarlet fever, in her red dress. But then, plague is necessary to destroy a rotten, false humanity.

Pearl, the devilish girl-child, who can be so tender and loving and *understanding*, and then, when she has understood, will give you a hit across the mouth, and turn on you with a grin of sheer diabolic jeering.

Serves you right, you shouldn't be *understood*. That is your vice. You shouldn't want to be loved, and then you'd not get hit across the mouth. Pearl will love you: marvellously. And she'll hit you across the mouth: oh, so neatly. And serves you right.

Pearl is perhaps the most modern child in all literature.

Old-fashioned Nathaniel, with his little-boy charm, he'll tell you what's what. But he'll cover it with smarm.

Hester simply *hates* her child, from one part of herself. And from another, she cherishes her child as her one precious treasure. For Pearl is the continuing of her female revenge on

life. But female revenge hits both ways. Hits back at its
own mother. The female revenge in Pearl hits back at Hester,
the mother, and Hester is simply livid with fury and "sadness",
which is rather amusing.

"The child could not be made amenable to rules. In giving
her existence a great law had been broken; and the result was
a being whose elements were perhaps beautiful and brilliant,
but all in disorder, or with an order peculiar to themselves,
amidst which the point of variety and arrangement was difficult
or impossible to discover."

Of course, the order is peculiar to themselves. But the
point of variety is this: "Draw out the loving, sweet soul,
draw it out with marvellous understanding; and then spit in
its eye."

Hester, of course, didn't at all like it when her sweet child
drew out her motherly soul, with yearning and deep understanding: and then spit in the motherly eye, with a grin. But
it was a process the mother had started.

Pearl had a peculiar look in her eyes: "a look so intelligent,
yet so inexplicable, so perverse, sometimes so malicious, but
generally accompanied by a wild flow of spirits, that Hester
could not help questioning at such moments whether Pearl was
a human child."

A little demon! But her mother, and the saintly Dimmesdale,
had borne her. And Pearl, by the very openness of her perversity, was more straightforward than her parents. She flatly
refuses any Heavenly Father, seeing the earthly one such a
fraud. And she has the pietistic Dimmesdale on toast, spits
right in his eye: in both his eyes.

Poor, brave, tormented little soul, always in a state of recoil,
she'll be a devil to men when she grows up. But the men
deserve it. If they'll let themselves be "drawn", by her loving
understanding, they deserve that she shall slap them across
the mouth the moment they *are* drawn. The chickens! Drawn
and trussed.

Poor little phenomenon of a modern child, she'll grow up
into the devil of a modern woman. The nemesis of weak-
kneed modern men, craving to be love-drawn.

The third person in the diabolic trinity, or triangle, of the
Scarlet Letter, is Hester's first husband, Roger Chillingworth.

He is an old Elizabethan physician, with a grey beard and a long-furred coat and a twisted shoulder. Another healer. But something of an alchemist, a magician. He is a magician on the verge of modern science, like Francis Bacon.

Roger Chillingworth is of the old order of intellect, in direct line from the medieval Roger Bacon alchemists. He has an old, intellectual belief in the dark sciences, the Hermetic philosophies. He is no Christian, no selfless aspirer. He is not an aspirer. He is the old authoritarian in man. The old male authority. But without passional belief. Only intellectual belief in himself and his male authority.

Shakespeare's whole tragic wail is because of the downfall of the true male authority, the ithyphallic authority and master-hood. It fell with Elizabeth. It was trodden underfoot with Victoria.

But Chillingworth keeps on the *intellectual* tradition. He hates the new spiritual aspirers, like Dimmesdale, with a black, crippled hate. He is the old male authority, in intellectual tradition.

You can't keep a wife by force of an intellectual tradition. So Hester took to seducing Dimmesdale.

Yet her only marriage, and her last oath, is with the old Roger. He and she are accomplices in pulling down the spiritual saint.

"Why dost thou smile so at me——" she says to her old, vengeful husband. "Art thou not like the Black Man that haunts the forest around us? Hast thou not enticed me into a bond which will prove the ruin of my soul?"

"Not thy soul!" he answered with another smile. "No, not thy soul!"

It is the soul of the pure preacher, that false thing, which they are after. And the crippled physician—this other healer —blackly vengeful in his old, distorted male authority, and the "loving" woman, they bring down the saint between them.

A black and complementary hatred, akin to love, is what Chillingworth feels for the young, saintly parson. And Dimmesdale responds, in a hideous kind of love. Slowly the saint's life is poisoned. But the black old physician smiles, and tries to keep him alive. Dimmesdale goes in for self-torture, self-lashing, lashing his own white, thin, spiritual saviour's body. The dark old Chillingworth listens outside the door and laughs, and prepares another medicine, so that the game can go on longer. And the saint's very soul goes rotten. Which is the supreme triumph. Yet he keeps up appearances still.

The black, vengeful soul of the crippled, masterful male, still dark in his authority: and the white ghastliness of the fallen saint! The two halves of manhood mutually destroying one another.

Dimmesdale has a "coup" in the very end. He gives the whole show away by confessing publicly on the scaffold, and dodging into death, leaving Hester dished, and Roger as it were, doubly cuckolded. It is a neat last revenge.

Down comes the curtain, as in Ligeia's poem.

But the child Pearl will be on in the next act, with her Italian Count and a new brood of vipers. And Hester greyly Abelling, in the shadows, after her rebelling.

It is a marvellous allegory. It is to me one of the greatest allegories in all literature, *The Scarlet Letter*. Its marvellous under-meaning! And its perfect duplicity.

The absolute duplicity of that blue-eyed *Wunderkind* of a Nathaniel. The American wonder-child, with his magical allegorical insight.

But even wonder-children have to grow up in a generation or two.

And even SIN becomes stale.

[From *Studies in Classic American Literature*, 1924]

[99]

HERMAN MELVILLE'S *TYPEE* AND *OMOO*

THE greatest seer and poet of the sea for me is Melville. His vision is more real than Swinburne's, because he doesn't personify the sea, and far sounder than Joseph Conrad's, because Melville doesn't sentimentalise the ocean and the sea's unfortunates. Snivel in a wet hanky like Lord Jim.

Melville has the strange, uncanny magic of sea-creatures, and some of their repulsiveness. He isn't quite a land animal. There is something slithery about him. Something always half-seas-over. In his life they said he was mad—or crazy. He was neither mad nor crazy. But he was over the border. He was half a water animal, like those terrible yellow-bearded Vikings who broke out of the waves in beaked ships.

He was a modern Viking. There is something curious about real blue-eyed people. They are never quite human, in the good classic sense, human as brown-eyed people are human: the human of the living humus. About a real blue-eyed person there is usually something abstract, elemental. Brown-eyed people are, as it were, like the earth, which is tissue of bygone life, organic, compound. In blue eyes there is sun and rain and abstract, uncreate element, water, ice, air, space, but not humanity. Brown-eyed people are people of the old, old world: *Allzu menschlich*. Blue-eyed people tend to be too keen and abstract.

Melville is like a Viking going home to the sea, encumbered with age and memories, and a sort of accomplished despair, almost madness. For he cannot accept humanity. He can't belong to humanity. Cannot.

The great Northern cycle of which he is the returning unit has almost completed its round, accomplished itself. Balder the beautiful is mystically dead, and by this time he stinketh. Forget-me-nots and sea-poppies fall into water. The man who came from the sea to live among men can stand it no longer. He hears the horror of the cracked church bell, and goes back down the shore, back into the ocean again, home, into the salt water. Human life won't do. He turns back to the elements. And all the vast sun-and-wheat consciousness of his day he plunges back into the deeps, burying the flame in the deep, self-conscious and deliberate. As blue flax and sea-poppies fall into the waters and give back their created sun-stuff to the dissolution of the flood.

The sea-born people, who can meet and mingle no longer: who turn away from life, to the abstract, to the elements: the sea receives her own.

Let life come asunder, they say. Let water conceive no more with fire. Let mating finish. Let the elements leave off kissing, and turn their backs on one another. Let the merman turn away from his human wife and children, let the seal-woman forget the world of men, remembering only the waters.

So they go down to the sea, the sea-born people. The Vikings are wandering again. Homes are broken up. Cross the seas, cross the seas, urges the heart. Leave love and home. Leave love and home. Love and home are a deadly illusion. Woman, what have I to do with thee? It is finished. *Consummatum est.* The crucifixion into humanity is over. Let us go back to the fierce, uncanny elements: the corrosive vast sea. Or Fire.

Basta! It is enough. It is enough of life. Let us have the vast elements. Let us get out of this loathsome complication of living humanly with humans. Let the sea wash us clean of the leprosy of our humanity and humanness.

Melville was a northerner, sea-born. So the sea claimed him. We are most of us, who use the English language, water-people, sea-derived.

Melville went back to the oldest of all the oceans, to the Pacific. *Der Grosse oder Stille Ozean.*

Without doubt the Pacific Ocean is æons older than the Atlantic or the Indian Oceans. When we say older, we mean it has not come to any modern consciousness. Strange convulsions have convulsed the Atlantic and Mediterranean peoples into phase after phase of consciousness, while the Pacific and the Pacific peoples have slept. To sleep is to dream: you can't stay unconscious. And, oh heaven, for how many thousands of years has the true Pacific been dreaming, turning over in its sleep and dreaming again: idylls: nightmares?

The Maoris, the Tongans, the Marquesans, the Fijians, the Polynesians: holy God, how long have they been turning over in the same sleep, with varying dreams? Perhaps, to a sensitive imagination, those islands in the middle of the Pacific are the most unbearable places on earth. It simply stops the heart, to be translated there, unknown ages back, back into that life, that pulse, that rhythm. The scientists say the South Sea Islanders belong to the Stone Age. It seems absurd to class people according to their implements. And yet there is something in it. The heart of the Pacific is still the Stone Age; in spite of steamers. The heart of the Pacific seems like a vast vacuum, in which, mirage-like, continues the life of myriads of ages back. It is a phantom-persistence of human beings who should have died, by our chronology, in the Stone Age. It is a

phantom, illusion-like trick of reality: the glamorous South Seas.
Even Japan and China have been turning over in their sleep
for countless centuries. Their blood is the old blood, their
tissue the old soft tissue. Their busy day was myriads of years
ago, when the world was a softer place, more moisture in the air,
more warm mud on the face of the earth, and the lotus was
always in flower. The great bygone world, before Egypt. And
Japan and China have been turning over in their sleep, while we
have "advanced". And now they are starting up into night-
mare.

The world isn't what it seems.

The Pacific Ocean holds the dream of immemorial centuries.
It is the great blue twilight of the vastest of all evenings:
perhaps of the most wonderful of all dawns. Who knows?

It must once have been a vast basin of soft, lotus-warm
civilisation, the Pacific. Never was such a huge man-day
swung down into slow disintegration, as here. And now the
waters are blue and ghostly with the end of immemorial
peoples. And phantom-like the islands rise out of it, illusions
of the glamorous Stone Age.

To this phantom Melville returned. Back, back, away from
life. Never man instinctively hated human life, our human life,
as we have it, more than Melville did. And never was a man
so passionately filled with the sense of vastness and mystery
of life which is non-human. He was mad to look over our
horizons. Anywhere, anywhere out of *our* world. To get away.
To get away, out!

To get away, out of our life. To cross a horizon into another
life. No matter what life, so long as it is another life.

Away, away from humanity. To the sea. The naked, salt,
elemental sea. To go to sea, to escape humanity.

The human heart gets into a frenzy at last, in its desire to
dehumanise itself.

So he finds himself in the middle of the Pacific. Truly over
a horizon. In another world. In another epoch. Back, far
back, in the days of palm trees and lizards and stone implements. The sunny Stone Age.

Samoa, Tahiti, Raratonga, Nukuheva: the very names are
a sleep and a forgetting. The sleep-forgotten past magnificence
of human history. "Trailing clouds of glory."

Melville hated the world: was born hating it. But he was looking for heaven. That is, choosingly. Choosingly, he was looking for paradise. Unchoosingly, he was mad with hatred of the world.

Well, the world is hateful. It is as hateful as Melville found it. He was not wrong in hating the world. *Delenda est Chicago.* He hated it to a pitch of madness, and not without reason.

But it's no good *persisting* in looking for paradise "regained".

Melville at his best invariably wrote from a sort of dream-self, so that events which he relates as actual fact have indeed a far deeper reference to his own soul, his own inner life.

So in *Typee* when he tells of his entry into the valley of the dread cannibals of Nukuheva. Down this narrow, steep, horrible dark gorge he slides and struggles as we struggle in a dream, or in the act of birth, to emerge in the green Eden of the Golden Age, the valley of the cannibal savages. This is a bit of birth-myth, or rebirth-myth, on Melville's part—unconscious, no doubt, because his running underconsciousness was always mystical and symbolical. He wasn't aware that he was being mystical.

There he is then, in Typee, among the dreaded cannibal savages. And they are gentle and generous with him, and he is truly in a sort of Eden.

Here at last is Rousseau's Child of Nature and Chateaubriand's Noble Savage called upon and found at home. Yes, Melville loves his savage hosts. He finds them gentle, laughing lambs compared to the ravening wolves of his white brothers, left behind in America and on an American whale-ship.

The ugliest beast on earth is the white man, says Melville.

In short, Herman found in Typee the paradise he was looking for. It is true, the Marquesans were "immoral", but he rather liked that. Morality was too white a trick to take him in. Then again, they were cannibals. And it filled him with horror even to think of this. But the savages were very private and even fiercely reserved in their cannibalism, and he might have spared himself his shudder. No doubt he had partaken of the Christian Sacraments many a time. "This is my body, take and eat. This is my blood. Drink it in remembrance of me." And if the savages liked to partake of their sacrament without raising the transubstantiation quibble, and if they liked to say, directly: "This is thy body, which I take from thee and eat. This is thy blood, which I sip in annihilation of thee," why surely their sacred ceremony was as awe-inspiring as the one Jesus substituted. But Herman chose to be horrified. I confess, I am not horrified; though, of course, I am not on the spot. But the savage sacrament seems to me more valid than the Christian: less side-tracking about it. Thirdly, he was shocked by their wild methods of warfare. He died before the great European war, so his shock was comfortable.

Three little quibbles: morality, cannibal sacrament, and stone axes. You must have a fly even in Paradisal ointment. And the first was a ladybird.

But Paradise. He insists on it. Paradise. He could even go stark naked, as before the Apple episode. And his Fayaway, a laughing little Eve, naked with him, and hankering after no apple of knowledge, so long as he would just love her when he felt like it. Plenty to eat, needing no clothes to wear, sunny, happy people, sweet water to swim in: everything a man can want. Then why wasn't he happy along with the savages?

Because he wasn't.

He grizzled in secret, and wanted to escape.

He even pined for Home and Mother, the two things he had run away from as far as ships would carry him. Home and Mother. The two things that were his damnation.

There on the island, where the golden-green great palm-trees chinked in the sun, and the elegant reed houses let the sea-breeze through, and people went naked and laughed a great deal, and Fayaway put flowers in his hair for him—great red hibiscus flowers, and frangipani—O God, why wasn't he happy? Why wasn't he?

Because he wasn't.

Well, it's hard to make a man happy.

But I should not have been happy either. One's soul seems under a vacuum, in the South Seas.

The truth of the matter is, one cannot go back. Some men can: renegade. But Melville couldn't go back: and Gauguin couldn't really go back: and I know now that I could never go back. Back towards the past, savage life. One cannot go back. It is one's destiny inside one.

There are these peoples, these "savages". One does not despise them. One does not feel superior. But there is a gulf. There is a gulf in time and being. I cannot commingle my being with theirs.

There they are, these South Sea Islanders, beautiful big men with their golden limbs and their laughing, graceful laziness. And they will call you brother, choose you as a brother. But why cannot one truly be brother?

There is an invisible hand grasps my heart and prevents it opening too much to these strangers. They are beautiful, they are like children, they are generous: but they are more than this. They are far off, and in their eyes is an easy darkness of the soft, uncreate past. In a way, they are uncreate. Far be it from me to assume any "white" superiority. But they are savages. They are gentle and laughing and physically very handsome. But it seems to me, that in living so far, through all our bitter centuries of civilisation, we have still been living onwards, forwards. God knows it looks like a *cul-de-sac* now. But turn to the first negro, and then listen to your own soul. And your own soul will tell you that however false and foul our forms and systems are now, still, through the many centuries since Egypt, we have been living and struggling forwards along some road that is no road, and yet is a great life-development. We have struggled on, and on we must still go. We may have to smash things. Then let us smash. And our road may have to take a great swerve, that seems a retrogression.

But we can't go back. Whatever else the South Sea Islander is, he is centuries and centuries behind us in the life-struggle, the consciousness-struggle, the struggle of the soul into fulness. There is his woman, with her knotted hair and her dark, inchoate, slightly sardonic eyes. I like her, she is nice. But I would never want to touch her. I could not go back on myself so far. Back to their uncreate condition.

She has soft warm flesh, like warm mud. Nearer the reptile, the Saurian age. *Noli me tangere.*

We can't go back. We can't go back to the savages: not a stride. We can be in sympathy with them. We can take a great curve in their direction, onwards. But we cannot turn the current of our life backwards, back towards their soft warm twilight and uncreate mud. Not for a moment. If we do it for a moment, it makes us sick.

We can only do it when we are renegade. The renegade hates life itself. He wants the death of life. So these many "reformers" and "idealists" who glorify the savages in America. They are death-birds, life-haters. Renegades.

We can't go back, and Melville couldn't. Much as he hated the civilised humanity he knew. He couldn't go back to the savages; he wanted to, he tried to, and he couldn't.

Because, in the first place, it made him sick; it made him physically ill. He had something wrong with his leg, and this would not heal. It got worse and worse, during his four months on the island. When he escaped, he was in a deplorable condition—sick and miserable, ill, very ill.

Paradise!

But there you are. Try to go back to the savages, and you feel as if your very soul was decomposing inside you. That is what you feel in the South Seas, anyhow: as if your soul was decomposing inside you. And with any savages the same, if you try to go their way, take their current of sympathy.

Yet, as I say, we must make a great swerve in our onward-going life-course now, to gather up again the savage mysteries. But this does not mean going back on ourselves.

Going back to the savages made Melville sicker than anything. It made him feel as if he were decomposing. Worse even than Home and Mother.

And that is what really happens. If you prostitute your psyche by returning to the savages, you gradually go to pieces. Before you can go back, you *have* to decompose. And a white man decomposing is a ghastly sight. Even Melville in Typee.

We have to go on, on, on, even if we must smash a way ahead.

So Melville escaped, and threw a boat-hook full in the throat of one of his dearest savage friends, and sank him, because that savage was swimming in pursuit. That's how he felt about the savages when they wanted to detain him. He'd have murdered them one and all, vividly, rather than be kept from escaping. Away from them—he must get away from them—at any price.

And once he has escaped, immediately he begins to sigh and

pine for the "Paradise"—Home and Mother being at the other end even of a whaling voyage.

When he really was Home with Mother, he found it Purgatory. But Typee must have been even worse than Purgatory, a soft hell judging from the murderous frenzy which possessed him to escape.

But once aboard the whaler that carried him off from Nukuheva, he looked back and sighed for the Paradise he had just escaped from in such a fever.

Poor Melville! He was determined Paradise existed. So he was always in Purgatory.

He was born for Purgatory. Some souls are purgatorial by destiny.

The very freedom of this Typee was a torture to him. Its ease was slowly horrible to him. This time *he* was the fly in the odorous tropical ointment.

He needed to fight. It was no good to him, the relaxation of the non-moral tropics. He didn't really want Eden. He wanted to fight. Like every American. To fight. But with weapons of the spirit, not the flesh.

That was the top and bottom of it. His soul was in revolt, writhing for ever in revolt. When he had something definite to rebel against—like the bad conditions on a whaling ship—then he was much happier in his miseries. The mills of God were grinding inside him, and they needed something to grind on.

When they could grind on the injustice and folly of missionaries, or of brutal sea-captains, or of governments, he was easier. The mills of God were grinding inside him.

They are grinding inside every American. And they grind exceeding small.

Why? Heaven knows. But we've got to grind down our old forms, our old selves, grind them very very small, to nothingness. Whether a new somethingness will ever start, who knows? Meanwhile the mills of God grind on, in American Melville, and it was himself he ground small: himself and his wife, when he was married. For the present, the South Seas.

He escapes on to the craziest, most impossible of whaling ships. Lucky for us Melville makes it fantastic. It must have been pretty sordid.

And anyhow, on the crazy *Julia*, his leg, that would never heal in the paradise of Typee, began quickly to get well. His life was falling into its normal pulse. The drain back into past centuries was over.

Yet, oh, as he sails away from Nukuheva, on the voyage that will ultimately take him to America, oh, the acute and intolerable nostalgia he feels for the island he has left.

The past, the Golden Age of the past—what a nostalgia we all feel for it. Yet we don't want it when we get it. Try the South Seas.

Melville had to fight, fight against the existing world, against his own very self. Only he would never quite put the knife in the heart of his paradisal ideal. Somehow, somewhere, somewhen, love should be a fulfilment, and life should be a thing of bliss. That was his fixed ideal. *Fata Morgana*.

That was the pin he tortured himself on, liked a pinned-down butterfly.

Love is never a fulfilment. Life is never a thing of continuous bliss. There is no paradise. Fight and laugh and feel bitter and feel bliss: and fight again. Fight, fight. That is life.

Why pin ourselves down on a paradisal ideal? It is only ourselves we torture.

Melville did have one great experience, getting away from humanity: the experience of the sea.

The South Sea Islands were not his great experience. They were a glamorous world outside New England. Outside. But it was the sea that was both outside and inside: the universal experience.

The book that follows on from *Typee* is *Omoo*.

Omoo is a fascinating book; picaresque, rascally, roving. Melville, as a bit of a beachcomber. The crazy ship *Julia* sails to Tahiti, and the mutinous crew are put ashore. Put in the Tahitian prison. It is good reading.

Perhaps Melville is at his best, his happiest, in *Omoo*. For once he is really reckless. For once he takes life as it comes. For once he is the gallant rascally epicurean, eating the world like a snipe, dirt and all baked into one *bonne bouche*.

For once he is really careless, roving with that scamp, Doctor Long Ghost. For once he is careless of his actions, careless of his morals, careless of his ideals: ironic, as the epicurean must be. The deep irony of your real scamp: your real epicurean of the moment.

But it was under the influence of the Long Doctor. This long and bony Scotsman was not a mere ne'er-do-well. He was a man of humorous desperation, throwing his life ironically away. Not a mere loose-kneed loafer, such as the South Seas seem to attract.

That is good about Melville: he never repents. Whatever he did, in Typee or in Doctor Long Ghost's wicked society, he never repented. If he ate his snipe, dirt and all, and enjoyed it at the time, he didn't have bilious bouts afterwards, which is good.

But it wasn't enough. The Long Doctor was really knocking about in a sort of despair. He let his ship drift rudderless.

Melville couldn't do this. For a time, yes. For a time, in this Long Doctor's company, he was rudderless and reckless. Good as an experience. But a man who will not abandon himself to despair or indifference cannot keep it up.

Melville would never abandon himself either to despair or' indifference. He always cared. He always cared enough to hate missionaries, and to be touched by a real act of kindness. He always cared.

When he saw a white man really "gone savage", a white man with a blue shark tattooed over his brow, gone over to the savages, then Herman's whole being revolted. He couldn't bear it. He could not bear a renegade.

He enlisted at last on an American man-of-war. You have the record in *White Jacket*. He was back in civilisation, but still at sea. He was in America, yet loose in the seas. Good regular days, after Doctor Long Ghost and the *Julia*.

As a matter of fact, a long thin chain was round Melville's ankle all the time, binding him to America, to civilisation, to democracy, to the ideal world. It was a long chain, and it never broke. It pulled him back.

By the time he was twenty-five his wild oats were sown; his reckless wanderings were over. At the age of twenty-five he came back to Home and Mother, to fight it out at close quarters. For you can't fight it out by running away. When you have run a long way from Home and Mother, then you realise that the earth is round, and if you keep on running you'll be back on the same old doorstep—like a fatality.

Melville came home to face out the long rest of his life. He married and had an ecstasy of a courtship and fifty years of disillusion.

He had just furnished his home with disillusions. No more Typees. No more paradises. No more Fayaways. A mother: a gorgon. A home: a torture box. A wife: a thing with clay feet. Life: a sort of disgrace. Fame: another disgrace, being patronised by common snobs who just know how to read.

The whole shameful business just making a man writhe.

Melville writhed for eighty years.

In his soul he was proud and savage.

But in his mind and will be wanted the perfect fulfilment of love; he wanted the lovey-doveyness of perfect mutual understanding.

A proud savage-souled man doesn't really want any perfect lovey-dovey fulfilment in love: no such nonsense. A mountain lion doesn't mate with a Persian cat; and when a grizzly bear roars after a mate, it is a she-grizzly he roars after—not after a silky sheep.

But Melville stuck to his ideal. He wrote *Pierre* to show that the more you try to be good the more you make a mess of things: that following righteousness is just disastrous. The better you are, the worse things turn out with you. The better you try to be, the bigger mess you make. Your very striving after righteousness only causes your own slow degeneration.

Well, it is true. No men are so evil to-day as the idealists, and no women half so evil as your earnest woman, who feels herself a power for good. It is inevitable. After a certain point, the ideal goes dead and rotten. The old pure ideal becomes in itself an impure thing of evil. Charity becomes pernicious, the spirit itself becomes foul. The meek are evil. The pure in heart have base, subtle revulsions: like Dostoievsky's Idiot. The whole Sermon on the Mount becomes a litany of white vice.

What then?

It's our own fault. It was *we* who set up the ideals. And if we are such fools, that we aren't able to kick over our ideals in time, the worse for us.

Look at Melville's eighty long years of writhing. And to the end he writhed on the ideal pin.

From the "perfect woman lover" he passed on to the "perfect friend". He looked and looked for the perfect man friend. Couldn't find him.

Marriage was a ghastly disillusion to him, because he looked for perfect marriage.

Friendship never even made a real start in him—save perhaps his half-sentimental love for Jack Chase, in *White Jacket.*

Yet to the end he pined for this: a perfect relationship; perfect mating; perfect mutual understanding. A perfect friend.

Right to the end he could never accept the fact that *perfect* relationships cannot be. Each soul is alone, and the aloneness of each soul is a double barrier to perfect relationship between two beings.

Each soul *should* be alone. And in the end the desire for a "perfect relationship" is just a vicious, unmanly craving. "*Tous nos malheurs viennent de ne pouvoir être seuls.*"

Melville, however, refused to draw his conclusion. *Life* was wrong, he said. He refused Life. But he stuck to his ideal of perfect relationship, possible perfect love. The world *ought* to be a harmonious loving place. And it *can't* be. So life itself is wrong.

It is silly arguing. Because after all, only temporary man sets up the "oughts".

The world ought *not* to be a harmonious loving place. It ought to be a place of fierce discord and intermittent harmonies; which it is.

Love ought *not* to be perfect. It ought to have perfect moments, and wildernesses of thorn bushes—which it has.

A "perfect" relationship ought *not* to be possible. Every relationship should have its absolute limits, its absolute reserves, essential to the singleness of the soul in each person. A truly perfect relationship is one in which each party leaves great tracts unknown in the other party.

No two persons can meet at more than a few points, consciously. If two people can just be together fairly often, so that the presence of each is a sort of balance to the other, that is the basis of perfect relationship. There must be true separatenesses as well.

Melville was, at the core, a mystic and an idealist.

Perhaps, so am I.

And he stuck to his ideal guns.

I abandon mine.

He was a mystic who raved because the old ideal guns shot havoc. The guns of the "noble spirit". Of "ideal love".

I say, let the guns rot.

Get new ones, and shoot straight.

[From *Studies in Classic American Literature,* 1924.]

[100]

HERMAN MELVILLE'S *MOBY DICK*

Moby Dick, or the White Whale.

A hunt. The last great hunt.

For what?

For Moby Dick, the huge white sperm whale: who is old, hoary, monstrous, and swims alone; who is unspeakably terrible in his wrath, having so often been attacked; and snow-white.

Of course he is a symbol.

Of what?

I doubt if even Melville knew exactly. That's the best of it.

He is warm-blooded, he is lovable. He is lonely Leviathan, not a Hobbes sort. Or is he?

But he is warm-blooded and lovable. The South Sea Islanders, and Polynesians, and Malays, who worship shark, or crocodile, or weave endless frigate-bird distortions, why did they never worship the whale? So big!

Because the whale is not wicked. He doesn't bite. And their gods had to bite.

He's not a dragon. He is Leviathan. He never coils like the Chinese dragon of the sun. He's not a serpent of the waters. He is warm-blooded, a mammal. And hunted, hunted down.

It is a great book.

At first you are put off by the style. It reads like journalism. It seems spurious. You feel Melville is trying to put something over you. It won't do.

And Melville really is a bit sentialious: aware of himself,

self-conscious, putting something over even himself. But then it's not easy to get into the swing of a piece of deep mysticism when you just set out with a story.

Nobody can be more clownish, more clumsy and sententiously in bad taste, than Herman Melville, even in a great book like *Moby Dick*. He preaches and holds forth because he's not sure of himself. And he holds forth, often, so amateurishly.

The artist was so *much* greater than the man. The man is rather a tiresome New Englander of the ethical mystical-transcendentalist sort: Emerson, Longfellow, Hawthorne, etc. So unrelieved, the solemn ass even in humour. So hopelessly *au grand sérieux*, you feel like saying: Good God, what does it matter? If life is a tragedy, or a farce, or a disaster, or anything else, what do I care! Let life be what it likes. Give me a drink, that's what I want just now.

For my part, life is so many things I don't care what it is. It's not my affair to sum it up. Just now it's a cup of tea. This morning it was wormwood and gall. Hand me the sugar.

One wearies of the *grand sérieux*. There's something false about it. And that's Melville. Oh, dear, when the solemn ass brays! brays! brays!

But he was a deep, great artist, even if he was rather a sententious man. He was a real American in that he always felt his audience in front of him. But when he ceases to be American, when he forgets all audience, and gives us his sheer apprehension of the world, then he is wonderful, his book commands a stillness in the soul, an awe.

In his "human" self, Melville is almost dead. That is, he hardly reacts to human contacts any more; or only ideally: or just for a moment. His human-emotional self is almost played out. He is abstract, self-analytical and abstracted. And he is more spellbound by the strange slidings and collidings of Matter than by the things men do. In this he is like Dana. It is the material elements he really has to do with. His drama is with them. He was a futurist long before futurism found paint. The sheer naked slidings of the elements. And the human soul experiencing it all. So often, it is almost over the border: psychiatry. Almost spurious. Yet so great.

It is the same old thing as in all Americans. They keep their old-fashioned ideal frock-coat on, and an old-fashioned silk hat, while they do the most impossible things. There you are: you see Melville hugged in bed by a huge tattooed South Sea Islander, and solemnly offering burnt offering to this savage's little idol, and his ideal frock-coat just hides his shirt-tails and prevents us from seeing his bare posterior as he salaams, while his ethical silk hat sits correctly over his brow the while. That is so typically American: doing the most impossible things without taking off their spiritual get-up. Their ideals are like armour which has rusted in, and will never more come off. And meanwhile in Melville his bodily knowledge moves naked, a living quick among the stark elements. For with sheer physical vibrational sensitiveness, like a marvellous wireless-station, he registers the effects of the outer world. And he records also, almost beyond pain or pleasure, the extreme transitions of the isolated, far-driven soul, the soul which is now alone, without any real human contact.

The first days in New Bedford introduce the only human being who really enters into the book, namely, Ishmael, the "I" of the book. And then the moment's hearts-brother, Queequeg, the tattooed, powerful South Sea harpooner, whom Melville loves as Dana loves "Hope". The advent of Ishmael's bedmate is amusing and unforgettable. But later the two swear "marriage", in the language of the savages. For Queequeg has opened again the flood-gates of love and human connexion in Ishmael.

"As I sat there in that now lonely room, the fire burning low, in that mild stage when, after its first intensity has warmed the air, it then only glows to be looked at; the evening shades and phantoms gathering round the casements, and peering in upon us silent, solitary twain: I began to be sensible of strange feelings. I felt a melting in me. No more my splintered hand and maddened heart was turned against the wolfish world. This soothing savage had redeemed it. There he sat, his very indifference speaking a nature in which there lurked no civilised hypocrisies and bland deceits. Wild he was; a very sight of sights to see; yet I began to feel myself mysteriously drawn towards him."—So they smoked together and are clasped in each other's arms. The friendship is finally sealed when Ishmael offers sacrifice to Queeqeug's little idol, Gogo.

"I was a good Christian, born and bred in the bosom of the infallible Presbyterian Church. How then could I unite with the idolater in worshipping his piece of wood? But what is worship?—to do the will of God—*that* is worship. And what is the will of God?—to do to my fellow-man what I would have my fellow-man do to me—*that* is the will of God."—Which sounds like Benjamin Franklin, and is hopelessly bad theology. But it is real American logic. "Now Queequeg is my fellow-man. And what do I wish that this Queequeg would do to me? Why, unite with me in my particular Presbyterian form of worship. Consequently, I must unite with him; ergo, I must turn idolater. So I kindled the shavings; helped prop up the innocent little idol; offered him burnt biscuit with Queequeg, salaamed before him twice or thrice; kissed his nose; and that done, we undressed and went to bed, at peace with our own consciences and all the world. But we did not go to sleep without some little chat. How it is I know not; but there is no place like bed for confidential disclosures between friends. Man and wife, they say, open the very bottom of their souls to each other; and some old couples often lie and chat over old times till nearly morning. Thus, then, lay I and Queequeg—a cosy, loving pair——"

You would think this relation with Queequeg meant something to Ishmael. But no. Queequeg is forgotten like yesterday's newspaper. Human things are only momentary excitements or amusements to the American Ishmael. Ishmael, the hunted. But much more Ishmael the hunter. What's a Queequeg? What's a wife? The white whale must be hunted down. Queequeg must be just "KNOWN", then dropped into oblivion.

And what in the name of fortune is the white whale?

Elsewhere Ishmael says he loved Queequeg's eyes: "large, deep eyes, fiery black and bold." No doubt like Poe, he wanted to get the "clue" to them. That was all.

The two men go over from New Bedford to Nantucket, and there sign on to the Quaker whaling ship, the *Pequod*. It is all strangely fantastic, phantasmagoric. The voyage of the soul. Yet curiously a real whaling voyage, too. We pass on into the midst of the sea with this strange ship and its incredible crew. The Argonauts were mild lambs in comparison. And

Ulysses went *defeating* the Circes and overcoming the wicked hussies of the isles. But the *Pequod*'s crew is a collection of maniacs fanatically hunting down a lonely, harmless white whale.

As a soul history, it makes one angry. As a sea yarn, it is marvellous: there is always something a bit over the mark, in sea yarns. Should be. Then again the masking up of actual seaman's experience with sonorous mysticism sometimes gets on one's nerves. And again, as a revelation of destiny the book is too deep even for sorrow. Profound beyond feeling.

You are some time before you are allowed to see the captain, Ahab: the mysterious Quaker. Oh, it is a God-fearing Quaker ship.

Ahab, the captain. The captain of the soul.

> I am the master of my fate,
> I am the captain of my soul!

Ahab!

"Oh, captain, my captain, our fearful trip is done."

The gaunt Ahab, Quaker, mysterious person, only shows himself after some days at sea. There's a secret about him! What?

Oh, he's a portentous person. He stumps about on an ivory stump, made from sea-ivory. Moby Dick, the great white whale tore off Ahab's leg at the knee, when Ahab was attacking him.

Quite right, too. Should have torn off both his legs, and a bit more besides.

But Ahab doesn't think so. Ahab is now a monomaniac. Moby Dick is his monomania. Moby Dick must DIE, or Ahab can't live any longer. Ahab is atheist by this.

All right.

This *Pequod*, ship of the American soul, has three mates.

1. Starbuck: Quaker, Nantucketer, a good responsible man of reason, forethought, intrepidity, what is called a dependable man. At the bottom, *afraid*.

2. Stubb: "Fearless as fire, and as mechanical." Insists on being reckless and jolly on every occasion. Must be afraid too, really.

3. Flask: Stubborn, obstinate, without imagination. To him "the wondrous whale was but a species of magnified mouse or water-rat——"

There you have them: a maniac captain and his three mates, three splendid seamen, admirable whalemen, first-class men at their job.

America!

It is rather like Mr. Wilson and his admirable, "efficient" crew, at the Peace Conference. Except that none of the Pequodders took their wives along.

A maniac captain of the soul, and three eminently practical mates.

America!

Then such a crew. Renegades, castaways, cannibals: Ishmael, Quakers.

America!

Three giant harpooners, to spear the great white whale.

1. Queequeg, the South Sea Islander, all tattooed, big and powerful.

2. Tashtego, the Red Indian of the sea-coast, where the Indian meets the sea.

3. Daggoo, the huge black negro.

There you have them, three savage races, under the American flag, the maniac captain, with their great keen harpoons, ready to spear the white whale.

And only after many days at sea does Ahab's own boat-crew appear on deck. Strange, silent, secret, black-garbed Malays, fire-worshipping Parsees. These are to man Ahab's boat, when it leaps in pursuit of that whale.

What do you think of the ship *Pequod*, the ship of the soul of an American?

Many races, many peoples, many nations, under the Stars and Stripes. Beaten with many stripes.

Seeing stars sometimes.

And in a mad ship, under a mad captain, in a mad, fanatic's hunt.

For what?

For Moby Dick, the great white whale.

But splendidly handled. Three splendid mates. The whole thing practical, eminently practical in its working. American industry!

And all this practicality in the service of a mad, mad chase.

Melville manages to keep it a real whaling ship, on a real

cruise, in spite of all fantastics. A wonderful, wonderful voyage. And a beauty that is so surpassing only because of the author's awful flounderings in mystical waters. He wanted to get metaphysically deep. And he got deeper than metaphysics. It is a surpassingly beautiful book, with an awful meaning, and bad jolts.

It is interesting to compare Melville with Dana, about the albatross—Melville a bit sententious. "I remember the first albatross I ever saw. It was during a prolonged gale in waters hard upon the Antarctic seas. From my forenoon watch below I ascended to the overcrowded deck, and there, lashed upon the main hatches, I saw a regal feathered thing of unspotted whiteness, and with a hooked Roman bill sublime. At intervals it arched forth its vast, archangel wings—wondrous throbbings and flutterings shook it. Though bodily unharmed, it uttered cries, as some King's ghost in supernatural distress. Through its inexpressible strange eyes methought I peeped to secrets not below the heavens—the white thing was so white, its wings so wide, and in those for ever exiled waters, I had lost the miserable warping memories of traditions and of towns. I assert then, that in the wondrous bodily whiteness of the bird chiefly lurks the secret of the spell——"

Melville's albatross is a prisoner, caught by a bait on a hook.

Well, I have seen an albatross, too: following us in waters hard upon the Antarctic, too, south of Australia. And in the Southern winter. And the ship, a P. and O. boat, nearly empty. And the lascar crew shivering.

The bird with its long, long wings following, then leaving us. No one knows till they have tried, how lost, how lonely those Southern waters are. And glimpses of the Australian coast.

It makes one feel that our day is only a day. That in the dark of the night ahead other days stir fecund, when we have lapsed from existence.

Who knows how utterly we shall lapse.

But Melville keeps up his disquisition about "whiteness". The great abstract fascinated him. The abstract where we end, and cease to be. White or black. Our white, abstract end!

Then again it is lovely to be at sea on the *Pequod*, with never a grain of earth to us.

"It was a cloudy, sultry afternoon; the seamen were lazily

lounging about the decks, or vacantly gazing over into the lead-coloured waters. Queequeg and I were mildly employed weaving what is called a sword-mat, for an additional lashing to our boat. So still and subdued, and yet somehow preluding was all the scene, and such an incantation of reverie lurked in the air that each silent sailor seemed resolved into his own invisible self——"

In the midst of this preluding silence came the first cry: "There she blows! there! there! there! She blows!" And then comes the first chase, a marvellous piece of true sea-writing, the sea, and sheer sea-beings on the chase, sea-creatures chased. There is scarcely a taint of earth—pure sea-motion.

" 'Give way men,' whispered Starbuck, drawing still further aft the sheet of his sail; 'there is time to kill fish yet before the squall comes. There's white water again!—Close to!— Spring!' Soon after, two cries in quick succession on each side of us denoted that the other boats had got fast; but hardly were they overboard when with a lightning-like hurtling whisper Starbuck said: 'Stand up!' and Queequeg, harpoon in hand, sprang to his feet.—Though not one of the oarsmen was then facing the life and death peril so close to them ahead, yet their eyes on the intense countenance of the mate in the stern of the boat, they knew that the imminent instant had come; they heard, too, an enormous wallowing sound, as of fifty elephants stirring in their litter. Meanwhile the boat was still booming through the mist, the waves curbing and hissing around us like the erected crests of enraged serpents.

" 'That's his hump. *There! There*, give it to him!' whispered Starbuck.—A short rushing sound leapt out of the boat; it was the darted iron of Queequeg. Then all in one welded motion came a push from astern, while forward the boat seemed striking on a ledge; the sail collapsed and exploded; a gush of scalding vapour shot up near by; something rolled and tumbled like an earthquake beneath us. The whole crew were half-suffocated as they were tossed helter-skelter into the white curling cream of the squall. Squall, whale, and harpoon had all blended together; and the whale, merely grazed by the iron, escaped——"

Melville is a master of violent, chaotic physical motion; he can keep up a whole wild chase without a flaw. He is as perfect at creating stillness. The ship is cruising on the Carrol Ground, south of St. Helena.—"It was while gliding through these latter waters that one serene and moonlight night, when all the waves rolled by like scrolls of silver; and by their soft, suffusing seethings, made what seemed a silvery silence, not a solitude; on such a silent night a silvery jet was seen far in advance of the white bubbles at the bow——"

Then there is the description of brit. "Steering north-eastward from the Crozello we fell in with vast meadows of brit, the minute, yellow substance upon which the right whale largely feeds. For leagues and leagues it undulated round us, so that we seemed to be sailing through boundless fields of ripe and golden wheat. On the second day, numbers of right whales were seen, secure from the attack of a sperm whaler like the *Pequod*. With open jaws they sluggishly swam through the brit, which, adhering to the fringed fibres of that wondrous Venetian blind in their mouths, was in that manner separated from the water that escaped at the lip. As moving mowers who, side by side, slowly and seethingly advanced their scythes through the long wet grass of the marshy meads; even so these monsters swam, making a strange, grassy, cutting sound; and leaving behind them endless swaths of blue on the yellow sea. But it was only the sound they made as they parted the brit which at all reminded one of mowers. Seen from the mast-heads, especially when they paused and were stationary for a while, their vast black forms looked more like masses of rock than anything else——"

This beautiful passage brings us to the apparition of the squid.

"Slowly wading through the meadows of brit, the *Pequod* still held her way northeastward towards the island of Java; a gentle air impelling her keel, so that in the surrounding serenity her three tall, tapering masts mildly waved to that languid breeze, as three mild palms on a plain. And still, at wide intervals, in the silvery night, that lonely, alluring jet would be seen.

"But one transparent-blue morning, when a stillness almost preternatural spread over the sea, however unattended with any stagnant calm; when the long burnished sunglade on the waters seemed a golden finger laid across them, enjoining secrecy; when all the slippered waves whispered together as they softly ran on; in this profound hush of the visible sphere a strange spectre was seen by Daggoo from the mainmast head.

"In the distance, a great white mass lazily rose, and rising higher and higher, and disentangling itself from the azure, at last gleamed before our prow like a snow-slide, new slid from the hills. Thus glistening for a moment, as slowly it subsided, and sank. Then once more arose, and silently gleamed. It seemed not a whale; and yet, is this Moby Dick? thought Daggoo——"

The boats were lowered and pulled to the scene.

"In the same spot where it sank, once more it slowly rose. Almost forgetting for the moment all thoughts of Moby Dick, we now gazed at the most wondrous phenomenon which the secret seas have hitherto revealed to mankind. A vast pulpy mass, furlongs in length and breadth, of a glancing cream-colour, lay floating on the water, innumerable long arms radiating from its centre, and curling and twisting like a nest of anacondas, as if blindly to clutch at any hapless object within reach. No perceptible face or front did it have; no conceivable token of either sensation or instinct; but undulated there on the billows, an unearthly, formless, chance-like apparition of life. And with a low sucking it slowly disappeared again."

The following chapters, with their account of whale-hunts, the killing, the stripping, the cutting up, are magnificent records of actual happening. Then comes the queer tale of the meeting of the *Jeroboam*, a whaler met at sea, all of whose men were under the domination of a religious maniac, one of the ship's hands. There are detailed descriptions of the actual taking of the sperm oil from a whale's head. Dilating on the smallness of the brain of a sperm whale, Melville significantly remarks—"for I believe that much of a man's character will be found betokened in his backbone. I would rather feel your spine than your skull, whoever you are——" And of the whale, he adds:

"For, viewed in this light, the wonderful comparative smallness of his brain proper is more than compensated by the wonderful comparative magnitude of his spinal cord."

In among the rush of terrible, awful hunts, come touches of pure beauty.

"As the three boats lay there on that gently rolling sea, gazing down into its eternal blue noon; and as not a single groan or cry of any sort, nay not so much as a ripple or a thought, came up from its depths; what landsman would have thought that beneath all that silence and placidity the utmost monster of the seas was writhing and wrenching in agony!"

Perhaps the most stupendous chapter is the one called "The Grand Armada", at the beginning of Volume III. The *Pequod* was drawing through the Sunda Straits towards Java when she came upon a vast host of sperm whales. "Broad on both bows, at a distance of two or three miles, and forming a great semicircle embracing one-half of the level horizon, a continuous chain of whale-jets were up-playing and sparkling in the noonday air." Chasing this great herd, past the Straits of Sunda, themselves chased by Javan pirates, the whalers race on. Then the boats are lowered. At last that curious state of inert irresolution came over the whales, when they were, as the seamen say, gallied. Instead of forging ahead in huge martial array they swam violently hither and thither, a surging sea of whales, no longer moving on. Starbuck's boat, made fast to a whale, is towed in amongst this howling Leviathan chaos. In mad career it cockles through the boiling surge of monsters, till it is brought into a clear lagoon in the very centre of the vast, mad, terrified herd. There a sleek, pure calm reigns. There the females swam in peace, and the young whales came snuffing tamely at the boat, like dogs. And there the astonished seamen watched the love-making of these amazing monsters, mammals, now in rut far down in the sea—"But far beneath this wondrous world upon the surface, another and still stranger world met our eyes, as we gazed over the side. For, suspended in these watery vaults, floated the forms of the nursing mothers of the whales, and those that by their enormous girth seemed shortly to become mothers. The lake, as I have hinted, was to a considerable depth exceedingly transparent; and as human infants while sucking will calmly and fixedly gaze away from the breast, as if leading two different lives at a time; and while yet drawing moral nourishment, be still spiritually feasting upon some unearthly reminiscence, even so did the young of these whales seem looking up towards us, but not at us, as if we were but a bit of gulf-weed in their newborn sight. Floating on their sides, the mothers also seemed quietly eyeing us.—Some of the subtlest secrets of the seas seemed divulged to us in this enchanted pond. We saw young Leviathan amours in the deep. And thus, though surrounded by circle upon circle of consternation and affrights, did these inscrutable creatures at the centre freely and fearlessly indulge in all peaceful concernments; yea, serenely revelled in dalliance and delight——"

There is something really overwhelming in these whale-hunts, almost superhuman or inhuman, bigger than life, more terrific than human activity. The same with the chapter on ambergris: it is so curious, so real, yet so unearthly. And again in the chapter called "The Cassock"—surely the oddest piece of phallicism in all the world's literature.

After this comes the amazing account of the Try-works, when the ship is turned into the sooty, oily factory in mid-ocean, and the oil is extracted from the blubber. In the night of the red furnace burning on deck, at sea, Melville has his startling experience of reversion. He is at the helm, but has turned to watch the fire: when suddenly he feels the ship rushing backward from him, in mystic reversion—"Uppermost was the impression, that whatever swift, rushing thing I stood on was not so much bound to any haven ahead, as rushing from all havens astern. A stark bewildering feeling, as of death, came over me. Convulsively my hands grasped the tiller, but with the crazy conceit that the tiller was, somehow, in some enchanted way, inverted. My God! What is the matter with me, I thought!"

This dream-experience is a real soul-experience. He ends with an injunction to all men, not to gaze on the red fire when its redness makes all things look ghastly. It seems to him that his gazing on fire has evoked this horror of reversion, undoing.

Perhaps it had. He was water-born.

After some unhealthy work on the ship, Queequeg caught a fever and was like to die. "How he wasted and wasted in those few, long-lingering days, till there seemed but little left of him but his frame and tattooing. But as all else in him thinned, and his cheek-bones grew sharper, his eyes, nevertheless, seemed growing fuller and fuller; they took on a strangeness of lustre; and mildly but deeply looked out at you there from his sickness, a wondrous testimony to that immortal health in him which could not die, or be weakened. And like circles on the water, which as they grow fainter, expand; so his eyes seemed rounding and rounding, like the circles of Eternity. An awe that cannot be named would steal over you as you sat by the side of this waning savage——"

But Queequeg did not die—and the *Pequod* emerges from the Eastern Straits, into the full Pacific. "To my meditative Magian rover, this serene Pacific once beheld, must ever after be the sea of his adoption. It rolls the utmost waters of the world——"

In this Pacific the fights go on: "It was far down the afternoon, and when all the spearings of the crimson fight were done, and floating in the lovely sunset sea and sky, sun and whale both died stilly together; then such a sweetness and such a plaintiveness, such inwreathing orisons curled up in that rosy air, that it almost seemed as if far over from the deep green convent valleys of the Manila Isles, the Spanish land-breeze had gone to sea, freighted with these vesper hymns. Soothed again, but only soothed to deeper gloom, Ahab, who has steered off from the whale, sat intently watching his final wanings from the now tranquil boat. For that strange spectacle, observable in all sperm whales dying—the turning of the head sunwards, and so expiring—that strange spectacle, beheld of such a placid evening, somehow to Ahab conveyed wondrousness unknown before, 'He turns and turns him to it; how slowly, but how steadfastly, his home-rendering and invoking brow, with his last dying motions. He too worships fire . . .' "

So Ahab soliloquises: and so the warm-blooded whale turns for the last time to the sun, which begot him in the waters.

But as we see in the next chapter, it is the Thunder-fire which Ahab really worships: that living sundering fire of which he bears the brand, from head to foot; it is storm, the electric storm of the *Pequod*, when the corposants burn in high, tapering flames of supernatural pallor upon the masthead, and when the compass is reversed. After this all is fatality. Life itself seems mystically reversed. In these hunters of Moby Dick there is nothing but madness and possession. The captain, Ahab, moves hand in hand with the poor imbecile negro boy, Pip, who has been so cruelly demented, left swimming alone in the

vast sea. It is the imbecile child of the sun hand in hand with
the northern monomaniac, captain and master.

The voyage surges on. They meet one ship, then another.
It is all ordinary day-routine, and yet all is a tension of pure
madness and horror, the approaching horror of the last fight.
"Hither and thither, on high, glided the snow-white wings of
small unspecked birds; these were the gentle thoughts of the
feminine air; but to and fro in the deeps, far down in the
bottomless blue, rushed mighty leviathans, sword-fish and
sharks; and these were the strong, troubled, murderous
things of the masculine sea——" On this day Ahab confesses
his weariness, the weariness of his burden. "But do I look very
old, so very, very old, Starbuck? I feel deadly faint, and bowed,
and humped, as though I were Adam staggering beneath the
piled centuries since Paradise——" It is the Gethsemane of
Ahab, before the last fight: the Gethsemane of the human soul
seeking the last self-conquest, the last attainment of extended
consciousness—infinite consciousness.

At last they sight the whale. Ahab sees him from his hoisted
perch at the masthead—"From this height the whale was now
seen some mile or so ahead, at every roll of the sea revealing
his high, sparkling hump, and regularly jetting his silent spout
into the air."

The boats are lowered, to draw near the white whale. "At
length the breathless hunter came so nigh his seemingly un-
suspectful prey that his entire dazzling hump was distinctly
visible, sliding along the sea as if an isolated thing, and continually set in a revolving ring of finest, fleecy, greenish foam.
He saw the vast involved wrinkles of the slightly projecting
head, beyond. Before it, far out on the soft, Turkish-rugged
waters, went the glistening white shadow from his broad, milky
forehead, a musical rippling playfully accompanying the shade;
and behind, the blue waters interchangeably flowed over the
moving valley of his steady wake; and on either side bright
bubbles arose and danced by his side. But these were broken
again by the light toes of hundreds of gay fowl softly feathering
the sea, alternate with their fitful flight; and like to some flag-
staff rising from the pointed hull of an argosy, the tall but
shattered pole of a recent lance projected from the white whale's
back; and at intervals one of the clouds of soft-toed fowls

hovering, and to and fro shimmering like a canopy over the fish, silently perched and rocked on this pole, the long tail-feathers streaming like pennons.

"A gentle joyousness—a mighty mildness of repose in swift ness, invested the gliding whale——"

The fight with the whale is too wonderful, and too awful, to be quoted apart from the book. It lasted three days. The fearful sight, on the third day, of the torn body of the Parsee harpooner, lost on the previous day, now seen lashed on to the flanks of the white whale by the tangle of harpoon lines, has a mystic dream-horror. The awful and infuriated whale turns upon the ship, symbol of this civilised world of ours. He smites her with a fearful shock. And a few minutes later, from the last of the fighting whale-boats comes the cry: " 'The ship! Great God, where is the ship?' Soon they, through the dim, bewildering mediums, saw her sidelong fading phantom, as in the gaseous *fata Morgana*; only the uppermost masts out of the water; while fixed by infatuation, or fidelity, or fate, to their once lofty perches, the pagan harpooners still maintained their sinking lookouts on the sea. And now concentric circles seized the lone boat itself, and all its crew, and each floating oar, and every lance-pole, and spinning, animate and inanimate, all round and round in one vortex, carried the smallest chip of the *Pequod* out of sight——"

The bird of heaven, the eagle, St. John's bird, the Red Indian bird, the American, goes down with the ship, nailed by Tastego's hammer, the hammer of the American Indian. The eagle of the spirit. Sunk!

"Now small fowls flew screaming over the yet yawning gulf; a sullen white surf beat against its steep sides; then all collapsed; and then the great shroud of the sea rolled on as it rolled five thousand years ago."

So ends one of the strangest and most wonderful books in the world, closing up its mystery and its tortured symbolism. It is an epic of the sea such as no man has equalled; and it is a book of exoteric symbolism of profound significance, and of considerable tiresomeness.

But it is a great book, a very great book, the greatest book of the sea ever written. It moves awe in the soul.

The terrible fatality.

Fatality.

Doom.

Doom! Doom! Doom! Something seems to whisper it in the very dark trees of America. Doom!

Doom of what?

Doom of our white day. We are doomed, doomed. And the doom is in America. The doom of our white day.

Ah, well, if my day is doomed, and I am doomed with my day, it is something greater than I which dooms me, so I accept my doom as a sign of the greatness which is more than I am.

Melville knew. He knew his race was doomed. His white soul, doomed. His great white epoch, doomed. Himself, doomed. The idealist, doomed. The spirit, doomed.

The reversion. "Not so much bound to any haven ahead, as rushing from all havens astern."

That great horror of ours! It is our civilisation rushing from all havens astern.

The last ghastly hunt. The White Whale.

What then is Moby Dick? He is the deepest blood-being of the white race; he is our deepest blood-nature.

And he is hunted, hunted, hunted by the maniacal fanaticism of our white mental consciousness. We want to hunt him down. To subject him to our will. And in this maniacal conscious hunt of ourselves we get dark races and pale to help us, red, yellow, and black, east and west, Quaker and fire-worshipper, we get them all to help us in this ghastly maniacal hunt which is our doom and our suicide.

The last phallic being of the white man. Hunted into the death of upper consciousness and the ideal will. Our blood-self subjected to our will. Our blood-consciousness sapped by a parasitic mental or ideal consciousness.

Hot-blooded sea-born Moby Dick. Hunted by monomaniacs of the idea.

Oh God, oh God, what next, when the *Pequod* has sunk?

She sank in the war, and we are all flotsam.

Now what next?

Who knows? *Quien sabe? Quien sabe, señor?*

Neither Spanish nor Saxon America has any answer.

The *Pequod* went down. And the *Pequod* was the ship of the white American soul. She sank, taking with her negro and Indian and Polynesian, Asiatic and Quaker and good, business-like Yankees and Ishmael: she sank all the lot of them.

Boom! as Vachel Lindsay would say.

To use the words of Jesus, IT IS FINISHED.

Consummatum est!

But *Moby Dick* was first published in 1851. If the Great White Whale sank the ship of the Great White Soul in 1851, what's been happening ever since?

Post-mortem effects, presumably.

Because, in the first centuries, Jesus was Cetus, the Whale. And the Christians were the little fishes. Jesus, the Redeemer, was Cetus, Leviathan. And all the Christians all his little fishes.

[From *Studies in Classic American Literature*, 1924.]

[101]

WHITMAN

POST-mortem effects?

But what of Walt Whitman?

The "good grey poet".

Was he a ghost, with all his physicality?

The good grey poet.

Post-mortem effects. Ghosts.

A certain ghoulish insistency. A certain horrible pottage of human parts. A certain stridency and portentousness. A luridness about his beatitudes.

DEMOCRACY! THESE STATES! EIDOLONS! LOVERS, END-LESS LOVERS!

ONE IDENTITY!

ONE IDENTITY!

I AM HE THAT ACHES WITH AMOROUS LOVE.

Do you believe me, when I say post-mortem effects?

When the *Pequod* went down, she left many a rank and dirty steamboat still fussing in the seas. The *Pequod* sinks with all her souls, but their bodies rise again to man innumerable tramp steamers, and ocean-crossing liners. Corpses.

What we mean is that people may go on, keep on, and rush

on, without souls. They have their ego and their will; that is enough to keep them going.

So that you see, the sinking of the *Pequod* was only a metaphysical tragedy after all. The world goes on just the same. The ship of the *soul* is sunk. But the machine-manipulating body works just the same: digests, chews gum, admires Botticelli and aches with amorous love.

I AM HE THAT ACHES WITH AMOROUS LOVE.

What do you make of that? I AM HE THAT ACHES. First generalisation. First uncomfortable universalisation. WITH AMOROUS LOVE! Oh, God! Better a bellyache. A bellyache is at least specific. But the ACHE OF AMOROUS LOVE!

Think of having that under your skin. All that!

I AM HE THAT ACHES WITH AMOROUS LOVE.

Walter, leave off. You are not HE. You are just a limited Walter. And your ache doesn't include all Amorous Love, by any means. If you ache you only ache with a small bit of amorous love, and there's so much more stays outside the cover of your ache, that you might be a bit milder about it.

I AM HE THAT ACHES WITH AMOROUS LOVE.

CHUFF! CHUFF! CHUFF!

CHU-CHU-CHU-CHU-CHUFF!

Reminds one of a steam-engine. A locomotive. They're the only things that seem to me to ache with amorous love. All that steam inside them. Forty million foot-pounds pressure. The ache of AMOROUS LOVE. Steam-pressure. CHUFF!

An ordinary man aches with love for Belinda, or his Native Land, or the Ocean, or the Stars, or the Oversoul: if he feels that an ache is in the fashion.

It takes a steam-engine to ache with AMOROUS LOVE. All of it.

Walt was really too superhuman. The danger of the superman is that he is mechanical.

They talk of his "splendid animality". Well, he'd got it on the brain, if that's the place for animality.

> I am he that aches with amorous love:
> Does the earth gravitate, does not all matter, aching, attract all matter?
> So the body of me to all I meet or know.

What can be more mechanical? The difference between life and matter is that life, living things, living creatures, have the instinct of turning right away from *some* matter, and of blissfully ignoring the bulk of most matter, and of turning towards only some certain bits of specially selected matter. As for living creatures all helplessly hurtling together into one great snowball, why, most very living creatures spend the greater part of their time getting out of the sight, smell or sound of the rest of living creatures. Even bees only cluster on their own queen. And that is sickening enough. Fancy all white humanity clustering on one another like a lump of bees.

No, Walt, you give yourself away. Matter *does* gravitate, helplessly. But men are tricky-tricksy, and they shy all sorts of ways.

Matter gravitates because it *is* helpless and mechanical.

And if you gravitate the same, if the body of you gravitates to all you meet or know, why, something must have gone seriously wrong with you. You must have broken your mainspring.

You must have fallen also into mechanisation.

Your Moby Dick must be really dead. That lonely phallic monster of the individual you. Dead mentalised.

I only know that my body doesn't by any means gravitate to all I meet or know. I find I can shake hands with a few people. But most I wouldn't touch with a long prop.

Your mainspring is broken, Walt Whitman. The mainspring of your own individuality. And so you run down with a great whirr, merging with everything.

You have killed your isolate Moby Dick. You have mentalised your deep sensual body, and that's the death of it.

I am everything and everything is me and so we're all One in One Identity, like the Mundane Egg, which has been addled quite a while.

> Whoever you are, to endless announcements——
> And of these one and all I weave the song of myself.

Do you? Well then, it just shows you haven't *got* any self. It's a mush, not a woven thing. A hotch-potch, not a tissue. Your self.

Oh, Walter, Walter, what have you done with it? What have you done with yourself? With your own individual self? For it sounds as if it had all leaked out of you, leaked into the universe.

Post-mortem effects. The individuality had leaked out of him. No, no, don't lay this down to poetry. These are post-mortem effects. And Walt's great poems are really huge fat tomb-plants, great rank graveyard growths.

All that false exuberance. All those lists of things boiled in one pudding-cloth! No, no!

I don't want all those things inside me, thank you.

"I reject nothing," says Walt.

If that is so, one must be a pipe open at both ends, so everything runs through.

Post-mortem effects.

"I embrace ALL," says Whitman. "I weave all things into myself."

Do you really! There can't be much left of *you* when you've done. When you've cooked the awful pudding of One Identity.

"And whoever walks a furlong without sympathy walks to his own funeral dressed in his own shroud."

Take off your hat then, my funeral procession of one is passing.

This awful Whitman. This post-mortem poet. This poet with the private soul leaking out of him all the time. All his privacy leaking out in a sort of dribble, oozing into the universe.

Walt becomes in his own person the whole world, the whole universe, the whole eternity of time, as far as his rather sketchy knowledge of history will carry him, that is. Because to *be* a thing he had to know it. In order to assume the identity of a thing he had to know that thing. He was not able to assume one identity with Charlie Chaplin, for example, because Walt didn't know Charlie. What a pity! He'd have done poems, pæans and what not, Chants, Songs of Cinematernity.

Oh, Charlie, my Charlie, another film is done——

As soon as Walt *knew* a thing, he assumed a One Identity with it. If he knew that an Eskimo sat in a kyak, immediately there was Walt being little and yellow and greasy, sitting in a kyak.

Now will you tell me exactly what a kyak is?

Who is he that demands petty definition? Let him behold me *sitting in a kyak*.

I behold no such thing. I behold a rather fat old man full of a rather senile, self-conscious sensuosity.

DEMOCRACY. EN MASSE. ONE IDENTITY.

The universe in short, adds up to ONE.

ONE.

. 1.

Which is Walt.

His poems, *Democracy, En Masse, One Identity*, they are long sums in addition and multiplication, of which the answer is invariably MYSELF.

He reaches the state of ALLNESS.

And what then? It's all empty. Just an empty Allness. An addled egg.

Walt wasn't an Eskimo. A little, yellow, sly, cunning, greasy little Eskimo. And when Walt blandly assumed Allness, including Eskimoness, unto himself, he was just sucking the wind out of a blown egg-shell, no more. Eskimos are not minor little Walts. They are something that I am not, I know that. Outside the egg of my Allness chuckles the greasy little Eskimo. Outside the egg of Whitman's Allness too.

But Walt wouldn't have it. He was everything and everything was in him. He drove an automobile with a very fierce headlight, along the track of a fixed idea, through the darkness of this world. And he saw everything that way. Just as a motorist does in the night.

I, who happen to be asleep under the bushes in the dark, hoping a snake won't crawl into my neck; I, seeing Walt go by in his great fierce poetic machine, think to myself: What a funny world that fellow sees!

ONE DIRECTION! toots Walt in the car, whizzing along it.

Whereas there are myriads of ways in the dark, not to mention trackless wildernesses, as anyone will know who cares to come off the road—even the Open Road.

ONE DIRECTION! whoops America, and sets off also in an automobile.

ALLNESS! shrieks Walt at a cross-road, going whizz over an unwary Red Indian.

ONE IDENTITY! chants democratic En Masse, pelting behind
in motor-cars, oblivious of the corpses under the wheels.

God save me, I feel like creeping down a rabbit-hole, to get
away from all these automobiles rushing down the ONE
IDENTITY track to the goal of ALLNESS.

A woman waits for me——

He might as well have said: "The femaleness waits for my
maleness." Oh, beautiful generalisation and abstraction! Oh,
biological function.

"Athletic mothers of these States——" Muscles and wombs.
They needn't have had faces at all.

As I see myself reflected in Nature,
As I see through a mist, One with inexpressible complete-
    ness, sanity, beauty,
See the bent head, and arms folded over the breast, the
    Female I see.

Everything was female to him: even himself. Nature just
one great function.

This is the nucleus—after the child is born of woman, man
    is born of woman,
This is the bath of birth, the merge of small and large,
    and the outlet again——

"The Female I see——"
If I'd been one of his women, I'd have given him Female,
with a flea in his ear.

Always wanting to merge himself into the womb of something or other.

"The Female I see——"
Anything, so long as he could merge himself.

Just a horror. A sort of white flux.

Post-mortem effects.

He found, as all men find, that you can't really merge in
a woman, though you may go a long way. You can't manage
the last bit. So you have to give it up, and try elsewhere if
you *insist* on merging.

In *Calamus* he changes his tune. He doesn't shout and thump and exult any more. He begins to hesitate, reluctant, wistful.

The strange calamus has its pink-tinged root by the pond, and it sends up its leaves of comradeship, comrades from one root, without the intervention of woman, the female.

So he sings of the mystery of manly love, the love of comrades. Over and over he says the same thing: the new world will be built on the love of comrades, the new great dynamic of life will be manly love. Out of this manly love will come the inspiration for the future.

Will it though? Will it?

Comradeship! Comrades! This is to be the new Democracy of Comrades. This is the new cohering principle in the world: Comradeship.

Is it? Are you sure?

It is the cohering principle of true soldiery, we are told in *Drum Taps*. It is the cohering principle in the new unison for creative activity. And it is extreme and alone, touching the confines of death. Something terrible to bear, terrible to be responsible for. Even Walt Whitman felt it. The soul's last and most poignant responsibility, the responsibility of comradeship, of manly love.

> Yet you are beautiful to me, you faint-tinged roots, you make me think of death.
> Death is beautiful from you (what indeed is finally beautiful except death and love?)
> I think it is not for life I am chanting here my chant of lovers, I think it must be for death,
> For how calm, how solemn it grows to ascend to the atmosphere of lovers,
> Death or life, I am then indifferent, my soul declines to prefer,
> (I am not sure but the high soul of lovers welcomes death most)
> Indeed, O death, I think now these leaves mean precisely the same as you mean——

This is strange, from the exultant Walt.

Death!

Death is now his chant! Death!

Merging! And Death! Which is the final merge.

The great merge into the womb. Woman.

And after that, the merge of comrades: man-for-man love.

And almost immediately with this, death, the final merge of death.

There you have the progression of merging. For the great mergers, woman at last becomes inadequate. For those who love to extremes. Woman is inadequate for the last merging. So the next step is the merging of man-for-man love. And this is on the brink of death. It slides over into death.

David and Jonathan. And the death of Jonathan.

It always slides into death.

The love of comrades.

Merging.

So that if the new Democracy is to be based on the love of comrades, it will be based on death too. It will slip so soon into death.

The last merging. The last Democracy. The last love. The love of comrades.

Fatality. And fatality.

Whitman would not have been the great poet he is if he had not taken the last steps and looked over into death. Death, the last merging, that was the goal of his manhood.

To the mergers, there remains the brief love of comrades, and then Death.

> Whereto answering, the sea
> Delaying not, hurrying not,
> Whispered me through the night, and very plainly before
>   daybreak,
> Lisp'd to me the low and delicious word death,
> And again death, death, death, death.
> Hissing melodious, neither like the bird nor like my
>   arous'd child's heart,
> But edging near as privately for me rustling at my feet,
> Creeping thence steadily up to my ears and laving me
>   softly all over,
> Death, death, death, death, death——

Whitman is a very great poet, of the end of life. A very great post-mortem poet, of the transitions of the soul as it loses its integrity. The poet of the soul's last shout and shriek, on the confines of death. *Après moi le déluge.*

But we have all got to die, and disintegrate.

We have got to die in life, too, and disintegrate while we live. But even then the goal is not death.

Something else will come.

> Out of the cradle endlessly rocking.

We've got to die first, anyhow. And disintegrate while we still live.

Only we know this much: Death is not the *goal*. And Love, and merging, are now only part of the death-process. Comradeship—part of the death-process. Democracy—part of the death-process. The new Democracy—the brink of death. One Identity—death itself.

We have died, and we are still disintegrating.

But IT IS FINISHED.

Consummatum est.

Whitman, the great poet, has meant so much to me. Whitman, the one man breaking a way ahead. Whitman, the one pioneer. And only Whitman. No English pioneers, no French. No European pioneer-poets. In Europe the would-be pioneers are mere innovators. The same in America. Ahead of Whitman, nothing. Ahead of all poets, pioneering into the wilderness of unopened life, Whitman. Beyond him, none. His wide, strange camp at the end of the great high-road. And lots of new little poets camping on Whitman's camping-ground now. But none going really beyond. Because Whitman's camp is at the end of the road, and on the edge of a great precipice. Over the precipice, blue distances, and the blue hollow of the future. But there is no way down. It is a dead end.

Pisgah. Pisgah sights. And Death. Whitman like a strange, modern, American Moses. Fearfully mistaken. And yet the great leader.

The essential function of art is moral. Not æsthetic, not decorative, not pastime and recreation. But moral. The essential function of art is moral.

But a passionate, implicit morality, not didactic. A morality which changes the blood, rather than the mind. Changes the blood first. The mind follows later, in the wake.

Now Whitman was a great moralist. He was a great leader. He was a great changer of the blood in the veins of men.

Surely it is especially true of American art, that it is all essentially moral. Hawthorne, Poe, Longfellow, Emerson, Melville: it is the moral issue which engages them. They all feel uneasy about the old morality. Sensuously, passionally, they all attack the old morality. But they know nothing better, mentally. Therefore they give tight mental allegiance to a morality which all their passion goes to destroy. Hence the duplicity which is the fatal flaw in them: most fatal in the most perfect American work of art, *The Scarlet Letter*. Tight mental allegiance given to a morality which the passional self repudiates.

Whitman was the first to break the mental allegiance. He was the first to smash the old moral conception that the soul of man is something "superior" and "above" the flesh. Even Emerson still maintained this tiresome "superiority" of the soul. Even Melville could not get over it. Whitman was the first heroic seer to seize the soul by the scruff of her neck and plant her down among the potsherds.

"There!" he said to the soul. "Stay there!"

Stay there. Stay in the flesh. Stay in the limbs and lips and in the belly. Stay in the breast and womb. Stay there, O Soul, where you belong.

Stay in the dark limbs of negroes. Stay in the body of the prostitute. Stay in the sick flesh of the syphilitic. Stay in the marsh where the calamus grows. Stay there, Soul, where you belong.

The Open Road. The great home of the Soul is the open road. Not heaven, not paradise. Not "above". Not even "within". The soul is neither "above" nor "within". It is a wayfarer down the open road.

Not by meditating. Not by fasting. Not by exploring heaven after heaven, inwardly, in the manner of the great mystics. Not by exaltation. Not by ecstasy. Not by any of these ways does the soul come into her own.

Only by taking the open road.

Not through charity. Not through sacrifice. Not even

through love. Not through good works. Not through these does the soul accomplish herself.

Only through the journey down the open road.

The journey itself, down the open road. Exposed to full contact. On two slow feet. Meeting whatever comes down the open road. In company with those that drift in the same measure along the same way. Towards no goal. Always the open road.

Having no known direction even. Only the soul remaining true to herself in her going.

Meeting all the other wayfarers along the road. And how? How meet them, and how pass? With sympathy, says Whitman. Sympathy. He does not say love. He says sympathy. Feeling with. Feel with them as they feel with themselves. Catching the vibration of their soul and flesh as we pass.

It is a new great doctrine. A doctrine of life. A new great morality. A morality of actual living, not of salvation. Europe has never got beyond the morality of salvation. America to this day is deathly sick with saviourism. But Whitman, the greatest and the first and the only American teacher, was no Saviour. His morality was no morality of salvation. His was a morality of the soul living her life, not saving herself. Accepting the contact with other souls along the open way, as they lived their lives. Never trying to save them. As leave try to arrest them and throw them in gaol. The soul living her life along the incarnate mystery of the open road.

This was Whitman. And the true rhythm of the American continent speaking out in him. He is the first white aboriginal.

"In my Father's house are many mansions."

"No," said Whitman. "Keep out of mansions. A mansion may be heaven on earth, but you might as well be dead. Strictly avoid mansions. The soul is herself when she is going on foot down the open road."

It is the American heroic message. The soul is not to pile up defences round herself. She is not to withdraw and seek her heavens inwardly, in mystical ecstasies. She is not to cry to some God beyond, for salvation. She is to go down the open road, as the road opens, into the unknown, keeping company with those whose soul draws them near to her, accomplishing nothing save the journey, and the works incident to the journey, in the long life-travel into the unknown, the soul in her subtle sympathies accomplishing herself by the way.

This is Whitman's essential message. The heroic message of the American future. It is the inspiration of thousands of Americans to-day, the best souls of to-day, men and women. And it is a message that only in America can be fully understood, finally accepted.

Then Whitman's mistake. The mistake of his interpretation of his watchword: Sympathy. The mystery of SYMPATHY. He still confounded it with Jesus's LOVE, and with Paul's CHARITY. Whitman, like all the rest of us, was at the end of the great emotional highway of Love. And because he couldn't help himself, he carried on his Open Road as a prolongation of the emotional highway of Love, beyond Calvary. The highway of Love ends at the foot of the Cross. There is no beyond. It was a hopeless attempt to prolong the highway of Love.

He didn't follow his Sympathy. Try as he might, he kept on automatically interpreting it as Love, as Charity. Merging!

This merging, *en masse*, One Identity, Myself monomania was a carry-over from the old Love idea. It was carrying the idea of Love to its logical physical conclusion. Like Flaubert and the leper. The decree of unqualified Charity, as the soul's one means of salvation, still in force.

Now Whitman wanted his soul to save itself; *he* didn't want to save it. Therefore he did not need the great Christian receipt for saving the soul. He needed to supersede the Christian Charity, the Christian Love, within himself, in order to give his Soul her last freedom. The highroad of Love is no Open Road. It is a narrow, tight way, where the soul walks hemmed in between compulsions.

Whitman wanted to take his Soul down the open road. And he failed in so far as he failed to get out of the old rut of Salvation. He forced his Soul to the edge of a cliff, and he looked down into death. And there he camped, powerless. He had carried out his Sympathy as an extension of Love and Charity. And it had brought him almost to madness and soul-death. It gave him his forced, unhealthy, post-mortem quality.

His message was really the opposite of Henley's rant:

I am the master of my fate,
I am the captain of my soul.

Whitman's essential message was the Open Road. The leaving
of the soul free unto herself, the leaving of his fate to her and to
the loom of the open road. Which is the bravest doctrine man
has ever proposed to himself.

Alas, he didn't quite carry it out. He couldn't quite break
the old maddening bond of the love-compulsion; he couldn't
quite get out of the rut of the charity habit—for Love and
Charity have degenerated now into habit: a bad habit.

Whitman said Sympathy. If only he had stuck to it! Because
Sympathy means feeling with, not feeling for. He kept on
having a passionate feeling *for* the negro slave, or the prostitute,
or the syphilitic—which is merging. A sinking of Walt Whitman's soul in the souls of these others.

He wasn't keeping to his open road. He was forcing his soul
down an old rut. He wasn't leaving her free. He was forcing
her into other people's circumstances.

Supposing he had felt true sympathy with the negro slave?
He would have felt *with* the negro slave. Sympathy—compassion—which is partaking of the passion which was in the
soul of the negro slave.

What was the feeling in the negro's soul?

"Ah, I am a slave! Ah, it is bad to be a slave! I must free
myself. My soul will die unless she frees herself. My soul says
I must free myself."

Whitman came along, and saw the slave, and said to himself:
"That negro slave is a man like myself. We share the same
identity. And he is bleeding with wounds. Oh, oh, is it not
myself who am also bleeding with wounds?"

This was not *sympathy*. It was merging and self-sacrifice.
"Bear ye one another's burdens": "Love thy neighbour as
thyself": "Whatsoever ye do unto him, ye do unto me."

If Whitman had truly *sympathised*, he would have said:
"That negro slave suffers from slavery. He wants to free
himself. His soul wants to free him. He has wounds, but they
are the price of freedom. The soul has a long journey from
slavery to freedom. If I can help him I will: I will not take
over his wounds and his slavery to myself. But I will help

him fight the power that enslaves him when he wants to be free, if he wants my help, since I see in his face that he needs to be free. But even when he is free, his soul has many journeys down the open road, before it is a free soul."

And of the prostitute Whitman would have said:

"Look at that prostitute! Her nature has turned evil under her mental lust for prostitution. She has lost her soul. She knows it herself. She likes to make men lose their souls. If she tried to make me lose my soul, I would kill her. I wish she may die."

But of another prostitute he would have said:

"Look! She is fascinated by the Priapic mysteries. Look, she will soon be worn to death by the Priapic usage. It is the way of her soul. She wishes it so."

Of the syphilitic he would say:

"Look! She wants to infect all men with syphilis. We ought to kill her."

And of still another syphilitic:

"Look! She has a horror of her syphilis. If she looks my way I will help her to get cured."

This is sympathy. The soul judging for herself, and preserving her own integrity.

But when, in Flaubert, the man takes the leper to his naked body; when Bubu de Montparnasse takes the girl because he knows she's got syphilis; when Whitman embraces an evil prostitute: that is not sympathy. The evil prostitute has no desire to be embraced with love; so if you sympathise with her, you won't try to embrace her with love. The leper loathes his leprosy, so if you sympathise with him, you'll loathe it too. The evil woman who wishes to infect all men with her syphilis hates you if you haven't got syphilis. If you sympathise, you'll feel her hatred, and you'll hate too, you'll hate her. Her feeling is hate, and you'll share it. Only your soul will choose the direction of its own hatred.

The soul is a very perfect judge of her own motions, if your mind doesn't dictate to her. Because the mind says Charity! Charity! you don't have to force your soul into kissing lepers or embracing syphilitics. Your lips are the lips of your soul, your body is the body of your soul; your own single, individual soul. That is Whitman's message. And you soul hates syphilis and leprosy. Because it *is* a soul, it hates these things, which are against the soul. And therefore to force the body of your soul into contact with uncleanness is a great violation of your soul. The soul wishes to keep clean and whole. The soul's deepest will is to preserve its own integrity, against the mind and the whole mass of disintegrating forces.

Soul sympathises with soul. And that which tries to kill my soul, my soul hates. My soul and my body are one. Soul and body wish to keep clean and whole. Only the mind is capable of great perversion. Only the mind tries to drive my soul and body into uncleanness and unwholesomeness.

What my soul loves, I love.

What my soul hates, I hate.

When my soul is stirred with compassion, I am compassionate.

What my soul turns away from, I turn away from.

That is the *true* interpretation of Whitman's creed: the true revelation of his Sympathy.

And my soul takes the open road. She meets the souls that are passing, she goes along with the souls that are going her way. And for one and all, she has sympathy. The sympathy of love, the sympathy of hate, the sympathy of simple proximity; all the subtle sympathisings of the incalculable soul, from the bitterest hate to passionate love.

It is not I who guide my soul to heaven. It is I who am guided by my own soul along the open road, where all men tread. Therefore, I must accept her deep motions of love, or hate, or compassion, or dislike, or indifference. And I must go where she takes me, for my feet and my lips and my body are my soul. It is I who must submit to her.

This is Whitman's message of American democracy.

The true democracy, where soul meets soul, in the open road. Democracy. American democracy where all journey down the open road, and where a soul is known at once in its going. Not by its clothes or appearance. Whitman did away with that. Not by its family name. Not even by its reputation. Whitman and Melville both discounted that. Not by a progression of piety, or by works of Charity. Not by works at all. Not by anything, but just itself. The soul passing unenhanced, passing on foot and being no more than itself. And recognised, and passed by or greeted according to the soul's dictate. If it be a great soul, it will be worshipped in the road.

The love of man and woman: a recognition of souls, and a communion of worship. The love of comrades: a recognition of souls, and a communion of worship. Democracy: a recognition of souls, all down the open road, and a great soul seen in its greatness, as it travels on foot among the rest, down the common way of the living. A glad recognition of souls, and a gladder worship of great and greater souls, because they are the only riches.

Love, and Merging, brought Whitman to the Edge of Death! Death! Death!

But the exultance of his message still remains. Purified of MERGING, purified of MYSELF, the exultant message of American Democracy, of souls in the Open Road, full of glad recognition, full of fierce readiness, full of the joy of worship, when one soul sees a greater soul.

The only riches, the great souls.

[From *Studies in Classic American Literature,* 1924.]

BOTTOM DOGS

By Edward Dahlberg

WHEN we think of America, and of her huge success, we never realise how many failures have gone, and still go, to build up that success. It is not till you live in America, and go a little under the surface, that you begin to see how terrible and brutal is the mass of failure that nourishes the roots of the gigantic tree of dollars. And this is especially so in the country, and in the newer parts of the land, particularly out west. There you see how many small ranches have gone broke in despair, before the big ranches scoop them up and profit by all the back-breaking, profitless, grim labour of the pioneer. In the west you can still see the pioneer work of tough, hard first-comers, individuals, and it is astounding to see how often these individuals, pioneer first-comers who fought like devils against their difficulties, have been defeated, broken, their efforts and their amazing hard work lost, as it were, on the face of the wilderness.

But it is these hard-necked failures who really broke the resistance of the stubborn, obstinate country, and made it easier for the second wave of exploiters to come in with money and reap the harvest. The real pioneer in America fought like hell and suffered till the soul was ground out of him: and then, nine times out of ten, failed, was beaten. That is why pioneer literature, which, even from the glimpses one has of it, contains the amazing Odyssey of the brute fight with savage conditions of the western continent, hardly exists, and is absolutely unpopular. Americans will not stand for the pioneer stuff, except in small, sentimentalised doses. They know too well the grimness of it, the savage fight and the savage failure which broke the back of the country but also broke something in the human soul. The spirit and the will survived: but something in the soul perished: the softness, the floweriness, the natural tenderness. How could it survive the sheer brutality of the fight with that American wilderness, which is so big, vast, and obdurate!

The savage America was conquered and subdued at the expense of the instinctive and intuitive sympathy of the human soul. The fight was too brutal. It is a great pity some publisher does not undertake a series of pioneer records and novels, the genuine, unsweetened stuff. The books exist. But they are shoved down into oblivion by the common will-to-forget. They show the strange brutality of the struggle, what would have been called in the old language the breaking of the heart. America was not colonised and "civilised" until the heart was broken in the American pioneer. It was a price that was paid. The heart was broken. But the will, the determination to conquer the land and make it submit to productivity, this was not broken. The will-to-success and the will-to-produce became clean and indomitable once the sympathetic heart was broken.

By the sympathetic heart, we mean that instinctive belief which lies at the core of the human heart, that people and the universe itself are *ultimately* kind. This belief is fundamental and, in the old language, is embodied in the doctrine: God is good. Now given an opposition too ruthless, a fight too brutal, a betrayal too bitter, this belief breaks in the heart, and is no more. Then you have either despair, bitterness, and cynicism, or you have the much braver reaction which says: God is not good, but the human will is indomitable, it cannot be broken, it will succeed against all odds. It is not God's business to be good and kind, that is man's business. God's business is to be indomitable. And man's business is essentially the same.

This is, roughly, the American position to-day, as it was the position of the Red Indian, when the white man came, and of the Aztec and of the Peruvian. So far as we can make out, neither Redskin nor Aztec nor Inca had any conception of a "good" God. They conceived of implacable, indomitable Powers, which is very different. And that seems to me the essential American position to-day. Of course the white American believes that man should behave in a kind and benevolent manner. But this is a social belief and a social gesture, rather than an individual flow. The flow from the heart, the warmth of fellow-feeling which has animated Europe and been the best of her humanity, individual, spontaneous, flowing in thousands of little passionate currents often conflicting, this seems unable to persist on the American soil. Instead you get the social creed of benevolence and uniformity, a mass *will*, and an inward individual retraction, an isolation, an amorphous separateness like grains of sand, each grain isolated upon its own will, its own indomitableness, its own implacability, its own unyielding, yet heaped together with all the other grains. This makes the American mass the easiest mass in the world to rouse, to move. And probably, under a long stress, it would make it the most difficult mass in the world to hold together.

The deep psychic change which we call the breaking of the heart, the collapse of the flow of spontaneous warmth between a man and his fellows, happens of course now all over the world. It seems to have happened to Russia in one great blow. It brings a people into a much more complete social unison, for good or evil. But it throws them apart in their private, individual emotions. Before, they were like cells in a complex tissue, alive and functioning diversely in a vast organism composed of family, clan, village, nation. Now, they are like grains of sand, friable, heaped together in a vast inorganic democracy.

While the old sympathetic flow continues, there are violent hostilities between people, but they are not secretly repugnant to one another. Once the heart is broken, people become repulsive to one another, secretly, and they develop social benevolence. They smell in each other's nostrils. It has been said often enough of more primitive or old-world peoples, who live together in a state of blind mistrust but also of close physical connexion with one another, that they have no noses. They are so close, the flow from body to body is so powerful, that they hardly smell one another, and hardly are aware at all of offensive human odours that madden the new civilisations. As it says in this novel: The American senses other people by their sweat and their kitchens. By which he means, their repulsive effluvia. And this is basically true. Once the blood-sympathy breaks, and only the nerve-sympathy is left, human beings become secretly intensely repulsive to one another, physically, and sympathetic only mentally and spiritually. The secret physical repulsion between people is responsible for the perfection of American "plumbing", American sanitation, and American kitchens, utterly white-enamelled and antiseptic. It is revealed in the awful advertisements such as those about "halitosis", or bad breath. It is responsible for the American nausea at coughing, spitting, or any of those things. The American townships don't mind hideous litter of tin cans and paper and broken rubbish. But they go crazy at the sight of human excrement.

And it is this repulsion from the physical neighbour that is now coming up in the consciousness of the great democracies, in England, America, Germany. The old flow broken, men could enlarge themselves for a while in transcendentalism, Whitmanish "adhesiveness" of the social creature, noble supermen, lifted above the baser functions. For the last hundred years man has been elevating himself above his "baser functions" and posing around as a transcendentalist, a superman, a perfect social being, a spiritual entity. And now, since the war, the collapse has come.

Man has no ultimate control of his own consciousness. If his nose doesn't notice stinks, it just doesn't, and there's the end of it. If his nose is so sensitive that a stink overpowers him, then again he's helpless. He can't prevent his senses from transmitting and his mind from registering what it does register.

And now, man has begun to be overwhelmingly conscious of the repulsiveness of his neighbour, particularly of the physical repulsiveness. There it is, in James Joyce, in Aldous Huxley, in André Gide, in modern Italian novels like *Parigi*—in all the very modern novels, the dominant note is the repulsiveness, intimate physical repulsiveness of human flesh. It is the expression of absolutely genuine experience. What the young feel intensely, and no longer so secretly, is the extreme repulsiveness of other people.

It is, perhaps, the inevitable result of the transcendental bodiless brotherliness and social "adhesiveness" of the last hundred years. People rose superior to their bodies, and soared along, till they had exhausted their energy in this performance. The energy once exhausted, they fell with a struggling plunge, not down into their bodies again, but into the cesspools of the body.

The modern novel, the very modern novel, has passed quite away from tragedy. An American novel like *Manhattan Transfer* has in it still the last notes of tragedy, the sheer spirit of suicide. An English novel like *Point Counter Point* has gone beyond tragedy into exacerbation, and continuous nervous repulsion. Man is so nervously repulsive to man, so screamingly, nerve-rackingly repulsive! This novel goes one further. Man just *smells*, offensively and unbearably, not to be borne. The human stink!

The inward revulsion of man away from man, which follows on the collapse of the physical sympathetic flow, has a slowly increasing momentum, a wider swing. For a long time, the *social* belief and benevolence of man towards man keeps pace with the secret physical repulsion of man away from man. But ultimately, inevitably, the one outstrips the other. The benevolence exhausts itself, the repulsion only deepens. The benevolence is external and extra-individual. But the revulsion is inward and personal. The one gains over the other. Then you get a gruesome condition, such as is displayed in this book.

The only motive power left is the sense of revulsion away from people, the sense of the repulsiveness of the neighbour. It is a condition we are rapidly coming to—a condition displayed by the intellectuals much more than by the common people. Wyndham Lewis gives a display of the utterly repulsive effect people have on him, but he retreats into the intellect to make his display. It is a question of manner and manners. The effect is the same. It is the same exclamation: They stink! My God, they stink!

And in this process of recoil and revulsion, the affective consciousness withers with amazing rapidity. Nothing I have ever read has astonished me more than the "orphanage" chapters of this book. There I realised with amazement how rapidly the human psyche can strip itself of its awarenesses and its emotional contacts, and reduce itself to a sub-brutal condition of simple gross persistence. It is not animality—far from it. Those boys are much less than animals. They are cold wills functioning with a minimum of consciousness. The amount that they are *not* aware of is perhaps the most amazing aspect of their character. They are brutally and deliberately *unaware*. They have no hopes, no desires even. They have even no will-to-exist, for existence even is too high a term. They have a strange, stony will-to-persist, that is all. And they persist by reaction, because they still feel the repulsiveness of each other, of everything, even of themselves.

Of course the author exaggerates. The boy Lorry "always had his nose in a book"—and he must have got things out of the books. If he had taken the intellectual line, like Mr. Huxley or Mr. Wyndham Lewis, he would have harped on the intellectual themes, the essential feeling being the same. But he takes the non-intellectual line, is in revulsion against the intellect too, so we have the stark reduction to a persistent minimum of the human consciousness. It is a minimum lower than the savage, lower than the African Bushman. Because it is a *willed* minimum, sustained from inside by resistance, brute resistance against any flow of consciousness except that of the barest, most brutal egoistic self-interest. It is a phenomenon, and pre-eminently an American phenomenon. But the flow of repulsion, inward physical revulsion of man away from man, is passing over all the world. It is only perhaps in America, and in a book such as this, that we see it most starkly revealed.

After the orphanage, the essential theme is repeated over a wider field. The state of revulsion continues. The young Lorry is indomitable. You can't destroy him. And at the same time, you can't catch him. He will recoil from everything, and nothing on earth will make him have a positive feeling, of affection or sympathy or connexion. His mother?—we see her in her decaying repulsiveness. He has a certain loyalty, because she is his sort: it is part of his will-to-persist. But he must turn his back on her with a certain disgust.

The tragedian, like Theodore Dreiser and Sherwood Anderson, still dramatises his defeat and is in love with himself in his defeated role. But the Lorry Lewis is in too deep a state of revulsion to dramatise himself. He almost deliberately finds himself repulsive too. And he goes on, just to see if he can hit the world without destroying himself. Hit the world not to destroy it, but to experience in himself how repulsive it is.

Kansas City; Beatrice, Nebraska; Omaha; Salt Lake City; Portland, Oregon; Los Angeles, he finds them all alike, nothing if not repulsive. He covers the great tracts of prairie, mountain, forest, coast-range, without seeing anything but a certain desert scaliness. His consciousness is resistant, shuts things out, and reduces itself to a minimum.

In the Y.M.C.A. it is the same. He has his gang. But the last word about them is that they stink, their effluvia is offensive. He goes with women, but the thought of women is inseparable from the thought of sexual disease and infection. He thrills to the repulsiveness of it, in a terrified, perverted way. His associates—which means himself also—read Zarathustra and Spinoza, Darwin and Hegel. But it is with a strange external, superficial mind that has no connexion with the affective and effective self. One last desire he has—to write, to put down his condition in words. His will-to-persist is intellectual also. Beyond this, nothing.

It is a genuine book, as far as it goes, even if it is an objectionable one. It is, in psychic disintegration, a good many stages ahead of *Point Counter Point*. It reveals a condition that not many of us have reached, but towards which the trend of consciousness is taking us, all of us, especially the young. It is, let us hope, a *ne plus ultra*. The next step is legal insanity, or just crime. The book is perfectly sane; yet two more strides, and it is criminal insanity. The style seems to me excellent, fitting the matter. It is sheer bottom-dog style, the bottom-dog mind expressing itself direct, almost as if it barked. That directness, that unsentimental and non-dramatised thoroughness of setting down the under-dog mind surpasses anything I know. I don't want to read any more books like this. But I am glad to have read this one, just to know what is the last word in repulsive consciousness, consciousness in a state of repulsion. It helps one to understand the world, and saves one the necessity of having to follow out the phenomenon of physical repulsion any further, for the time being.

[Preface to *Bottom Dogs*, London, 1929.]

[103]

AMERICANS

By Stuart P. Sherman

Professor Sherman once more coaxing American criticism the way it should go.

Like Benjamin Franklin, one of his heroes, he attempts the invention of a creed that shall "satisfy the professors of all religions, and offend none".

He smites the marauding Mr. Mencken with a velvet glove, and pierces the obstinate Mr. More with a reproachful look. Both gentlemen, of course, will purr and feel flattered.

That's how Professor Sherman treats his enemies: buns to his grizzlies.

Well, Professor Sherman, being a professor, has got to be nice to everybody about everybody. What else does a professor sit in a chair of English for, except to dole out sweets?

Awfully nice, rather cloying. But there, men *are* but children of a later growth.

So much for the professor's attitude. As for his "message". He steers his little ship of Criticism most obviously between the Scylla of Mr. Mencken and the Charybdis of Mr. P. E. More. I'm sorry I never heard before of either gentleman: except that I dimly remember having read, in the lounge of a Naples hotel, a bit of an article by a Mr. Mencken, in German, in some German periodical: all amounting to nothing.

But Mr. Mencken is the Scylla of American Criticism, and hence, of American democracy. There is a verb "to menckenize", and a noun "menckenism". Apparently to *men-*

ckenize is to manufacture jeering little gas-bomb phrases against everything deep and earnest, or high and noble, and to paint the face of corruption with phosphorus, so it shall glow. And a *menckenism* is one of the little stink-gas phrases.

Now the *nouveau riche jeune fille* of the *bourgeoisie*, as Professor Sherman puts it; in other words, the profiteers' flappers all read Mr. Mencken and swear by him: swear that they don't give a nickel for any Great Man that ever was or will be. Great Men are all a bombastical swindle. So asserts the *nouveau riche jeune fille*, on whom, apparently, American democracy rests. And Mr. Mencken "learnt it her". And Mr. Mencken got it in Germany, where all stink-gas comes from, according to Professor Sherman. And Mr. Mencken does it to poison the noble and great old spirit of American democracy, which is grandly Anglo-Saxon in origin, but absolutely American in fact.

So much for the Scylla of Mr. Mencken. It is the first essay in the book. The Charybdis of Mr. P. E. More is the last essay: to this monster the professor warbles another tune. Mr. More, author of the *Shelburne Essays*, is learned, and steeped in tradition, the very antithesis of the nihilistic stink-gassing Mr. Mencken. But alas, Mr. More is remote: somewhat haughty and supercilious at his study table. And even, alasser! with all his learning and remoteness, he hunts out the risky Restoration wits to hob-nob with on high Parnassus; Wycherley, for example; he likes his wits smutty. He even goes and fetches out Aphra Behn from her disreputable oblivion, to entertain her in public.

And there you have the Charybdis of Mr. More: snobbish, distant, exclusive, disdaining even the hero from the Marne who mends the gas bracket: and at the same time absolutely *preferring* the doubtful odour of Wycherley because it is—well, malodorous, says the professor.

Mr. Mencken: Great Men and the Great Past are an addled egg full of stink-gas.

Mr. P. E. More: Great Men of the Great Past are utterly beyond the *mobile vulgus*. Let the *mobile vulgus* (in other words, the democratic millions of America) be cynically scoffed at by the gentlemen of the Great Past, especially the naughty ones.

To the Menckenites, Professor Sherman says: Jeer not at the Great Past and at the Great Dead. Heroes are heroes still, they do not go addled, as you would try to make out, nor turn into stink-bombs. Tradition is honourable still, and will be honourable for ever, though it may be splashed like a futurist's picture with the rotten eggs of menckenism.

To the smaller and more select company of Moreites: Scorn not the horny hand of noble toil: "—the average man is, like (Mr. More) himself, at heart a mystic, vaguely hungering for a peace that diplomats cannot give, obscurely seeking the permanent amid the transitory: a poor swimmer struggling for a rock amid the flux of waters, a lonely pilgrim longing for the shadow of a mighty rock in a weary land. And if 'P. E. M.' had a bit more of that natural sympathy of which he is so distrustful, he would have perceived that what more than anything else to-day keeps the average man from lapsing into Yahooism is the religion of democracy, consisting of a little bundle of general principles which make him respect himself and his neighbour; a bundle of principles kindled in crucial times by an intense emotion, in which his self-interest, his petty vices, and his envy are consumed as with fire; and he sees the common weal as the mighty rock in the shadow of which his little life and per-sonality are to be surrendered, if need be, as things negligible and transitory."

All right, Professor Sherman. All the profiteers, and shovers, and place-grabbers, and bullies, especially bullies, male and female, all that sort of gentry of the late war were, of course, outside the average. The supermen of the occasion.

The Babbitts, while they were on the make.

And as for the mighty rocks in weary lands, as far as my experience goes, they have served the pilgrims chiefly as sanitary offices and places in whose shadows men shall leave their offal and tin cans.

But there you have a specimen of Professor Sherman's "style". And the thin ends of his parabola.

The great arch is of course the Religion of Democracy, which the professor italicises. If you want to trace the curve you must follow the course of the essays.

After Mr. Mencken and Tradition comes Franklin. Now Benjamin Franklin is one of the founders of the Religion of Democracy. It was he who invented the creed that should satisfy the professors of all religions, not of universities only, and offend none. With a deity called Providence. Who turns out to be a sort of superlative Mr. Wanamaker, running the globe as a revolving dry-goods store, according to a profit-and-loss system; the profit counted in plump citizens whose every want is satisfied: like chickens in an absolutely coyote-proof chicken-run.

In spite of this new attempt to make us like Dr. Franklin, the flesh wearies on our bones at the thought of him. The professor hints that the good old gentleman on Quaker Oats was really an old sinner. If it had been proved to us, we *might* have liked him. As it is, he just wearies the flesh on our bones. *Religion civile*, indeed.

Emerson. The next essay is called "The Emersonian Liberation". Well, Emerson is a great man still: or a great individual. And heroes are heroes still, though their banners may decay, and stink.

It is true that lilies may fester. And virtues likewise. The great Virtue of one age has a trick of smelling far worse than weeds in the next.

It is a sad but undeniable fact.

Yet why so sad, fond lover, prithee why so sad? Why should Virtue remain incorruptible, any more than anything else? If stars wax and wane, why should Goodness shine for ever unchanged? That too makes one tired. Goodness sweals and gutters, the light of the Good goes out with a stink, and lo, somewhere else a new light, a new Good. Afterwards, it may be shown that it is eternally the same Good. But to us poor mortals at the moment, it emphatically isn't.

And that is the point about Emerson and the Emersonian Liberation—save the word! Heroes are heroes still: safely dead. Heroism is always heroism. But the hero who was heroic one century, uplifting the banner of a creed, is followed the next century by a hero heroically ripping that banner to rags. *Sic transit veritas mundi.*

Emerson was an idealist: a believer in "continuous revelation", continuous inrushes of inspirational energy from the Oversoul. Professor Sherman says: "His message when he leaves us is not, 'Henceforth be masterless', but, 'Bear thou henceforth the sceptre of thine own control through life and the passion of life'."

When Emerson says: "I am surrounded by messengers of God who send me credentials day by day," then all right for him. But he cosily forgot that there are many messengers. He knew only a sort of smooth-shaven Gabriel. But as far as we remember, there is Michael too: and a terrible discrepancy between the credentials of the pair of 'em. Then there are other cherubim with outlandish names bringing very different messages than those Ralph Waldo got: Israfel, and even Mormon. And a whole bunch of others. But Emerson had a stone-deaf ear for all except a nicely aureoled Gabriel *qui n'avait pas de quoi.*

Emerson listened to one sort of message and only one. To all the rest he was blank. Ashtaroth and Ammon are gods as well, and hand out their own credentials. But Ralph Waldo wasn't having any. They could never ring *him* up. He was only connected on the Ideal phone. "We are all aiming to be idealists," says Emerson, "and covet the society of those who make us so, as the sweet singer, the orator, the ideal painter."

Well, we're pretty sick of the ideal painters and the uplifting singers. As a matter of fact we have worked the ideal bit of our nature to death, and we shall go crazy if we can't start working from some other bit. Idealism now is a sick nerve, and the more you rub on it the worse you feel afterwards. Your later reactions aren't pretty at all. Like Dostoievsky's Idiot, and President Wilson sometimes.

Emerson believes in having the courage to treat all men as equals. It takes some courage *not* to treat them so now.

"Shall I not treat all men as gods?" he cries.

If you like, Waldo, but we've got to pay for it, when you've made them *feel* that they're gods. A hundred million American godlets is rather much for the world to deal with.

The fact of the matter is, all those gorgeous inrushes of exaltation and spiritual energy which made Emerson a great man, now make us sick. They are with us a drug habit. So when Professor Sherman urges us in Ralph Waldo's footsteps, he is really driving us nauseously astray. Which perhaps is hard lines on the professor, and us, and Emerson. But it wasn't I who started the mills of God a-grinding.

I like the essay on Emerson. I like Emerson's real courage. I like his wild and genuine belief in the Oversoul and the

inrushes he got from it. But it is a museum-interest. Or else it
is a taste of the old drug to the old spiritual drug-fiend in me.

We've got to have a different sort of sardonic courage. And
the sort of credentials we are due to receive from the god in the
shadow would have been real bones out of hell-broth to Ralph
Waldo. *Sic transeunt Dei hominorum.*

So no wonder Professor Sherman sounds a little wistful,
and somewhat pathetic, as he begs us to follow Ralph Waldo's
trail.

Hawthorne: A Puritan Critic of Puritanism. This essay is
concerned chiefly with an analysis and praise of *The Scarlet
Letter.* Well, it is a wonderful book. But why does nobody give
little Nathaniel a kick for his duplicity? Professor Sherman
says there is nothing erotic about *The Scarlet Letter.* Only
neurotic. It wasn't the sensual act itself had any meaning for
Hawthorne. Only the Sin. He knew there's nothing deadly
in the act itself. But if it is Forbidden, immediately it looms
lurid with interest. He is not concerned for a moment with
what Hester and Dimmesdale really felt. Only with their
situations as Sinners. And Sin looms lurid and thrilling, when
after all it is only just a normal sexual passion. This luridness
about the book makes one feel like spitting. It is somewhat
worked up: invented in the head and grafted on to the lower
body, like some serpent of supposition under the fig-leaf. It
depends so much on *coverings.* Suppose you took off the fig-leaf,
the serpent isn't there. And so the relish is all two-faced and
tiresome. *The Scarlet Letter* is a masterpiece, but in duplicity
and half-false excitement.

And when one remembers *The Marble Faun*, all the parochial
priggishness and poor-bloodedness of Hawthorne in Italy, one
of the most bloodless books ever written, one feels like giving
Nathaniel a kick in the seat of his poor little pants and landing
him back in New England again. For the rolling, many-
godded medieval and pagan world was too big a prey for such
a ferret.

Walt Whitman. Walt is the high priest of the Religion of
Democracy. Yet "at the first bewildering contact one wonders
whether his urgent touch is of lewdness or divinity", says
Professor Sherman.

"All I have said concerns you." But it doesn't. One ceases

to care about so many thing. One ceases to respond or to react. And at length other things come up, which Walt and Professor Sherman never knew.

"Whatever else it involves, democracy involves at least one grand salutary elementary admission, namely, that the world exists for the benefit and for the improvement of all the decent individuals in it." O Lord, how long will you submit to this Insurance Policy interpretation of the Universe! How "decent"? Decent in what way? Benefit! Think of the world's existing for people's "benefit and improvement".

So wonderful says Professor Sherman, the way Whitman identifies himself with everything and everybody: Runaway slaves and all the rest. But we no longer want to take the whole hullabaloo to our bosom. We no longer want to "identify ourselves" with a lot of other things and other people. It *is* a sort of lewdness. *Noli me tangere*, "you". I don't want "you".

Whitman's "you" doesn't get me.

We don't want to be embracing everything any more. Or to be embraced in one of Waldo's vast promiscuous armfuls. *Merci, monsieur!*

We've had enough democracy.

Professor Sherman says that if Whitman had lived "at the right place in these years of Proletarian Millennium, he would have been hanged as a reactionary member of the *bourgeoise*". ('Tisn't my spelling.)

And he gives Whitman's own words in proof: "The true gravitation hold of liberalism in the United States will be a more universal ownership of property, general homesteads, general comforts—a vast intertwining reticulation of wealth. . . . She (Democracy) asks for men and women with occupations, well-off, owners of houses and acres, and with cash in the bank and with some craving for literature too"—so that they can buy certain books. Oh, Walt!

Allons! The road is before us.

Joaquin Miller: Poetical Conquistador of the West. A long essay with not much spirit in it, showing that Miller was a true son of the Wild and Woolly West, in so far as he was a very good imitation of other people's poetry (note the Swinburnian bit) and a rather poor assumer of other people's played-out poses. A self-conscious little "wild" man, like the rest of the "wild" men. The Wild West is a pose that pays Zane Grey to-day, as it once paid Miller and Bret Harte and Buffalo Bill.

A note on Carl Sandburg. That Carl is a super-self-conscious literary gent stampeding around with red-ochre blood on his hands and smeared-on soot darkening his craggy would-be-criminal brow: but that his heart is as tender as an old tomato.

Andrew Carnegie. That Andy was the most perfect American citizen Scotland ever produced, and the sweetest example of how beautifully the *Religion Civile* pays, in cold cash.

Roosevelt and the National Psychology. Theodore didn't have a spark of magnanimity in his great personality, says Professor Sherman, what a pity! And you see where it lands you, when you play at being pro-German. You go quite out of fashion.

Evolution of the Adams Family. Perfect Pedigree of the most aristocratic Democratic family. Your aristocracy is played out, my dear fellows, but don't cry about it, you've always got your Democracy to fall back on. If you don't like falling back on it of your own free will, you'll be shoved back on it by the Will of the People.

"Man is the animal that destiny cannot break."

But the Will of the People can break Man and the animal man, and the destined man, all the lot, and grind 'em to democratic powder, Professor Sherman warns us.

Allons! en-masse is before us.

But when Germany is thoroughly broken, Democracy finally collapses. (My own prophecy.)

An Imaginary Conversation with Mr. P. E. More: You've had the gist of that already.

Well there is Professor Sherman's dish of cookies which he bids you eat and have. An awfully sweet book, all about having your cookies and eating 'em. The cookies are Tradition, and Heroes, and Great Men, and $350,000,000 in your pocket. And eating 'em is Democracy, Serving Mankind, piously giving most of the $350,000,000 back again. "Oh, nobly and heroically get $350,000,000 together," chants Professor Sherman in this litany of having your cookies and eating 'em, "and then piously and munificently give away $349,000,000 again."

P.S. You can't get past Arithmetic.

[Review in *Dial*, May 1923.]

[104]

FOUR AMERICAN NOVELS

Nigger Heaven, by Carl Van Vechten; *Flight*, by Walter
White; *Manhattan Transfer*, by John Dos Passos; *In Our
Time*, by Ernest Hemingway

NIGGER HEAVEN is one of the negro names for Harlem, that
dismal region of hard stone streets way up Seventh Avenue
beyond One Hundred and Twenty-Fifth Street, where the
population is all coloured, though not much of it is real black.
In the daytime, at least, the place aches with dismalness and a
loose-end sort of squalor, the stone of the streets seeming
particularly dead and stony, obscenely stony.

Mr. Van Vechten's book is a nigger book, and not much of a
one. It opens and closes with nigger cabaret scenes in feeble
imitation of Cocteau or Morand, second-hand attempts to be
wildly lurid, with background effects of black and vermilion
velvet. The middle is a lot of stuffing about highbrow niggers,
the heroine being one of the old-fashioned school-teacherish sort,
this time an assistant in a public library; and she has only one
picture in her room, a reproduction of the Mona Lisa, and on
her shelves only books by James Branch Cabell, Anatole
France, Jean Cocteau, etc.; in short, the literature of disillusion. This is to show how refined she is. She is just as refined
as any other "idealistic" young heroine who earns her living,
and we have to be reminded continually that she is golden-
brown.

Round this heroine goes on a fair amount of "race" talk,
nigger self-consciousness which, if it didn't happen to mention
it was black, would be taken for merely another sort of self-
conscious grouch. There is a love-affair—a rather palish-
brown—which might go into any feeble American novel
whatsoever. And the whole coloured thing is peculiarly
colourless, a second-hand dish barely warmed up.

The author seems to feel this, so he throws in a highly-spiced nigger in a tartan suit, who lives off women—rather in the distance—and two perfect red-peppers of nigger millionairesses who swim in seas of champagne and have lovers and fling them away and sniff drugs; in short, altogether the usual old bones of hot stuff, warmed up with all the fervour the author can command—which isn't much.

It is a false book by an author who lingers in nigger cabarets hoping to heaven to pick up something to write about and make a sensation—and, of course, money.

Flight is another nigger book; much more respectable, but not much more important. The author, we are told, is himself a negro. If we weren't told, we should never know. But there is rather a call for coloured stuff, hence we had better be informed when we're getting it.

The first part of *Flight* is interesting—the removal of Creoles, just creamy-coloured old French-negro mixture, from the Creole quarter of New Orleans to the negro quarter of Atlanta. This is real, as far as life goes, and external reality: except that to me, the Creole quarter of New Orleans is dead and lugubrious as a Jews' burying-ground, instead of highly romantic. But the first part of *Flight* is good negro *data*.

The culture of Mr. White's Creoles is much more acceptable than that of Mr. Van Vechten's Harlem golden-browns. If it is only skin-deep, that is quite enough, since the pigmentation of the skin seems to be the only difference between the negro and the white man. If there be such a thing as a negro soul, then that of the Creole is very very French-American, and that of the Harlemite is very very Yankee-American. In fact, there seems no blackness about it at all. Reading negro books, or books about negroes written from the negro standpoint, it is absolutely impossible to discover that the nigger is any blacker inside than we are. He's an absolute white man, save for the colour of his skin: which, in many cases, is also just as white as a Mediterranean white man's.

It is rather disappointing. One likes to cherish illusions about the race soul, the eternal negroid soul, black and glistening and touched with awfulness and with mystery. One is not allowed. The nigger is a white man through and through. He even sees himself as white men see him, blacker than he ought to be. And his soul is an Edison gramophone on which one puts the current records: which is what the white man's soul is, just the same, a gramophone grinding over the old records.

New York is the melting-pot which melts even the nigger. The future population of this melting-pot will be a pale-greyish-brown in colour, and its psychology will be that of Mr. White or Byron Kasson, which is the psychology of a shrewd mixture of English, Irish, German, Jewish, and negro. These are the grand ingredients of the melting-pot, and the amalgam, or alloy, whatever you call it, will be a fine mixture of them. Unless the melting-pot gets upset.

Apparently there is only one feeling about the negro, wherein he differs from the white man, according to Mr. White: and this is the feeling of warmth and humanness. But *we* don't feel even that. More mercurial, but not by any means warmer or more human, the nigger seems to be: even in nigger books. And he sees in himself a talent for life which the white man has lost. But remembering glimpses of Harlem and Louisiana, and the down-at-heel greyness of the colourless negro *ambiente*, myself I don't feel even that.

But the one thing the negro *knows* he can do, is sing and dance. He knows it, because the white man has pointed it out to him so often. There, again, however, disappointment! About one nigger in a thousand amounts to anything in song or dance: the rest are just as songful and limber as the rest of Americans.

Mimi, the pale-biscuit heroine of *Flight*, neither sings nor dances. She is rather cultured and makes smart dresses and passes over as white, then marries a well-to-do white American, but leaves him because he is not "live" enough and goes back to Harlem. It is just what Nordic wives do, just how they feel about their husbands. And if they don't go to Harlem, they go somewhere else. And then they come back. As Mimi will do. Three months of Nigger Heaven will have her fed up, and back she'll be over the white line, settling again in the Washington Square region, and being "of French extraction". Nothing is more monotonous than these removals.

All these books might as well be called *Flight*. They give one the impression of swarms of grasshoppers hopping big hops, and buzzing occasionally on the wing, all from nowhere to no-where, all over the place. What's the point of all this flight, when they start from nowhere and alight on nowhere? For the Nigger Heaven is as sure a nowhere as anywhere else.

Manhattan Transfer is still a greater ravel of flights from nowhere to nowhere. But at least the author knows it, and gets a kind of tragic significance into the fact. John Dos Passos is a far better writer than Mr. Van Vechten or Mr. White, and his book is a far more real and serious thing. To me, it is the best modern book about New York that I have read. It is an endless series of glimpses of people in the vast scuffle of Manhattan Island, as they turn up again and again and again, in a confusion that has no obvious rhythm, but wherein at last we recognise the systole-diastole of success and failure, the end being all failure, from the point of view of life: and then another flight towards another nowhere.

If you set a blank record revolving to receive all the sounds, and a film-camera going to photograph all the motions of a scattered group of individuals, at the points where they meet and touch in New York, you would more or less get Mr. Dos Passos's method. It is a rush of disconnected scenes and scraps, a breathless confusion of isolated moments in a group of lives, pouring on through the years, from almost every part of New York. But the order of time is more or less kept. For half a page you are on the Lackawanna ferry-boat—or one of the ferry-boats—in the year 1900 or somewhere there—the next page you are in the Brevoort a year later—two pages ahead it is Central Park, you don't know when—then the wharves— way up Hoboken—down Greenwich Village—the Algonquin Hotel—somebody's apartment. And it seems to be different people, a different girl every time. The scenes whirl past like snowflakes. Broadway at night—whizz! gone!—a quick-lunch counter! gone!—a house on Riverside Drive, the Palisades, night—gone! But, gradually, you get to know the faces. It is like a movie picture with an intricacy of different stories and no close-ups and no writing in between. Mr. Dos Passos leaves out the writing in between.

But if you are content to be confused, at length you realise that the confusion is genuine, not affected; it is life, not a pose. The book becomes what life is, a stream of different things and different faces rushing along in the consciousness, with no apparent direction save that of time, from past to present, from youth to age, from birth to death, and no apparent goal at all. But what makes the rush so swift, one gradually realises, is the wild, strange frenzy for success: egoistic, individualistic success.

This very complex film, of course, does not pretend to film *all* New York. Journalists, actors and actresses, dancers, unscrupulous lawyers, prostitutes, Jews, out-of-works, politicians, labour agents—that kind of gang. It is on the whole a gang, though we do touch respectability on Riverside Drive now and then. But it is a gang, the vast loose gang of strivers and winners and losers which seems to be the very pep of New York, the city itself an inordinately vast gang.

At first it seems too warm, too passionate. One thinks: this is much too healthily lusty for the present New York. Then we realise we are away before the war, when the place was steaming and alive. There is sex, fierce, ranting sex, real New York: sex as the prime stimulus to business success. One realises what a lot of financial success has been due to the reckless speeding-up of the sex dynamo. Get hold of the right woman, get absolutely rushed out of yourself loving her up, and you'll be able to rush a success in the city. Only, both to the man and woman, the sex must be the stimulant to success; otherwise it stimulates towards suicide, as it does with the one character whom the author loves, and who was "truly male".

The war comes, and the whole rhythm collapses. The war ends. There are the same people. Some have got success, some haven't. But success and failure alike are left irritable and inert. True, everybody is older, and the fire is dying down into spasmodic irritability. But in all the city the fire is dying down. The stimulant is played out, and you have the accumulating irritable restlessness of New York of to-day. The old thrill has gone, out of socialism as out of business, out of art as out of love, and the city rushes on ever faster, with more maddening irritation, knowing the apple is a Dead Sea shiner.

At the end of the book, the man who was a little boy at the beginning of the book, and now is a failure of perhaps something under forty, crosses on the ferry from Twenty-third Street, and walks away into the gruesome ugliness of the New Jersey side. He is making another flight into nowhere, to land upon nothingness.

"Say, will you give me a lift?" he asks the red-haired man at the wheel (of a furniture-van).

"How fur ye goin'?"

"I dunno . . . Pretty far."

The End.

He might just as well have said "nowhere!"

In Our Time is the last of the four American books, and Mr. Hemingway has accepted the goal. He keeps on making flights, but he has no illusion about landing anywhere. He knows it will be nowhere every time.

In Our Time calls itself a book of stories, but it isn't that. It is a series of successive sketches from a man's life, and makes a fragmentary novel. The first scenes, by one of the big lakes in America—probably Superior—are the best; when Nick is a boy. Then come fragments of war—on the Italian front. Then a soldier back home, very late, in the little town way west in Oklahoma. Then a young American and wife in post-war Europe; a long sketch about an American jockey in Milan and Paris; then Nick is back again in the Lake Superior region, getting off the train at a burnt-out town, and tramping across the empty country to camp by a trout-stream. Trout is the one passion life has left him—and this won't last long.

It is a short book: and it does not pretend to be about one man. But it is. It is as much as we need know of the man's life. The sketches are short, sharp, vivid, and most of them excellent. (The "mottoes" in front seem a little affected.) And these few sketches are enough to create the man and all his history: we need know no more.

Nick is a type one meets in the more wild and woolly regions of the United States. He is the remains of the lone trapper and cowboy. Nowadays he is educated, and through with everything. It is a state of *conscious*, accepted indifference to everything except freedom from work and the moment's interest. Mr. Hemingway does it extremely well. Nothing matters. Everything happens. One wants to keep oneself loose. Avoid one thing only: getting connected up. Don't get connected up. If you get held by anything, break it. Don't be held. Break it, and get away. Don't get away with the idea of getting somewhere else. Just get away, for the sake of getting away. Beat it! "Well, boy, I guess I'll beat it." Ah, the pleasure in saying that!

Mr. Hemingway's sketches, for this reason, are excellent: so short, like striking a match, lighting a brief sensational cigarette, and it's over. His young love-affair ends as one throws a cigarette-end away. "It isn't fun any more."—"Everything's gone to hell inside me."

It is really honest. And it explains a great deal of sentimentality. When a thing has gone to hell inside you, your sentimentalism tries to pretend it hasn't. But Mr. Hemingway is through with the sentimentalism. "It isn't fun any more. I guess I'll beat it."

And he beats it, to somewhere else. In the end he'll be a sort of tramp, endlessly moving on for the sake of moving away from where he is. This is a negative goal, and Mr. Hemingway is really good, because he's perfectly straight about it. He is like Krebs, in that devastating Oklahoma sketch: he doesn't love anybody, and it nauseates him to have to pretend he does. He doesn't even *want* to love anybody; he doesn't want to go anywhere, he doesn't want to do anything. He wants just to lounge around and maintain a healthy state of nothingness inside himself, and an attitude of negation to everything outside himself. And why shouldn't he, since that is exactly and sincerely what he feels? If he really *doesn't* care, then why should he care? Anyhow, he doesn't.

[Review in *Calendar of Modern Letters,* April 1927.]

Index

Abercrombie, Lascelles, 73, 81–2
Adams family (in U.S.A.), 421
Aeschylus, 185–6, 191, 226
Alcibiades, 70
Aldington, Richard, 83
All Things are Possible (Shestov),
  242–4
Allegory, 157–9
Americans ('good at "occasional"
  verse'), 93; ('consciousness pot-
  bound'), 96; ('no new feelings'),
  258–9; ('saving American tale from
  American artist'), 296–8; (opposi-
  tion to Europe), 298–303; (and
  Red Indians), 302–5; (tourists in
  Europe), 307–8; (ideals), 310–3;
  (sloughing the old European con-
  sciousness), 319–21; ('ship of the
  American soul'), 380–1; (and
  'Whitman's message'), 402–3;
  (pioneers heart-broken), 407–9; (no
  'warmth of fellow-feeling'), 409–14
Americans (Sherman), 414–21
Anderson, Sherwood, 413
Anna Karenina (Tolstoi), 39, 177,
  178, 189, 286, 287
Anna of the Five Towns (Bennett), 131
Annie Laurie, 36
Annunzio, Gabriel d', 272, 283, 291,
  292, 294
Apocalypse, 156–9, 164–6
Apocalypse of our Times (Rozanov),
  247, 249
Apple Tree, The (Galsworthy), 126–7
Aretino, 35, 53
Aquinas, Thomas, 117
Arabian Nights (Burton), 50
Aristophanes, 32
Aristotle, 117
Ashenden (Maugham), review of, 144
Austen, Jane, 120, 292
"Autobiographical Sketch", 1

Babbitt (Lewis), 116
Babylonians, 161, 163
Baring, Maurice, 143–4
Barker, Granville, 132
Barrie, James, 5, 22

Baudelaire, 148, 306
Beethoven, 91
Belloc, Hilaire, 138
Bennett, Arnold ('an old imitator'),
  20; (his 'resignation'), 131; ('sort of
  pig in clover'), 145
Berenice (Poe), 340
Bible, The (in Lawrence's childhood)
  9, 164; ('a great confused novel'),
  105; (modern translations), 165
Blake, William, 63, 338
Boccaccio, 35, 36, 37, 39, 40, 50, 51
Bohemians, modern, 45–7
Botticelli, 59, 68, 69, 192, 195, 226
Bottom Dogs (Dahlberg), review of, 407
Bottomley, Gordon, 73, 74
Bourget, Paul, 272
Braque, 67
Brentford, Viscount, 49
Brontë, Charlotte, 37, 39, 54
Brontë, Emily, 294
Brooke, Rupert, 73, 74, 75
Brothers Karamazov, The (Dos-
  toievsky), 230–1, 233, 276
Brown, Curtis, letter to, 20
Buddenbrooks (Mann), 260
Bumppo, Natty (Fenimore Cooper
  character), 316–26
Burns, Robert, 44, 52, 54
Burton, Richard, 50
Buzzi, Paolo, 19
Byron, Lord, 71, 76, 148, 270
Byron, Robert, 140–2, 144

Calamus (Whitman), 398
Carnegie, Andrew, 421
Carswell, Catherine (book on Burns),
  52; (letters to), 83, 242
Carswell, Donald, letter to, 52
Carter, Frederick, 153–66
Casanova, 254
Cask of Amontillado, The (Poe), 344
Cavalier poetry, 54
Cavalleria Rusticana (Verga), 271,
  272, 275, 279–91
Cellini, Benvenuto, 50
Cézanne, 64, 66, 67
Chaldeans, 160–5

Chambers, Robert, 114
"Chaos in Poetry", extract from, 89
Chaplin, Charlie, 395
Chateaubriand, 367
Chardin, 62
Chaucer, 53, 54, 57
Chavannes, Puvis de, 65
Christianity ('got over Christian dogma at 16'), 8; (demolished by Nietzsche), 72; ('love it for what it brought us'), 74; (and the Apocalypse), 156; ('ends in submission'), 224; (Christian ecstasy), 230–1; (the ideal but impossible), 235; (and Dostoievsky's Grand Inquisitor), 236–41, 245; (Rozanov's attack on), 247–8
Christmas Carol, A (Dickens), 272
Clarissa Harlowe (Richardson), 36
Cocteau, Jean, 422
Collings, Ernest, letters to, 21, 76
Conrad, Joseph, 132, 363
Constable, John, 64
Constant Nymph, The (Kennedy), 112
Cooper, Fenimore, 303–29, 330
Corot, 75, 261
Correggio, 67, 68
Corvo, Baron, 149 53
Country House, The (Galsworthy), 129
Courbet, 66
Crèvecœur, Hector St. John de, 304
Crime and Punishment (Dostoievsky), 111
Criticism ('can never be a science'), 118; (requirements in a critic), 118–9
Crome, John, 64
Crosby, Harry, letters to, 25, 149
Crosland, T. W. H., 138

Dahlberg, Edward, 407
Dana, Richard, 377, 382
Dante, 71, 91, 225, 226
Darwin, Charles, 121, 146, 195
Daumier, 66
Davies, Rhys, letter to, 242
Davies, W. H., 74; ('a shorn lamb'), 77–8
De la Bretonne, Restif, 255
De la Mare, Walter, 74
De Quincey, Thomas, 345
Debussy, 225
Decameron, 50
Deerslayer (Cooper), 317, 326–9
Degas, 66
Dekker, E. D., 266–70
Del Sarto, Andrea, 68
Deledda, Grazia, 276, 291–5
Derain, 67

Desperate Remedies (Hardy), 169, 179, 181, 182
Dickens, Charles (*Dombey and Son*), 116; (Sairey Gamp), 120; (his Agnes), 203; 272, 273, 274, 292
Diderot, Denis, 255
Dobson, Austin, 306
Donne, John, 54
Dos Passos, John, 425–6
Dostoievsky, 17, 225, 226, 229–41, 242, 245, 246, 247, 248, 249, 250, 251, 252, 268, 269, 275–6, 297, 374
Doyle, Conan, 340
Dragon of the Apocalypse, The (Carter), 153–66
Dreiser, Theodore, 413
Drinkwater, John, 73
Drum Taps (Whitman), 398
Du bist wie eine Blume, 44, 46
Dürer, 68
Dynasts, The (Hardy), 189

Eleanora (Poe), 340
Eliots, the, 21
Emerson, R. W., 377, 401, 417–9
England and the Octopus (Williams-Ellis), review of, 143
Ernst, Morris L., letter to, 30
Eros (Verga), 280
Etty, William, 63
Eumenides, 53, 191, 226
Euripides, 185–6, 207
Eva (Verga), 280
Eve Effingham (Cooper), 306

Fall of the House of Usher, The (Poe), 331, 341–4
Fallen Leaves (Rozanov), 245, 249–54
Far from the Madding Crowd (Hardy), 169, 181
Faux Monnayeurs (Gide), 147
Feuillet, Octave, 271
Fielding, Henry, 54; (his Amelia), 203
Flaubert, Gustave, 72, 131, 226, 260, 265, 273–4
Flecker, J. E., 77; (*Golden Journey to Samarkand*), 80
Flight (White), 423–4
Fogazzaro, 291
Ford, Henry, 309
Forster, E. M., 139
Fra Angelico, 68, 69
Francis of Assisi, 91, 104, 148
Franklin, Benjamin, 303, 304, 379, 414, 416–7
Fraternity (Galsworthy), 122, 125, 129
Free Verse, 87–89

French, the (as painters), 65–7; ('Frenchy mind'), 148; ('minds of domestic cats'), 149; (eighteenth century literature), 254–60; ('creed of self-effacement'), 288
Futurists, 17, 19

Gainsborough, Thomas, 62
Galsworthy, John (Essay on), 118–31; (as dramatist), 132; 145
Gardiner, Rolf, letters to, 22, 24
Garnett, David, 140
Garnett, Edward, letters to, 12, 13, 14, 15, 16, 17, 76, 132
Gauguin, 67
Georgian Poetry: 1911–1912, review of, 72
Gibson, W. W., 73, 81, 82
Gide, André, 411
Giorgione, 59
Goethe, 6, 13, 71, 144, 148, 226, 261
Gogol, Nikolai, 270
Gold Bug, The (Poe), 345
Golden Journey to Samarkand, The (Flecker), 80
Gollerbach, E., 245, 247, 249
"Good Man, The," 254
Goncourts, the, 272, 280
Goulds, the, 21
Grand Inquisitor, The (Dostoievsky), 233–41, 245–6
Greeks, (vases), 50–1; (tragedy), 53; (and Homer), 84; (conception of Law), 185; ('never pitied Woman'), 207; (Law and Love), 225; (and Sicilians), 276–7; ('old Greek singleness'), 278
Grey, Zane, 114, 116, 421

H. C., letter to, 11
Hadrian the Seventh (Corvo), review of, 149
Hamlet, 32, 53, 57, 121, 177, 178, 184, 226, 275, 276
Hand of Ethelberta, The (Hardy), 170, 181
Hardie, Keir, 52
Hardy, Thomas, 14, 67, 72, 132; ("Study of"), 166–228; 272, 292, 328
Harte, Bret, 324, 421
Hawthorne, Nathaniel, 273, 296, 297, 347–63, 377, 401, 419
Heinemann, William, 3
Hemingway, Ernest, 427–8
Henley, W. E., 403
Hodgson, Ralph, 78
Hogarth, 62

Homer, 84, 90, 105, 165
Homeward Bound (Cooper), 306
Horace, 70, 81
House by the Medlar Tree, The (Verga), 273
Howard's End (Forster), 139
Hueffer, Ford Madox (publishes Lawrence) 2–3
Hugo, Victor, 70, 288
Huxley, Aldous (likes Lady C.), 23; letters to, 145, 146, 147, 148, 149; ('continuous nervous repulsion'), 411, 412
Huxley, Thomas, 195
Huysmans, J. K., 149
"Hymns in a Man's Life," 6

I Malavoglia (Verga), 272, 273–4
I Promessi Sposi (Manzoni), 270–1
Ibsen, Henrik, 72
Idiot, The (Dostoievsky), 229, 230, 231, 374
If Winter Comes (Hutchinson), 111, 116
Iliad, 85
Impressionists, 66–7
In Our Time (Hemingway), 427–8
Ingres, 62
Intelligent Woman's Guide, The (Shaw), 133
"Introduction to these Paintings" extract from, 52
Island Pharisees, The (Galsworthy), 125, 128, 129
Italians ('always acting up'), 272
Ivanhoe (Scott), 271

James, William, 340
Jane Eyre (Brontë), 36, 37, 39
Jefferies, Richard, 12
Job, Book of, 226
John, St., 70, 154, 157, 164
John Thomas and Lady Jane (Lawrence), 23
Joyce, James, 114–5, 148, 149, 291, 411
Jude the Obscure (Hardy), 167, 198–222, 275

Kant, Immanuel, 117
Keats, John, 6, 54, 64, 85, 90; (and the nightingale), 98–101
King Lear, 121, 123, 184
Königliche Hoheit (Mann), 260

La Bruyère, 27, 346
Lady Chatterley's Lover (Lawrence), 23, 24, 25, 146

Lady into Fox (Garnett), 140
Landscape painting ('English excel at'), 63–4
Laodicean, The (Hardy), 179, 180, 181
Lang, Andrew, 306
Lasca, 40
Last of the Mohicans, The (Cooper), 317, 323, 325–6
Lauzun, Duc de, 255, 258
Lawrence, D. H. (autobiographical), 1–5; (hymns in childhood), 6–11; ('give myself away so much'), 12; ('written a great book'), 13; ('cannot trim and garnish'), 14; ('I write because I want folk to have more sense'), 14; ('going through transition stage'), 16; ('a passionately religious man'), 17; ('I shall get my reception'), 18; ('the animal that I am'), 21; ('how I serve God'), 75; ('me alive'), 102–5
Lawrence, Sir Thomas, 63
Leatherstocking novels (Cooper), 306, 314–29
Lederhandler, D. V., letter to, 25
Leighton, Lord, 63
Leonardo da Vinci, 91, 148
Lewis, Wyndham, 411, 412
Ligeia (Poe), 331, 332, 333–40, 343, 363
Lincoln, Abraham, 320
Lockhart (life of Burns), 52
Longfellow, Henry, 347, 377, 401
Louis XIV, 148
Louis XV, 259
Lupa, La (Verga), 288, 289
Lynds, the, 21
Lys dans la Vallée (Balzac), 273

Macbeth, 177, 178, 184, 265
Macaulay, Thomas, 119
McLeod, A. W., letters to, 14, 19, 131, 133, 138
Mackenzie, Compton, 139
Madame Bovary (Flaubert), 265, 273–4, 275, 288
Maeterlinck, 19
Mallarmé, 225
Man of Property, The (Galsworthy), 122, 128, 129
Manhattan Transfer (Dos Passos), 411, 425–7
Mann, Thomas, 260–5
Mansfield, Katherine (letter to), 229, 233, 271
Manzoni, 270–1, 272
Marinetti, 17, 18, 19
Marble Faun, The (Hawthorne), 419

Marsh, Edward, letters to, 77, 79, 81
Mascagni, 271, 291
Masefield, John, 73, 74, 76, 82
Mastro-Don Gesualdo (Verga), 270–9, 281
Matisse, 67
Maugham, W. Somerset, 144–5
Maupassant, Guy de, 272, 288
Max Havelaar (Dekker), 266–70
Mayor of Casterbridge, The (Hardy), 179, 181
Meredith, George, 82, 120, 272
Mérimée, Prosper, 288
Metre, poetic, 79–81
Melville, Herman, 363–92, 401, 406
Mencken, H. L., 414–6
Michelangelo, 68, 70, 71, 75, 148
Mill on the Floss, The (Eliot), 39
Millais, John, 65
Miller, Joaquin, 420–1
Milton, John, 61, 71, 81
Moby Dick (Melville), 376–92, 394
Moffatt translation of Bible, 165
Monroe, Harriet, letter to, 83
More, P. E., 414–6, 421
Mother, The (Deledda), 291–5
"Morality and the Novel," 108
Morrell, Lady Ottoline, letters to, 21, 25, 147, 229
Morrison, Nelly, letter to, 254
Mozart, 36
Muir, Edwin, 145
Multatuli, 266
Murders in the Rue Morgue (Poe), 345
Murry, J. Middleton, 21, 22, 233; letters to, 21, 139, 140, 229, 232
My love is like a red, red rose, 44
Myth, 158

Napoleon, 121
New Machiavelli (Wells), 14, 133
New Numbers, 81
New Poems (Lawrence), Introduction to, 84
Nietzsche (demolishing Christian religion), 72; (*Wille zur Macht*), 201
Nigger Heaven (Van Vechten), 422–3
"Nightingale, The", extract from, 98
Norris, Frank, 324
Novel, the, (Lawrence 'a stratum deeper than anybody has ever gone'), 14; ('the old stable ego of the character'), 18; ('rules of construction'), 20; (its importance), 102–8; (and morality), 108–13; (its present state and future), 114–8; ('nervous repulsion' in modern novel), 411
Novelle Rusticane (Verga), 272, 281

Octopus, The (Norris), 324
Odyssey, 84, 177, 178, 279, 317
Œdipus, 53, 121, 184
Old People and the Things that Pass (Couperus), 267
Omoo (Melville), 363–76
Orestean trilogy, 53, 184, 185, 191, 198, 224, 226, 302

Pamela (Richardson), 36, 39
Pansies (Lawrence), Introduction to, 26
Pair of Blue Eyes, A (Hardy), 169, 182
Paradise Lost, 61
Pascal, 27
Passage to India (Forster), 139
Pater, Walter, 119
Pathfinder, The (Cooper), 317, 326
Paul et Virginie, 271
Paul, Jean, 268, 270
Paul Morel, 12–13
Paul, St., 70, 71
Pawling, S. S., letter to, 11
Pearn, Miss, letter to, 23
Petronius, 229
Phædra, 121
Phidias, 70
Pierre (Melville), 374
Pilgrim's Progress, The (Bunyan), 157, 232
Pilot, The (Cooper), 306
Pinker, J. B., letters to, 20, 138
Pioneers (Cooper), 317, 321–3
Pirandello, Luigi, 272
Plato, 69, 70, 71, 105, 225, 226, 297
Plumed Serpent, The (Lawrence), 20
Poe, Edgar Allan, 296, 330–46, 379, 401
Poetry, War Number, 83
Point Counter Point (Huxley), 146, 147, 411, 413
Pointed Roofs (Richardson), 114
Pollinger, L. E., 23, letter to, 24
Pope, Alexander, 260
"Pornography and Obscenity", 32
Possessed, The (Dostoievsky), 229–30, 231
Poussin, 62
Prairie, The (Cooper), 317, 323–4
Pre-Raphaelites, 63
Proper Studies (Huxley), 145
Proust, Marcel, 48, 114, 147, 148
Puritanism, 9, 32, 37, 39, 40, 58; (opposed to Cavalier type), 197

Rabelais, 35, 37
Raeburn, 63

Rainbow, The (Lawrence), 15
Ramie, Marian, 83
Raphael, 68, 69, 70, 71, 112, 225, 226
Rembrandt, 62, 68, 226
Renaissance, ('gay Renaissance stories'), 37; ('fear entered English soul'), 53; ('heavens rolled up'), 95; (began conscious woman-reverence), 200; ('the great pause') 225; ('kingship and fatherhood fell'), 302; ('Europe sloughed her last skin'), 319
Renoir, 36, 39, 65, 67
Restoration dramatists, 54, 415
Return of the Native, The (Hardy), 170–8, 181, 189
Revelation, St. John's, 154, 156, 157, 164
Revolution in Tanner's Lane (Rutherford), 138
Reynolds, Sir Joshua, 62
Rhythm (D. H. L.'s), 77; (Catherine Carswell's), 84; (and free verse), 87
Richardson, Dorothy, 114–5
Richardson, Samuel, 54, 274
Rolfe, Frederick ('Baron Corvo'), 149–53
Roosevelt, Theodore, 152, 421
Rosso Malpelo (Verga), 289
Rouge et le Noir, Le (Stendhal), 12
Rousseau, Jean-Jacques, 148, 255, 256, 259, 367
Rozanov, V. V., 245–54
Ruskin, John, 13
Russians ('destroyed the Tsar to have Lenin'), 234; ('Bolshevist bread barren'), 239; ('meant an enormous amount to me'), 242; ('the Russian spirit'), 242–3; ('Russianism' and Rozanov), 245–53; ('of the old regime'), 252–3; ('Bolshevist Russia only a sort of America'), 258; ('subjectively intense'), 275–6; ('pouring out tea and their souls'), 278
Rutherford, Mark, 138

Saga of Siegfried, The (Lawrence), 11
Sainte-Beuve, 119
Sandburg, Carl, 421
Sardinia (and Deledda's novels), 292–5
Sargent, Edmund Beale, 74
Sargent, J. S., 63
Satire, ('ridicules the social being'), 123; (in *Max Havelaar*), 268
Scarlet Letter, The (Hawthorne), 347–63, 401, 419
Scansion of verse, 79–80

Schiller, 70
Scrutinies, 145
Scott, Sir Walter, 270
Secker, Martin, letters to, 23, 132, 139
Second Contemporary Verse Anthology, A, review of, 92
Serao, Matilda, 271, 292
Shakespeare, 6, 53, 57, 70, 71, 91, 105, 177, 226, 261, 274
Shaw, G. Bernard, 58, 132, 133, 266
Sheik, The, 36, 114, 116
Shelley, P. B., 54, 64, 70, 71, 81, 85, 187, 226
Sherman, Stuart P., 414–21
Shestov, Leo, 242–4
Sicilian, ('doesn't have any soul'), 276
Silas Marner (Eliot), 272
Sinister Street (Mackenzie), 139
Sisters, The (Lawrence), 15, 16
Sitwells, 140, 141, 142
Socrates, 70
Soffici, 19
Solitaria (Rozanov), 245–9, 250
Song of Solomon, 36
Sons and Lovers (Lawrence), 12, 14, 15, 82
Sophocles, 70, 177
Spencer, Herbert, 195
Spenser, Edmund, 71
"Spirit of Place, The", 296
Spoon River Anthology, 84
Spy, The (Cooper), 306
Squire, Jack, 22 ('the Squires'), 21
Station, The: Athos, Treasures and Men (Byron), review of, 140
Stein, Gertrude, 148, 149
Stendhal, 12
Sterne, Lawrence, 54, 255
Strindberg, August, 132
Stopes, Dr. Marie, 45, 46
Storia di Una Capinera (Verga), 272
Story of My Heart, The (Jefferies), 12
"Study of Thomas Hardy", extracts from, 67–71, 166–228
"Surgery for the Novel—or a Bomb", 114
Swift, Jonathan, 26, 29, 30, 54, 270
Swinburne, A. C., 54, 74, 187, 363
Symbolistes, 19
Symbols, ('images of myth'), 157–9
Synge, J. M., 132
Syphilis, effect of its appearance, 54–58, 60, 65

Tchekhov, 132, 242, 250, 251, 271, 275–6, 288
Tennyson, 70
Tess of the d'Urbervilles (Hardy), 181, 192–8, 272

Theocritus, 283
Tigre Reale (Verga), 271, 280
Titian, 36, 39, 62
Tod in Venedig, Der (Mann), 260, 262–5
To Let (Galsworthy), 129
To the Pure, 30
Tolstoi, 17, 70, 71, 177, 183, 188–9, 226, 242, 253, 286, 287
Tonio Kröger (Mann), 260, 261
Tragedy (Greek and Renaissance), 53; (in Hardy), 167–70; (Egdon Heath the tragic power), 172–3; (Hardy compared with Shakespeare, Sophocles, Tolstoi), 177–8; (Aeschylus and Euripides), 185–6; (*Tess* contains elements of greatest tragedy), 198; (Flaubert's sense of tragedy), 274
Transition, 148, 149
Trespasser, The (Lawrence), 11, 12
Trevelyan, Sir G., 52
Tristan (Mann), 260
Tristan and Isolde (Wagner), 36, 39
Trumpet Major, The (Hardy), 181
Turgenev, 17, 70, 242
Turner, J. M. W., 64, 195, 225, 226
Twain, Mark, 268, 270
Two on a Tower (Hardy), 176, 179, 181, 182
Typee (Melville), 363–76

Uncle Tom's Cabin (Stowe), 266, 267
Under the Greenwood Tree (Hardy), 169, 181
Ulysses (Joyce), 114

Vagabondaggio (Verga), 272
Van Gogh, 64, 108
Van Vechten, Carl, 422–3, 425
Velasquez, 62
Verga, Giovanni, 270–91, 295
Verlaine, 6
Vlaminck, 67
Voltaire, 121, 247, 270

Wagner, Richard, 36, 39
Watteau, 62
Watts, G. F., 63, 65
Wedding Ring, The (Lawrence), 15, 17
Well-Beloved, The (Hardy), 189
Wells, H. G., 5, 14, 22; (*Country of the Blind*), 82; (Wellsian heroine), 126; (*New Machiavelli*), 133; (review of *The World of William Clissold*), 133
Werther (Goethe), 271
White Fox, 22
White Jacket (Melville), 373, 375

White Peacock, The (Lawrence), 2, 3
White, Walter, 423–5
Whitman, Walt, 77, 87, 89, 91, 92, 392–407, 419–20
Who is Sylvia, what is she?, 44
"Why the Novel Matters", 102
Wilde, Oscar, 54, 148, 149, 257
Wilhelm Meister (Goethe), 148
William Wilson (Poe), 345
Williams-Ellis, Clough, 142–3
Wilson, Richard, 64
Wilson, Woodrow, 152, 255, 381

Woodlanders, The (Hardy), 176, 179, 182, 192
Wordsworth, William, 6, 71, 91, 226
World of William Clissold, The (Wells), review of, 133
Wuthering Heights (Brontë), 273, 294

Yeats, W. B., 75
Yoni Noguchi, 77

Zola, Émile, 283